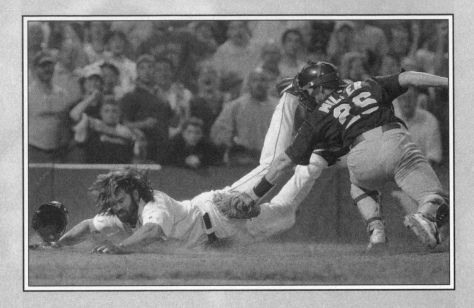

FAITHFUL

TWO DIEHARD BOSTON RED SOX FANS
CHRONICLE THE HISTORIC 2004 SEASON

STEWART O'NAN

STEPHEN KING

SCRIBNER
New York   London   Toronto   Sydney

SCRIBNER
1230 Avenue of the Americas
New York, NY 10020

SCRIBNER and design are trademarks of Macmillan Library Reference USA, Inc.,
used under license by Simon & Schuster, the publisher of this work.

For information about special discounts for bulk purchases,
please contact Simon & Schuster Special Sales:
1-800-456-6798 or business@simonandschuster.com

DESIGNED BY ERICH HOBBING

Text set in Adobe Garamond

Manufactured in the United States of America

1   3   5   7   9   10   8   6   4   2

Library of Congress Control Number: 2004063398

ISBN 0-7432-6752-4

CREDITS
AP/Wide World Photos (pages ii–iii, 1, 29, 145, 235, 275, 335, and 349);
Brian Snyder/Reuters/Corbis (page 179); Robert Galbraith/Reuters/Corbis (page 383);
Republished with permission of Globe Newspaper Company, Inc. (page 405).

Dirty Water: Words and music by Ed Cobb. Copyright © 1965 (Renewed)
by Embassy Music Corporation (BMI). International copyright secured.
All rights reserved. Reprinted by permission.
I Put a Spell on You: Words and music by JAY HAWKINS. Copyright © 1956 (Renewed 1984)
EMI UNART CATALOG INC. All rights controlled by EMI UNART CATALOG INC.
and WARNER BROS. PUBLICATIONS U.S. INC. All rights reserved. Used by permission.
Warner Bros. Publications U.S. Inc., Miami, Florida 33014.

For Victoria Snelgrove,
Red Sox fan

CONTENTS

Down by the river,
down by the banks of the River Charles.
That's where you'll find me,
along with
muggers, lovers and thieves.

THE STANDELLS

I put a spell on you,
cause you're mine.

SCREAMIN' JAY HAWKINS

INTRODUCTION

I wasn't always like this. I was born a World Champion, a third-generation Pirates fan, in early 1961.

A few short months before, the Bucs had taken the heavily favored Yankees to Game 7 in Forbes Field. The Yanks seemed to have the series in hand, up 7–4 in the eighth when Bill Virdon hit a simple double-play ball to short. As Tony Kubek charged, the ball took a bad hop off the alabaster plaster, hitting him in the Adam's apple, and both runners were safe. Two singles later, it was 7–6. The next batter, backup catcher Hal Smith, caught up to a Bobby Shantz fastball and parked it over the left-field wall for a 9–7 lead.

But the Pirates couldn't close it out, surrendering two in the next frame. With the game tied at nine, second baseman Bill Mazeroski led off the bottom of the ninth. He took the first pitch from Ralph Terry for a ball, and then, as every Pirates and Yankees fan knows, Maz cranked a high fastball over Yogi Berra and everything in left, and the fans stormed the field.

As a longtime Red Sox fan, I appreciate this history even more now, but, as a kid then, my perspective was limited. Living so close to the real-life setting of the legend (our library was right across the parking lot, and we'd walk over and touch the brick wall the ball cleared), I grew up pitying the Yankees as hard-luck losers.

As the '60s turned into the '70s, nothing happened to refute this. We won it all again in '71, beating an Orioles team with four 20-game winners, and made the playoffs nearly every year before succumbing to the Dodgers or the Big Red Machine. Roberto Clemente, tragically, was gone, but his spirit lingered over the Lumber Company, a colorful and monstrous offensive club that included hitters like Willie Stargell, Dave Parker, Al Oliver, Richie Zisk, Rennie Stennett and Manny Sanguillen. Earl Weaver's O's and Charlie Finley's A's ruled the AL. The bumbling Yankees, like the Brooklyn

Dodgers or New York Giants, belonged to a flannel, white-bread past, hope-lessly square.

About the time George Steinbrenner took them over, I traded my inter-est in baseball for cooler high school pursuits: music and cars, girls and cig-arettes. I noticed with an offhand disgust that the Yankees had bought the heart of the A's dynasty to "win" two cheapies, but it didn't mean much to me. I was too busy messing around to bother with a kid's game.

That probably wouldn't have changed if the Pirates didn't go and win it all again in '79. I was going to school in Boston, lost in engineering problems and partying, but one of my best friends was an Orioles fan. Game 7 was excruciating for him. Just like in '71, they were playing in Baltimore, and just like in '71, the three-run homer the O's were waiting for never showed up. Rather than rub it in, I did my best to console my friend. That's just how it went with the Pirates in Game 7—like the Steelers in the Super Bowl.

By Opening Day of 1980, the glow from winning it all hadn't worn off, and, living two blocks from Kenmore Square, I decided to take advantage of the neighborhood and visit Fenway Park for the first time. I didn't expect much. AL ball back then seemed boring to me, a slow, low-scoring game like soccer (since then, the leagues have swapped styles, maybe due to the DH, or the AL teams' new, smaller parks), but bleacher seats were only three dollars. The park reminded me of long-gone Forbes Field, with its green girders and cramped wooden seats and oddball dimensions. And that wall, the top hung with sail-like nets to catch home run balls. It made me think of the wire screen in right and the way Clemente anticipated every weird carom off it, gunning down runners chugging into second.

And the Sox surprised me. They played like an NL club—all hitting, no pitching. No speed or defense either. The stars of the great '75 and '78 teams were gone, sacrificed to free agency by the old-school Yawkeys. The only sur-vivors were Jim Rice, Dwight Evans and the fast-aging Yaz, anchoring a lineup of journeymen. They were a slower, less talented version of the old Pirates, a Lumbering Company, just hoping to outslug the other team. They weren't good but they weren't really bad either. They were entertaining, and Fenway provided me with the amenities of an actual park—a green space in the middle of the city where I could pass the hours reading and doing my homework. I watched the games and I liked the team enough, but I didn't kid myself that they were contenders.

And that was okay. Between championships the Pirates went through long stretches in the cellar. This was better, skirting .500. The farm system was in good shape, and eventually we'd develop some pitchers.

You could say I didn't know what I was getting myself into, but game after game I happily shelled out my three bucks at the barred ticket window outside Gate C and staked my claim to Section 34 in straight center, right beside Channel 38's camera, where you could call balls and strikes and let the opposing center fielder know he was on the road.

The Sox weren't a tough ticket then, and I was surrounded by a scruffy tribe of regulars. My favorite was the General, a scrawny, grizzled guy in his late twenties with rotten teeth who wore a squashed Civil War cap and challenged all comers with his portable Othello board. And then there was the husky dude with receding hair who always came late with his dinner in a Tupperware bowl and bellowed, "WAAAAAAAAAAAAADE!"

After the '84 season, I left for a job on Long Island, and was living there when Roger Clemens and the '86 club made the playoffs. I was there for Game 6 of the World Series, deep in the heart of Mets country. I remember us being one strike away again and again. I was ready to jump up from my chair and dance. It was late, and I was watching by myself, the TV turned down so it wouldn't wake the baby. When the ball rolled through Billy Buck's legs, I heard the cheers of my neighbors.

One pitch—say, one of Pedro's change-ups—and I wouldn't be writing this. But no, we placed our faith in Calvin Schiraldi (who blew leads in both the eighth *and* the tenth in Game 6).

I've been to disappointing games since then—a string of playoff losses to Cleveland, the phantom-tag game in the '99 ALCS, last year's Pedro-Zimmer brawl—but none of those teams, no matter how far they went, even last year's overachievers, were true contenders. We were always at least two players away, and one of those was usually a closer. Even in '86, the odds were on the Mets (who, if you remember, were touted as one of the greatest teams of all time, a claim that now seems like the New York hype it was).

This year was different. With the addition of Curt Schilling and Keith Foulke, it looked like we had the horses. Months before pitchers and catchers were scheduled to report, the pressure on the team was already intense. Anything short of a World Championship would be considered a failure, and with the new owners trying to juggle too many high-priced contracts (including Nomar and Pedro in the last year of their deals), it appeared this was the only shot the Sox would have for a long time.

Add to that a new, largely unproven manager, Terry Francona, whose previous experience with the Phillies had been less than successful. After last year's Game 7 debacle, the front office (led by whiz kid and Bill James disciple Theo Epstein) canned the Chauncey Gardner–like Grady Little, the latest in a parade of weak field managers with no input into personnel moves. Francona inherited a team with several notorious prima donnas, a brutal local media and a demanding fan base. He had a three-year contract, but if he didn't produce a winner immediately, he knew he might as well pack his bags.

Along with those overarching dramas, there were questions about how the failed A-Rod deal would play out with Nomar and Manny Ramirez. The Yankees also picked up former Sox closer Tom Gordon, who they hoped would be the missing setup man they'd needed since promoting Mariano Rivera to closer. The Sox were still hoping Ramiro Mendoza would come around, and submariner Byung-Hyun Kim, but, emotionally, Sox fans were pulling harder for prodigal sons Brian Daubach and Ellis Burks. (Daubach's drama started early: he was a nonroster invitee to training camp, and, as has been the case his entire career, had to scrap to stay in the majors.) And of course there was the question of Pedro and his shoulder, Pedro and his back, Pedro and his mouth. Plus whatever controversy came up. This Sox clubhouse, like the Yankees' back when they had personality, was known for soap opera.

It would be an interesting year, whichever way it went. If the Sox contended, all of New England would catch pennant fever. If they tanked, the carnage would be spectacular. Either way, Steve and I would be following them, watching them, listening to them, taking in games at Fenway, reading the box scores, checking the website, discussing them endlessly with friends and family and total strangers. Like any devoted Sox fans, we'd been waiting for this season since the end of Game 7, and our hopes were both impossibly high and cautiously guarded. Because as much as we love them, the Sox had broken our hearts over and over, and that probably wouldn't change.

But what if? No one expected the Patriots to *ever* win a Super Bowl, let alone two. Our rotation was the best in the majors, and we actually had a closer now. Last year's offense had outslugged the '27 Yankees. More than any team we'd fielded since '78 (that wonderful, terrible season), this squad had a bona fide shot. In February, before a single pitch had been thrown, millions of us believed this would be the year.

This book should reflect the depth of our obsession as well as how quickly the tone of a season changes. To get the emotions while they were fresh, the book is in double diary form. We didn't chase the team like journalists, looking for total coverage. We just did our best to have a regular Sox-filled summer. For each day or game that we naturally came in contact with the Sox and found something remarkable—from spring training to the very last out—we wrote separate entries or reflections.

Besides the diary entries, for games or streaks that especially thrilled us or pissed us off (and with the Sox, we didn't lack for those), we've attached spur-of-the-moment e-mail exchanges that show us firmly in the grip of the beast, feeding it.

In baring our relationship with the Sox, we hope to illuminate readers' feelings for their own favorite teams. We also hope there's something funny about owning up to the silliness of obsession yet being unable to break free of it—like Woody Allen or David Foster Wallace being painfully aware of their neuroses even as they navigate situations bound to freak them out. Sox fans are like any anxious sports fans, except we have good reason to be paranoid, so that even an 8–1 laugher against Tampa Bay can turn—in a matter of a couple of base runners, a couple of knuckleheaded pitching changes—into pure torture. And like hardcore followers of any sport, Sox fans are expert at taking a game apart and examining its most intricate components, especially when the worst happens.

We knew all of this coming into the 2004 season, and yet, for all the heartbreak, there we were again, psyched that Tommy Brady and the Pats might show up on Opening Day the way they did in 2002. Fenway was sold out for the season, and ticket prices on eBay were through the roof. The Sox and Yanks were both stocked and talking smack, from the front office down to the scalpers. The waiting was over—finally, it was next year.

Stewart O'Nan, February 29th, 2004

Welcome to Next Year

February 21st

After the Schilling acquisition, and during the A-Rod negotiations, I felt distinctly weird . . . out of kilter as a Red Sox fan. I started to think, "I'm going to come back to a team of superhero strangers wearing Red Sox uniforms. Who are these guys?" It was a dreamlike feeling, both pleasant and unpleasant . . . like getting gas at the dentist and knowing it's going to hurt like almighty hell later on. Then the A-Rod deal fell through—the same old Red Sox problem: lots of cash, just not quite enough cash. And the Yankees got him. And the tabloids gloated. And even the *New York Times,* that supposedly staid gray lady, got in a crack; the Yankees, one of their columnists said, continued to show the Red Sox how to win, winter and summer. That was when the unpleasant dreamlike feeling burst, and I woke up to real life, smelling not the coffee but the peanuts and Cracker Jacks: Ah yes, screwed again. Hello, world, I'm a Red Sox fan. For better or worse, I'm a Red Sox fan, and I've just been screwed again. Same as it ever was. So bring on the Yankees, and may Alex Rodriguez bat .240.

We're going to spring training, the whole family. It's a surprise, my birthday present, a long weekend in Fort Myers. I've always wanted to go, ever since I was a kid in Pittsburgh listening to the Bucs warm up in sunny Bradenton. Trudy says she's sick of listening to me yap about it, so here it is, a folder with the plane tickets, the hotel reservations, the rental-car agreement. We can't afford it, but I can't say that.

And there's the envelope with the game tickets and the diagram of City of Palms Park. We're going to see the Sox play their traditional game against Boston College on Friday, then the first game of the year against the Yankees Sunday and finally a Monday game against the Twins, who also train in Fort Myers. I forget about the money for a second and check out where we're sitting.

I hit the Sox website to find out more about the training complex. I figure my son Steph and I can hang out and watch the players while Trudy and Caitlin beach it. I check the schedule, thinking the BC game is the very first of the spring.

It's not. We're playing the Twins at their place on Thursday. I go to their website and buy four tickets for it.

We're also playing Northeastern at home on Friday night. I buy four more.

February 23rd

My brother John calls from Pittsburgh and asks me who he should draft from the Sox for his AL fantasy team. He's a Pirates fan and doesn't follow the junior circuit closely. Personally, I don't like fantasy leagues, the way they make you root for individual players over team performance, but I do my best for him.

"Keith Foulke should get forty saves no matter how badly he pitches."

"Last year you told me Mendoza."

"Bronson Arroyo."

"He's no good. At least he wasn't when he was with us. Who else?"

"Pokey Reese."

"We had him. He's always injured."

I hang up feeling unhelpful, all of my arcane knowledge useless.

Second base is the one big question mark this season, besides not having a lefty starter. Pokey Reese has missed the better part of the last two seasons with leg and thumb injuries. He's a little guy, a speedster who played option QB in high school, but suddenly he's become delicate. He could be the Gold Glover he was a few years back and hit a respectable .260, or he could tank. Already the Sox are looking at Mark Bellhorn, Tony Womack and Terry Shumpert as insurance policies.

Nomar says he's excited about playing beside such a slick fielder. Every spring it seems he says the same thing, because it's been ten years since we've had the same Opening Day second baseman in consecutive seasons. We let playoff hero Todd Walker walk. Rey Sanchez got the boot after a decent year. Before that we had Jose Offerman, ex–general manager Dan Duquette's laughable answer to losing Mo Vaughn.

Duquette, you'll remember, is the genius who said Roger Clemens was "in the twilight of his career" and let him go off to Toronto, where he won

4

back-to-back Cy Youngs. In the '80s there was continuity at second. Jerry Remy, Marty Barrett and Jody Reed all enjoyed long stays, and were fan favorites (Jerry still is, doing color for NESN). Duquette, trading our top prospects yearly in his attempt to build an instant champion, stripped the farm system, and now our second baseman—like our closer—is a replacement player.

February 25th

I'm trying to get tix for Stewart (and Stewart's wife Trudy) and me to the annual game pitting the Red Sox B-team (invitee Brian "Dauber" Daubach should be starting for the Sox) against the Boston College baseball team. Ordinarily these would be a slam dunk—prime real estate up in Owner's Country at City of Palms Park, and maybe a couple of spots among the Escalades and Navigators in the players' parking lot— but my main man, Kevin Shea, has moved on, and so it's nervous-making time. How about the satellite connection? Can I get New England Sports Network (aka NESN, aka The Home of the Free and Land of the Eck) down here? Yes. Thank God. But my subscription from last year has lapsed. Oh shit. And how many spring training games will they carry, anyway? Oh shit, maybe Joe Castiglione can help me with tix to the Sox/BC game . . . but he wanted me to blurb his book, and it deserves a blurb, but I haven't done it yet . . .

It's nervous time.

Oh God, I wish Curt Schilling was only thirty-two.

February 27th

I've been trying to nail down tickets to the home opener for months now. It's been sold out since five minutes after seats went on sale, but I've got an in. Last year I managed to score some last-minute seats—field boxes ten rows behind home plate. Took the kids out of school, only to sit in the freezing rain for three hours before the game was called. I figured we'd get the same seats, but when the replacements came they were grandstands. I sent them back, but the ticket office never got back to me. At the end of the season, I called and asked what the deal was, and Naomi there said they'd give me two field boxes for this year's opener and a chance to buy two more.

But so far I've been having trouble getting through to Naomi. My great fear is that she's changed jobs and we'll be stuck watching the game on TV.

February 28th

I vet the depth chart on the website as if I'm Theo, trying to figure out who to keep, who to cut, who to ship to Pawtucket. We've brought the expanded forty-man roster to camp, along with twelve nonroster invitees. By Opening Day, management will whittle these fifty-two down to twenty-five, and of the twenty-five spots, twenty are already filled. Essentially, thirty-two players, most with big league experience, are fighting for five spots reserved for middle relievers and backup position players.

One guy who I hope makes it is Brian Daubach. Even though he's a millionaire, fans still see him as a scrappy blue-collar player. He paid his dues in the minors with the Marlins and Devil Rays before getting his chance with the Sox, and played well as a platoon guy before getting demoted for Tony Clark (who he outplayed to win his job back), then dumped for the awful Jeremy Giambi. "We want Dauber!" we'd shout after Giambi struck out looking again.

Now he's back, and his main competition is David McCarty, a good defensive first baseman we picked up from Oakland at the end of last season. As a lefty hitter with power, Dauber has the edge, but since David Ortiz already fills that bill, McCarty's glove might be more valuable in the late innings. McCarty, weirdly, also plans on trying to pitch, and we're so desperate for lefties that Francona's going to let him.

SK: Dauber was a real old-time Red Sox player. Like he was born to play for the Red Sox. Millar is that way; and Varitek, of course. And you know, Pedro Martinez wasn't born a Red Sox guy, but has become one. He finished his becoming in the seventh game of the ALCS last year, don't you think? Came out covered in mud and blood and shit, soul brother to Pumpsie Green. Man, I root for the Dauber . . . but I don't give him a dog's chance. Sure wish I had my DAUBACH IS MY DADDY shirt. I'd wear it to the Sox/BC game. God, no one ever tried harder in the clutch.

SO: And, like Fisk, he always took it out on his old clubs. He wore out Tampa Bay, and last year when he beat us he was smiling for Tom

Caron [NESN's roving on-field reporter] like a new dad. No doubt Pedro's paid his dues. Manny, well, it's close. Johnny D's still too new, and Bill Mueller (pronounced Miller), and David Ortiz. The Sox need more Sox!

SK: Some of what happens to Daubach is down to pure luck—who gets hurt and who stays healthy. But you know he's on the edge of being back in civvies. Or a minor league uni. Hope he made some good investments over the years.

February 29th

Reporters following Byung-Hyun Kim say he stays till 1 A.M. working out, but that he naps at all times. I wonder if BK's regimen is like the Japanese, who throw two hundred pitches a day. He's young and talented, with that weird submarine delivery, but he's never thrown a full season as a starter. If he can give us two hundred innings and twenty quality starts, we should win the East. The worry is that he's a head case. He gave Fenway the finger when we booed him during the introductions before the ALCS, and in the off-season he smashed a photographer's camera. I guess he's this year's Oil Can Boyd or Cowboy Carl Everett.

March 1st

Steve calls as Trudy's microwaving her lunch. I can barely hear him through the Geiger-like static. For the BC game, we're parking in the players' lot and sitting in the owner's booth. As a bleacher rat, I'm a little nervous. What do you say to an owner—"Way to own"?

March 2nd

Oops—Yankees Jason Giambi and Gary Sheffield received steroids from Barry Bonds's trainer, according to the ongoing federal probe. Giambi showed up at camp looking shrunken. Sheffield says he'll pee in a cup any-time anyplace, but when a reporter produces a cup, Sheff backs down. Makes me wonder if Steinbrenner went out and got A-Rod and Travis Lee in case the league suspends the BALCO Boys.

March 3rd

All day an unreal, nearly paralyzing feeling. It seems so impossible that we're blowing off work and school that we have to keep repeating the news to each other like lottery winners: "We're going to Florida!"

In the Charlotte airport, waiting for our connection to Fort Myers, I look around the gate for fellow pilgrims, but the one kid wearing a cap is a Brewers fan. It's only when we're on board that the hard core begin dribbling in—four single guys in their twenties, all big enough to be players, in various Sox hats.

We get in after midnight and the airport's crazy. In the long line at the rental-car center, half the people are in Boston garb. Fort Myers is an endless grid of strip malls and stoplights, and everyone drives like they're either having a heart attack or trying to find an emergency room for someone who is. We fly past Mattress World, Bath World, Rug World. It's Hicksville, Long Island, with palm trees and pelicans.

Our hotel has personality—unfortunately it's the personality of a lunch lady turned crack whore. Bikers and twentysomethings early for spring break wander the parking lot, knocking back Coronas and margaritas to the thumping of a ragged cover band. The hotel's assurance on their website that they don't rent to anyone under twenty-one seems less a defensive measure now than an admission of a long-standing problem. It's one-thirty and the music is thundering up from the stage, one floor below our balcony. The song ends and the drunk girls scream. The drunk guys go "Wooooo!"

March 4th

I want to get up and be at the practice fields by nine. I expect it'll be just me and Steph, but Trudy comes too, driving while I navigate. We peel off the Tamiami Trail and in a few blocks we see City of Palms Park. According to the website, the training complex is two and a half miles straight down Edison, but there's no parking. You're supposed to park here and ride a shuttle bus to the practice fields.

City of Palms Park is understated and classic from the outside, a plain white concrete facade three stories tall, with flags for all the AL teams flying atop the roof, and one window-sized Sox logo over the green main gates. There's no one on the plaza in front, just the stalky palm trees. I don't see anywhere to park, so I tell Trudy to go ahead and cruise the practice fields.

We get lucky—the lot for the practice facility is half-empty. The clear-coated monster trucks and chrome-wheeled Escalades are obviously the players'. We park in a far corner and head for the nearest gate. AUTHORIZED ACCESS ONLY, a sign says. As we walk through, I look for other fans, but only see a few people who might be players' relatives.

There are five fields and, closest to us, a roofed arcade. Someone's in there smacking balls, but it's too dim to see who, and we're trying to act cool. We head for a field where the players are stretching. No one challenges us. When we reach the team, we see why—it's not the big club but the rookie and minor league invitees, guys with no shot this year, but who may develop and move up through the system.

The pitchers run bunt drills. The outfielders handle line-drive singles silently fired from a rubber-wheeled machine. Former players Luis Alicea and U L Washington coach the infielders, tossing short-hops the players have to backhand barehanded. The range of skill is evident. Some never miss while others are lucky to pick one cleanly.

Summers, we see a lot of the triple-A PawSox over in Pawtucket and the double-A Portland Sea Dogs when they visit New Britain, but the only player I recognize is Hanley Ramirez. He's the number one prospect in our farm system, a shortstop with speed and power. He's only twenty, and rumor is he might be promoted from single-A Augusta to Portland, with an eye towards taking Nomar's place in 2005. One problem is he made 36 errors last year and hit only .275 after batting over .330 at lower levels. Another is that he's a hothead, earning a ten-game suspension for making an obscene gesture to the crowd. Here, in practice, he moves like he's already a superstar, cool and loose and slouchy.

There are three seniors watching with us, a woman and two men, one of whom is wearing a Springfield Elks cap. The woman has a camera, a couple signed balls and a handful of minor league cards. She wants to get Jamie Brown to sign his. She knows all the players taking batting practice. This is what they do, she says. They're mad at the Sox for forcing them to buy ticket packages that include three crummy games to get the one good one against the Yanks, so now they just come to the complex and watch the kids.

BP wraps, so we ramble along the road beyond the last field. It's hot, and Steph's cheeks are red. We've circled the entire complex, and walk through the lot just as two women in a '69 Firebird convertible pull up. They're older than any of the guys here, but beach-tanned and gym-tight. I don't think

Steph's seen *Bull Durham* or knows what a Baseball Annie is, but he probably wouldn't be interested anyway.

We come back in the players' entrance, which has a Boston *Globe* honor box beside it. The batting alleys are full of guys getting extra swings in. By the backstop, the old lady is getting Jamie Brown to sign. We've only been here a few hours, but it's enough. It's only our first day and we're already wilting.

After putting in some beach time, we get caught in traffic and are nearly late for the night game. Hammond Stadium holds only 7,500, but it seems they've all brought their cars. The Twins have elected to park the overflow on the outfields of their practice facility. We just shrug and follow the soft ruts in front of us and nose it in against the 330 sign by the foul pole.

"The temperature at game time here in Fort Myers is seventy-nine degrees," the PA announcer informs us, to applause. "In Minneapolis, it's thirty-four with a mix of rain and snow."

Besides the ailing Johnny Damon and Trot Nixon sitting out, the starting lineup is most decidedly the A-team. Gabe Kapler, a solid backup outfielder, leads off, followed by last year's surprise batting champ Bill Mueller, Manny, Nomar, David Ortiz, Kevin Millar, Jason Varitek, PawSock Adam Hyzdu subbing in right for Trot, and in the nine-spot, Pokey Reese.

The Twins roll out their postseason lineup, including outfielders Shannon Stewart and Torii Hunter, and first baseman Doug Mientkiewicz, as well as phenom Joe Mauer at catcher.

It's the first inning of the first exhibition game, but when Bill Mueller launches one to deep center, Torii Hunter gets on his horse and runs it down, diving at full extension like it's the playoffs.

The intensity only lasts a couple of innings. By the fourth the substitutions are wholesale and the game takes on a double-A flavor. The Sox win on a broken-bat bleeder by prospect Jeremy Owens, and we leave happy, picking up our free grapefruit, two each in a yellow mesh bag. In the lot I spy an old orange VW bus with RED SOX NATION handpainted in red across the back window. Three guys in their early twenties are piling in the side door, and for a second I envy them the trip. Then I remember that I'm on it too.

March 5th

It's sunny and eighty-four in Fort Myers, the sort of faux summer day that fills Florida's west coast with tourists in the month of March and makes driving a pain in the ass—often a dangerous pain in the ass, as many of the people with whom one is sharing the road are old, bewildered, and heavily medicated. All the same, I'm in a chipper mood as I stash my car among the Hummers and Escalades in the players' parking lot (I have a special dispensation from Kerri Moore, the new Public Relations gal). It's a perfect day for my first game of the year.

Well, okay, so it's not really a game; more of a seven-inning scrimmage against the Boston College baseball team, which is down to take its annual pasting from the experienced teams along the Sun Coast and Alligator Alley (Florida college teams get to play and practice year-round, which hardly seems fair) before swinging north to play under usually cloudy skies and in cutting winds that make fifty degrees feel like thirty. But they are naturally juiced to be playing against the big boys, and in front of an audience that numbers in the thousands instead of the hundreds or—sometimes, early on—the mere dozens.

City of Palms Park in Fort Myers is Fenway's sunnier-tempered little brother. The aisles are wider, the concession lines are shorter, the prices are saner, the pace is slower, and the mood is laid-back. One hears the occasional cry of *You suck!*—these are Boston fans after all—but they are isolated, and often draw disapproving looks. This is a mellow crowd, and hey, why not? We're still in first place—along with the Yankees, and the Orioles, and even the Devil Rays, who dwell in their somehow dingy dome up the road in Tampa—and all things are possible. Curse? What curse? As if to underline this, a grinning bald guy holds up a sign for Pokey Reese. OKEY DOKEY, POKEY, it reads.

It's an afternoon for saying hello to old friends from previous springs going back—can it be?—six years, now; everyone from the parking-lot attendant and the elderly security guard outside the elevator going up to the offices and the press boxes to a laid-back Larry Lucchino, who wants to know if I'm over my bout of pneumonia. And Stewart O'Nan is here, looking exactly as he did last October during the American League Championship Series against the Yankees. Maybe a little more gray in the goatee—being a Red Sox fan will do that to you—but otherwise he looks like the same old Stew. He could even be munching from the same bag of peanuts. The wonderful Kerri Moore (who I still haven't met, although I did leave her a signed copy of *The Girl Who Loved Tom Gordon* as a thank-you) has gotten us seats directly behind the screen, and the grass is so green it almost looks painted on.

Tim Wakefield starts for Boston and gets a solid round of applause: these people remember the games he won in postseason, not the catastrophic season-ending home run he gave up to Aaron Boone. He throws more hard stuff than I'm used to seeing, but Wake's bread-and-butter pitch is the knuckleball, and to him the really hard stuff is a heater that clocks in at 81 miles an hour (the scoreboard down here gives no radar-gun readout, so we just have to guess). The top of the BC lineup hits him pretty well, and after half an inning they've put up a two-spot on four hits. This is a pretty typical early-spring outing for Wakefield, who just throws the one inning. At thirty-seven he's not only the dean of the Red Sox pitching staff, but the player who's been with the club longest.

A lot of the guys who see action in the Sox-BC scrimmage (which the Sox eventually win, 9–3, big surprise there) are a lot less familiar. There's Jesus Medrano, for instance, and career minor leaguer Andy Dominique; there's Tony Schrager, who is wearing the highest number I've ever seen: 95. Holy shit, I think, that could almost be his temperature. These guys and plenty of others will undoubtedly be on their way back to the Pawtucket Red Sox, the Portland Sea Dogs, and the Lowell Spinners (where the team mascot, Stew informs me, is the world-famous Canalligator) when the forty-man roster starts to shrink. For others, so-called invitees like Terry Shumpert, Tony Womack, and the world-famous Dauber, things are more serious. If it doesn't work here for them, it may not work anywhere. The career of a pro baseball player is longer than that of the average pro basketball or football player, but it is still short compared to that of your average account executive or ad salesman, and although the pay is better, the end can come with shocking suddenness.

But no one worries too much about stuff like that on a day like this. It's only the second game-day of the short spring season, the weather's beautiful, and everyone's loose. Around the fourth inning, Red Sox radio broadcaster Joe Castiglione comes down and sits with Stewart and me for a little while. Like the players, Joe looks trim, tanned and relaxed. He has his own book coming out in a month or so, a wonderful, anecdote-crammed trip down memory lane called *Broadcast Rites and Sites,* subtitled *I Saw It on the Radio with the Boston Red Sox.* (One of the best is about the grand slam Boston catcher Rich Gedman hit off Detroit screwballer Willie Hernandez back in '86.) He tells us more stories as he sits on the step at the end of the aisle, watching Boston College bat in the top of the fifth. Baseball is a leisurely game, and those of us who love it fill its pauses with stories of other games and other years. When I mention how hard I'm pulling for Brian Daubach to find a home with the '04 Red Sox, Joe tells us how he set Dauber up with the woman who became his wife. "She said she didn't like ballplayers because they were always hitting on her," Joe says, smiling in the warm afternoon sun. "I told her she ought to meet this guy. I told her he was really different. Really nice." Joe's smile widens into a grin. "Then I sent Dauber in to get his hair cut," he finishes. "Case closed."

Stew and I look at each other and say the same thing at exactly the same moment: What hair? The Dauber's got a quarter of an inch, at most. And we all laugh. It's good to be laughing at a baseball game again. God knows the laughs were hard to come by last October.

I ask Joe if the college kids get excited about these games with the pros (I'm thinking of the BC pitcher who struck out big David Ortiz in the third, and wondering if he'll still be telling people about it when he's forty-five and paunchy). "Oh, like you wouldn't believe," Joe says, and then goes on to tell us the Red Sox player the college kids liked the most was the much maligned Carl Everett, who was dubbed Jurassic Carl by Boston *Globe* columnist Dan Shaughnessy (for his temper as much as his fundamentalist Christian beliefs), and who has since been traded to the Montreal Expos. "He was great to the [college players]," Joe says. "He'd spend lots of time talking to them and give them all kinds of equipment." He pauses, then adds, "I bet he prospers in Montreal, because there's no media coverage. People won't be watching him so closely."

By now it's the bottom of the sixth, and Joe excuses himself. He and his broadcast partner, Jerry Trupiano ("Troop"), are doing the evening game (another slo-mo scrimmage, this time against Northeastern, with a fellow named Schilling starting for the Sox), and he has to prepare. But, like everything else that happens this day, the preparations will be leisurely, more pleasure than business. Joe knows a lot of people back home in New England will be listening, but not exactly paying attention—it's the Sox versus Northeastern, after all . . . but it's also baseball, Schilling on the mound, Garciaparra at short, and Varitek behind the plate (at least for a while, then maybe Kelly Shoppach, another guy with a high number). It's the fact of it that matters, like that first robin you see on your still-snowy front lawn.

It's too early to play really hard, and too early to wax really lyrical, either (God knows there's too much labored lyricism in baseball writing these days; it's even crept into the newspapers, which used to be bastions of statistics and hard-nosed reality—what sports reporters used to call "the agate"). But it can't hurt to say that being here—especially after a serious bout of pneumonia—feels pretty goddamn wonderful. It's like putting your hand out and touching a live thing—another season when great things may happen. Miracles, even. And if that isn't touching grace, it's pretty close.

Oh, shit, that's too close to lyrical for comfort, but it's been a good day. There was baseball. So let it stand.

March 6th

After a sloppy loss at the Twins' place, we run into Dauber by the players' lot. Everyone pushes toward him; it's not a surge, more of a controlled approach, lots of jockeying. There's a space of two feet around him that we seem to agree is forbidden. You can reach a ball or a card into it, but anything more would be a violation. No one tries to shake his hand or put an arm around him for a picture, as if that would be too personal.

I'm lucky enough to be in the front, in the middle.

"Welcome back," I tell him.

"Thank you." He's surprisingly soft-spoken, you might even say shy.

"Have you noticed everyone's been cheering the loudest for you, even here on the road."

"It means a lot."

I back off after he signs my ball, and see a Navigator with Illinois plates rolling up. I know Dauber's the pride of Belleville, Illinois (along with Wilco's Jeff Tweedy), so I call, "Your ride's here."

"Thanks," he says, and he's off.

When we get back to the hotel, I'm unwinding on the balcony when I see a woman on the beach in an old Lou Merloni shirt. "Loooooooo ooooooooouuuuuuu!" I hoot, and she turns around but doesn't see me.

For years Lou Merloni—the Pride of Framingham, Massachusetts—was our regular schlub and native son. He could play anywhere in the infield or outfield, and was a reliable pinch hitter. Someone would get hurt, and he'd end up starting, hit .330, and then sit when the guy came back. He was Nomar's best friend, yet Sox management seemed to delight in shipping him down to Pawtucket and calling him back up, a crazy yo-yo motion. Two years ago we shipped him to San Diego, only to get him back in midseason.

Lou's gone, off to Cleveland. Lou, who last year Ben Affleck (post-*Dogma*, pre-*Gigli*) called a joke during a visit to the Sox broadcast booth. Dauber's our Lou now.

March 7th

There's no point trying to beat the crowd today. People will be camping out for this one. Scalpers line Edison like hitchhikers, holding up signs: I NEED TICKETS.

The lot's almost full two hours before game time. People are tailgating, barbecuing on hibachis. A few rows closer to the park, four cotton-headed grandmothers in full Yankee regalia have their lawn chairs arranged under a shade tree.

Inside, it's a mini-invasion. The Yanks have brought their A-team: Jeter's at short and A-Rod, weirdly, is at third. It seems crazy to pay a guy that kind of money to play a corner. It must be ego: A-Rod's got better range, a better glove, a better arm. Jeter seems to have lost his concentration the last few years.

A-Rod lets a grounder skip under his glove into left, and the crowd cheers.

I notice the Yanks have a #22—Clemens's old number. After all Roger's talk of wanting to go into the Hall wearing a Yankee cap, it seems a calculated insult. While the Sox haven't officially retired his 21, it's one of the few numbers that hasn't been assigned.

I don't see Giambi or Sheffield, and wonder if the Yankees are protecting them from us. Our seats are down the right-field line, and I'd been looking forward to listening to the fans peppering Sheffield and waving signs like JUICIN' JASON.

There's a commotion down by the Sox dugout, and a cheer. Nomar's come out to shake hands with A-Rod. I only see their heads for an instant before the photographers swamp them. A few minutes later the scene repeats when Nomar greets Jeter.

The Yanks finish hitting—unimpressive except for this huge lefty I don't recognize. No Giambi or Sheffield. Maybe they're replacing their blood somewhere like Keith Richards did. And no sign of former Sox closer Tom Gordon, who would be sure to elicit a mixed reaction. I've got to ask Steve: Does that girl still love him?

Our lineup's disappointing: Nomar's sitting, so are Johnny D, Yankee killer David Ortiz and Dauber, and Trot's still out. Bronson Arroyo, who threw a perfect game for Pawtucket, is our starter. He may not be Pedro or Schilling but he looks good in the first, getting Kenny Lofton, Jeter and A-Rod in order.

Kapler leads off with an easy grounder to Jeter, who throws it away.

"A-Rod's smiling," a guy behind me says.

Kapler steals on Contreras and scores on a single by Bill Mueller. Contreras slows the pace down to Cuban National Team speed, hoping to take away our momentum, but Ellis Burks smacks a single, Kevin Millar whomps a double and we're up 3–0.

There's a lot of taunting in the stands, and a Yankee fan snaps back, "Yeah, you guys are great in March."

"What do Yankee fans use for birth control?" one guy asks, then answers, "Their personalities."

In the bottom of the second, Pokey Reese, subbing for Nomar, takes Contreras deep. The Yanks bring in Rivera to stop the bleeding, as if this is Game 7.

The Sox counter with minor leaguer Jason Shiell, who melts down. Francona makes no concessions to the rivalry, or even the game. This is spring training, and he leaves Shiell in to see if he can fight his way out.

The big lefty who was blasting them in batting practice turns out to be veteran Tony Clark, who golfs a three-run shot.

"Let's go Mets!" someone yells.

"Let's go Tigers!"

"Let's go Sox!"

The Yankees are still worried, it seems, because they bring in Felix Heredia to pitch the seventh and eighth. McCarty, who's played the whole game, hits into a 4-6-3 double play in the eighth, making him 0 for 4. In the top of the ninth he blocks a hot smash at first, then kicks the ball away.

"How's the weather in Pawtucket?" someone yells.

Hyzdu strikes out to end it. The final's 11–7. Unsatisfying, but we did win the A game, knocking Contreras around, and Arroyo looked good.

Outside, we walk by the players' lot, ogling a classic tomato-red GTO convertible. Someone says it's Nomar's, except he's already left with Mia Hamm in her car.

A Jeep Cherokee with BK in it flies by us.

"You're making friends," someone shouts after him.

Several people confirm a new trade rumor: BK and Trot for Randy Johnson.

Most of the big names are long gone, but first-base coach Lynn Jones rolls down his window and signs, as does Cesar Crespo, driving a pimped-out Integra with Konig rims. Terry Francona doesn't stop—"Another bad decision!"

A young guy pulls up in a Taurus. No one can place him. He stops and rolls down his window, but no one approaches.

"I'm only a rookie," he says. "You probably wouldn't want my autograph."

He's right, but we can't say that to his face.

"Sure we do." A couple of parents push their kids forward.

It's Josh Stevens, a pitcher for the PawSox.

There are only four people left when we take off. It's almost five.

Driving back to the hotel, I say, "I wonder if the Twins are playing tonight."

"You want a divorce?" Trudy asks.

March 9th

We're home, it's snowing, and summer seems a long way off. Maybe it's the weather, but that connection to the Sox that felt so strong just yesterday feels tenuous. I tell Steve it's like getting a taste of high summer and then having it snatched away. By season's end, I imagine it will seem Edenic, all possibility and perfect weather.

That night while we're watching TV, Dunkin' Donuts runs a commercial starring Curt Schilling. Schilling sits by his locker, eating a breakfast sandwich and listening to a language tape teaching him Bostonspeak. "Wicked hahd," he repeats between bites. "Pahk. Play wicked hahd when I go to the pahk." For several years now the spokesperson for Dunkin' Donuts has been Nomar. Another sign he's leaving?

March 12th

I catch an interview with PawSock third baseman Kevin Youkilis at the practice fields. In Michael Lewis's *Moneyball*, A's general manager Billy Beane champions Youkilis as "The Greek God of Walks." He's the kind of player Beane loves: average glove, so-so wheels, but a great eye, quick bat and astonishing on-base percentage. Likewise, Bill James, the Sox's statistical guru, is high on the guy's numbers. The interviewer is optimistic about Youkilis's chances of making the team, which I think is crazy. He's fourth on the depth chart behind Shump, and Shump's probably not going to make it.

Youkilis is positive but realistic. "Hopefully I'll make it up to Fenway this year"—meaning a cup of coffee in September when they expand the roster. Clips roll of the Monster seats and Pedro going up the ladder on a flailing Devil Ray, and again I'm ready for the season to start.

March 13th

Mr. Kim has a sore shoulder. I'm not surprised, with that goofy motion. Bronson Arroyo may take his slot, though the *Courant* says that during the first few weeks of the season the schedule's spread out enough that we can go with a four-man rotation.

Steve's not upset. He says Kim looked lost out there in the playoffs, as if he didn't know where the ball was going.

"He's only twenty-five," I say, "and he's already pitched in a lot of big games."

"That's part of his problem." Stat maven Bill James found that the more innings pitchers threw before the age of twenty-three, the more problems they had later in their careers.

"What about Clemens?"

"James doesn't count college. Clemens is actually one of the guys he uses to make his case. And Clemens is an exception, he's a workhorse. Dan Duquette found that out when he looked at his stats and said his career was over."

I don't see how James can have it both ways—an example *and* an exception—and it seems notable that the only championship Clemens ever really led his team to was the College World Series, but even the devil can quote Scripture for his purposes.

• • •

In bed, in the dark, I match last year's rotation to this year's. Schilling's a major upgrade from John Burkett, but who is Kim—now Arroyo—replacing? It takes me a minute to recall Casey Fossum—or Blade, as we called him, since he weighed about 140 pounds, his front literally concave. He was the guy we wouldn't trade last spring to get Bartolo Colon, hoping he'd develop into a steady lefty starter. He was in and out all year with injuries and never got it going. Kim is an improvement on him, but Arroyo is in pretty much the same place Blade was two years ago, a triple-A player trying to earn that number five slot. We'll be stronger, but there'll still be a weak spot other managers can attack, stealing series by feeding their weaker pitchers to our aces, matching their ace against Lowe and then throwing their number two and three guys against Wake and Arroyo.

Should I be worrying about this now?

Terry Francona better be.

March 14th

In the Sunday sports section are two pictures of Jason Giambi, a before and after comparison that makes me go, "Whoa." In the one from last year he's pudgy-cheeked, a pad of fat under his chin, his biceps filling his sleeves. The one from a couple weeks ago shows a drawn, scrawny guy, rock-star thin, as if he's been hit by some wasting disease. My immediate reaction isn't partisan but humane: God, I hope he's okay.

I don't catch the final of today's game until the late news. Pedro had control problems and walked in a run, but Johnny D homered and we beat the O's 5–2. I'm glad we won, but it doesn't really matter. I'm more concerned with Pedro's walk total from last year, and the trouble he had finding the plate in the playoffs. It's been three years since he's been consistently dominant, and I wonder if he'll ever get back to that level.

Because back then, there was no doubt. In 2001, we went to a game he was supposed to throw against Seattle, when Seattle was the hottest team in the majors. The game was delayed by rain about two hours, and we were worried that Pedro wouldn't start because of the cold. He came out in the first and got Ichiro on three pitches, then John Olerud on three pitches, and then Edgar Martinez on three pitches. Nine pitches, nine strikes. I looked at Steph like, what did we just see?

It was a strange realization, witnessing him strike out seventeen or spin a one-hitter. Then, when you were watching Pedro, you knew you were watching the best pitcher—out of the millions of people to pick up a base-ball and try to throw it past a batter—in the entire world. But that was three years ago.

March 17th

Tonight the high school dedicates Caitlin's choral concert to a beloved cus-todian who died suddenly of a heart attack. The teacher reading a speech about him confesses that they bonded as Sox fans, and that "the morning after the Sox had blown another sure thing, we knew not to talk about the game until we'd had our coffees."

An easel at the front of the auditorium holds a picture of him. He couldn't be more than fifty-five, and I think how unfair it is that he never got to expe-rience the Sox winning it all—like Trudy's uncle Vernon, who died last year in his sixties. Whenever I saw him, we talked Sox. It was our one point of connection, a joshing, bitching camaraderie shared over beers. This sum-mer's going to be different without him, emptier. I think of the millions of Sox fans who rooted their entire lives and never felt that giddy vindication the Pats have given us twice now. There has to be a tremendous psychic charge built up from those faithful generations. This year, if we do it, we'll be doing it for them too.

I don't want to spend a long time maundering over mortality, but you know, when I was eighteen and Lonnie was pitching for the Sox, I *knew* I'd be around to see them win the Series. You know how it is when you're eighteen and bulletproof. Now, holy shit, I'm fifty-seven, I've been hit by a car, I had a lung practically go up in smoke this winter, and I realize maybe it really won't happen. And still I look at our team and sometimes wonder . . . *Who are these guys?* Oh well. I used to joke, you know, about having a tombstone that read: STEPHEN KING with the dates, and then, below that, a single sock, and below that: NOT IN MY LIFETIME. And below that: NOT IN YOURS, EITHER. Not a bad tagline, huh?

March 18th

I'm shocked to read in the paper that Nomar is 0 for spring—0 for 8, really—and has missed four straight games with that bruised heel. Cesar Crespo's seizing the opportunity, hitting .435. Maybe he can take that extra roster spot.

March 19th

Trot flies out to L.A. to get checked by a specialist and looks doubtful for Opening Day. Kapler, who took a pay cut to stay with the Sox, must be cursing his agent.

Nomar shows up at the clubhouse with a boot on his foot. The trainer's diagnosed him with Achilles tendinitis, but an MRI shows no structural damage. And Manny, I discover, is hitting .172. Now I'm glad we've got a few weeks to get things together.

The lottery for Green Monster seats begins, one entry per e-mail address. After getting aced out of regular tickets, I'm resigned, punching in our two entries.

Then I get an idea. I have dozens of friends who have no interest in Monster seats. I can use their names, and if by some chance they win, I can pay them face value for the tickets. I imagine scalpers are using dozens, even hundreds, of e-mail addresses.

The comparison's unavoidable. Now I'm like them, bending the rules in my greed for the seats. It feels decidedly squirmy, and yet for the next few hours I span the continent, tapping Oklahoma and the Rockies and San Francisco and Edmonton for names, addresses, phone numbers and birthdays donated by pitying friends.

March 20th

The team dwindles as Theo assigns seven players to the minors, including optioning Kevin Youkilis to Pawtucket.

Steve's worried about Trot, and brings up Tim Naehring, our ill-fated third baseman of the nineties. Naehring was that agonizing player who's vastly talented but always hurt. At 6'2", 205, he wasn't delicate, but he broke his wrist, he broke his ankle, he had a bad back. He was on the DL so much that he came to seem like a platoon player. When he finally retired at age thirty, it seemed possible that he was just hurt again. That's not how Trot wants to go out.

March 21st

This morning Philadelphia blew up the Vet. While Phillies fans remembered their one World Series win, Eagles fans hoped it would change their luck. Back when our old owners were planning to build a new Fenway, I heard the same kind of superstitious talk out of stalwarts like Ted Williams (who always hated the Monster's effect on Sox pitchers). So, if we win, do we have to keep it as a good-luck charm? The Vet, like Three Rivers Stadium or the Kingdome, bit the dust not because it was unlucky or falling down, but because it just wasn't a fun place to watch a ball game. That's not true of Fenway, unless you're stuck behind a pole or in line for the bathroom. The true test of a ballpark, and maybe a ball club, is percent capacity—how many butts versus how many seats—and Fenway's aced that test every year since 1967.

Steve couldn't even scrounge a ticket to the Sox-Jays game yesterday—at *their* place.

SO: I can see you in the parking lot, wagging a finger, waylaying strangers—"Need one."

SK: The Sox are a hot ticket everywhere they go in Florida. Folks think they are a genna-wine Team of Destiny. They banged out Ed Wood Stadium, or whatever they call the place here in Sarasota where Cincy plays; first time in two years. And were turning them away at the door. All that and Air-Cast Nomar didn't even play. It will be interesting to see if the phenomenon carries over into the regular season.

Remember the year the Orioles were relatively stacked and started 0-21? Or was it 0-22?

Go you big David Ortiz.

I call up the website and find we've shipped Tony Womack to the Cards. With Womack gone, we don't have a designated late-inning base-stealer, unless Shump is showing flashes of his old speed. I feel bad for Womack, his salary and Lamborghini notwithstanding. He bunted and ran better than anyone on the team this spring, but not being able to play the field, he never had a chance.

Shump takes advantage of this break by straining a hamstring in the night game. So after finally outlasting Womack, he essentially hands McCarty the twenty-fifth spot.

March 24th

The drawing for Monster seats was yesterday. All morning I avoid opening my e-mail, not wanting to jinx our shot. It's noon when I finally check, expecting dozens of forwards from my co-conspirators. There's a piece of spam from priceline.com, that's it.

At five there's still nothing, good or bad.

The Sox are playing the Yanks on NESN. Trudy says I can watch it, but there's an interesting documentary on, and I say, "That's okay. It's just pre-season."

The documentary's short, and we catch up to the game late. We're behind 8–5, but when we rally in the bottom of the ninth, there aren't enough Yankee fans left to overcome a hearty "Let's go, Red Sox!" chant. It's a classic Red Sox moment, that refusal to give in, even with Lowell Spinner Iggy Suarez stepping to the plate as our last hope. Iggy, feeling it, singles. With two on and two out, Dauber hits a flare to left, and it's 8–6 with men on second and third and Hyzdu coming up. The chanting grows frantic, like we might actually pull it out. Hyzdu's batting .173. He shows us why, taking three late, waving swings, and for the second time this spring we lose to the Yankees.

I turn the channel. I know it's only exhibition, and that it's classier not to chase after meaningless wins, but it's irritating.

By midnight I still haven't gotten any e-mail about Monster tickets. I think that can't be good, but, like losing to the Yanks, there's nothing I can do but eat it.

March 25th

I'm hoping/expecting to shove all the work off my desk and get down to City of Palms to see the Sox on Saturday. I've got an invite to watch the game with Dan "Curse of the Bambino" Shaughnessy, the writer most New England fans (at least those who read the Boston *Globe*) most readily associate with the Olde Towne Team. And this Curse thing has really entered the New England stream of consciousness, as I'm sure you know— it's right up there with the Salem witch trials and Maine lobstah, up there to the point where some wit with a spray can (or tortured sports fan/artist, take your choice) has turned a traffic sign reading REVERSE CURVE on Storrow Drive into one reading REVERSE THE CURSE. Of course you and I know the so-called Curse of the Bambino is about as real as the so-called Books of Mormon, supposedly discovered in a cave and read with the help of "magic peekin' stones" (true!), but like all those Mormons, I kind of believe in spite of the thing's patent absurdity.

March 27th

At three the remaining Green Monster seats go on sale. Considering we went 0 for 34 during the online lottery, I can't imagine there are any left, but at 2:57 I'm watching the seconds tick off on the Weather Channel. I've enlisted Trudy, against her will, to take the other phone, and at exactly three we bombard the old info line.

Forty minutes into it, Trudy breaks through and hands over the phone. "I did my duty."

I wait through "Hot Fun in the Summertime," and Boz Scaggs's "It's Over," and "(Na Na Hey Hey) Kiss Him Good-bye." When I finally get a human, he says there are actual seats left, which I think is wrong.

"Anything for the Yankees?"

"I can get you second row for April eighteenth."

"I'll take 'em," I say, thinking I'm getting away with something.

March 28th

Now they're saying Nomar probably won't make the opener. Francona, trying to play it down, says Nomar would be starting if it were September—as if he doesn't know all the games count the same.

March 30th

The Yomiuri (Tokyo) Giants, who Matsui played for, are Japan's answer to the Yankees—based in the largest city, with dozens of championships. My friend Phil in Tokyo has told me the Hanshin Tigers from Osaka-Kyoto are their Sox, a hard-luck club with fans who are devoted beyond all reason. Last year they won the Central League, beating the Giants, then lost a heartbreaker of a Series to the Daiei Hawks. For a couple weeks, people all over Japan were wearing their Hanshin Tigers gear, even in Tokyo.

It makes sense—Osaka-Kyoto is like Boston, a proud, much smaller city in the shadow of a megalopolis, and like the Yankees, the Giants have the most money and generate the most media coverage.

WELCOME TO NEXT YEAR

Yesterday the Hanshin Tigers pounded Donovan Osborne and the Yanks, 11–7. Their first baseman, with the un-Japanese-sounding name of Arias, has a sweet line in the box score: 4 2 3 5. Go Tigers!

Today the Yanks open the regular season there—in fact, with the time difference, they're losing to Lou Piniella's Devil Rays as I read the morning paper.

SK: I got down to the game yesterday and saw my man Tim Wakefield go a strong six. We won, 8–3. He gave up two long balls, but the second was a pop-fly type of deal that just kind of got up in the slipstream and carried over the wall. It would have been caught by Trot (in Fenway). I spent a lot of time in the booth with Joe Castiglione and Jerry Trupiano. Troop told me a really terrible joke. Janet Jackson decides to rehab her tattered reputation by becoming the first woman to play major league baseball, right? But it doesn't work. Her first at-bat in Kansas City . . . she pops out again.

BOOO!

In between half-innings in the sixth—this could only happen to a writer—I was proofing some copy for the final Dark Tower book and working out with my eraser. The Sox come up just as I'm finishing. The first pitch produces a line foul that missed my nose by less than an inch. I swear this is a true thing I'm telling you. I saw it go between my nose and the little pile of manuscript I had in my hands, also heard the baleful whiz of the ball, which hit an old guy behind me pretty hard. My seatmates are going, "Did you see that? Pokey Reese almost nailed Stephen King!" Etc, etc. Well, the lady next to me was into her third or fourth beer—enough so she was willing to be disapproving no matter who I was. She said, "We're sitting right behind the dugout, in case you didn't notice. You should be paying attention." I replied—and I really believe this to be true—that if I had been watching, I would have involuntarily jerked right into it and gotten my friggin' face rearranged (some would say that might be an improvement). I mean, that thing was a rocket.

I'm back for more abuse tomorrow. That's the last spring training tilt. Then things get serious.

SO: Glad you're okay, and congratulations on finishing. Now the important question: Who got the ball?

March 31st

Before I've eaten breakfast, the Yanks have crushed the D-Rays 12–1, and the division's knotted at .500 again. We play the Twins at Hammond tomorrow, then head to Atlanta for two against the Braves before opening in Baltimore.

By Sunday, the club has to make eleven more cuts to get down to the final twenty-five-man roster. On the bubble: Dauber, McCarty, Crespo, Hyzdu and Shump. Three of the bubble guys and one lucky pitcher (maybe a second lefty to go with Embree) should make the team, at least for the next month. The trouble is, we're short on outfielders. Theo and Francona may have to keep Hyzdu, who's had the worst spring of any Red Sock, and send down Shump and Crespo, who's had the best.

April 1st

On the very last day he could, Shump exercises an out clause in his contract and is free to sign with another club (eventually the Pirates), meaning Cesar Crespo, hitting .361, has earned a spot on the roster.

Met vet Bobby Jones and Tim Hamulack will fight for the final bullpen spot. They'll both travel to Atlanta—as will Adam Hyzdu, who's already been told by Francona he'll start the year in Pawtucket. He's the twenty-sixth man, the last one cut, and knows he could have made the team if he'd only hit the ball. With Trot out and Kapler starting, our backup outfielders are the thirty-eight-year-old, leg-injury-prone Ellis Burks, first baseman/aspiring pitcher David McCarty and fullbacks Brian Daubach and Kevin Millar.

The roster's set, if not the lineup. The bench may not be as deep as the Yankees', but it's a good club, a 95–100 win club. My only worry now is health, with Nomar, Trot and BK already out. If we lose anyone else important, this could quickly turn into a lost season, like the Angels' last year.

April 2nd

I drive to Boston to meet my friend Lowry's lit class at Simmons College, right down Brookline Ave from Fenway. All the way up, I wrestle with the question of whether to drop in on Naomi. I don't want to freak her out, but she hasn't returned my calls, and we're a week away from the home opener.

I'm early, there's a parking spot, and I can't resist. From the sidewalk, the office looks dark, but that's just the tinted windows. The big tally board with all the games broken down by sections is covered with X's. Everything's sold-out except some August games against Tampa Bay and Toronto.

A young guy at a desk is on the phone with someone who got aced out of the Monster seats. "I'm sorry, sir," the guy says, "but it did say first-come first-serve."

I'm loitering, and he looks up from the phone in mid-conversation.

"Is Naomi expecting you?"

He calls her, then explains that she's all the way on the other side of the park (there *is* no other side of the park—that would be where the batting cages are, under the center-field bleachers). She says not to worry, it's going to happen. It's going to be a day-of-game thing, I'll have to pick them up at the Will Call window.

Outside, a crew is fixing pennants over Gate A. The one they're working on as I pass says 1918 WORLD CHAMPIONS.

I go down Lansdowne and look up at the Monster seats. Green metal stools perch upside-down on the counters, like a bar after closing. I try to imagine sitting up there, but the wind's so cold it's hard to believe the season's only two days away.

It's after dinner when I finally catch up to yesterday's game. We beat the Twins 4–3, taking three out of five from them to win Fort Myers's Mayor's Cup. The hero, ironically, was Adam Hyzdu, who homered to break the tie in the ninth. Too little, too late.

April 3rd

Last night we beat the Braves 7–3. Exhibition results mean even less the day before the opener, but I'm glad to see Manny pick up his first homer of the spring.

Today the Braves shut us out, 5–0, with Foulke giving up two runs in a third of an inning. I tell myself it means nothing, but neither does our 17-12 Grapefruit League record (a half game, I'm sorry to report, behind the Yanks).

In the last meaningful action of the spring, lefty Bobby Jones's slider and

1.74 ERA win him the final roster spot over the less experienced Tim Hamulack.

The Weather Channel's predicting snow here tomorrow night. In Baltimore, for the first pitch, it's supposed to be thirty-nine degrees.

Who Are These Guys?

April 4th

Opening Day: *Notes on Addiction*

I've written about substance abuse a good many times, and see no need to rehash all that in a book about baseball . . . but because this also happens to be a book about *rooting*, the subject at least has to be mentioned, it seems to me. These are a fan's notes, after all, and when used in the context of rooting, the word *fan* ain't short for *fantastic*.

I don't booze it up anymore, and I don't take the mind- or mood-altering drugs, but over a good many years of staying away from those things one day at a time, I've come to a more global view of addiction. Sometimes I think of it as the Lump in the Sofa Cushion Theory of Addiction. This theory states that addiction to booze or dope is like a lump in a sofa cushion. You can push it down . . . but it will only pop up somewhere else. Thus a woman who quits drinking may start smoking again. A guy who quits the glass pipe may rediscover his sex drive and become a serial womanizer. A gal who quits drinking and drugging may put Twinkies and strawberry ice cream in their place, thus adding forty or fifty pounds before putting on the brakes.

Hey, I've been lucky. No sex issues, no gambling issues, moderate food issues. I do, however, have a serious problem with the Boston Red Sox, and have ever since they came so damned close to winning the whole thing in '67. Before then, I was what you might call a recreational Red Sox user. Since then I've been a full-blown junkie, wearing my hat with the scarlet *B* on the front for six months straight and suffering a serious case of hat-head while I obsess over the box scores. I check the Boston Red Sox official website, and all the unofficial ones as well (most of them fucking dire); I scoff at the so-called Curse of the Bambino, believing completely in my

31

heart even though I know it is the bullshit creation of one talented and ambitious sportswriter.*

Worst of all, during the season I become as much a slave to my TV and radio as any addict ever was to his spike. I have been asked by several people if working on this book is a hardship, given the fact that I have two *other* books coming out this year (the final novels in the Dark Tower cycle), a television series still in production (that would be *Kingdom Hospital* on ABC, the Detroit Tigers of network broadcasting), and a half-finished *new* novel sitting on my desk. The answer is no—it's not a hardship but a relief. I would either be sitting at Fenway or in my living room with the TV tuned to NESN (the New England Sports Network, the regional pusher that services addicts like me) in any case; this book legitimizes my obsession and allows me to indulge it to an even greater degree. In the language of addiction, the book's publisher has become my enabler and my colleague, Stewart O'Nan, is my codependent.

Now, nine hours before Sidney Ponson of the Orioles throws his first pitch to the first Red Sox batter of the season, I can look at my situation coldly and clearly: I am a baseball junkie, pure and simple. Or perhaps it's even more specific than that. Perhaps I'm a *Red Sox* junkie, pure and simple. I'm hoping it's choice B, actually. If it is, and the Sox win the World Series this year, this nearly forty-year obsession of mine may break like a long-term (*very* long-term) malarial fever. Certainly this team has the tools, but Red Sox fans do not need the bad mojo of some false "curse" to appreciate the odd clouds of bad luck that often gather around teams that seem statistically blessed. Outfitted in the off-season with strong pitching and defense to go with their formidable hitting, the Sox suddenly find themselves short two of their most capable players: Nomar Garciaparra and Trot Nixon. 2003 batting champ Bill Mueller, suffering supposed elbow problems (from swinging a leaded bat in the on-deck circle?—I wonder), has seen little spring training action. And Cadillac closer Keith Foulke has been, let's face it, nothing short of horrible.

But for the true junkie—er, fan, I mean, true *fan*—such perverse clouds of darkness do not matter. The idea of starting 0 and 22, for instance (as the Orioles once did), is pushed firmly to the back of the mind.† There will be no *Sopranos* tonight at 9 P.M., even if the Sox trail by

---

*The Boston *Globe*'s Dan Shaughnessy.
†Where it festers.

five in the seventh inning; there will be no *Deadwood* tonight at 10 P.M. even if Keith Foulke comes on in the eighth, blows a three-run Sox lead, and then gives up an extra three for good measure. Tonight, barring a stroke or a heart attack, I expect to be in until the end, be it bitter or sweet. And the same could be said for the season as a whole. I'm going to do pretty much what I did last year, in other words (only this year I expect to get paid for it). Which is pretty much addiction in a nutshell: doing the same thing over and over, and expecting a different result.

Right now it's only 10 A.M., though, and the house is quiet. No one's playing baseball yet. I'm fever-free for another nine hours, and I'm enjoying it. Don't get me wrong, I'll enjoy the baseball game, too. The first one's always a thrill. I think that's true even if you're a Tigers or Devil Rays fan (a team that looks much improved this year, by the way). But by August, in the heat of a pennant race, I always start to resent the evenings spent following baseball and to envy the people who can take it or just turn it off and read a good book. Myself, I've never been that way. I'm an addict, you see. And I'm a fan. And if there's a difference, I don't see it.

Opening on the road sucks. You can't feel the perfect newness of the season up close. A true home opener's a pearl, smooth and untouched. Not this year. By the time the team gets to Fenway, whether we're 4-0 or 0-4, the season will have been rubbed up, scuffed, cut. And it'll still be cold.

It's forty-three and breezy in Baltimore. Hot dog wrappers and plastic bags drift by behind the home-plate ump. I'm at home, digging the game on NESN from my cozy couch. Don Orsillo and Jerry Remy talk about Opening Day jitters, and to prove them right, in the first Bill Mueller throws one wide of Millar. Melvin Mora lets him off the hook by trying to take third on a bloop single, and Manny easily guns him down. In the top of the next inning, Mora lifts his glove and lets a grounder go through his legs.

The heart of the O's lineup is made of their big off-season free agents—former MVP Miguel Tejada and All Stars Rafael Palmeiro and Javy Lopez. In the second, Lopez, seeing his first pitch as an O, plants a high fastball from Pedro in the left-field seats, and the crowd chants, "Ja-vy, Ja-vy." Don points out that the fastball was clocked at 89.

Pedro's missing the plate, pulling his hard curve a good two feet outside on righties. Gibbons singles, then Pedro plunks David Segui. There are no outs. Bigbie hits an excuse-me roller to Pedro, who checks second and goes

33

to first. The throw's to the home side of the bag, and looks like Millar can handle it, but it tips off his glove and skips away. Gibbons scores and the runners move up. "Payyyyd-rooooo, Payyyyd-rooooo," the crowd taunts. He leaves a change-up up to Matos, who singles in Segui. Matos steals second. In the bullpen Bronson Arroyo is warming.

Don and Jerry debate the possibility that something's physically wrong with Pedro; maybe he's having trouble gripping the ball in the cold. Pedro quiets them (and the crowd) by striking out Roberts and Mora, bringing up Tejada, who looks thicker around the middle, positively husky for a short-stop. He hits one deep to right-center that Johnny Damon tracks down, and we're out of it.

Jerry says we're lucky to be down only three runs, and while he's right, I don't feel lucky. Two innings into the opener and the season's turning to shit.

We get a run back in the top of the third when Manny rips a single off Ponson's back leg. In the bottom, Bellhorn and Pokey turn a nifty two to end the inning and touch gloves on their way to the dugout. So some things are working.

In the fourth, on a ball to the right-field corner with two down and the number nine hitter coming up, Dale Sveum holds Kapler at third, though the throw goes into second without a cutoff man. "Don't be stupid," I plead, too late. And then Pokey, for no reason I can see, tries to sneak a bunt past Ponson and is an easy third out.

Pedro's settled down, giving up only two hits since the second. It's still only 3–1 in the seventh when David Ortiz launches one down the right-field line—foul.

In the seventh, Timlin comes in and walks two, gives up a bloop to Tejada and a Palmeiro single through a shifted infield, and it's 4–1. Dave Wallace makes a visit to the mound but doesn't take Timlin out. The next batter, Javy Lopez, hits a long fly to right-center that hangs up. Johnny D tracks it as the wind takes it away from him. Kapler's angling in from right to back up the play. Johnny looks up, then looks over at Kapler. Kapler looks at Johnny. The ball lands between them. With two outs, everyone's running, and Palmeiro hoofs it all the way around from first.

This is when everyone leaves, including Trudy. It's eleven o'clock on a Sunday, and the game has been plain ugly. It continues that way. The reliever for the O's walks the bases loaded and gives up a run on a fielder's choice. Later, Cesar Crespo makes a throw in the dirt that Millar should scoop but doesn't, letting in another run. In the top of the ninth it's 7–2 and thirty degrees and Camden Yards is empty, yet the fans I see behind the dugout—this is so typical it makes me laugh—are all Red Sox fans. And here I am, the only one left awake in the house, watching to the bitter end.

Tom Caron and Dennis Eckersley break it down on *Extra Innings,* but really, what can you say about a game like this? The most obvious stat is 14 men left on base. Johnny D went 0 for 5 in the leadoff spot, Tek went 0 for 4. Timlin gave up three earned runs in two-thirds of an inning (and one of those outs was Tek cutting down a runner on a risky pitchout). They pick on Pokey, showing the bunt attempt. Eck says he understands the strategy but, "If it doesn't work, it looks horrible." They also examine Millar's footwork on the throwing error charged to Pedro that kept the O's rally going. Instead of posting up at the front corner of the bag with his right foot so he can stretch towards Pedro with his left (and his glove), Millar is facing the bag with his left foot in the center so that he has to reach across his body to handle the throw. Basically, he nonchalanted it and cost us a couple of runs.

I turn it off. What's demoralizing isn't losing—we'll lose 60–70 games this year (knock wood)—it's playing badly. If this had been the first week of the NFL season, the announcers would have said this team has a lot of work to do.

April 5th

I can't help running a quick postmortem, scanning the story in the morning paper. Francona stands by his man Sveum, saying Kapler would have been meat if he'd gone. I hope this kind of denial isn't indicative of the new emperor.

SK: The bad news this morning is that the Red Sox lost their opener and Pedro looked *very* mortal. The good news is that there *was* baseball.

SO: Pedro had a bad inning, helped along by Millar. Still, he settled down after the second, and we were in the game till Timlin let it get away.

Think Pokey bunted on his own? Is he going to be like Steve "Psycho" Lyons?

SK: Yeah, I think Pokey Reese bunted on his own, and I think it was the break point in the game for the Red Sox. You can say there are a lot of games left and I would agree, but Gil Hodges (I think it was Hodges) said, "First games are big games," and if he meant they set the tone, I agree. And I know, I know, two-out rallies are always chancy. All the more reason to play it straight, right? Here's your situation: Millar, who really only hits middle relievers with reliability, opens the fourth by flying out to center. Kapler singles. Tek-money—Tek-small-change in April—hits a bat-busting pop to short. Two out. Bellhorn doubles. Runners at second and third, that sets the stage for Mr. Reese, who can tie the game with a righteous single. Instead, he bunts—hard—and is out easily, pitcher to first. Easy to read his thinking: Ponson's a porker, if I place it right, I get on to load 'em up for Johnny Damon, or maybe Kapler scores. But even if Kapler *does* score, we're still behind, and that early in the game, you'd think he'd be swinging away. So yeah— I think it was a plan he hatched in his own head, and a classic case of a baseball player taking dumb pills. Which leads me to something my elder son said this afternoon: "Dad, I don't envy you this book—you could have picked the wrong year. A team this high-octane could stall with the wrong manager and be out of it in the first month." I don't say it will happen, but he's got a point, and I hope the Pokester got a stern talking-to about that bunt.

I don't intend to deconstruct every game—or even most of them— but that bunt made me a lot more uneasy than the way Pedro Martinez threw on a cold night.

It's Opening Day for the rest of the league, and ESPN has wall-to-wall coverage. I catch pieces of the Cubs-Reds game (Sean Casey, a Pittsburgh native, blasts a two-run double off of Kerry Wood); a rare TV appearance by the Pirates taking on Kevin Millwood and the Phils (my brother's somewhere in the freezing center-field bleachers); and the Astros with Nolan Ryan in the dugout hosting Barry Bonds, Willie Mays and the Giants (lots of home run talk but not a word about steroids from Joe Morgan). I watch the games with mild interest, but can't commit to any of them. I wish the Sox were playing today so we could get back on the winning track and ditch this bad morning-after feeling. It's just impatience. I've waited all winter for Schilling. I can wait one more day.

April 6th

I have to do a reading over in Bristol, Rhode Island. It's a gig I set up months ago, hoping it wouldn't interfere with Opening Day. It won't, but today's game in Baltimore starts at 3:05, and I'm meeting a class then, and dining with the faculty at 5:30.

My host, Adam, says we could have a beer in between and catch a few innings. We find a bar down by the water with the sun flooding through the windows. The place must have six TVs. None of them is showing the game. We start some chatter about Schilling making his debut, and a pair of regulars join the chorus. The barmaid finds NESN for the big-screen on the wall. Beside it is a printout of a picture I've seen on eBay: a little towheaded boy about three years old in a Sox shirt on someone's shoulders. He's leaning toward the field, screaming and giving someone a tiny finger.

There's Schilling, sitting on the bench, going over something on a clipboard. It's 3–1 Sox in the seventh, and Embree's in. The O's only have six hits, so I assume Schilling threw well.

The two locals at the bar next to us start grousing about Pedro leaving Sunday's game before it was over. "When are they gonna do something about him?"

In the eighth, Melvin Mora hits a medium-deep fly to right-center. Johnny D drifts over. It's his ball, obviously, but Millar, unaccustomed to playing right, keeps coming. The memory of the pop falling between Johnny and Kapler Sunday night is still fresh, and neither takes his eyes off the ball. Johnny gets there first. As he makes the catch, his shoulder catches Millar flush in the face, knocking him on his ass like a vicious blindside on a kick return. Millar stays down.

The guys in the truck roll the collision between Johnny and Damian Jackson in last year's playoffs, Johnny's head snapping back and then the ambulance idling on the outfield grass. They show it twice, both times getting a vocal reaction from the whole bar. Then they show today's collision two more times. Millar spits a little blood, but he looks more dazed than anything, blinking and squeezing the bridge of his nose. He comes out and Cesar Crespo makes his debut as a right fielder.

The next batter, Tejada, hits a fly to deep right-center. This time Johnny waves his throwing hand high above his head to call off Crespo, and that's the inning.

Foulke is warming, but we have to go to dinner—we're already twenty minutes late.

"They look like they're in good shape," Adam says as we head to the restaurant.

"Never say that," I say.

SK: Nice game today. It went almost exactly the way the BoSox geneticists would like them to go. You get six innings from Schilling, who gives up a single run. One inning from Embree (no runs), one inning from Timlin (no runs), and one from Foulke, who gets the save. Also on the plus side is my BOSOX CLUB hat, which seems to be quite lucky. I plan to wear it until the lining falls out.

P.S. More questions about Francona: (1) Was Pedro consciously testing the new manager's authority by leaving when he did during the first game? (2) Was F. wrong to pull Manny from the field when he did, thus denying Manny the chance to bat in the ninth inning? (3) What's up with his unwillingness to sacrifice the runners to the next base(s)?

SO: (1) Dunno what's up with Pedro, but it seems early to be riding the guy. (2) Yes, definitely a mistake to pull Manny when Millar's the non-outfielder out there (see what happened?). (3) His distaste for the sac bunt is straight from the Bill James bible: don't give up any outs, even what we might think are necessary ones.

SK: Also, the guy just doesn't look like a manager to me. Yon Francona has a lean and stupid look.

SO: Well, Grady didn't exactly strike me as a Stephen Hawking figure.

April 7th

Not only did the Sox win, but the Yanks lost. The D-Rays beat on Mussina again, so they're on top of the division. Go, you crazy Lou!

Schilling threw 109 pitches yesterday, topping out at 98 mph. I know the gun down there is fast, because it clocked Ponson at 97, but still, knowing Schilling's strong makes me optimistic about the season.

While I was out yesterday, Matt from my agent's office called and left a message with Steph that says he wants to talk about Opening Day. I'm thinking it has to do with tickets, but it's about Opening Day in Baltimore. He went. A friend came up with tickets at the last minute, and he put everything aside and hopped on a cheap flight. He says the wind was crazy; the two big oriole weather vanes on top of the scoreboard in center were spinning in opposite directions.

He was surprised at the venom of the O's fans. After Pedro hit Segui, they were chanting "Pedro Sucks." I'm not surprised. Pedro can come off as arrogant, and after dominating for so long, he's earned some payback. The same with the Sox lately. They're a high-paid, high-profile club, and the second-division teams have a right to dislike them.

Tonight's game is a pitching mismatch, D-Lowe versus the young Kurt Ainsworth. This is one main strength of the 2004 Sox. Over the last two years, Lowe's won more games that any AL pitcher except the Jays' Roy Halladay. Part of the reason: last year he led the league in run support, with over 7 runs a start.

Ainsworth looks okay through the first, getting Ortiz and Manny (batting cleanup again). In the second he has runners on first and second with two out when Pokey hits a hopper to the hole. Tejada nabs it cleanly. He's moving toward third, and looks to Mora for the force, but Mora—not having the instincts of a third baseman—is lagging behind the runner, and Tejada has to plant and throw across his body to first. After hesitating, there's no way he's getting Pokey, so now the bases are loaded. Johnny D slaps a single to left. Sveum, bizarrely, sends Bellhorn. The throw beats him by twenty feet, but comes in on a short-hop and Javy Lopez can't get a handle on it. 2–0, second and third. Bill Mueller hits a single to center. This time the trailing runner is Johnny, and he scores easily.

Ainsworth's upset and can't find the plate now, walking Ortiz. He goes

3-1 on Manny before Manny flies to center. It's well hit but should be caught. Ainsworth takes a few steps toward the dugout, watching Matos, who holds up both arms as if beseeching the sky. He's lost it in the twilight. It hits the track by the base of the wall and bounces high, giving Ortiz more than enough time to chug around. 6–0. Millar rips a single to center. Matos has a shot at Manny, but his throw is off-line.

And that's it, that's more than enough. Johnny goes 5 for 5 and makes a spectacular grab, going over the fence in front of the O's bullpen to take a three-run homer away from David Segui; David Ortiz cranks a three-run shot down the line in right; Lowe throws well, and Pokey and Bellhorn do a nice job behind him; even Mendoza gets some work in; but really it's a one-inning game. It's the kind of win that makes you complacent—that makes you see the O's as a bad club.

It's not true. Like the opener, it's just one game. We still have to beat them tomorrow with Wake to take the series.

April 8th

SK: How about Damon's catch last night? I saw it on tape. That was *my* game to miss, except for the eighth and ninth. Dinner with friends. Isn't it annoying, the way life keeps intruding on baseball?

SO: Besides Johnny having a big night, you didn't miss much. I think Baltimore needs to rethink trying to change Melvin Mora into a third baseman. He's just lost out there—like Todd Walker, no instincts. Then after Lee Mazzilli and the media ream him out, he gets to go home to his wife and their two-year-old quints. No wonder he looks like he's going to break into tears any second.

You want to hear life intruding on baseball? I've been planning for months to take T to Chicago for our twentieth anniversary—got the plane tickets, hotel reservations, everything. Our first day there is the first game of the World Series. I say, "Hey, maybe we'll be playing the Cubs." She says, "We're not going there for the World Series. I'm not playing second fiddle to the Red Sox."

SK: Oh God, does that ever sound familiar. They're playing our song.

There's an official tally of the Opening Day payrolls. Once again, the Yankees top the majors at 183 million. The Sox are second at 125, the Angels third at 101.

By three I'm getting antsy, and call Naomi. I call five times before I get her machine and leave a message. Before I pack the family in the car and drive a hundred miles, I want to know the tickets are going to be there.

At a quarter to five, Naomi calls. She's still not sure of the exact location, and the seats may be piggybacked—two in front, two behind—but they'll be there. Thank you, Naomi; you came through like Tommy Brady. I'm sorry I ever doubted you.

It's sprinkling at Camden Yards and the stands are half-empty. Wake's going against a young lefty named Matt Riley who's coming off Tommy John surgery. Ortiz sits, Millar plays right, Burks DHs and McCarty gets a start at first. Mirabelli, who usually handles Wake, is behind the plate. Along with Bellhorn and Pokey, it's not the most power-packed lineup, so I'm hoping Riley doesn't have much.

He doesn't need much. Through eight, our five through nine guys are 0 for 10. The starters leave with the score tied 2–2, and then it's the game that won't end. By the twelfth, only Dauber and Mendoza haven't seen action (they show Dauber in the dugout in a Sox watch cap, bent over, his chin propped on the knob of his bat like the one kid who wasn't picked). It's been four hours now; everyone else has long since turned off *ER* and gone to bed, and with the Sox not scoring in the top of the innings, the bottoms are like a death watch, just waiting for the bad thing to happen.

The twenty-fifth man, Bobby Jones, is on for us, and gives up a leadoff single to Bigbie. Mazzilli chooses to play by the book and has Roberts bunt him over. With two outs and Jones behind 2-0 on Tejada, we walk him intentionally and then get Palmeiro to ground out on a nice charging play by Bellhorn that Todd Walker wouldn't have made.

We do nothing in the thirteenth. It's raining again, and it's past 11:30. Jones, who's been going deep in the count to every batter, walks Lopez to start the inning. Bautista tries to bunt him across only once, then strikes out.

41

The ump's noticeably squeezing the zone on Jones on righties, where, in the tenth, he called two pitches well up and in strikes to lefties Tek and Bill Mueller. On 3-1, Segui swings but steals a walk by running down to first. On 3-2, Matos takes an agonizingly close pitch. The ump gives him the home call, and with one out the bases are loaded. Bigbie's up. Jones has him struck out on a 1-2 pitch—down the pipe, not a nibble job—but, again, the ump doesn't call it. Part of it's the lateness of the hour, part of it's the weather, and part has to be just a lack of respect. Jones dips his head and walks in a circle behind the mound. Ortiz visits from first to calm him down. A borderline pitch and it's 3-2. And then the payoff pitch is up and out, and the game's over. The camera follows Jones off, expecting he'll say something in the direction of the ump. To his credit, he doesn't.

I only watch *Extra Innings* for a minute, just long enough to hear Eck say, "Not pretty."

As I get ready for bed, I keep replaying the game in my mind, running over the what-ifs, worrying that we'll need this game somewhere down the road. And it was winnable. There was no good reason we lost it, just a terrible ump. I make a note to find his name in the paper tomorrow.

April 9th

His name is Alfonso Marquez. It's said an umpire's done a good job when no one notices him or her. Hey, Marquez, I got my eye on you.

The paper says Nomar, though he's still on the DL, will be in uniform for the opener today, as if that will placate the crowd.

We get going a half hour late, but still arrive a good hour before game time. Parking is horrific. The main lot by the hospital is full, and we cruise Beacon Street down to Coolidge Corner, then try the side streets. We find a spot in a quiet neighborhood about a half mile away and hump it in.

"Anyone sellin'?" the scalpers call, but no one is.

The Will Call windows are mobbed, and incredibly slow. I wait in line for half an hour, and fear we're going to miss the first pitch.

As we cut in to get to our section, I realize we're right at Canvas Alley, where the grounds crew hangs out. Up the stairs, and there's the green of the field and the Monster and the jammed bleachers with the scoreboard on top. Our seats are right on the alley, about ten rows back. We've missed the first pitch from Arroyo, but he's still working on the first batter.

"The milk bottle's gone," Trudy says, and I look up to the roof in right field. The light stanchion there is bare, looming above three tiers of new tables squeezed in beneath a long BUDWEISER sign. The Hood milk bottle used to flash whenever a Sox pitcher struck someone out, and Hood would donate money in the pitcher's name to the Jimmy Fund. I guess milk and beer don't mix.

Also new are Toronto's black road uniforms, which I don't like. They look exactly like the D-Rays'.

Arroyo gets through the first, but makes his own trouble in the second by walking two. The bases are loaded when Reed Johnson doubles off the Monster. 2–0 Jays.

Behind us are four guys in the brewpub business. One of them is constantly on the phone, trying to cut a deal, hollering as if he doesn't believe the signal will reach. "We can bring a hundred thousand to start," he says. "I want to say we can go one-ten, one-twenty if we have to." He has this conversation with a dozen people, as if he's clearing the deal with his partners. Buddy, it's Opening Day. TURN OFF YOUR CELL PHONE.

In the third Bellhorn's on second with two down when Johnny comes up. "Save us, Jebus!" a girl beside us yells, a nifty *Simpsons* reference. Johnny fouls one off his knee that puts him on the ground. He can't be hurt, we can't afford it, and everyone cheers when he stands in again and bloops one down toward us that drops, making it 2–1. The next batter, Bill Mueller, hits another bloop toward us, spinning foul. Delgado's got no shot at it, but Orlando Hudson sprints all the way from second to the line and dives. I see the ball land in his glove just as he disappears, thumping into the padded wall. I have to check the first-base ump shadowing the play: he clenches his fist in the out sign. Hudson's still not up, we can't see him at all, and then Delgado pulls him to his feet. His whole left side including his hat is covered with dirt, and we give him a standing O. That is some major league baseball. I hope I catch the replay on ESPN to see how he did it.

By now the crowd's settled and Trudy and Steph make a run to the concession stand. There's a new 3-D cup this year with the four starters on it, along with Fenway, a flag and an eagle left over from the 2002 model. The company hasn't proofread the thing: Schilling is spelled SHILLING. And will be all season long.

In the fourth, Arroyo lets in two more. He's just not sharp. But in the bottom of the inning Manny turns on an inside pitch and rips one off of Hinske at third (the ball rolling into the dugout, giving him second—it's not an error for Hinske, just a hard chance and a bruise), Ortiz doubles to knock him in, and with two gone we load the bases for Pokey. He hits a floating liner to left. It looks like it should be caught, but it sails over Frank Catalanotto's head to the base of the wall, and the game's tied at 4.

When the inning ends, I head for the restroom and the concession stand. Everyone else has the same idea, and after I've tracked down some commemorative Opening Day balls, a Cuban sandwich for Trudy and a bag of Swedish fish for Caitlin, I'm walking across the big concourse behind right field when a roar goes up from the crowd, and then a roar on top of that that makes everyone turn. I hustle with my arms full to a TV monitor in time to see Tek jog across the plate. He's homered to put us on top, 5–4.

To preserve the lead in the seventh, Francona brings in lefty Mark Malaska, who didn't even make the club, but who we've brought up from Pawtucket because we went through the entire pen last night. Malaska is asked to get the good-hitting Catalanotto and then last year's #2 and #1 RBI guys, Vernon Wells and Carlos Delgado. And he does, one-two-three. Mystery Malaska!

In the Toronto eighth, righty Josh Phelps leads off, so Francona opts to go with Mike Timlin, who only threw two-thirds of an inning last night. Timlin Ks Phelps, but then has to face lefty Eric Hinske, who singles, and the switch-hitting Hudson, who doubles to the left-center gap, tying the game. Timlin gets pinch hitter Simon Bond, but number nine hitter Kevin Cash doubles to the exact same spot, and the crowd boos. There's nobody warming—again, the effect of last night. Timlin hits Johnson with a pitch, and people are screaming. Catalanotto lines one over Millar's head. Millar turns and does his impression of running, giving a blind wave of his glove. We're lucky—the ball hops into the stands for a ground-rule double, and Johnson has to go back to third. When Timlin finally gets Wells to pop up for the third out, it's 7–5 Toronto.

We do nothing with our half of the eighth.

Embree comes on in the ninth and gives up a rocket of a homer to Delgado. Phelps flies deep to right, and then Embree walks Hinske. Francona, I suppose to prove he has a sense of humor (and to test ours), brings in McCarty. "You should have brought him in for Timlin!" someone yells.

McCarty actually doesn't look bad, throwing in the mid-to-high eighties and going to his curve. He gets Hudson to ground one to him, moving Hinske over. Two down. When he goes to a full count on Chris Gomez, the crowd rises, cheering the absurdity of it. McCarty reaches back and throws one by Varitek all the way to the backstop, walking Gomez and giving Hinske third. The crowd subsides, and then groans when Cash blasts a double to the triangle in center, scoring both runners. It's 10–5, and the casual fans head for the exits, while the diehards sneak down to steal their seats.

The good news is that they've changed the numbers on the scoreboard for the Yankees–White Sox game. Chicago's up 5–1 in the fifth.

In the bottom of the ninth, with one down and Bellhorn up, Brian Daubach comes out and walks over to the on-deck circle. Bellhorn flies out, and the crowd rises for Dauber (Eminem's on the PA: "Guess who's back, back again"), hoping he'll give us something to cheer about. He grounds weakly to second, and we've lost the home opener.

The walk to the car seems long. At least it's nice out. We mutter about Timlin, and laugh at how I missed the one great moment of the game. It's still a good day.

On the Mass Pike, we pass a car with a bumper sticker that says JOB WAS THE FIRST RED SOX FAN, and it's early enough in the year that it's still funny. We tune into the PawSox playing Buffalo and catch the final of the Yankee game: White Sox 9, Yankees 3. It's the Buffalo station we're pulling in, and as we head west into the night and traffic thins, the signal grows stronger. The PawSox are leading 5–4, and mile after mile we get to catch up with Kevin Youkilis.

Today was the first game I missed from beginning to end: I even dipped into last night's Late Show, catching the tenth and eleventh of the game versus Baltimore the Sox ended up dropping in thirteen. My younger son Owen called me with an update on this one in the fourth, with the Sox down 4–1 ("Whoa, make that 4–2," he said in the middle of the call, adding that Manny had hit the hardest line shot he—Owen—had ever seen; claimed it even looked like a bullet in slo-mo). Red Sox ended up losing 10–5, according to the Fox New England Sports Network ticker, which I for some reason get down here in Florida (ubiquitous Fox!). Man, Stewart! I'll wait for the highlights (lowlights? deadlights?), but that doesn't sound like Moneyball, that sounds like Uglyball. I'll bet you anything that what's-his-face, the converted fielder, pitched at least two innings. And the Yankees lost again. The AL East is looking My-T-Sof-Tee, at least in the early going. If I can get the game tomorrow, I intend to be there for the whole deal. It's pretty important, I think, that Pedro be able to play the stopper and get us back to .500 early. Can't wait for the standings tomorrow; .500 should be good enough to lead this fool's parade.

April 10th

While we were waiting in the Will Call line, we missed Nomar and Yaz and Dewey and Tommy Brady. Damn you, unwieldy ticketing process!

The paper says that Mendoza was moved to the DL, and that Johnny will be out for a few days with a "golf ball–sized lump" on his knee. Yesterday before his first at-bat, they played "Ironman" for him, and here a foul ball takes him out.

It also says the plane the Sox were supposed to take from Baltimore after the thirteen-inning game had mechanical problems, and with the delays, the team bus didn't get to Fenway until 7:30 yesterday morning, which might account for their sleepwalking performance.

Because we spent all day at the park yesterday, I can't persuade anyone to go to tonight's game, even with the Pedro–Roy Halladay matchup. It frees me to leave early. I rocket across the Mass Pike and get there a full two and a half hours before game time. I'm the first one in the lot (now twenty-five bucks, though the attendant assures me they raised the price last August). I score my Will Call tickets and head for Lansdowne, thinking I might shag some home runs. Like a little kid, I'm lugging my glove.

On Brookline Ave a billboard with a big picture of Nomar asks us to KEEP THE FAITH.

Before I turn the corner, I find a scalper leaning against a wall, muttering, "Anyone buyin', anyone sellin'." I tell him I have one, and we haggle. Even though it's hours before game time, it's Pedro-Halladay, and I want at least face value. He lowballs so I walk, but there's a young Korean tourist lurking behind him who steps forward and offers to trade me a Yankee ticket for it—the Patriots' Day game, which starts at 11 A.M., way too early for us to get here. I jump on the trade, then turn and sell the $20 bleacher seat to the scalper for well more than the face value of today's ticket, and walk away grinning. It's rare that you scalp a scalper.

On Lansdowne the Sausage King and the souvenir guys by Gate E are setting up. A band of college kids wearing long dark wigs and beards walks by; their shirts say DAMON'S DISCIPLES. I stake my claim to a pillar by the entrance to the elevated parking lot, leaning against it to hide my glove behind my back, and watch the Monster. I'm almost under the Coke bottles, between them and Fisk's foul pole, the perfect spot for dead-pull hitters. But nothing's coming over. It's too early; they're still running the tour groups through.

A father and son join me. They've got standing rooms on the Monster and they're hoping to catch a ball. I wish them luck and post up by Gate E, hoping to be the first one in so I can grab my favorite corner spot down the left-field line.

After a nervous five minutes waiting for them to roll open the corrugated-steel doors, I'm the second one through the turnstiles and the first into the grandstand. The Sox are already batting. As I make my way down to the empty corner, I see Johnny Pesky walking out toward left field with a fungo bat and hail him. Johnny joined the club as a shortstop in 1942. He's eighty-five and still putting on the uniform. He waves back, a Fenway benediction.

Bending over the low wall and reaching with my glove, I can just touch the plastic left-field foul line (yeah, weird, not chalk but a permanent strip of plastic). I wait for a hot grounder into the corner, pounding my glove.

Nothing comes. The Sox finish and the Jays take the field. A liner hooks over us for Section 33—"Heads up!"—and bangs into the seats. A few balls off the wall end up in the corner, but these the outfielders toss up or hand to little kids.

Out in left, #27 for the Jays has been shagging flies. As he comes in for his turn in the cage, I see he has a ball in his mitt. "Hey, two-seven," I holler, and he looks around and tosses it to me.

It's Frank Catalanotto, their left fielder and number two hitter, whose triple started them off yesterday.

Still nothing down the line. A lot of balls are banging off the Monster or reaching the seats. One arcs down into the front row, where a big guy in a windbreaker catches it barehanded against his chest and gets a hand. It's the dad from Lansdowne. The kid's all excited.

Later, on his way back out to left, Catalanotto picks up a ball from the grass behind third and—amazingly—tosses it to me. When he comes off, I ask if he'll sign one, and he does. It's the only autograph he gives, and while he's not a star, I feel lucky, singled out.

BP's finished, and I wander over to Steve's seats behind the Sox on-deck circle. They're dream seats, so close that, say, Manny swinging his taped-up piece of rebar intrudes on your view of Ortiz at the plate. Julie, the assistant who's babysitting Steve's tickets, might be there, and I need to talk to her. I plant myself in his seat and admire the balls and Catalanotto's illegible signature. As game time nears, I wonder if Julie's coming. If not, fine. I'll just sit here.

Before the game starts, there's already good news on the scoreboard:

CWS 7
NYY 3

Pedro comes out throwing 89–90. Catalanotto singles sharply to center, but that's it in the first. Halladay's up at 93, 95. He's 6'4" with a patchy beard, and on the mound he looks Randy Johnson tall. Crespo leads off, and Halladay blows two by him, then freezes him with a backdoor curve. Bill Mueller and Ortiz barely get wood on the ball. Looks like it's going to be a quick game.

Josh Phelps leads off the top of the second with a drive down the right-field line. It looks like it's going to drop, but Kapler digs hard and dives, tumbles in the dust and comes up with it. It's even bigger when the next batter, Hinske, rips a single. There's some muttering in the seats, but Pedro bears down and gets Hudson, then gets a borderline call on Woodward, and the Faithful stand and cheer him off.

When Kapler stands on deck that inning, I call, "Great catch, Gabe," and he turns in profile and nods. I'm so close I can read the writing on his T-shirt under his white home jersey. It's a new tradition with the club; last year with Grady, the players wore all kinds of inside motivational slogans. Backwards across Gabe's shoulders, it says ZAGGIN LAER. When he pops to third to end the inning, the ump inspects the scuffed ball and gives it to the Sox batboy (bat-man, really, because he's a pro) Andrew. As Andrew's coming back toward the circle, I call his name and hold up my glove, and he hits me. "Thanks, Andrew."

Ortiz is wearing a slogan too. ARE YOU GONNA— That's all I can get.

Both pitchers settle in. There are no rallies, no tight spots, just solo base runners stranded at first, and lots of strikeouts.

In the bottom of the sixth, Crespo leads off with a slow roller to short. He busts it down the line and dives headfirst for the bag—safe. It's a spark. Bill Mueller rolls one to Delgado, who makes the right decision and goes to second to get Crespo. David Ortiz comes up ("El Jefe!") and after seeing a few pitches blasts one deep to right that makes us all rise. It carries the wall and caroms off the roof of the Sox bullpen. In the stands we're high-fiving. David touches the plate, lifts his eyes and points with both hands to God.

First pitch, Manny lines one for a single. Maybe Halladay's tired. He's thrown 80 pitches—120 Canadian. He blows away Kapler to end the inning.

Pedro's having a quick top of the seventh when, with two down, he gets behind Hudson 2-1. Hudson's the number seven hitter, a second baseman and not a big guy, so Pedro goes after him. He can't get his 90 mph fastball past him, and Hudson parks it in the Jays' bullpen.

It's only 2–1 for one batter, as Bellhorn leads off the bottom with a slicing Pesky Pole homer.

Pedro Ks the first batter in the top of the eighth. It's his last inning, and as he sometimes does, he's going to sign the win by striking out the side. Except after Catalanotto takes a backdoor curve for strike three, here comes Francona from the dugout. Pedro looks around, surprised. He glances out to the bullpen where Foulke is warming, as if he had no idea. Francona chucks Pedro on the shoulder as if to say good job and takes the ball from him. *Boooooo!* Pedro high-fives everyone in conference at the mound, then, as he's walking off, before crossing the first-base line, touches his heart, kisses his pitching hand and points to God. Huge standing O. At the top of the dugout steps he stops and points to God again, holding the pose a little too long, but hey, that's Pedro. (This is the kind of showboating that gets him booed in other parks, but here, after taking on Halladay, it's okay.)

Petey's thrown 106 pitches, but I wonder if it's more of a power move on Francona's part, taking an early opportunity to show the media and the talk-radio fans that this is his club and he can make Pedro do something he doesn't want to do (as opposed to Grady, who couldn't take the ball from him when it was clear he needed to come out). Foulke gets Vernon Wells on a roller, so it's a good move, or at least not a bad one.

Manager Carlos Tosca decides to close the Mike Scioscia way, bringing in a lefty to get Ortiz, then pulling him for a righty to face Manny. Manny uncharacteristically swings at the first pitch, and greets Aquilino Lopez with a bomb to center that just keeps going. It's hit into the wind but ends up a few rows deep in Section 36, somewhere around 450 feet. 4–1 Sox. After that, Tosca says the hell with it and leaves Lopez in to finish.

As we start the ninth, the crowd's singing "Sweet Caroline" a cappella long after Neil Diamond's finished. It's a party, and when the folks in the front row take off to beat the traffic, I move up and stand at the wall with my hands on the bunting (real cloth, not plastic, as you might expect) as Foulke closes.

It's only 9:30. It's been the fast, clean game you'd expect from two Cy Youngs, all the scoring on longballs.

The high floats me home. Traffic's light, and I'm entirely satisfied. There's nothing to nitpick or second-guess, no needling what-ifs. Pedro wasn't dominant, but he was very, very good. Ortiz delivered the big blow, Manny was 3 for 4, Kapler made that great diving catch. And—this is silly, since it's not even Easter yet—with Baltimore whipping up on Tampa Bay, I do believe we own a share of first place.

SK: Well, well, good game. Petey looked like Petey and Roy Halladay surely looked like he was saying "FUCK! SHIT!!" after the Ortiz home run in the sixth. On the replay, too. So the Red Sox climb to .500 for the third time in the young season. Now, for the really interesting question—since most of us watch these things on TV (hell, I'm 1000 miles from Fenway, give or take a few), who pays the freight? Mostly Dad-oriented companies, as you might guess, but one of the heavy-rotation sponsors, McDonald's, features hungry ladies leaving a baby shower and booking straight for Mickey D's, where they gobble turkey clubs on pita bread. And maybe that's not so strange; I watched tonight with my eighty-year-old mother-in-law, who went directly from the BoSox game upstairs to Maine-Denver Frozen Four hockey down-stairs.

Also, for your consideration, the following big-league sponsors:

Tweeter ("Just sit back and enjoy")

Dunkin' Donuts (Curt Schilling with a Walkman, learning to speak New England)

Foxwoods Casino ("The wonder of it all")

Geico Insurance ("Good news, your rap sucks but I saved a bundle")

Xtra Mart ("Fuel up on Brewboy coffee")

SBC Phone Service ("Old farts, please phone home")

Friendly's Restaurants ("Sorry, Dad, no sports car for you")

TD Waterhouse ("Know your investment risk")

Cool TV (i.e., "Watch more Boston Bruins hockey")

Funny Bears Drink Pepsi Cola

Volvo ("Official car of the Boston Red Sox")

Camry, the Car of Caring Dads

Ricoh Color Printers ("Because, face it, black and white sucks")

Dunkin' Donuts again (Curt again: "Wicked haaa-aaaad")

Albert Pujols for DirecTV ("Mah bat iss alwaysss talkun to me . . ." Seek help, Albert, seek help)

AFLAC, the Anthrax Duck

Interestingly enough, no beer ads until after 9 P.M., when they come in a suds . . . er, flood. And goodness, are they ever suggesting young men should drink a lot, especially the Coors Light ads.

Also, Foxwoods advertises a lot. The strong suggestion of the ads being that "the wonder of it all" involves pulling a great many chrome-plated handles a great many times.

I thought you—and possibly TV-watching fans everywhere—should know these things. Now, all together: AAAAAFFFFLACK!

P.S. Did you see Johnny's Cavemen? Are they the perfect Bleacher Creatures or what?

SO: Speaking of advertising, for the first time the dugouts are plastered with Ford ovals—like the Jays' wallpapered with Canadian Tire ads.

I saw Damon's Disciples before, during and after the game. A shame Johnny didn't play. Crespo hustled (two infield hits) and played center passably. Let's hope Millar's days roaming Trot's yard are over.

April 11th

Poor ol' Dauber. Because we've been eating up the pen, we need fresh arms, and ship him to Pawtucket to bring up a ghost—Frank Castillo, who we dumped last year and then re-signed this February. Dauber will have to clear waivers before reporting. The odds are slim that anyone will claim him, but why take the chance if he's really part of the team?

Johnny says he saw his disciples as he was coming out of the players' lot. "They have shirts that said, 'We have Jesus on our side.'"

It's Schilling's Fenway debut, and I'm not going. For the first time in my life I'm going to be a no-show, eating a pair of grandstands along with Easter dinner. I tell Steph that Schilling better not throw a no-hitter. "A perfect game," he says.

Instead, it's an extra-inning nail-biter that takes all day. Mystery Malaska battles again, taking us into the thirteenth.

"So who do we bring in next," Steph asks, "Williamson?"

"We won't have to," I say. "We're doing it here." To seal the oath, we high-five around the room.

It's Aquilino Lopez's game. He walks Bill Mueller, bringing up David Ortiz. With Manny next, Lopez has to throw to him. He tries to nibble, then gives in and puts one over the plate. Ortiz hits a rainbow that brings us to our feet. "Get out!" It's headed for deep left-center. It's going to make the wall, and now it's clear it's going to carry it. The ball lands in the second row of the Monster seats, in the aisle between M7 and M8, ricocheting off a fan who scrambles after the magical souvenir. The Sox win 6–4, and the whole club gathers at home to pound David on the helmet and bounce up and down as a team. Too bad Dauber missed this one. Now I wish I'd gone—a walk-off job's rare—but we're celebrating here too, hooting and running to the kitchen to mob Trudy as if she hit it.

"Now it is officially a happy Easter," I say.

The temptation is to see this as a defining moment, proof that we're in for a wild year. It's a win, that's all, but a very satisfying one. Though it's only April, with one swing, emotionally, we've made up for blowing both openers.

April 12th

In the mail there's a promotional postcard for Steph, a handsomely designed riff on a fight poster that says SHOWDOWN IN BEANTOWN, touting Friday's Yankee game on Fox—the network's first regular-season game in prime time in years.

We've got Monster seats for Sunday's Yankee game, and I'm hoping to cadge two field boxes from Steve for Friday's "showdown." Francona says he's not going to use the off day to give Pedro an extra day of rest, meaning we'll skip Arroyo and Petey will go in his normal slot Thursday night against the O's (maybe a revenge game for him?). This way, Schilling stays on track for thirty-five starts rather than thirty-three, and Pedro sees the Yanks down in the Stadium the weekend after next. So Schilling will go this Friday, as he's planned since February. Steph and I figure out we'll see Wake on Sunday, and then, on Thursday against Tampa Bay, Wake again. (It's a good thing Steph likes Tim-may. Last year we went through a goofy stretch where he saw five straight home starts of his.)

But that's only if the weather holds. "It's spring," Steph reminds me. "We're probably going to have some rainouts."

April 13th

A dark, cold day. It pours all afternoon, and the Sox cancel tonight's game early. There's no reschedule date, and no rush, since Baltimore comes through again in July and September. The rainout itself is depressing, as if a party's been called off, and makes the day that much gloomier.

SK: It was an insult that they shipped Dauber. The injury was that they shipped him for Frank.

SO: Funny how Crespo's turned into our utility everything. Had a big spring, beating out Shump and Tony Wo, and now he's playing infield *and* outfield and getting four or five at-bats a game, while Dauber's rotting in Pawtucket. You can't teach speed.

April 14th

My 2004 Media Guide arrives, with a picture of D-Lowe on the cover, celebrating the Game 5 win over Oakland, except the background isn't from that game, but from the wild-card clincher at Fenway, with the fans on their feet and the whole bench bolting from the dugout. Matted in below this are press-conference shots of Schilling, Francona and Foulke holding up their new Sox unis, the symbolism unmistakable, as if adding these three elements together will produce a championship.

Just for fun, the text of the guide is printed in blue and red ink this year, 627 pages of stats and oddball facts like: last year with the White Sox, Dauber stole home; in college Mark Malaska was a slugging outfielder; Cesar Crespo's brother Felipe played for the Giants, and homered twice in the same game in which Cesar hit his first major league homer with the Padres. Among the career highlights and personal trivia, I recognize dozens of lines I've already heard from Don and Jerry.

As if 627 pages aren't enough, I hit the local bookstore and pick up Jerry Remy's *Watching Baseball*, just out. As a color analyst, he's usually pretty good with strategy, and I'm always willing to learn. I'm not disappointed. While a lot of it is basic, he also talks a fair amount about setting the defense according to the batter, the count and the pitch, and how important it is not to give your position away. He also lays out the toughest plays for each position, and the slight advantages base runners can take of pitchers and out-fielders.

I'm psyched to use some of my new knowledge watching the game, but the website says it's been cancelled due to "inclement weather and unplayable field conditions." It's a letdown, as if I was supposed to play. After Sunday's walk-off homer, I'm feeling a little withdrawal.

April 15th

It's raining when I wake up, but by midmorning the sun's out, so I think we're okay. Even better: in the mail are Steve's dream seats for tomorrow night's game, along with a parking pass. Look for me on Fox. (Last year, for one nationally televised game, we noticed that Todd Walker was miked, a transmitter tucked in his back pocket. Every time he was on deck, we yelled "Rupert Murdoch sucks!")

Sunday's game is On-Field Photo Day. I call up Sox customer service to find out more, but the woman there doesn't know when it starts or what gate you need to go in or where the line will form.

In the paper, the Yanks asked UConn men's hoops coach Jim Calhoun if he'd throw out the first ball at one of their games. Coach Calhoun's a serious Sox fan; after his squad won it all in '99 (beating a Yankee-like Duke team), he threw out the first pitch up at Fenway. "No chance," he tells the Yanks. "Sixty years of torment is enough."

The confusion the Yanks had is natural. The monied southwestern corner of Connecticut drains toward New York, and historically supports the more established Gotham teams. For a couple years, before moving to Jersey, the football Giants played in the Yale Bowl. The northern and eastern edges of the state, butted up against Massachusetts and Rhode Island, are country, decidedly New England. The suburban middle, where I live, is disputed territory. On the Sox website, there's a petition for Connecticut residents to sign, pledging their loyalty based on "traditional New England values of hard work and fair play," and denouncing the encroachment of, yes, the evil empire. I've signed, though what good it does against George's bounty hunters and clone army, I have no idea.

The game goes on as scheduled. Ben Affleck's in the front row beside the Sox dugout (he emceed the Sox Welcome Back luncheon the other day), and I expect he'll be there tomorrow against the Yanks. With the rainouts, neither pitcher's seen action for a while. Pedro gives up a leadoff home run to Roberts. He's missing spots, walking people, giving up another run in the second, but Ponson loads the bases and Johnny singles to right, and then Bill Mueller breaks an 0-for-20 drought with a Pesky Pole wraparound, and we're up 5–2. It's early, but the game seems in hand, and the home folks have shows they want to watch, so we switch over to *Survivor* and then *The Apprentice* (don't worry, Steve, we're taping *Kingdom Hospital*), clicking back to NESN every so often.

It's 5–4 Sox in the fourth when we check in, just in time to see Johnny knock in Bellhorn. Ponson's struggling, and Tejada doesn't help him by dropping the transfer on a sure DP. Ortiz grounds to the right side and Pokey scores. 7–4.

When we check in again, it's 7–7 in the top of the fifth and Pedro's still in there. What the hell? (Palmeiro hit a three-run shot into the Sox bullpen.) He's given up 8 hits and 4 walks. Yank him already!

Ponson's gone after four, and Malaska comes on for us in the top of the sixth. It's the big finale of *The Apprentice,* and for two hours we play peekaboo with the relievers: Lopez, Williamson, Timlin, Ryan, Foulke, Embree.

The Apprentice ends just in time for us to catch the biggest play of the game. It's the bottom of the tenth, bases loaded and two out for Bill Mueller. He lifts one high and deep to left-center that looks like it'll scrape the Monster. I'm up, cheering, thinking this is the game—that we'll have a little cushion going into the Yankee series—but the wind knocks the ball down. Bigbie is coming over from left, and Matos from center, on a collision course. Bigbie cuts in front, Matos behind, making the grab on the track in front of the scoreboard, and that's the inning.

Arroyo starts the top of the eleventh against Tejada. He hangs a curve, and Tejada hits it off the foot of the light tower on the Monster for his first homer of the year. 8–7 O's. In a long and ugly sequence, they pile on four more. We go one-two-three, and that's the game, a painful, bullpen-clearing, four-and-a-half-hour extra-inning loss very much like last week's in Baltimore. Not the way we wanted to go into tomorrow's opener against the Yanks, and not how I wanted to go to bed—late and pissed-off.

April 16th

The Sox are unveiling a statue of Ted Williams today outside Gate B—the gate no one uses, way back on Van Ness Street, behind the right-field concourse. The statue's part of an ongoing beautification effort. We've already widened the sidewalks and planted trees to try to disguise the fact that Van Ness is essentially a gritty little backstreet with more than its share of broken glass. I'm surprised there's not a statue of Williams already, the way the Faithful venerate him. During the Pedro-Halladay game, I chanced across a rolling wooden podium with a bronze plaque inlaid on top honoring Ted; it looked like something from the sixties, coated with antique green milk paint. It was pushed against a wall in the hallway inside Gate A next to the old electric organ no one ever plays. I'd never seen it before, and wondered why it was shoved to the side. In Pittsburgh there was a statue of Honus Wagner by the entrance of Forbes Field, and when the Bucs moved to Three Rivers, it moved with them, to be joined by a statue of Clemente, and now, at PNC Park, one of Willie Stargell. I wonder how long it will take the Sox to commission one of Yaz.

Because the game's on Fox, the start time's been pushed back to 8:05, giving me some extra time to deal with Friday rush hour. All the way up 84 and across the Mass Pike I see a lot of New York and New Jersey plates. When I pull into the lot behind Harvard Med Center a good hour before the gates open, it's already half-filled.

I head for Lansdowne, but BP hasn't started yet. There are some Yankee fans outside the Cask 'n Flagon having their pictures taken—skinny college girls in pink Yankee T-shirts and hats with a hefty dude in an A-Rod jersey. I pass a woman wearing a T-shirt that says THIS IS YOUR BRAIN (above a Red Sox logo), THIS IS YOUR BRAIN ON DRUGS (and a Yankees logo). TV crews are wandering around doing stand-ups, shooting B-roll of people eating by the Sausage Guy. Above, banner planes and helicopters crisscross.

I walk down Lansdowne past the nightclubs, figuring I'll go around the long way and check out the statue. Fuel is playing the Avalon Ballroom; their fans are sitting against the wall to be the first in, and seem disgusted that their good time has been hijacked by a bunch of dumb jocks. When I turn the corner onto Ipswich, I find another line of young people waiting at the entrance of a parking lot. Everyone has an ID on a necklace, as if they're all part of a tour group. Then I notice the yellow Aramark shirts hidden under their jackets. It's the vendors, queuing up so they can get ready for a big night. It's already cold in the shadows, and I pity the guys trying to move ice cream.

I expect the Williams statue to be ringed by fans taking pictures or touching it for luck, the way they do in Pittsburgh with Clemente and Stargell (if you reach up you can balance a lucky penny on Willie's elbow), but it's just standing there alone while a line waits about thirty feet away for day-of-game tickets.

It's uninspired and uninspiring, a tall man stooping to set his oversized cap on a little bronze kid's head. It's not that Ted didn't love kids (his work with the Jimmy Fund is a great legacy), it's just that I expected something more dynamic for the greatest hitter that ever lived. In Pittsburgh, Clemente's just finished his swing and is about to toss the bat away and dig for first; he's on his toes, caught in motion, and there's a paradoxical lightness to the giant structure that conveys Clemente's speed and grace. Stargell's cocked and waiting for his pitch, his bat held high; you can almost see him waggling the barrel back and forth behind his head. This Williams is static and dull and carries none of The Kid's personality. He could be any Norman Rockwell shmoo making nice with the little tyke.

I take a couple of pictures anyway, then head back to Gate E to wait for my friend Lowry. Before a big game like this, people are handing out all sorts of crummy free stuff, and I accept a *Globe* just to have something to read (okay, and for the poster of Nomar). I buy a bag of peanuts and lurk at the corrugated door, and when Lowry comes, we're first in line and then the first in and the first to get a ball, tossed to me by David McCarty in left. I snag a grounder by Kapler, and later an errant warm-up throw by Yanks coach (and former Pirate prospect) Willie Randolph—picking the neat short-hop out of sheer reflex.

A-Rod comes out to warm, and the fans boo. Some migrate over from other sections just to holler at him while he plays long toss, chucking the ball from the third-base line out to deep right-center. "Hey, lend me a hundred bucks, huh?" "How you liking third?" "Hey, A-Rod, break a leg, and I mean that."

We boo Jeter when he steps in to hit. And Giambi ("*Bal*-co") and Sheffield ("*Ballll*-coooo").

The rest of the Yanks are friendly enough. Jose Contreras and Kevin Brown banter with the fans; even hothead Jorge Posada jokes with us. When Mussina comes by and chats and smiles, someone calls, "You're the *good* Yankee, Mike."

Miguel Cairo, one of the last Yankees to bat, smokes a grounder down the line. It's mine. I catch it off-center, and it bends the fingers of my mitt back. The ball knocks off the wall and rolls away, out of reach, gone forever. It's a play I'll make 99 times out of 100, even if it was hit hard.

"Hey," Lowry says, "you've got three."

Yeah, I say, I know, but it's always the one that gets away that you remember.

We stop by El Tiante's for an autographed picture, saying hey to Luis and picking up some Cuban sandwiches, then fight the crowd to reach our seats. The choke point's right behind home, where the concourse narrows to feed the first ramp to the stands. The crush is worse than Opening Day, and I think they've got to fix it somehow before something very bad happens.

The tide of people separates us. I find Lowry at our seats just as the anthem begins. As always, I'm overwhelmed by how good these seats are. One section over, one row in front of us, is the governor of Massachusetts, Mitt Romney.

The Yanks send Kenny Lofton, Jeter and A-Rod to face Wake in the first. The boos grow louder with each at-bat, peaking with A-Rod, who gets a *standing* excoriation—something only Clemens has managed over the years. "Gay-Rod," some wags are chanting. When Tim's first pitch is a strike, the crowd explodes, as if we've won.

Johnny opens with a hopper to first that hits Giambi in the middle and gets through him for an E. "*Bal*-co!" Vazquez has Bill Mueller 0-2, but gets impatient, aiming a fastball that Billy cranks into the Sox bullpen, and we're up 2–0. Manny hits a slicing liner down the right-field line that disappears from view. The ump signals fair, then twirls one finger in the air for a homer. Somehow the Yanks are able to relay the ball in—they're arguing that it never went out. We don't get a replay. (Later, I hear that the ball hit the top of the wall and caromed back in off Sheffield, so it wasn't a homer.) With two down and Ellis Burks on second, Doug Mirabelli grounds one to Jeter. It's an easy play, but Jeter comes up and lets it through the five-hole and into left, and with two outs Burks scores easily.

Posada gets one back with a solo homer in the second. In the fourth, Mirabelli—who, like Wake, is only making his second start—takes Vazquez deep on the first pitch. 5–1.

A great moment in the sixth when the Yanks try a double steal (or is it a blown hit-and-run?). Sheffield doesn't make contact, and A-Rod's meat at third. The crowd taunts him into the dugout.

It's 6–2 with two out in the eighth when Giambi lofts a fly to Manny in left. "Good inning," I holler to Doug Mirabelli, heading off, and then I see the ball glance off Manny's glove and bounce in the grass. He Charlie Browned it!

I look around to verify that this has actually happened. No one else can believe it either.

Things get a little shaky when Sheffield and Posada both work walks to load the bases. "A home run here and the game's tied," a neighbor says. I know where this is coming from, but come on, we're up 6–2 with four outs to go. Have some faith.

Embree gets Matsui, and the Yanks never threaten again, and when Jeter makes the last out and the PA plays "Dirty Water," all the different TV crews hustle to set up their tall director's chairs for the postgame shows.

April 17th

Steve and I have been going back and forth about the Yankees' place in our cosmos. I've been trying to argue that they've only gotten in our way a few times across our overall history. In the fifties and sixties (besides the Impossible Dream year), we were so bad that it didn't matter. '78's a fluke, and people forget that after our big fold in August we came back and won our last eight to gain the tie for the division. The Winfield-Mattingly Yanks never gave us any problems; were, in fact, massive chokers, consistently finishing second to Toronto, Baltimore and us. In '86 we stood in our own way (or

Calvin Schiraldi did). In '99, we were lucky to get by Cleveland, and last year we pulled a rabbit out of our hat to beat Oakland, and were playing on the road the whole time. Plus we took enough out of the Yanks that they had nothing left for the Marlins. We were *their* stumbling block, beating them twice at the Stadium, putting their weaknesses on display. All the Marlins had to do was mop them up.

SK: Your rationalizations can't stand up to the killer graphics Fox put up on the screen last night. I'll get the facts for my little Yankees-Sox piece (and no, it hasn't always been the Yankees, just the Dent home run, the Boston Massacre, and last year . . . plus the Boston-Yankees all-time numbers, which are all New York). But while we've been starving, New York has been feasting. How many consecutive years have they gone to the postseason now? Twelve? Come on, ya gotta hate 'em! Fear 'em and hate 'em!

SO: You forget—my roots are in Pittsburgh, and Maz's homer is our Excalibur. We not only slew the beast, we broke their damn hearts, and the Sox can do it too. Shoot, if we really wanted to win one, we could go the '97 Marlins' route, or the 2001 D-Backs'. We're almost there but not quite. But that's not an honorable way. That's why all the Steinbrenner titles don't count. The last time the Yanks really won anything was 1962.

SK: "Maz's homer is our Excalibur." Mine too. I LOVED that series. Remember that Baltimore chop that hit Tony Kubek in the Adam's apple? Of course you do, you devil, you.

SO: As Bob Prince used to say, "We had 'em all the way!"

SK: The game last night was the perfect antidote (except for Scott Williamson in the eighth . . . PRETTY SCARY, HALLOWEEN MARY). A measure of payback for Tim-MAY Wakefield after the heartbreaking home run to Aaron Boone. One game down, eighteen to go.

• • •

One luxury of having two bona fide aces is the constant possibility of a marquee matchup. Last Saturday it was Pedro-Halladay, this Saturday it's Schilling-Mussina. With the watering down of pitching talent around the league, these games are rare, and I'd be at Fenway except that I have to tape an interview for Canadian TV.

Moose is rocky from the start, and Schilling's solid. Bill Mueller goes deep, and Manny. It's 4–1 in the seventh when Schilling's 121st pitch freezes Jeter for the first out—and suddenly here comes Francona from the dugout. Like Pedro against Toronto, Schilling looks around, surprised someone is warming. He turns his head and swears, but gives up the ball and gets a big hand. A few minutes later the camera shows him in the dugout, going over his charts. Another power move by Francona? Or just notice that he won't be like Grady? I think it's no coincidence that he pulled both aces at home during high-profile wins.

Johnny doubles in an insurance run in the eighth, and the Yanks get a cheapie in the ninth, but this one's over. Schilling beats Moose and we've taken the first two. On *Extra Innings*, Tom Caron says, "So the worst we can do is split." Why think of the worst, especially right now? We've got D-Lowe going against Contreras tomorrow. It's this kind of fatalism—from the Sox's own network!—that drives me crazy. You never hear this kind of hedging from the Yankees' YES-men.

April 18th

We get going early so we can be the first ones on the Monster, but as we're driving up I read in the Sunday paper that there's no BP today. While it doesn't mention it anywhere, and even the Sox ticket office and the guys who let us in through Gate C aren't sure where we're supposed to go, it's On-Field Photo Day. We take a right toward the stairs up to the Monster and notice the garage door to center's open. We fall in behind a staff member escorting two kids and then we're on the warning track in the bright sunshine. A yellow rope cordons off the grass, but we can walk all the way around to the dugout, where Schilling is sitting, being interviewed by a writer.

The PA tells us the plan. The Sox will come out and walk all the way around so we can take photos. Each player has a handler to make sure they don't sign autographs. Still, I've got to try. "No, I'll get in trouble," Bill Mueller says, like a little kid.

The guys are nice, shaking hands and posing. I get Steph with hitting coach Ron "Papa Jack" Jackson and Keith Foulke. Trudy's being crowded and can't get clean shots, so she moves out to the warning track in right where it's empty. Johnny Pesky's sitting in the dugout with Andrew, and I toss him a ball to sign. I notice Manny on the other end of the dugout, signing, and make my way over there, scissoring over the wall and then high-stepping over the railings between sections. The mob around him is packed tight, but I finally get through and have him sign my ball.

The Monster seats are a dream—a counter for your stuff, a swiveling barstool and room behind it to stand or lean against the wall. We're in the second row. In the first row, there are new signs that read: WARNING: FOR YOUR SAFETY PLEASE DO NOT REACH OVER WALL. The one drawback is that we're a long way from the plate. It's a little breezy, but when the wind is blowing right you can smell the burgers grilling. The sun's out, Lowry's with us, and when Kevin Millar doubles into the corner in the first, scoring Bill Mueller, the day seems ideal.

The pitching matchup's in our favor, or should be. Contreras is their fourth starter, and a weak link. The worry is that Lowe, working on ten days' rest, will be too strong and leave the ball up. In the third that's exactly what happens. After he walks A-Rod, he gives up a single to Giambi, a double to Sheffield, a single to Matsui and a double to Posada—all of them down the line in left. Lowe strikes out Travis Lee, but Enrique Wilson singles to right, scoring Matsui to make it 4–1. Jeter grounds out, scoring Posada, then Bernie Williams doubles down the left-field line. That's it for Lowe: 2⅔ innings, 8 hits, 7 runs.

The Sox get two back in the bottom of the inning, chasing Contreras. We should have more except for a blown call. With two on and two out, Tek slaps one down the first-base line that Travis Lee has to dive to spear. Reliever and ex-Sock Paul Quantrill beats Tek to the bag, but Lee has trouble getting the ball out of his glove, and by the time the throw arrives, Quantrill's well past the base. The ump punches Tek out to end the inning, bringing Francona from the dugout to argue, though by then it's pointless.

Also during this inning, the Yanks haul out their Cuban National Team tactics, slowing down the pace of the game in the middle of our rally to quiet the crowd and throw off the hitters' timing. Posada visits the mound. They send the trainer out in midcount, as if the pitcher has some injury. He doesn't, but because the trainer accompanies Torre, the visit doesn't count as a visit by the manager. They send the pitching coach. They change pitchers. They change pitchers. They have an infield conference. They send the pitching coach again in midcount. The pitcher himself wanders behind the mound to stall. They change pitchers again. Technically it's only semilegal, a judgment call with the league's new rules requiring umps to pick up the pace of the game. A good crew chief wouldn't put up with this nonsense.

It stays 7–3. There's not much action, and the crowd's grumpy and distracted. From time to time the bleachers rise and roar, signaling a fight. The cops haul some Yankee fans away, and everyone cheers, "Yank-ees suck! Yank-ees suck!" In the seventh, Tom Gordon comes in to some moderate boos, but it's hard to get too excited, down by four runs. The sole highlight of the late innings is an awkward sliding catch by Sheffield along the right-field line. The crowd salutes him with the old Atlanta tomahawk chop, with the finger attached.

We lose 7–3. It was basically a one-inning game, over after the third. The loss can't ruin the day—walking on the field, seeing the guys, sitting on the Monster—but it makes for a quiet ride home. And tomorrow's their matchup: Kevin Brown against Bronson Arroyo. Okay, now who's the fatalist?

SK: Not quite s'good t'day, and with KBrown tomorrow, the Yanks look good for the split, curse them.

SO: It was a dull game, even up on the Monster. The wind was blowing in hard, and knocked down two balls from Manny that would have been gone any other day.

Saw the new Williams statue by Gate B—pure schmaltz. He deserves better.

SK: Yep. Putting his hat on the little kiddie's head. Cute. And, out of the side of his mouth: "Now get outta my way, you little rat-bastard."

SO: Hey, imagine what Steinbrenner's statue'll be doing.

SK: Cast in bronze with his wallet out.

The Rivalry—April 18th

The Yankees have never beaten the Red Sox in the World Series; with both teams in the American League, that, of course, is impossible. Nevertheless, the Yankees (who are playing the Red Sox in the third game of their first four-game set of 2004 as I write this) have become the Sox's principal rival over the last fifty or sixty years, and as someone who has written a great many scary stories during his career, I almost *have* to write about them. For Red Sox fans, the Yankees are the thing under the bed, the boogeyman in the closet. When they come to us, we expect bad luck on horseback; when we go to them, we expect, in our hearts, not to return alive.*

The rivalry has captured hearts in both Boston and New York, with fans cross-pollinating freely (and sometimes fistily) at the games. On April 16th, the *New York Post*'s front page showed a pin-striped Darth Vader with a Yankees logo on his helmet and a bat on his shoulder. It quoted Red Sox president Larry Lucchino, who in 2002 called the Yankees "the Evil Empire," and trumpeted MAY THE CURSE BE WITH YOU. On the Fox Game of the Week that night (of *course* it was the Game of the Week, are you kidding), the announcers displayed a souvenir T-shirt proclaiming SHOWDOWN IN BEANTOWN. That one must have been officially sanctioned by Red Sox management. In the bleachers, the ones reading JETER SUCKS are much more popular. I understand there's one featuring A-Rod with an even more obscene sentiment, but I haven't seen that one yet (I'm sure I will). And how many fightin' fans have been ejected by the security people over the years? I have no idea, but as Ole Casey used to say, "You could look it up."

When there are fights, the first blows are usually thrown by Red Sox fans; the jeers and epithets chiefly come from Sox fans, too. Maybe Billy Herman, who managed the club from 1964 to 1966 (not stellar years), explained it best: "For Red Sox fans, there are only two seasons: August and winter." Losing makes us sad . . . except when it doesn't. Then it

---

*In the first two meetings of this year, we beat them by scores of 6–2 and 5–2, and the Yankees' big off-season acquisition, Alex Rodriguez (who Red Sox fans see, rightly or wrongly, as a player stolen out from under our very noses by George "I'll Spend Anything" Steinbrenner) went 0 for 8. Well enough. In the third game, however, The Team That Will Not Die is leading the Sox 7–3 in the fourth inning.

makes us pissed. The attitude of your average pinstripe fan, on the other hand—unless and until directly attacked—tends to be one of indulgent, slightly patronizing good nature. Arguing with a Yankee fan is like arguing with a real estate agent who voted for Ronald Reagan.

I date the Sox/Yanks rivalry of the Modern Age from October 3rd, 1948, a day on which the Red Sox actually *beat* the Yankees, 10–5. What's wrong with that, you say? Well, it got us into a one-game playoff game with the Cleveland Indians, one we lost, 8–3. That's Heartbreak Number One.

Fast-forward past 1951 (Mickey Mantle makes his major league debut versus the Red Sox, Yanks win 4–0), and 1952–53 (the Red Sox lose thirteen in a row to the Yankees), and 1956 (Ted Williams fined for spitting at Boston fans after misplaying a Mickey Mantle fly ball, an incident Williams will never live down). Let us forget 1960, when the Yankees set the record for team home runs (192) . . . against Boston. And let us by all means wince past Roger Maris's 61st home run, which came against Tracy Stallard . . . who pitched for Boston.

No, let's move directly to 1978. "Nothing compares," says Dan Shaughnessy in *The Curse of the Bambino*. "The mind calcifies. This was the apocalyptic, cataclysmic fold by which all others must be measured." Yeah, and it was pretty bad, too. On July 20th of that year, the Red Sox led the Yankees by fourteen games.* Then came the infamous Boston Massacre, in which the Red Sox were swept—not at Yankee Stadium but at *Fenway*—by the Bombers in a four-game series. The Sox ended the season in a flat-footed tie with the Yankees, and lost the playoff game on Monsieur Dent's Punch-and-Bucky home run, the pop fly heard 'round the world. That's Heartbreak Number Two.

In 1999, the Red Sox went into postseason as the wild-card team and once again faced the Yankees. The Yanks won both of the first two games in the Stadium, both by one run; they qualify as Heartbreaks Number Three-A and Three-B. (Game 1 of this series, you may remember, was

---

*Shaughnessy again: ". . . only three collapses approximate this one: the 1915 Giants led the Boston Braves by fifteen games on the Fourth of July and finished ten and a half behind; the 1951 Brooklyn Dodgers led the Giants by thirteen games August 11, got tied on the final day of the season, then lost the playoff; and the 1964 Phillies led the Cardinals by six and a half games with twelve to play, then lost ten straight. The Giants, Dodgers and Phillies eventually won championships. The Red Sox . . ." Well, do we need to finish that? Fuck, no, we's *fans*.

the one in which Chuck Knoblauch dropped a throw from Scott Brosius; the ump then ruled he'd dropped the ball while transferring it from his glove to his hand.) The third game, the first played at Fenway in the '99 series, offered some small measure of revenge. In that game, Sox batters pummeled first Roger Clemens and then a parade of relievers, Pedro Martinez fanned twelve, and the Red Sox won, 13–1. It was the most lopsided loss in the Yankees' postseason history, but in the end it made no difference; you can't carry any of those runs over to later games, can you? In the following game, the Red Sox were victimized by another bad call, this time by Tim Tschida,* and the Red Sox ended up losing, 9–2. The Yankees won the final game, 6–1. That's Heartbreak Number Three-C.

Whenever the eye of Red Sox management falls on a likely player, it seems that the Eye of Steinbrenner (like the Eye of Sauron in his tower) has also fallen there. It was very likely frustration as much as anything else that prompted Larry Lucchino's "Evil Empire" comment following the signing of Jose Contreras† in 2002; there was even more frustration following the signing of Alex Rodriguez. A-Rod was willing to come to Boston; it was the Players' Union that balked, citing a $15 million shortfall in Boston's offer and claiming it would set a disastrous precedent (bullshit—ballplayers are even more egregiously overpaid than best-selling novelists). The fans understand the truth: George Steinbrenner's your basic fat-cat owner. His pockets are deeper because his fan base is deeper. Current capacity at Fenway is about 35,000; at Yankee Stadium, it's 58,000. And that's only the tip of the iceberg. The differences carry over to all the ancillary goodies, from T-shirts to the big casino, TV telecast rights. Hummmm, baby . . . and while you're at it, gimme that cable deal, sweetheart.

But enough dallying. We've reached Heartbreak Number Four, the one I've been putting off but can put off no longer. Worse than the Boston Massacre? Yes. Worse than the ground ball through Bill Buckner's wickets? Yes. Worse, even, than the Bucky Dent cheap home run? Yes, because more recent. The wound is fresher; still bleeding, in fact. Part of me just wants to say, "If you don't know what happened, look it up or go rent a

---

*Who went to the unusual length of issuing an apology after the game—fat lot of good it did us.

†Who will not be eligible for the win today, I'm happy to report.

videotape somewhere. It hurts to even think about it, let alone write about it." Because, I think, we did more than come back; we were ahead. We were five outs away from beating the hated, feared Yankees (in their own house!) in the American League Championship Series and going back to the World Series for the first time since 1986. We had our fingers around that puppy, and it just . . . slipped . . . away.

The smart money had the Yankees winning that series, but the Red Sox took the first and fourth games behind Tim Wakefield, who simply bamboozled the Yankee hitters with his knuckleball . . . and who would issue the Final Heartbreak in the eleventh inning of Game 7. In between was the famous Game 3 rhubarb—more bad blood between two teams that have had it in for each other for what seems like a thousand years.

The trouble started when Pedro Martinez hit Karim Garcia in the back (narrowly missing his head). After Garcia was forced at second (taking Red Sox second baseman Todd Walker out with an ugly spikes-up slide), Yankee catcher Jorge Posada yelled at Martinez from the dugout. Martinez reputedly responded in charming fashion. "I'll hit your head, too, smartass!" cried he.

In frame number four, Roger Clemens—never a gentleman—threw at Manny Ramirez, who responded by telling the Rocket he could go fuck himself. Roger responded by telling Manny that no, Manny could go fuck *him*self. A real meeting of the minds, you see. The benches erupted. Don Zimmer, the aging Yankee coach,* ended up rolling around on the ground, courtesy of Pedro Martinez. Later, Zim made a tearful apology . . . behavior which cost fellow New Englander Edmund Muskie his shot at the presidency, but maybe that's neither here nor there.

In any case, the Yankees won the game. They also won Game 5 behind David ("Bostonians Are Psycho") Wells. The 2003 ALCS returned to Yankee Stadium with the Bronx Bombers needing only one more win to go on to the World Series. But the Sox won ugly in Game 6, 9–6.

So, Game 7. The Red Sox got off to a 4–0 lead behind Pedro, the ace of the staff. Jason Giambi then hit a pair of solo home runs for the Yanks; David Ortiz hit one for the Sox. It was 5–2 Red Sox in the eighth inning. Mayor Rudy Giuliani thought the Red Sox were finally going to

---

*When Zim was the Red Sox field general, Sox pitcher Bill Lee once called him "the designated gerbil."

win it.* Martinez got the first batter (Nick Johnson) he faced in that inning, and the Red Sox were five outs away from the World Series. For we Red Sox fans, that was the 2003 equivalent of Pickett's Charge: as close as we ever got. Jeter (Jeter the Horrible, to Sox fans) doubled to right. Bernie Williams singled, driving in Jeter. Matsui hit a ground-rule double after Grady conferred with the tiring but game Martinez and decided to leave him in (hell, it had worked once or twice during the regular season). And still left him in to face Posada, who dumped one over second base to tie the game. The Red Sox manager finally came with the hook . . . but Red Sox Nation would pretty much agree it was too Little, too late. In the bottom of the eleventh inning, Mayor Giuliani told his wife and daughter, "You're going to see your first walk-off home run."† The batter was Aaron Boone, and he made the mayor a prophet. Tim Wakefield, the man who was arguably the most responsible for getting the Red Sox as far as they were able to go, served up the fatal pitch, but had nothing to hang his head about. The real damage was done with one out in the eighth.

And is there a reason to drag all this history into a book about the 2004 Red Sox? There sure is. More than one, actually. First, baseball is a *game* of history, and those who don't learn from it are condemned to get drubbed by it. Second, even in a much improved American League East, the Yankees and Red Sox still seem, at this point in the young season, like the two dominant teams.‡ The tradition and history will hang over each of these matches like grandstand shadows over the infield at 5 P.M. The Red Sox half of the tradition, unfortunately, is one of losing the big games. The history half is one of snatching defeat from the jaws of victory, as on the night of October 17th, 2003.

Looking the other way, into the future (into the outfield, where the shadows have not yet reached, if you will), is the simple fact that the landscape of the American League East *has* changed since 2003; even two weeks into the season, that seems apparent. The lowly Tampa Bay Devil Rays (the

*Harvey Frommer and Frederic J. Frommer, *Red Sox vs. Yankees: The Great Rivalry* (Sports Publishing/Boston Baseball, 2004). This is a Boston-biased book, but most of the color photographs show celebrating Yankees and downcast Red Sox . . . wonder why.

†Ibid.

‡The Yankees won today's game, 7–3. The final game of the series will be played tomorrow at 11 A.M. (it's the annual Patriots' Day game in Boston), and with today's win and tomorrow's matchup—Boston's Bronson Arroyo versus the Yankees' Kevin Brown—the Yankees have an excellent chance of earning a split . . . curse them.

previously lowly D-Rays) are at .500, and the previously lowly Baltimore Orioles are in first place. Those things will very likely change, but I think it's likely that the Blue Jays, also improved, won't finish thirty games below .500, as they would if they continued along at their current pace.

What all this means to the Sox/Yanks rivalry is that one team is apt to be called when the postseason bell rings, but probably not both. And that makes the knees of every Red Sox fan tremble, no matter what they may tell you, no matter what sentiments they wear on their T-shirts, no matter what vile canards they may call down upon Yankee outfielders from the Monster seats high above.

There is no calculus here; the math is simple. We all hate what we fear, and sensible Red Sox fans fear the Yankees. Now, on the eighteenth of April, the Red Sox lead the nineteen-game regular-season series two games to one. A great many other games will be played with a great many other clubs before the dust settles and the 2004 season is in the record books . . . but in my heart, I believe the American League East will come down to Them, or to Us. And because we fear what we hate, in my heart I always dread it when they come to us. The only thing I dread more is when we must go to them. I suppose it would be different if I could play, but of course I can't; I'm helpless, doomed to only watch. To believe in the Curse of the Bambino even though I don't believe in it. And to think of the late Stephen Jay Gould, who somehow rooted for *both* teams (maybe in the end that was what killed him, not the cancer), and who once said, "The deepest possible anguish . . . [is] running a long hard course again and again to the very end, and then self-destructing one inch from the finish line."

Postscript—April 19th

This is Patriots' Day, which is a holiday only in Maine, where it chiefly means no mail delivery, and Massachusetts, where it means the Boston Marathon and an 11 A.M. Red Sox game at Fenway. Today the Red Sox spotted the Yankees leads of 3–0 and 4–1, but "Bronson Arroyo settled down and pitched a good game," in ESPN *SportsCenter* argot, and the Red Sox won it by a final score of 5–4.* I'm happy to report that A-Rod's

---

*The loser, I'm very sorry to say, happened to be ex–Red Sox closer Tom Gordon, the star of a book I wrote . . . and in *The Girl Who Loved Tom Gordon,* Flash will be the Red Sox closer forever. Sorry, Mr. Steinbrenner, but there's not a thing you can do about that one.

woes continue; he went 1 for 17 in the four-game series (hee-hee), the one hit was a meaningless single, and he made a throwing error in today's tilt that basically cost the Yankees the game. So now we're 3-1 with the Yanks, and can get back to the more normal business of playing baseball.

Whew.

April 20th

I read in the paper that in his first home game Dauber hit two homers, leading the PawSox to a 3–2 victory over Rochester. And to replace Frank Castillo, the Red Sox have activated lefty Lenny DiNardo, giving us four lefties in the pen for the first time I can remember. Must be setting up for this weekend's series in the Bronx, that short porch in right. I hope these PawSox can get it done. I'd start resting Embree now.

The crowd in the Skydome tonight is around 6,000, despite the Pedro-Halladay rematch. The Maple Leafs are playing the Ottawa Senators in Game 7 of their playoff series, and at one point Eric Frede, NESN's new man-in-the-stands, says there are more people in the concourse watching hockey than there are in the seats. Oh, Canada.

Pedro throws well and we win easily, but there's a little bad blood in the ninth when reliever Terry Adams goes up and in on Manny. Manny ducks away, tossing his helmet aside, and stands squared with the mound, arms out, calling, "What do you want?" Earlier, reliever Valerio de los Santos knocked Ortiz on his ass with a pitch aimed at his face, so it's not an over-reaction on Manny's part, as Jerry claims. When their no-name pitchers throw at your big three and four guys, it's on. The benches clear, and while there are no punches thrown, it's a signal that we're not going to take that shit. Expect newbie Lenny DiNardo to dust someone like Delgado tomorrow, or Timlin to plunk Wells or Phelps.

SK: Petey looked a lot better than Doc, didn't he? Are the Yankees playing tonight? I tried to get 'em on the satellite, and they were playing some weepy old Thurman Munson short instead of the ChiSox. Red Sox win, Martinez goes 2-1. Time for Tom Caron and Bob Tewksbury, aka The Talking Board.

SO: Rain delay. The Yanks scored 7 in the first, so maybe that'll get erased.

Tewks! You'll notice he changed his hair from that '50s style to something from the mid-to-late '70s. And where the hell is Bob Rodgers? Do they have him in a cage under Car Talk Plaza?

SK: I think I'll Google the sumbitch.

SO: Google away, dude, but I think Carmen Sandiego is working him over in a dank room with a DieHard and some piano wire. Long live TC and the new man-in-the-stands who looks like Ross Perot's love child.

SK: According to the *Globe* (March 2nd, 2004), Rodgers left Fort Myers to coach a Whitman-Hanson boys' basketball game in the MIAA Tournament. He left a recorded *SportsDesk* segment but did not get permission to do this. Both NESN and Red Sox management weren't happy, and although the public word is that Bobby the Serial Killer "has left NESN to pursue other opportunities" (Sean McGrail), the fact is they canned his ass. According to *Globe* writer Bill Griffith, Red Sox management "has sent a message that there are new sheriffs in town."

In a totally unrelated development, you should know that ex–Red Soxer Mo Vaughn is going to be the Grand Marshal of the fifteenth annual Hot Dog Safari on May 16th, at Suffolk Downs. It's being billed "The Hit Dog and the Hot Dog."

How the mighty have fallen.

By the way, Stew, Google also reports that a Bob Rodgers is reffing college soccer in the Boston area, but that may not be the same one.

SO: So he's just out there somewhere, like Michael Myers.

SK: Dude! That's it! Or Jason, only with a wimp-mask, sorta.

April 21st

A package arrives from the Souvenir Store (which is in fact Twins Enterprises now; the Sox have made it their official store) with the glossy 2004 yearbook,

71

a blue windbreaker made in Korea and a T-shirt made in Uzbekistan. Now I'm outfitted for the summer. The yearbook must have been put to bed in late March, because there, sharing the same page, are Shump and Tony Wo.

UPS brings another present, a rough cut of a future episode of *Kingdom Hospital* called "Butterfingers." The story line is familiar to Sox fans: Earl Candleton, the first baseman for the long-suffering New England Robins, drops a pop-up that would have won them the '87 World Series. From then on he's hounded by fans who call him Butterfingers and pelt him with balls. He descends into alcoholism, living in a fleabag of a mission in Lewiston. When the Robins go to Game 7 of the Series, with the game on the line in the bottom of the ninth, Earl holds a revolver to his temple. If the Robins win, he lives; if they fold, he dies.

Of course, they fold and he pulls the trigger and drops into a cobwebby purgatory as the doctors and kinder spirits of Kingdom Hospital try to save him. (The F/X haven't been matted in yet, so there are scenes where a grip follows the waif ghost Mary around with the head of the benevolent beast Antubis on a stick.) In the end, the spirits, with the help of Peter, the artist in a car-crash-induced coma, allow Earl to go back to that moment in '87 and make the catch, changing himself and the world. The two Down syndrome dishwashers who serve as oracles have the last word: "Baseball's not always a sad game. Sometimes the good guys win."

Tonight the matchup is Wake versus Ted Lilly, who beat us on Opening Day. Wake's sharp and Doug Mirabelli, happy to be starting, wallops two homers to give us a 3–0 lead, but the Jays chip away.

SK: 3–2 in the sixth. This is turning into a nail-biter. Damn, I hate seeing all those .250 hitters in the lineup. Thank God for Douglas "Miracle" Mirabelli. Speaking of hockey, did you see his shot off the glass?

SO: Doug also came through big-time Friday night against the Yanks. Amazing that he can be this hot when he sits four days between starts. And Tek's hot too. But Pokey, oh my, he's just struggling.

It's still 3–2 in the eighth when Tosca brings in Valerio de los Santos once more to face David Ortiz. Last night de los Santos put David on his ass; tonight he hangs a breaking ball that David stings down the right-field line. It bounces fair and caroms off the stands right to the right fielder Reed Johnson, and David has to sprint for second. He's a big man, and looks silly running way up on his toes, arms pumping. He slides headfirst, bouncing off the dirt, and he's in there. We shouldn't laugh but can't help it. Part of it is how sweet his revenge is. De los Santos is scowling as Tosca comes to take the ball from him. David hustles over to third on a long sac fly by Manny (only a great leaping catch against the wall by Johnson saves extra bases), then, on a wild pitch, scoots for home, sliding feetfirst this time, safe, adding an earned run to de los Santos's stats (the camera finds him brooding in the dugout).

We win 4–2. After the postgame show, Steve and I are still debating hope and fatalism.

SO: I think it's neat how our attitudes are so different. After '86, last year didn't feel that drastic to me. I mean, sure, it hurt, but I'd been through worse, and we weren't even supposed to get that far (we were at least three players away), so I thought everything after Trot's shot was gravy and just dug the ride. This year I have higher hopes because of Schilling and Foulke.

And here's some history: the Angels, prior to 2001, were all-time chokers. Remember? No, you can't, at least not emotionally, because their win has forever changed the way we see the club and its past. It's a line you cross, and when the Sox cross it, our hindsight will be softened, and all these close calls will lose their power to wound us. Like the Pats, we'll no longer be hapless. Ask the old hard-luck UConn Huskies of Jim Calhoun, the 1980 Phillies, the last two Elway Bronco squads, etc., etc. So good-bye, Tony Eason, good-bye, Donnie Moore.

SK: "Donnie Moore." Now there's a horror story.

I've been thinking about this, and I've decided that the age difference makes a difference here. What is it, fourteen years between us? Which means I remember Williams and you don't. I remember Maz leaping joyously around the bases when he hit that home run and you've only seen the kinescopes. I'm not trying to pull rank or make you feel like a kid, I'm just trying to get a focus on how we can approach this so differently. Maybe I've got it. I've been suffering fourteen more years. Why, that's almost a generation!

SO: I see it as partly geographical—that winning Pittsburgh experience—but part of it's also that I waited for both the Oakland Raiders and New York Rangers to finally win their championships after years and years of their great (and heavily favored) teams choking, and for two truly hapless clubs, the Pats and Penguins, to win theirs (only to have lightning strike not once but twice). All four of these teams put a shitload of history behind them with one big cleansing win, and that's what the Sox will do too.

SK: But don't you see? Your very argument proves what a striking anomaly the Red Sox are. All the clubs you've mentioned—in all the various sports—in this and in previous e-mails have won it all at least once in the last eighty or so years. Do I need to finish this thought? I mean, hello? "One of these things is not like the others / One of these things just doesn't belong / One of these things is not like the others / Tell me while I sing this song."

SO: By the same token, *all* of these teams were in our strikingly anomalous position (which we share with the Cubs, White Sox, Brewers, Mariners, Astros, Rangers, D-Rays, Padres, Expos, Rockies, not to mention dozens of NFL clubs (the St. Louis/Arizona Cards have never won one, or the Saints, or the Bills, the Minny Vikes, etc., etc.), dozens of NBA and NHL franchises, whole boatloads of NCAA Division I schools, etc.) up until t = +0, when all their troubled histories were redeemed by the one resource the world can count on: time. It's inevitable. Maybe not in our lifetimes, but that just means our faith has to be strong.

Which is one reason why I dug "Butterfingers" so much—how you framed Earl Candleton's life (and error) in terms of salvation or damnation. Take Me Out to the Ballgame/Shall We Gather at the River. Hail-Marymotherofgrace . . . "I thought I was in Hell." You really made us feel for the guy, so when the dishwashing kids came out after you'd used the old rewind to redeem #11 and said, "Sometimes the good guys win," damned if I didn't get a little teary for Billy Buck and for all of us.

And Billy Buck, you know we don't blame you. It was that lousy Schiraldi.

SK: I think Schiraldi might have been in some form of analysis or therapy following that season—I'm almost sure of this. And he was my daughter's first crush . . . a young man, and fair.

SO: He shoulda gone into analysis before the Angels series. And McNamara should have had his head examined for using him in both.

I guess some young girls just dig troubled guys.

SK: "Brewers, Mariners, Astros, Rangers, D-Rays, Padres, Expos, Rockies." Johnny-come-latelies.

"But Pokey, oh my, he's just struggling." Yeah, but he's a PR Mastuh!

SO: I'll cop to the Rocks and Rays being latecomers, but the Pods and Spos are looking at 30+ years of futility, the Stros at 40+, and the Rangers (as the Senators) have to go back to 1924 for their sole crown (compared to our five during that era).

Y'know, I just flat-out LIKE Pokey, despite him hitting .182 (67 points higher than Ellis Burks). He's got a major league glove, and we haven't seen much of that over the years.

SK: So do I—you just can't NOT like him, can you? And he's been steady-Eddie with the glove.

April 22nd

The Yanks won, but the O's lost, so guess who's all alone in first?

So far Doug Mirabelli has 3 homers in 9 at-bats. He sees his success as a product of his extra preparation. Playing once every five days, "I can put all my focus into that pitcher and watch video or whatever for four days and try to get a little edge for myself to feel confident going in there." Which at least partially explains why over his career he's a .270 hitter as a Sock and .213 as a Giant and Ranger.

The matchup tonight is in our favor again—Schilling-Batista—and the game goes as planned early on. Ortiz hits a two-run shot in the first and we hang on through six, when Toronto goes to their pen. Francona's said that he'll close with Williamson instead of Foulke, who's thrown three straight days now, and maybe he's worried about conserving the pen for this weekend in New York, because he leaves Schilling in too long in the seventh, and the Jays tie the game with four straight hits. "Take him out!" we're screaming at the set.

In the eighth, Schilling comes back out. We just look at each other. Would Francona have done this at Fenway?

Mystery Malaska's the only one warming as the Jays load the bases. Schilling's pitch count's above 120, and he's consistently leaving the ball up. Number nine hitter Chris Gomez makes the decision for Francona, hooking a grand slam over the left-field fence, and Toronto wins their first home game, 7–3.

Put this one on the list of games we should have won. When Schill struggles in the seventh, go to a stopper like Embree, then use any of your setup guys in the eighth and close with Williamson. What's the point of carrying extra arms if you don't use them?

At least the Yankees lost. The ChiSox got to Moose early and hung on, 4–3. It's slight consolation. I'm so disgusted I don't even watch the postgame, just turn the channel, as if I can make the loss go away.

SO: Captain, I'm detecting high levels of Gradium.

SK: Boy, you got that right.

April 23rd

The O's beat the D-Rays, so they're in first again.

The *Courant*'s all excited about the Sox-Yanks rivalry. Because Hartford's halfway between the two cities, the paper has a beat writer for both teams. The Yankee guy's a total homer, while the Red Sox guy, as befits the tradition, is a skeptic. Both dwell on Aaron Boone and Game 7, as if that's the only thing that happened last year.

We're headed down to New York to spend the weekend with Trudy's parents before they leave from the West Side piers for the transatlantic cruise they've always talked about. Trudy's sister and her boys will be there. We'll go to a few museums, take in a show, wander around Chinatown, but one thing we won't be doing is going to the games.

Tonight it's Red Sox–Yankees, Round 2, Game 1. So far the advantage goes to the Red Sox—they're up 6–0 in the fifth inning, courtesy of home runs by Millar, Bellhorn, and a three-run job by Bill Mueller. Do I need to bother with all this in-game detail? Probably not; O'Nan will have it. In fact I'm starting to suspect that O'Nan is going to finish the season with roughly seven hundred pages of manuscript. That man takes his baseball seriously.

The question I've been asking myself is whether or not I need to bother with a diary at all. I can hear my mother asking me, "Do you have to jump in the lake just because Stewart O'Nan does?" No, Ma. And certainly I don't expect to be scrivening away at this on every game day, but it seems to me that I *do* have to add something from time to time. Call it a kind of balance. Stewart's the brains of the operation, no doubt. He knows where all the fielders are playing at any given time, and who'll be covering second, Bellhorn or Reese (Garciaparra soon, if God is good), in any given situation. I'm more of a from-the-gut guy.

Also a superstitious guy. I don't necessarily know where the fielders are, but I *do* know enough to hit the MUTE button on the remote control when the opposing team's up, because everyone *knows* it's unlucky to listen to the announcers when the opposing team's at bat. They always score when fans do that. You should know that I'll be doing the MUTE thing for the Sox all season long, so relax. I'll also be turning my cap around when we're a run or two down in the late innings, and charting pitches when the opposing guy is really good—it's a helluva jinx. I got Moose Mussina that way, and expect to get Victor Zambrano (Devil Rays ace, currently 3-1) in the same fashion when he pitches against us.

And okay, quite often when the Red Sox are only up by a run or so in the late innings, I simply turn the idiot box off for a few minutes. Every superstitious fan knows that not watching for a while can also be good mojo, but basically I do it because I'm too scared to watch. Especially if there are men from the opposing team on base. I made it through *Night of the Living Dead* and *The Texas Chainsaw Massacre,* but baseball—especially stretch-run baseball—shreds my nerves. Now, though, it's 6–0 Red Sox in the fifth, and Derek Lowe doesn't look too bad (don't worry, I knocked on wood when I said it).

Oh yeah . . . and when Alex Rodriguez grounded out weakly, pitcher to first, in the fourth, the disgruntled fans in Yankee Stadium actually booed their preseason darling. Music to my ears. I'm also an *emotional* guy, at least when it comes to The Game. There's really nothing like baseball, especially when you don't have to freeze your ass off on a cold, rainy night in the Bronx.

And a postscript. Today the *New York Post* had fun comparing Johnny Damon, with his new beard and extralong hair, to a Cro-Magnon caveman. Johnny just scored Boston's seventh run of the night.

We take the Cross Bronx, driving by the Yankee Stadium exit right around game time. I don't turn on the radio. I'll let this one be a surprise—like opening a present or a door (the lady or the tiger?). There's so much chatter in New York, I figure I'll pick up bits of the game on the street, like a pulse underriding the city.

Our first hint is in the hotel bar—where I notice Steph is bravely wearing his Wake shirt. As we pass the bar, a TV tells us it's 6–0, but I'm not sure in whose favor. I see Billy Mueller make a nice off-balance throw to close an inning, and Lowe making a fist, so I'm hopeful. We're sitting so far in the dark back of the lounge that we can't see the TV, but when we come back out, it's 6–0 Sox and Donovan Osborne's in for the Yanks.

We make some noise, attracting the attention of a drunk Mets fan. "Red Sox, huh? All I gotta say is Bill Buckner, okay? Bill, Buckner."

"I hope you guys have a better year this year," I say.

Downstairs, the doorman's shaking his head at how bad the Yanks have been so far. "They'll be all right," he says. "George will pay."

A billboard for an investment firm in Times Square says BRAVE AS A RED SOX FAN IN THE BRONX. But all around me I'm seeing people in Sox caps and shirts laughing and giving each other the thumbs-up—something I've never experienced before in New York.

We're finishing dinner when Trudy's sister and her boys arrive with a new score: 10–2. The two were on a homer by Matsui, their only clutch guy.

We stop at a liquor store on the way back to the hotel for some champagne, and I can't resist asking the guy behind the counter in a Yanks hat who's winning the game.

As I write this, it's 11–2 in the eighth, and the only reason it isn't 11–0 is because Derek got a little tired there. I think we're gonna go up on 'em 4–1, which would be very swede. Knock on wood.
    Uh-oh, who's Lenny DiNardo? Still worrying even with one out.
    Red Sox win, 11–2 . . . and Eckersley's on *Extra Innings*! Whee!

Down in the city I don't get Eck, but at one in the morning I do get WCBS replaying the entire game, so here I am, half-buzzed and headachy from champagne, watching a game that's already long over in a darkened hotel room while everyone else sleeps, just for the sheer pleasure of seeing how we did it. Bill Mueller with a three-run shot, and, basically, they didn't throw a quality pitcher at us all night. Looks like Torre wrote this one off, knowing he's got the matchup tomorrow and hoping Vazquez can get Sunday's game to the pen.

April 24th

In the hotel, as I'm getting on the elevator to go down to Times Square, a woman in a Sox hat and shirt gets out—obviously going to today's game. And in the Guggenheim, as I wind my way down, I pass two boys in Sox hats, and their dad wearing a cherry red COWBOY UP T-shirt.

    In the taxi on the way to Chinatown, the radio's on low, but I can still hear that the Sox are up 2–1. Go ahead, Bronson (named, yes, after Charles Bronson).

    Hours later, back at the hotel, two decked-out Jets fans get on the elevator. I'd completely forgotten that today's the NFL draft. I've been seeing lots of Pats hats, but I just expect that now.

    It's almost five when we get back to the room. The game should be over, so I pop on the TV for the score. It's in extra innings, 2–2, and Foulke's on. There are two down in the eleventh and Sheffield's on first. I'm supposed to get dressed for dinner and the theater tonight, then jump a cab out to the airport to pick up Caitlin, and time's tight, but I sit on the edge of the bed with the boys and watch Tek gun down Sheff trying to get in scoring position for Bernie, with a nice slap tag by Crespo at second.

    In the top of the twelfth, Manny doubles to the base of the wall in right-center. Tek fights off three or four outside pitches from Quantrill before he gets one he can pull to the right side, moving Manny over with a ground out. Quantrill just nicks Millar's shirtfront with a pitch, and the double play's in order, but Bellhorn drives one medium deep to center, and Bernie, with his weak arm, has been playing in and has to go back to get it. Manny scores easily, 3–2 Sox.

Timlin comes on to close, but we've got to go. We call up from the lobby because we've forgotten Caitlin's flight information, and there are two outs, nobody on and a 1-2 count on Jeter, and then, in the cab, we hear that the Yanks have just lost to the Sox. This is the kind of demoralizing game we've already lost two of to Baltimore, and it's sweet to win one, especially in someone else's house. It's even sweeter because we're in New York, as if the city's ours now.

The local news at eleven has found a way to soften the blow. They open the sports with a long segment on the Giants trading for #1 pick Eli Manning, then show A-Rod making a nice backhand and getting Millar, then A-Rod homering, before showing Bellhorn's sac fly and the final score. The homer was the only hit Bronson Arroyo gave up in six innings, but you'd never know that.

Holy moly, the BoSox did it again. It took them twelve innings today, but they beat the Yankees 3–2. Keith Foulke got the win in relief ("vultured" the win is the term baseball players use for this type of win, I believe; Timlin pitched the bottom of the twelfth and got the save). If it were possible to feel sorry for the Yankees, who are now four full games out of first place—although whether behind us or Baltimore I don't at this moment know—I would feel *almost* sorry for them. Life being what it is, I don't feel a *bit* sorry. Derek Jeter—known in my household as Great Satan Jeter—is now 0 for his last thousand or so. The fans don't boo him, though. Jeter seems truly beyond the boo-birds. But the Yankees, man . . . I mean, how long can you go on saying, "Don't worry, it's only April"?

Another six days, actually.

Meanwhile, we're throwing Pedro at them tomorrow, and going for the sweep. We're only five wins away from taking the series . . . that's the series for *the year*. Man, I can't believe this. Something's *gotta* go wrong.

Unless dead or insane, I *will* be writing about tomorrow's game.

April 25th

It's the last game of Round 2, with the BoSox going for the sweep over the Yankees. In the top of the first inning, the young Yankee pitcher, Javier Vazquez, looked terrific—determined to be the stopper. Ortiz touched him for a single, but that was it. Now Pedro Martinez is on the mound for us, and the real question is which Pedro is going to show up: the mound-wise sharpie who pitched in Toronto last time, or the mediocre rag-arm who started the season against Baltimore at Camden Yards (and then left the park early, sparking a minor media flurry). He's 3-2 to Jeter to start with; Jeter, 0 for his last 21, strikes out to make that 0 for his last 22. It's the worst streak of Jeter's career, and given that sort of funk, tells us very little about the state of Pedro. But even as I write the words, there goes Bernie Williams, 3 to 1. That looks a little better, and has silenced the massive chant (another sellout today at the Stadium) of "Pedro sucks." And Kevin Millar just made an incredible sliding catch on A-Rod to finish the first: no runs and no runners for the Yankees.

The Yanks are, I should add, something of an anomaly: the only team against which I actively root (it was true for a while of Cleveland in the early nineties, but no more). And it seems to me that the Yankees almost have to have this third game, not to keep from falling five games off the pace early (although five really is quite a few, at *any* point in the season), but because it's the hated Red Sox and they are at home.

In the third inning, the story still seems to be young Vazquez, who gets six of the first nine outs by way of the K. Then, in the top of the fourth, Mark Bellhorn, batting today in the two-hole, walks (because that's what Mark Bellhorn does). After Ortiz strikes out looking—number seven for Vazquez—Manny Ramirez comes up. After getting ahead of Manny 0-2, Vazquez attempts to waste a curveball. He wastes it out over the plate, and . . . see ya. Over the Yankee bullpen and into the Bleacher Zone. We're up 2–0 in the middle innings.

Bottom of the fifth, Yankees threatening with runners on second and third, two out and Jeter (0 for 23) at the plate. Takes called strike one, outside corner; chases a fastball way up and out of the zone for strike two. Pedro sets, fires, teases Jeter outside, 1-2. Pedro's ready to go again but Jeter steps out, commanding right hand up to the ump in the old familiar gesture. Now he's back in, and Pedro immediately strikes him out looking with high, hard cheese. Jeter is 0 for 24, and the Yankees once more fail with two in scoring position (before Jeter, Enrique Wilson, who usually beats Pedro like a drum, popped out to Pokey).

Sweet!

In the sixth, A-Rod doubles with one out and goes to third on a Giambi groundout (Cesar Crespo in short right field—an almost comical overshift—makes the play on Giambi). Rodriguez, at least, has begun to come around (his average has crept up to something like .252), but it does the Yankees no good; Gary Sheffield fouls out to Varitek, and it's still 2–0 Sox, going into the lates.

Pedro's done after seven: his game to win, the bullpen's to lose. The bullpen hasn't given up a run in twentysome innings, but now Williamson's on, and he's a scary guy. Here's Jeter again. He tries to bunt; no joy. Fouls one away, and it's 0-2, a place Derek has gotten all too familiar with just lately. Let's see how Williamson plays this. He throws a low fastball, a true waste pitch, but Jeter goes fishing and strikes out. This time the crowd *does* boo, and even the resolutely upbeat Yankee announcers finally take notice. "Like booing Santa Claus," one of them remarks reprovingly.

It's the bottom of the ninth and last call for the Yankees. Here's Alex Rodriguez, and it's still Williamson to face him—no Keith Foulke, a little surprising. Williamson runs the count full on A-Rod, who has 7 of the last 22 Yankee hits; so much for *that* slump. Rodriguez, after fouling off one 3-2 pitch, grounds out, third to first. Now Jason Giambi grounds to Pokey Reese. Two out. Here's Gary Sheffield, who has one of the Yankees' four hits today. This time he strikes out, and suddenly—incredibly—the Red Sox have taken six of seven from the AL champs. The camera sneaks a look into their dugout, and the look on Jeter's face is one of pure amazement. And it's justified; this is the first time the Red Sox have beaten the Yankees six out of the first seven since 1913.

Sweet!

SK: I saw all the games and got six pages on the sweep in my newly inaugurated Sox diary—gloat-gloat. What it boils down to for the Yankees is that if they don't start playing pretty soon, it's gonna get late early and be lites-out in August. Remember when I said I liked them for third place?

SO: Gloating is such an ugly word for this creamy and delicious feeling. I think the Yanks' swoon will just make George bust out the wallet earlier for a starter or two. Lieber's still a ways away from filling the five slot, and Contreras looks terrible. Using Vazquez on three days' rest—even though he threw well—is a desperate move on ol' Joe's part. And after the day off tomorrow, they've got to face the A's three big aces. Who's going to throw that Thursday game—Vazquez on three days again? They're screwed. We trusted Bronson with the ball twice against them and he came through. And BK's not far from being ready.

Your third-place pick looks entirely possible. As expected, we're getting quality starts and our pen's much better, and those O's are pounding the ball. The Yanks right now are suffering from the revenge of Pettitte, Clemboy and Boomer.

April 26th

Tonight's the premiere of the Red Sox movie: *Still, We Believe.* Alyssa, my former student, has lined up a press pass for me, and while I've put together a short list of questions and fitted fresh batteries in the minicassette recorder, I've still got mixed feelings about crossing the line between fan and journalist.

We get to the Loews on the Common right on time, check in at the press table and claim a spot behind the velvet rope next to the red carpet. I've never had a press pass before, and I have no idea what secret powers it gives me. Outside, WEEI is doing a live feed from the street. It's raining and cold out, and the crowd's thin. As more people filter in, we're boxed and jostled by TV cameras. NESN's well represented, ESPN2, NECN, all the Boston channels. Nothing's happening, but there's some serious jockeying for position. Johnny Damon and Kevin Millar are definites, but those are the only two names mentioned. I'm hoping for Eck, maybe Yaz, Tim Wakefield, Pokey Reese.

Wally the Green Monster shows up in a tux, mugging for the cameras. "Hey Wally, who are you wearing?"

The fans featured in the film arrive, and the cameramen blind them with their lights, the sports anchors do their stand-ups. I'm not really interested in the fan-stars. I know I'll get their stories from the movie anyway.

Tom Caron stops at the press table, and Dan Shaughnessy. Big Sam Horn signs a ball for me—something a real journalist would never ever ask him to do—and there's Tom Werner and John Henry and Larry Lucchino, and Luis Tiant. Everyone but the players.

Outside, rented searchlights twirl across the night sky. It's nearly show-time when Kevin Millar arrives in a vintage Western print shirt, jeans and shiny black cowboy boots. He smiles as he shakes hands and signs, doing stand-up after stand-up as he inches down the red carpet. I bypass the clot of reporters and set up at an open spot a little farther down.

I catch him just as he's bouncing out. He's trailed by a guy my age dressed head to toe in Sox paraphernalia, with his huge, naked beer gut bulging out and painted with the Red Sox logo and STILL WE BELIEVE. WEEI has judged him the most outrageous fan and given him a ticket to the show. He shakes Millar's hand, pleased to meet him.

"Kevin," I say—and he talks to me just because I've got this recorder; it has power, like a gun—"what were *you* like as a fan, when you were younger?"

"Like this guy."

"You're kind of the official fan of the Sox with the Cowboy Up, but who was your team?"

"Dodgers. Grew up in Los Angeles. Dodgers were my team."

"Favorite player?"

"Steve Garvey."

"You wear the jersey?"

"Never had a jersey, but I was a big fan of the Dodgers. I'd go to a lot of games."

"Listen a lot on the radio?"

"Vin Scully."

"Ever get the autographs?"

"Went and got the autographs, did it all."

"Are you still a fan now? Can you be a fan now that you're a player?"

"No doubt about it."

"Are you still a Dodger fan?"

"Still a Dodger fan, still a fan of baseball."

"You check their box score every morning?"

"No, I don't check 'em, but I pull for 'em when I see 'em."

"So you hope to see 'em this fall?"

"That'd be nice."

And that's it, I thank him and he's gone to the next mike, the next camera. I've definitely crossed the line with my impersonation of a journalist, but, as a fan, it's my duty to take advantage of whatever access I can get, for the sheer thrill of it.

Johnny Damon's not here yet, but they're going to start the movie, so we crowd into the theater with Kevin Millar and the owners and everyone else. Down front, a radio team introduces all the Sox VIPs, who stand in turn to receive their applause. When they call Johnny Damon's name, Big Sam stands up as a joke. Finally the filmmaker, Paul Doyle, thanks everyone who helped and says, "The fans *are* the Red Sox," a sentiment which seems true even before he presents his evidence. When I was talking to a real journalist earlier, I mentioned that I've only been a Sox fan for twenty-five years, so I'm new. I was here before Clemens, and I'll be here long after Pedro. I've got a no-cut contract.

Steve's in the film—briefly, a shot of him chatting with John Henry before the ill-fated season opener in Tampa Bay. That was the one Chad Fox blew, and while the movie doesn't have the time to tell the rest of the story, after we dumped Fox he went on, along with former Sox closer Ugie Urbina, to defeat the Yanks and become a World Champion.

In trying to squeeze the whole season (and eight very different fans' lives) into two hours, the film can't connect all the dots. What strikes me most are all the Sox from last year's squad who are gone: Shea Hillenbrand, Todd Walker, Brandon Lyon, Damian Jackson, John Burkett, Jeff Suppan, Scott Sauerbeck and of course manager Grady Little, who, since we're in a room with the people who fired him, gets laughed at more than I find necessary. We witness Theo informing our number one prospect Freddy Sanchez that he's being traded to Pittsburgh (for Suppan and Sauerbeck, neither of whom panned out).

The main tension and source of comedy in the movie is the tug-of-war between hope and pessimism. Angry Bill, a diehard who's become a fixture on local call-in shows, vows that he'll never believe in the Sox again, and sees disaster everywhere—until we take the A's. Fireman Steve Craven is more laid-back. "We'll get 'em tomorrow," he says, and caps the film, after the disaster of Game 7, with his observation that all the losing will make finally winning it all that much sweeter, "don't you think?"

It's a fun film, but there's so much missing. Where's Bill James and his ridiculous bullpen-by-committee idea? Where's BK giving us the finger? Where's Roger's last win in Fenway? Where's Todd Walker's 2-out, 2-strike shot against Baltimore? Even the intricacies of the playoff games are glossed over, so while it gets some of the emotion of being a Sox fan, it still just skims the surface, and being a Sox fan is about total immersion.

The after-party at Felt is crowded and loud, but there's free Sam Adams, good hors d'oeuvres, and, for the brave, Fenway Franks served out of actual vendors' steamers. Beside us, Luis Tiant is chowing down. I want to talk to Larry Lucchino, maybe interview him about growing up a Pirates fan in Pittsburgh, but he's lost in the crowd, and then when I see him, he's on his way out. We've got to get going too. Tomorrow's a school day, it's raining like hell and we've got a long drive.

On the way home, Trudy says she was disappointed that only Kevin Millar showed. I am too, but big props to Mr. Millar, who did it all cheerfully. In his business a night off's a cherished rarity. I know I get on him for his lack of speed in the outfield, but, as with that difficult assignment, tonight he stepped up when no one else did.

April 27th

Ellis Burks's knee is hurting him, and his .133 batting average is hurting us, so he's on the DL and the Dauber's coming up from Pawtucket. In ten games there, he hit .350 with 5 homers and 11 RBIs, including a walk-off shot. "In baseball, you've got to keep plugging—until forever, I guess." Is there any wonder why we love this guy?

A strange front must be moving over New England, because it's been sunny all day here, but up in Boston it's pouring. To cheer us up during the rain delay, NESN shows clips of Nomar and BK working out at Fenway earlier today. Nomar's in shorts, taking grounders at half-speed and then talking with Mia Hamm over the low wall along third. BK's also in shorts, playing catch in the outfield grass; you think of him as this whip of a kid, but his thighs are massive and cut like early Arnold. Don and Jerry make it sound like he'll be our number five guy and Arroyo will go to the pen.

A good hour and a half after game time, the Sox call it.

April 28th

The team's so excited about BK's rehab that he's going to skip his last minor league start and pitch the first game of tomorrow's day-night double-header. Schilling will still go tonight, and Lowe tomorrow night, meaning Wake is sacrificing his start, something he's done throughout his long tenure with us, unselfish of him, and extremely valuable, giving his manager more flexibility.

Though he's running and taking infield, the team says Nomar's still at least two weeks away.

April 29th

After a rainout on the 27th, Schilling (and the bullpen) tossed another gem last night, beating Tampa Bay, 6–0. Tampa Bay only got a single runner as far as third base, and while I like the D-Rays (I sometimes think of the Red Sox as my baseball wife and Not-So-Sweet Lou Piniella's Devil Rays as my baseball mistress), I have to admit they are reverting to type after a hopeful start. But of course the Red Sox's 13-6 start is also part of a pattern I have observed over the years; call it BoSox Happy Hoop Days. The way it works is simple enough: the Red Sox have a tendency to tear up the American League until the NBA playoffs wrap up; after that, more often than not they sputter. And leave us face it, a two-game lead over Baltimore and a four-game lead over the Yankees, while better than a poke in the eye with a sharp stick, really ain't all that much. Of *course* it beats being behind, but I think I'll wait until after July Fourth to decide whether or not Schilling and Company are for real.

Footnote A on today's entry: Our Mr. Kim, he of the restless middle finger, is back from sore-shoulder woes (and a stint in Pawtucket) today. He's supposed to be limited to seventy-five pitches, after which Tim Wakefield will come in to relieve. Damn! It's a day-night doubleheader, and I was kind of hoping Timmy would pull a Wilbur Wood and start both games (nor am I joking).

Footnote B on today's entry: Although Derek Jeter's hitless streak has now reached 0 for 32, tying a Yankee record (the immortal Jimmy Wynn, in 1977), the Bombers beat the Oakland A's for the second straight night. They've only picked up half a game on Boston (because of that rainout), but the wins suggest that Boston's weekend sweep in the Bronx may have had more to do with Red Sox pitching, defense, and the bat of Manny Ramirez than it did with any Yankee funk. It may be too early to declare the Red Sox the class of the AL East, but it may *not* be too early to at least suspect that this year they *out*class the New York Yankees.

I check the standings to see how many games up we are on the O's (2) and discover we've got the best record in baseball. I think that's got to be wrong, since we opened 3-4, but no, only the Twins and the pitching-rich Marlins are anywhere near us.

Game 1 is BK versus Victor Zambrano, who's had some success against us. Dauber's starting at first base, and on the first play of the game lets a grounder slip under his glove for an E. Welcome back, Dauber.

It's a brilliant spring day, sunny, in the mid-seventies. Because this is a rainout of a night game, the Sox have to let ticket-holders sit in Sections 34 and 35 in dead center, which normally for day games are sealed off with a black tarp for the hitter's backdrop. The Sox have solved the problem by giving everyone sitting in the sections a T-shirt the same forest green as the seats.

Both pitchers are throwing well, but the defenses behind them are scuffling, as if the idea of playing an extra game today doesn't agree with either team. Bill Mueller and Doug Mirabelli lose a foul pop in the sun; it drops not between them but ten feet to the side. Later, Billy and Cesar Crespo go back for a short fly in left; Manny comes racing in, calling them off, almost collides with Crespo and drops the ball.

A play you rarely see in the second: Jose Cruz Jr.'s leading off first when Tino Martinez hits a screamer right at him. Cruz doesn't have time to go right or left, he just ducks. The liner skims off his back, barely nicking him, but Dauber points to let the ump know. The first-base ump says it never touched him, bringing Francona out to argue—at which time, without consulting anyone, the second-base ump calls Cruz out. Go Blue!

Kim looks sharp, getting groundouts with the ball down, then climbing the ladder with a good rising fastball. I saw his first start for the Sox last year in Pittsburgh, an efficient win, and he looks much the same. He's up to 70 pitches after five, and finishes the inning with a strikeout. As he walks off, the fans stand—remarkable, since this is the first time he's pitched since giving us the finger. Five innings, one hit, no runs. Come home, Byung-Hyun, all is forgiven.

Zambrano's cruising too, striking out the side in the fourth, but in the fifth, with a man on, he gets behind David Ortiz 3-0. Zambrano obviously hasn't read the scouting report, because David's always got the green light. He plants a meatball in the sea of green shirts in Section 35.

It's all we need, as Wake comes on to baffle the D-Rays for two more innings, then Timlin, then Embree. The final's 4–0, our third straight shutout. The pen hasn't been scored on in over 30 innings.

We get on the road to Game 2 just as Game 1's ending. We've got a table up in the new right-field roof terrace, and Steve's dugout seats. Trudy has papers to grade, so Caitlin and her friend Lindsay will take the good seats first and we'll switch after the fourth.

It's turned into a warm evening, and Yawkey Way is a carnival. A guy on stilts in a Sox uniform tosses a puffy ball to random people in the crowd. People are having their pictures taken with Wally in the big red chair on the sidewalk. The guys at Cambridge Soundworks are handing out their Sox bumper stickers—I BELIEVE and TURN IT UP—and we take a minute to gawk at the high-definition TVs in their little alcove. Then it's the long walk out to the big concourse in right field.

The stairs we take up to the roof are new, concrete and steep. The elevator shaft is in place, but there's no elevator in it yet. The views of Back Bay and the park at every turning are spectacular. I'm puffing by the time we make it to the top, and the low sun in the west is blinding. We get to our home-plate-shaped table in the second row and test the swiveling seats, the same as on the Monster. But there's not as much room as on the Monster—the wire fence digs into my knees when I try to turn toward home—and we're much farther from the action. On the way up, we passed the very last row of the bleachers in Section 43, joking that the corner seat there was probably the worst seat in Fenway. We're a good two stories higher, above the retired numbers attached to the roof's facing, nearly eye level with the top of the Pesky Pole. The view is the one you'd have if they built a second deck, as they were threatening to with the New Fenway. It's as far away as I've ever sat at a Red Sox game.

It's also windy, a breeze coming over the back of the deck whipping napkins off the tables and out over the front railing, where an updraft floats them high into the air. I'm glad it's warm now, because it's going to be cold later.

Lowe's going against lefty Damian Moss, a recent retread, so I think we've got the advantage. The first batter Lowe faces, speedburner Carl Crawford, bonks a double off the wall. Julio Lugo, known best for banging his ex-wife's head off the hood of a car ("Hey, Lugo, restrain yourself!"), bunts, and Lowe misplays it. A grounder by Woonsocket's own Rocco Baldelli scores Crawford, ending our scoreless streak, and the crowd's not happy. We're even less happy when Robert Fick doubles to right, scoring Lugo. Steph shakes his head; it's just like the Yankee game we saw Lowe throw here.

I overhear that Jeter's homered in the first at the Stadium, breaking his hitless streak. All good things must come to an end.

We come up to bat down 2–0. I realize the girls have forgotten to take my glove—for protection, seriously—and hustle down there. I'm underneath the grandstand when I hear the crowd cheer for Johnny. I guess that he's on base. Another cheer, this time for Bill Mueller. So probably a single. A bigger cheer (it's a long way), and I catch a monitor by a concession stand in time to see Johnny scoot home with our first run. I reach the seats as Manny's batting. The girls think I'm nuts, bringing down the glove, but I insist. "Lindsay," I say, "you're getting a ball tonight."

Moss is all over the place. He throws one to the backstop, moving Bill Mueller and Ortiz over. "Watch the ball," I tell the girls, because it's scuffed. The ump tosses it to Andrew, who looks back and sees me and the girls. Lindsay stands and Andrew throws it right to her—only to have this linebacker-sized guy in a muscle shirt in the front row reach back and snatch it away from her. The section boos, and the poacher realizes what he's done and dumps it in Caitlin's lap. So Lindsay gets her ball.

And Manny singles, scoring Bill Mueller to tie the game. Tek rocks a three-run shot. McCarty singles, Kapler doubles. That's it for Moss—7 earned runs in one-third of an inning. For a guy trying to make a comeback, that's got to hurt.

In the top of the third, Rocco Baldelli stings a tailing liner to right that Gabe Kapler makes a great diving catch on. When Kapler comes up with two down in the bottom of the inning, he must still be pumped, because he bunts for a base hit, digging hard and diving headfirst to beat the throw.

"I don't know," I say, and explain to Steph that with a big lead it's generally a sign of disrespect for the other club to bunt for a hit. Then Kapler steals second. "We'll see if they throw at one of our guys," I say.

Lowe's done after seven. Not a great start, but he'll get a W, thanks to good run support. Foulke closes, striking out Crawford and Lugo to finish it. It's a 7–3 final, a relatively uneventful game, and a sweep of the D-Rays. The Yanks have swept Oakland, who should be seriously worried. But no one's worried about the Yanks here, not tonight. We've won six in a row, and the crowd leaves the park happy. Even the talk radio guys on WEEI can't gripe—and whom should we hear but Angry Bill, who says, "Smooth sailing—that's what the captain of the *Titanic* said."

SK: Last time I looked in on the nightcap, the Sox were up 7–3, and Lowe was throwing in that queerly careless way he sometimes has, as though only a quarter of his mind is on the game. If we're going to lose one we should win, this would be my candidate. Second half of a doubleheader? D-Rays feeling embarrassed (by Gabe Kapler, for one)? Sure.

SO: So you caught Kapler's bunt and steal too. At first I thought it was unsporting, but hell, it was only the third. He didn't get plunked, but late in the game the ump rang him up on three pitches, only one of which was decidedly a strike. I guess the game polices itself.

April 30th

Thinking of Kapler last night, I wonder—with Trot due back soon—if he was trying to remind management of his special abilities. With Ellis Burks on the DL, he may be safe for a while, but there are no guarantees. So far Francona's shown he's willing to start Millar, Crespo and McCarty in the outfield, and I imagine we'll see Dauber out there eventually.

In the mail is a stack of scoresheets from the Remy Report. Now, instead of having to buy the same $4 program all month, I can just flip a single sheet over and fold it into my pocket when I'm done.

Also in the mail, a talisman: a ball signed by Sox playoff and World Series hero (how often do you hear those words together?) Dave Henderson. I add Hendu to the ball case like the crucial ingredient in a witch's brew.

We're still in a rain delay with Charlie Moore, NESN's Mad Fisherman, when the Yankee final crawls by—they beat KC for their fourth straight.

And ten minutes before midnight, when the Rangers finally call it (after the crowd's waited through a three-hour delay), the Yanks pick up a half game on us. The game's rescheduled for tomorrow at five Central time, meaning we'll be playing our second doubleheader in three days. Good thing our starting pitching's deep.

May 1st

SK: Good pitching = lots of wins. Also = short losing streaks, and hopefully = postseason. Nomah in thirteen days and counting. Speaking of days, I'll be out of touch for the next five or so as I drive back to God's country.

SO: Really, Nomie in thirteen days? That would be sweet. I expected Trot back first.

Last night after the game was called, Pedro mouthed off to reporters about his lack of a contract. He's pissed at the Red Sox for spreading rumors about his shoulder to drive his price down around the league. He says that he's decided to go free agent after the season, and that, if the situation's right, he could see signing with the Yankees. (All this I pick up from the *Courant*; later, when I see him making comments at his locker on TV, he says, "I want the fans to know my heart is here in Boston. I want to finish in Boston." He shrugs. "But I have to make a living." None of this is in the paper.) He also makes reference to Larry Lucchino's tenure with the Orioles, when they went from being a contender to a second-rate club. "Who was behind the Orioles?" he asks. "I'm not going to mention any names."

It's bad timing, with the Sox riding so high. Usually I'll stick up for Petey, but in this case all a fan has to do is look at Dauber or McCarty or Crespo. There are a lot of guys on this team who are just glad to be here, and rightfully so.

Jon Lieber's glad to be back pitching for the Yanks. He's the one wearing Roger Clemens's #22. Maybe it's an act of faith on the Yankees' part. It's unnecessary today; Lieber gets tons of run support and the Bombers whomp Tony Pena's struggling Royals 12–4.

I only catch the first inning of Game 1 against Texas before we go out to see *Kill Bill, Vol. 2*. By the time we get back, Game 1's over, and we've lost 4–3. Arroyo threw well, but the pen finally gave up some runs (it was just a matter of time; you can't throw scoreless ball forever). Williamson gave up the big hits, but it's Mystery Malaska, who faced only one batter, who gets the L. Manny, suddenly going cold, K'd four times.

I figure we'll get the split, with Pedro taking on green Joaquin Benoit, but Petey's awful from the start, giving up an opposite-field job to Hank Blalock in the first, then melting down in a 5-run third. Every pitch is up, nothing's working, as if he jinxed himself with last night's hissy fit. "Payyy-dro," the sparse crowd taunts. He's gone after four, and DiNardo's on for some garbage time. The final's 8–5, but it was never that close.

May 2nd

After the sweep yesterday, I'm ready for a solid win. Tonight's game is ESPN's *Sunday Night Baseball* feature, and starts an hour later than usual to make prime time. Once again, the pitching matchup's in our favor, Wake vs. R. A. Dickey, a junk-balling righty. His off-speed stuff looks hittable but isn't. Our whole lineup (except Bellhorn, who adds to his league-leading walk total) chases it. Dickey even throws a low knuckler called The Thing, the seams never turning. Wake, throwing his high, floating knuckler, matches him till the fourth, when Johnny misplays a liner into a triple, giving them a cheap run.

It's 1–0 most of the game, with few base runners. Wake tires in the seventh, giving up several foul-ball home runs. Francona wants him to finish the inning, and with two out and two strikes (including another foul-ball homer), David Dellucci straightens one out, and we're down 2–0. In the eighth Embree comes on and promptly gives up two runs.

In the ninth, the crowd chants, "Sweep, sweep," waving brooms. Buck Showalter leaves Dickey in to get the complete-game shutout, even though he's visibly tired. With one down, Manny hits a bloop single, Dauber crushes a liner right at the right fielder, Millar walks, and that's it for Dickey, no complete game. For the third time in two days, on comes Francisco Cordero. Bellhorn works the count deep, turns on a fastball and sticks it in the upper deck—foul—then walks to load the bases. The crowd's edgy now, and they're as pissed as Dickey when Cordero walks Tek to blow the shutout. 4–1, bases still loaded for Crespo, who, despite ample playing time, has yet to drive in a run. Our thin bench is showing, because Francona literally has no one to go to, and Crespo flies to center to end it.

A weak game, and that includes the Yankee-style rally in the ninth, groveling for walks. Ortiz and Bill Mueller aren't hitting, and Manny's in a rare cold spell. Last year the bottom of the order could pick us up, but that's when Bill Mueller was batting eighth and Trot ninth. Now we're trying to get run production out of Kapler, Crespo and Pokey, and it's not happening.

May 3rd

In anticipation of Saturday's front-row Monster seats, I drive around town in the rain trying to find a fishing net so we can haul in shots just short of the Wall. I go to Sears, figuring they might have a Ted Williams model in his fishing line. The floor associate there tells me they no longer carry fishing gear—or baseball gear, for that matter. All they have is home fitness equipment.

I find a net with a telescoping arm at the Sports Authority. It's big, and I doubt the gate attendants will let me in with it, but what the hell. Worst case, I take it back to the car. At home, the dogs are afraid of it. Trudy shakes her head. "How much?"

It's cold in Cleveland, and Lou Merloni's in the wrong dugout. Schilling's just getting warm in the first when he grooves one to cleanup man Victor Martinez, who cranks it into the right-field seats for a 2–0 lead. Schilling settles down after that, but we're just not hitting. The Indians' pitcher is Jake Westbrook, a kid who didn't make their rotation until last week. Ortiz ends two innings with men on; Bellhorn hits into a bases-loaded double play to kill a rally. I'm tired of being behind and wanting something good to happen.

We don't score till the seventh, and then it's on two walks given up by the aptly named David Riske and a blast to center by David Ortiz off retread reliever Rick White. The ball's deep, but it looks like center fielder Alex Escobar's going to make a great leaping catch against the wall. He's worried about the wall and jumps too early, and the ball bounces off him. The runners have to wait, and only Johnny scores. Even though we've had trouble scoring runs, Sveum's right not to send Bill Mueller. Ortiz ended up at second, and with first base open, it's a no-brainer to walk Manny and go after Dauber and Tek. White's a righty, but he's got a big twelve-to-six curve. That's all he throws to Dauber, and gets him easily. He quickly goes 0-2 on

Tek, who at least fouls a few off for drama before striking out on one in the dirt.

Embree throws a scoreless eighth, and we try to tie it in the ninth against former Sox farmhand Rafael Betancourt. Johnny slaps one through the left side. Bill Mueller Ks, but Johnny's running, and the throw from Martinez sails into center. Johnny at third with one down and Ortiz and Manny coming up. I think we've got a real chance to steal one here when Betancourt goes 2-0 on David. Here's where a hitter cuts his strike zone in half and only swings at a ball he knows he can drive. A fly ball's a run, and David's the guy we want up in this situation. He chases one at his knees and grounds out to second.

Two down, and it's up to Manny. Cleveland fans will never forgive him for taking the money and slouching off to Boston, and they're on their feet, cheering for some poetic justice. Betancourt (and manager Eric Wedge) foolishly pitch to him. Down 1-2, Manny fights back and finally walks. So there's no delicious revenge. First and third, two down. Dauber steps in and skies the first pitch to center, and the game's over.

"You guys suck!" I say, and change the channel. I don't want to hear the recap—I don't need to. We're 0 and 4 on the road trip, and have squandered that cushion from sweeping the Yanks. It's not that we're not hitting with men in scoring position, we're not hitting at all. Bill Mueller's not getting it done in the two slot, Ortiz and Millar are struggling, and there's no one to protect Manny. At least Francona acknowledged how desperate we are, running Pokey and Johnny to get something going in the late innings, but he may need to shake up the lineup. Trot and Nomar are still a long ways away.

May 4th

My brother John's visiting, and my friend Phil's flying in from Tokyo. His brother, Adam, has scored tickets to the only major league game within five hundred miles, the Mets and Giants at Shea. None of us is a Mets or Giants fan, but baseball's a fun way to spend time together—"a tonic," Phil calls it, and he's right. Watching baseball is the only way I naturally relax. If I care about the teams playing, I'm anxious, but the rest of my worries vanish.

The paper promises that Barry Bonds will play, but he has a sinus infection and sits. The only star on the field is Mike Piazza, but he's catching, and he can no longer play the position, he's just there until he breaks Fisk's home run record. Everyone knows it too, and in the second inning we're treated to some classic National League action as the Giants bunt three times, scoring an unearned run when Piazza throws wild down the first-base line.

It's a dull game, and a quiet crowd—very un-Fenway-like. Half the seats are empty, half the concession stands shuttered. Worse, the crowd expects nothing from the team. The biggest cheer is for the girls shooting bundled T-shirts into the stands with a CO_2 bazooka. On the small scoreboard, between innings, they run today's Wall Street ticker.

The one Met who impresses me is shortstop and Japanese import Kazuo Matsui, who has a coterie of fans right in front of us eating homemade rice balls. Kaz is 2 for 2 and makes a slick play in the hole. When he comes up next, Phil, a veteran of the Tokyodome, shouts, "Ganbatte!"—meaning "Persevere!" or "Do your best!"

"Ganbatte, Kaz!" we yell.

For me Shea's a break from the grind of the Sox's losing streak, but right beside us is the scoreboard. Cleveland's beating Lowe 2–0 in the second. 2–1 in the fourth. 3–1 in the fourth, 5–1, 6–1, 7–1—and Lowe's still in there. The way we've been hitting, I don't hold out much hope.

Here it's 6–2 Mets in the seventh, and the stadium's clearing out. By the middle of the eighth, there can't be more than 10,000 people, and it's not even ten o'clock.

In Cleveland the Sox rally in the ninth. Suddenly it's 7–6, and the Indians have changed pitchers. A couple minutes later they change again, to #63, Betancourt. I let the Mets distract me from the scoreboard. I keep thinking I'll look up and find us winning, but then the red light beside BOS goes out, the 9 turns into an F, and we've lost five in a row.

Ganbatte!

May 4th

SK: I got back to Maine this afternoon around 2 P.M. Spent the other night in a desperate little Quality Inn about five hundred yards off Route 84 in Sturbridge, Massachusetts, where every droning semi sounded like it was coming right through the bathroom wall, stacks blowing smoke and headlights glaring. But the first thing I did was to seize the little laminated channel card on top of the TV, and yes! Sho nuff! NESN on channel 37! Talk about your welcome back to New England! And a Red Sox welcome it was, as our guys managed to drop their fourth straight, this one by a score of 2–1. A real heartbreaker for Curt Schilling, who pitched like a hero after giving up that dinger.

Now a little editorial about Theo Epstein and his *Moneyball*-inspired gospel of the on-base percentage. I don't know how much or how little of his team-staffing strategy comes from that book, but I *do* know you only have to look at the roster and listen to the chatter from the sportswriters to know that on-base percentage is very important this year. In the last four games (and, to some extent, in the Oakland Athletics' postseason misadventures) you can see the strengths and weaknesses of the philosophy. God knows we've put enough men on base in this little skid; I count a total of *twenty-seven* left on in the four losses. Because, see, a player's on-base percentage will *never* guarantee that player's ability to get a key hit at a key moment. You saw it again and again in the game against Cleveland last night. Ortiz got it done once, with a double (I think on a warm summer night that ball's a home run), but he wasn't able to get Damon in with the tying run in the ninth. And who followed him? Was it Millar? Whoever it was just popped out, and there's your ball game. You can argue that this five-game skid is just one blip in a long season and I would tend to agree—working on this book really makes it clear what a long march a season of baseball is; the first pitch already seems a year gone—but all those men left on base is an interesting statistic, isn't it? It's like cooking enough to feed a family reunion and then only actually serving three people.

Meanwhile, the Yanks are winning again. Guess Derek Jeter won't have to hang up his spikes after all . . . but then, I never really thought he would. But we live in hope.

Chilly up here in God's country, but still—great to be home.

SO: Welcome back to the land of boulders and cold water.

You look at a guy like Bellhorn, and he's all about on-base percentage, working the walk early, middle and late, and he can still get the bat off his shoulder to knock a run in with a sac fly or a single. He's the guy they hoped Jeremy Giambi would be. But you're right, we need our big guys to be knocking these runners in. Ortiz is leaving lots of guys on. The problem is, once you get past Manny (by walking him or just not throwing him anything to hit), our five-thru-nine guys are struggling mightily. I don't expect Pokey to carry that weight, or Kapler or Bellhorn, but Tek, Millar and Dauber (who popped up first-pitch hitting to end that game) have to produce out of the 5 and 6 spots. And Bill Mueller—who got shoved down in the order last night—just hasn't been getting it done in the #2 hole. Lots of blame to go round. Our cushion over the Yanks is gone. Essentially, it's a brand-new season. Dammit.

May 5th

Mr. Kim's going tonight, his second start of the season. He's shaky, but Big David hits a solo homer and then a three-run shot to give him some breathing room. Which we immediately give back when, on three consecutive plays, Kim uncorks a wild pickoff throw, Bellhorn lets an easy grounder through his legs, and Millar kicks a single around right field. It's 5–5 and time for Mystery Malaska, who shuts Cleveland down. Bronson Arroyo's next out of the pen. He's in direct competition for the number 5 spot with Kim, and makes a statement by throwing two scoreless innings while risky David Riske comes in for Cleveland and surrenders a first-pitch three-run rainbow to Bill Mueller.

In the middle of the game, we switch to ESPN to check on the Pirates, who are facing Clemens, and find out that Piazza's hit the homer he's been waiting for so long, finally overtaking Pudge. The commentator says he's now "the greatest home-run-hitting catcher in history."

"No," I correct him, "he just has the most homers."

Each time Manny comes to the plate, everyone in Jacobs Field boos except for a woman's tiny voice picked up by the microphone: "We love you, Manny." With two down and two strikes on him in the ninth, the crowd rises, hoping for some payback, and Manny hits a screw-you double off the wall in right-center. When Tek singles, Sveum—up three runs—gets aggressive and sends Manny. Manny doesn't expect it; he hasn't been running hard from second and has to turn it on. The throw from Jody Gerut's a two-hopper, in time, but Victor Martinez is too worried about Manny and drops it. 9–5 Sox, and a very quiet crowd.

98

SK: So the five-game skid is history, Bronson Arroyo gets a W, and David Ortiz gets a couple of dingers. One more milepost on the long, long road. The important thing—the thing that absolutely *should* go in the book—is that I happened to watch one of those ads for Foxwoods Casino with the sound turned off and had a revelation: all of the people in the ad—gamblers, entertainers, cooks, waiters, and waitresses—look like *utter lunatics*.

We must go there, Stewart.

We must go there soon.

SO: If you really wanna go, let's go when we can catch a Norwich Navigators game (maybe against Portland); they're right up the road, and their little double-A park's nice. Great cheeseburgers too.

May 6th

When I went to bed last night, the Yanks were losing late in Oakland to Barry Zito. The first thing I do when I wake up is hit ESPN, and, perfect timing, they're showing the highlights. Both BALCO boys went deep for the Yanks. They're down 3–2 in the ninth when A-Rod's up with no outs and no one on. He swings, and just the way the camera pans toward the stands, zooming on the crowd, lets me know the ball's gone. Then with two down and two on, Tony Clark hits a quail toward the gap in left that the A's outfielder can't quite get to. 4–3 Yanks. And then there's Mariano Rivera dealing with two on and two out, and the A's last hope pops to second.

Not the way I wanted to start the day. So the Yanks are playing like the regular season means something. And the A's, for all of Billy Beane's genius, still haven't figured out that great starters are useless without a decent pen.

SK: Meet me at Foxwoods.

Meanwhile, as for Bronson versus BK, all I can say is that I have rarely seen any pitcher in my life who looked as uncomfortable on the mound as Mr. Kim did last night. Memo to Theo Epstein: It's time to rent that video, FINDING NOMO.

And the Yankees are apparently not going to lose again this season. Or so it looks now.

I still think this year's Yankee tootsies are made of clay.

SO: They scored on Mr. Kim every inning he was out there. If Theo doesn't get FINDING NOMO, he might be calling Bronson on the TELEFON.

The great Criswell predicts: The Yanks lose to-nite. Let it be so.

And that's clay and steroids.

A nice matchup for the final game of the Cleveland set: Pedro, who's undefeated lifetime in Jacobs Field, against their young ace C. C. Sabathia. Sabathia comes out blazing, while Matt Lawton puts Pedro's first pitch over the wall in dead center. Two hits and a grounder later, we're down 2–0.

It's a fast game, with both aces going right after batters. Old-time hockey, eh? Lou Merloni's playing third for them, which is just weird. Pokey triples, but we strand him.

In the sixth, Bellhorn doubles. Kapler singles, and Sveum, down two runs with nobody out, holds Bellhorn. Ortiz grounds into a DP, but Bellhorn scores, and then Manny, who owns Sabathia, plants one in the right-field stands to tie the game. Meanwhile, Pedro's only given up one hit since the first inning.

In the seventh, McCarty's on first with two down and Pokey at the plate. I tell Steph that Pokey's going to hit a double to the gap and we'll get to see big, gangly McCarty come wheeling all the way around. Unlike most of my hip-shot predictions, this one comes true—McCarty pumping his arms like a crazed windmill—and we've got the lead. Bellhorn comes up and doubles down the line in right, and Pokey scores easily. 4–2.

Pedro's been waiting awhile and struggles in the bottom of the inning, putting two on with one out, and who should step in but Lou. I've always had a soft spot for Lou, but we need a win here. He grounds one to Pokey—tailor-made double-play ball—and I'm pissed when Bellhorn loses his grip on the transfer. Millar, of all people, bails him out with the glove, making a tough catch in foul ground down the right-field line.

We add a run in the eighth, and on comes Embree to set up and Foulke to close.

May 7th

As the great Criswell predicted, the Yankees did indeed lose. Vazquez faltered in the middle innings, so we're a game up on them. The buzz is just temporary, since it appears now that Nomar won't be back till June, and Trot has problems with his left quad and is sitting. "We need those guys," David Ortiz says, "like a human being needs to be fed every day."

Last night Steph noticed that Ron Jackson was coaching first. The paper has the answer: Lynn Jones hurt his eye at home in northwestern Pennsylvania. It sounds serious, because Francona says, "There's a chance they can save some of his eyesight."

Our league-best record is long gone, obviously, but I'm shocked to find that distinction now belongs to the Angels, with the surprising White Sox right behind them. The season's so young that one hot streak puts you on top.

Tomorrow we've got Monster seats, front row, and I call the Sox customer service line to see if I can bring my fishing net for BP. The woman who answers doesn't know. She asks around the office; the consensus is that security will probably not let it in, but there's no set policy. I tell her I'll try. Got to make them make the play, right?

Tonight it's Wake and his 2.25 ERA against Jeremy Affeldt, who's yet to win a game. I'm thinking we should score a bunch of runs, but it's Wake who struggles. It's a windy night—usually good for a knuckler—but his ball looks awful straight. It also doesn't help that in the third we have Carlos Beltran picked off first but Bellhorn—maybe distracted by Desi Relaford trying to score from third—drops Millar's toss. It's 2–0, but not for long. In our half, Johnny answers with a leadoff shot over the Royals' pen. Bellhorn singles, Manny singles for the second time, Millar doubles. Tie game.

Between innings, the camera finds Trot in the dugout—a nice surprise—and there's Prince Nomar. Neither's close to being ready; it's more of a token appearance to raise morale.

Word on Lynn Jones is that somehow he gouged his eye with a screwdriver. They're still not sure if he'll regain sight in it. While he's out, former Sox catcher Bill Haselman, who played with the PawSox last year, will coach first.

In the sixth, Wake gives up five hits and Bill Mueller rushes a throw on a chopper, sailing it into the stands. The Royals score four runs before the creaky Benito Santiago grounds into a round-the-horn double play.

By the eighth Affeldt's pitch count is pushing 110. He's a young guy but he's never gone this deep in a game before. Tony Pena must want to conserve his pen for the rest of the series, because he leaves him in. Manny singles for the third time. Kapler hits a short fly to left that the wind takes away from Matt Stairs; it falls, and we've got first and second for Mirabelli, who lines one into the left-field corner. Stairs fires the ball in to second, but it's wide and gets by Relaford, and Kapler scoots in to make it 6–4.

Timlin throws a perfect top of the ninth. Before Johnny can lead off the bottom, two fans run out on the field, delighting the crowd. When Johnny finally gets up, he's laughing and loose, and walks on a pitch that's really too close to take. MacDougal, the Royals' young closer, stares in at veteran ump Joe West; West whips off his mask and stares back. A passed ball puts Johnny at second, so we don't have to worry about the double play. With Bellhorn up, I expect we're in for a long at-bat, but he gets a pitch belt-high and yanks it deep to right. Juan Gonzalez runs a few steps toward the corner, then pulls up as the ball lands a dozen rows in. The game's tied at 6 and Fenway's on its feet. Here in Avon, we're hollering and trading high fives.

They don't want to pitch to Manny with the game on the line, but they don't intentionally walk him either, just nibble a little and then stay away on 3-2.

MacDougal's gone and righty Scott Sullivan's on. With two down, Francona pinch-hits the switch-hitting Tek for the righty Kapler. Tek rips Sullivan's first pitch down the right-field line for a sure double. Manny's running on contact. The ball skims along the wall instead of kicking out. "Don't touch it!" I coach the fans past the Pesky Pole. I see other fans along the wall doing the same with their neighbors, holding their arms out wide as if to prove they're not fouling anyone. Gonzalez scoops the ball and fires to Relaford, whose relay to Santiago is just enough off the plate to the first-base side to let Manny tiptoe in standing up. He leaps into the arms of Kevin Millar and the Sox win 7–6. Here at home, Steph and I are jumping and high-fiving, slapping at each other like first-graders.

It's a huge win—a steal, really. Two in the eighth, then three in the ninth off a cold closer. Manny ran hard all the way and Sveum sent him in—classic strategy at home: play for the win and make them throw you out. I watch

Extra Innings, wallowing in the highlights and locker-room interviews. Sox win, Sox win!

SO: Man, what a wild one. I'm still short of breath from screaming. It's amazing how loud you have to yell at the TV so the players can hear you.

SK: . . . so it was spoken, and so it was. My God, Bellhorn's starting to look like the deal of the century, isn't he? (BELLHORN, BOOK, AND CANDLE, starring Spencer Tracy). He cranks one to get us even, and then Manny (MANNY THE TORPEDOES, starring Randolph Scott) struts across home plate three minutes later, arms raised like a ref signaling the extra point's good. And all at once we've got a little breathing room between us and the Yankees. Have you noticed, by the way, that on *Extra Innings* they now play Darth Vader music before giving the Yankees score? And call them the Evil Empire? Hee! Hating the Yankees is very much in vogue, but since we were doing it long before Yankee-hating was cool (outside of New England, that is), I'm sending you your own YANKEES HATER hat, with the spiffy **yh** intertwined logo on the front.

Also, the Coen Brothers remake: MUELLER'S CROSSING.

And the Hammer Horror remake: CURSE OF THE DAMON, titled JOHNNY EVIL for DVD release.

The art-film classic LEAVING NOMAR.

That gritty piece of '50s realism: I TROTTED ALL THE WAY HOME.

The soft-core classic PLEASE ME ORTIZ ME.

Nor can we forget the hardcore STROKE ME POKEY.

Bottom line? Baseball's a wonderful game. There's no greater thrill than when your team pulls one out. And you can't get that from a newspaper story. TV's better, but there's really nothing on God's earth like being at the ballpark and getting on your feet in the bottom of the ninth, hot dog still in hand, when the Sox pull one out. If Heaven's that good, I guess I wanna go.

Born Again in New England.

SO: Was at a game last year against Clemboy and the Yanks where John Williams threw out the first ball (I think he bounced it), and when

Clem jogged out to the pen, the PA played Lord Vader's March—perfect for a guy who started out as a headstrong young Jedi apprentice from a dusty, forlorn planet, then felt betrayed and hurt, grew power-mad and crossed over to the dark side.

May 8th

What's better than the Sox winning? The Sox winning and the Yanks losing. Last night the Mariners rocked Jon Lieber, so we're two games up. And we can't forget the O's, just a half game behind them. Toronto's under .500, and Tampa Bay's already in a death spiral. That's the kind of year a fan fears—out of the chase by May (like the Pirates, who got one-hit last night). As Sox fans, we need to remember how lucky we are.

And we're damn lucky today, with front-row seats on the Monster. All along Lansdowne, people stare at the net; Trudy pretends she's not with me. The guy at the turnstile asks me what I think I'm going to do with it, but just laughs and lets me through. Trudy and the kids can't believe I'm getting away with this.

The Royals are hitting, clumps of players spread around the outfield. It's a bright cool day up on the Monster, and the wind's in our faces, perfect for home runs. We're in M9, next to the second light standard, but that's too far toward center. I stake my claim to an empty spot in M5 above the power alley.

I've just started to extend the handle when a ball comes right at me. It's going to be short. I reach out and down. I'd have it if the handle were fully extended.

"Hey, no fair!" Trudy calls from M9. "That's cheating."

With the handle fully extended, the net's about ten feet long, giving me incredible range. It really *is* unfair.

Mike Sweeney's taking his cuts. He sends one directly over my head. I raise the net straight up and even jump, but the ball carries over it, banging off the third-row facade and then back past us and down to the field again.

A few swings later, Sweeney hits one just to my right. It's going to be close. I scoot a few steps and swing the net over. The ball clanks off the handle and drops at my feet. Inelegant, but hell, it's a ball, and Sweeney's as good a player as they've got.

I'm not sure who hits me the next one. It's right at me, and a few feet out from the lip, so I'm not taking it away from anyone, but I misjudge it and it bangs off the handle a good foot from the head of the net, and falls back to the field. The boos and laughs shower down, and I slump back in a stool and hang my head. "Nice going, Netman." "Netguy, you suck!"

The guy beside me points out a dent in the handle. It's a good-sized ding, the metal buckled inward. I can't close the handle all the way anymore.

Juan Gonzalez puts a bunch out by the Coke bottles, and then some guy in a blue fleece sweatshirt hits another right at me. It rises past the solid background of the roof and up into the blue sky, then falls fast. It's going to be short, and I dip the net out and down. I don't think I've got enough reach, but I must, because it's a swish, just a gentle tug on my arms and then the ball swinging in the mesh, caught. The crowd goes wild. "Yeah, go ahead, Netman!" "Hey, gimme one—isn't it catch and release?"

The ball has a pink stamp on the sweet spot: KCR enclosed by a thin circle, like something on special at CVS. The hitter was Benito Santiago—the BEN from his bathead's imprinted backwards across the cowhide.

Like Mark Bellhorn, I had a chance to redeem myself. And just in time too, because that's it for BP. Packing up, I'm visited by two people. A burly security dude who tells me I'll have to surrender the net to him before game time (so I don't interfere with play), and a reporter for the Greenfield, Mass, paper who saw the catch and wants to interview me. I get to use my Bellhorn analogy. "You're down one minute and the next you're up again. That's baseball." And, canned and corny as that sounds, it is: as long as you keep at it—stubbornly, dumbly—something good might happen.

It's a beautiful day, we're in the front row, and Schilling's on the mound. He's throwing 92–93, with great location. KC's throwing another kid, Jimmy Gobble, and I'm proud of the Faithful for not making turkey noises at him. He's throwing well too, mostly soft breaking stuff. We get a run off him in the third, Bellhorn doubling in Johnny. The Royals get it back in the fifth when Santiago homers to the exact spot in M5 where I was fishing. It's 1–1 in the fifth and the game's not even an hour old.

In the bottom of the fifth Pokey stings one down the right-field line. Gonzalez gets over to the wall by the Pesky Pole in time to cut the ball off—trying to hold Pokey to a single—but the ball slips through, bouncing past him along the wall and curling into the corner. Pokey's rounding third as the ball comes in to cutoff man Desi Relaford. The crowd's up—Sveum's sending him. Pokey's chugging now, and the throw's on the mark. Santiago lunges with the tag as Pokey dives flat-out and slides a hand across the plate—safe! The place goes insane, a good three-minute celebration that lasts halfway through Johnny's at-bat, and while we don't score again that inning, we're on our feet to salute Pokey when he trots out to short.

"I've never seen an inside-the-park home run live," Steph says. Neither have I.

Schill is cruising, really stretching his arm out, throwing 94 and 95 now. He's only given up three hits.

In our sixth, Gobble's breaking stuff stays up. Millar doubles, Manny doubles, Tek singles, Bill Mueller singles. It's 5–1, and Mr. Gobble is cooked. For the second straight game former Yankee Jason Grimsley provides little relief. With two down and Kapler on, he leaves one in Pokey's wheelhouse (it's a very small wheelhouse, but it still works), and Pokey turns on it and sticks it in M3. "*PO*-Key, *PO*-Key!" He comes back out of the dugout and tips his cap. Two homers in two innings—it looks awesome on the scorecard.

In the eighth, McCarty hits a two-run shot that keeps the party going, but the real ovation is reserved for Pokey. When he comes to bat the last time, the entire park rises. He's never had a two-homer game in his career, but he's been such a great defensive player, filling in for Nomar. Pokey pauses outside the batter's box, soaking in the moment, and I think it's a day he'll always keep—the way we will.

May 9th

Another matchup to love: D-Lowe against weak lefty Darrell May. After a brief rain delay, Bill Mueller gets us on the board in the second, driving a high change-up into M3 with Tek on base. 2–0 and all the mothers in the stands are happy.

The next inning, after Desi Relaford walks, David DeJesus hits a chopper to McCarty, who spins and fires to Pokey. DeJesus runs well, so the chances for two are slim, but it's a good play, cutting down the lead runner. The throw's perfect. Pokey comes off the bag for a look at first (there's no one there), and though the ball beat Relaford by a good five feet and the neighborhood play's in order, umpire Joe West calls him safe. Pokey can't believe it. Francona comes out to argue, but it's pointless. The replay shows that Pokey did indeed slide-step off the bag an instant before receiving the ball, so technically the runner would be safe, but in practice it's an out 99% of the time. Lowe battles and gets two outs, but then Sweeney pulls a grounder down the line past Bill Mueller for a game-tying double. On the replay, broken down, it makes no sense: Sweeney's a dead pull hitter and Lowe's been working him down and in, yet Bill Mill's playing him well off the line. Why isn't someone in the dugout waving him over?

The next inning, Pokey makes a leaping snag of a Joe Randa laser they have to show two or three times. In slow-mo it's even more impressive; Pokey heads back on contact and does a little stutter-step before going up for it like he's timing an alley-oop, leaps and snares it backhanded. The momentum of the ball sends him twisting around so he lands facing the Monster. "It's like watching *The Matrix*," Steph says.

It's a sedate game otherwise. May is spacing out the hits and Lowe's struggling with his control but seems to get a ground ball whenever he needs one.

That changes in the sixth. Joe Randa singles, and with two down, Lowe walks their eight and nine guys to load the bases. After Dave Wallace pays Lowe a visit, Angel Berroa, their leadoff man, hits a smash that Bill Mueller has to dive to stop. With Berroa's wheels, there's no chance at first, so he goes to Bellhorn for the force, but DeJesus is hustling and ties the throw. 3–2 Royals. Lowe's gone and Mystery Malaska's on to face the dangerous Carlos Beltran, now batting righty. He gets behind 3-0 and on 3-2 throws a fat pitch that Beltran pulls past Bill Mueller into the corner, clearing the bases. 6–2 Royals.

It's 8–3 in the bottom of the ninth and Steph and I are playing catch in the backyard, listening to the dregs of the game on the radio when Johnny knocks in Pokey. With two outs and Johnny on, Tony Pena—in a move I can only call paranoid, since he's up four runs—changes pitchers. It works—der—and the winning streak is over. We turn it off and keep tossing, dropping balls and making plays, banging throws off the downspout, off the porch railing, off the shed.

What's worse than the Red Sox losing? The Red Sox losing and the Yankees winning, which they do, coming back from a 6–0 deficit to nip the Mariners 7–6. Back to a one-game lead. Baltimore won as well. If this three-team race keeps up, we're in for a wild summer. It's kind of strange, knowing we won't see the Yanks again till the end of June, or the O's till late July. I'm ready *now*.

May 10th

Brigham's ice cream is coming out with a new flavor, Reverse the Curse. Vanilla with fudge sauce, caramel, chocolate and peanuts, the product looks suspiciously like their Big Dig, but I appreciate the sentiment. They say that after the Sox win this October, they'll have a contest to rename it.

The paper says Nomar took batting practice in the cage yesterday, another hopeful sign, but there's still no schedule for his return. Trot's headed back to Florida for more rehab on the quad. Also headed to Florida is Manny, to Miami, to become an American citizen. He'll miss tonight's game against Cleveland.

He's lucky. This one's a mess from the very beginning. Besides Lou Merloni's return to Fenway, there's not much to cheer about. Kim's ineffective, and the Indians can hit. They bang on the Monster three times in the first, giving Dauber a crash course in left field. He looks terrible on the first one—getting caught too close to the wall so Johnny has to come over and back him up—but on the last one he throws Ben Broussard out at second to end the inning.

Dauber provides some offensive highlights as well, lining a two-run double off the wall and later homering into the Indians' bullpen; he even backs up Johnny nicely on a double off the Bob's sign, but the story of the game is Kim. He's topping out at 86 and can't find the plate. He and Tek get their signs mixed up, and an elusive passed ball scores two more. When Kim leaves with one out in the top of the fourth, he's thrown 80 pitches, 46 for strikes, and it's 4–4 with the bases loaded. The sellout crowd boos. Lefty Lenny DiNardo comes in and gives up a single to outfielder Coco Crisp.

Cleveland leads the rest of the way, and the rest of the way is mighty ugly, a parade of relievers for both teams. DiNardo gives up a run of his own, Embree gives up a pair (thanks to Timlin, who walks the first guy he sees and can't wriggle out of the jam), Malaska lets one in. Foulke, at least, throws a clean inning. It's a long game, lots of base runners. Cleveland's line score says it all: 2 2 0 2 0 1 2 0 1.

The final's 10–6. No alibis, no one play to point to, we just plain stunk. The whole Kim-Arroyo debate's sure to heat up. I try not to overreact. It's just one game, and tomorrow we've got Pedro going.

May 11th

Theo and Francona don't waste any time: Kim's out of the rotation, Arroyo's in. They must have made the decision after the game, since it's in the morning paper.

SO: I really thought Mr. Kim would be an upgrade from John Burkett, but it sure doesn't look that way. As a manager, how do you rebuild his confidence? As a general manager, how do you showcase him so other teams don't quit on him?

SK: I'm really, really glad Kim is out of the starting ro.

SO: Me too, but I had such high hopes for him. 190 innings, 15 wins. All shot to hell.

Tonight it's Cleveland at the Fens, and a rematch of Pedro versus C. C. Sabathia, who has to be the pimpest pitcher in the American League (maybe in all of baseball): big, baggy uni, hat worn cocked arrogantly to one side. We're not off to a good start. After striking out the first batter, Pedro has allowed three straight hits (the second one tainted, a bouncer from Omar Vizquel off first baseman David Ortiz's glove) and Cleveland leads, 2–0.

At least it's a decent night for baseball. I may have said this before, but it bears repeating: spring baseball in New England is usually rotten for the fans and sometimes dangerous for the players (especially the pitchers). I mean, night baseball in April? In *Boston?* Where the temperature's forty-six degrees and the wind blowing in off the Back Bay makes it feel like twenty-seven? I'd say you've got to be kidding me, but we all know I'm not, just as we know it's all about the money. Baseball is a lazy game, meant to be played on long, lazy summer afternoons and into the purple twilight—when fans so inclined can exchange their iced tea or Cokes for cold beer—but money has changed all that. Tonight at least we have a foretaste of summer: eighty degrees at game time, according to Joe Castiglione in the radio booth, and coincidentally or not, it's also Boston's eightieth straight home sellout. Stewart O'Nan's there tonight, I think. Lucky dog. This older dog will be there a little later on this month, when the warmth may be a little more reliable.

Meantime, I have to look back on my own preseason musings about how much the AL East has improved—Orioles, Jays, D-Rays, blah-blah-blah—and smile a little bit. Because now, as the Red Sox play into the second inning of their thirty-second contest of the season, it's starting to look like a case of same as it ever was: Red Sox and Yankees, duking it out for first, with the long, hot summer stretching ahead. The Sox had a five-game bulge over the Yanks not long ago, but it's been years since Boston seemed comfortable with anything like a real lead; they went into tonight's game with just a half-game pad over the second-place Yankees and first place on the line. Baltimore is still in it, too, a game and a half back.

My mother-in-law, meanwhile, with whom I watched a good many games in Florida, is now in the hospital with respiratory problems, but I know she'll be watching on NESN. They're watching all over New England, tonight and every other night, in the hospitals, nursing homes, rehabs, and hospices. It's what we do, what we've done for going on a century now. They're hitting Pedro pretty well tonight, and we're down 2–0 in the second, Cleveland with two more in scoring position, but Pedro has also struck out the side in the first inning, and two more in the second. I pause in front of this keyboard every time he throws. I want him to get those six Ks. So does my mother-in-law, Sarah Jane, over in St. Joe's, not to mention Leo the short-order cook at Nicky's Diner down on Union Street, and Keith Jacubois at the Texaco station over in Montpelier. This is what we do, and we've finally got a decent night to do it on, and we may be behind, but there are no damn blackflies yet, and for the time being, we're still in first place.

Pedro walked Jody Miller, but now he's 0-2 on Red Sox killer Victor Martinez. He comes to the belt . . . and strikes Victor out swinging. And all over New England they're cheering in the hospitals, hospices, and road-side restaurants. When the Sox finally win this one two hours later, Pedro Martinez doesn't get the W; that goes to Alan Embree, who gives up a go-ahead gopher ball and then vultures the victory when the Sox come back in the bottom of the eighth.

The win allows the Sox to stay in first, because the Yankees beat the Angels—finally, after two rain delays, in front of approximately sixteen remaining fans—in the Bronx, in ten. The final score is high and Kevin Brown doesn't get the win. The Yankees have finally started to roll, but their pitching remains suspect as ever—a good sign.

And a rather endearing postscript having to do with our other Ramirez: to wit, one Manny. In Cleveland, he was usually silent and often viewed as sullen even when he was clearly enjoying the game. In Boston—a town where the sports reporters are often compared to the shark in *Jaws*—he has become more expansive with each passing year; not even management's efforts in the off-season to trade him for A-Rod seem to have fazed him in the slightest, and by the kickoff of the 2004 festivities, Manny was downright chatty. Not stupid, though. Asked for a comment following the Sox five-game massacre of the Yankees, Manny's deference was both charming and diplomatic: "They got all the World Series rings, man," he said. "We got nothing."

He has been the one completely dependable hitter in the Red Sox lineup this year, at this date in May batting roughly eighty points higher than Alex Rodriguez, the man for whom Theo Epstein hoped to trade him. He has played in every game of the season except for this Monday's (May 10th) trouncing by Cleveland, his old team. Manny was unavailable to play on that day because he was taking the U.S. citizenship test . . . which he passed. At the start of tonight's game he ran out to his position in left field with a big grin on his face and a small American flag in his right hand. Manny's People in left gave him a standing O.

Way to go, Manny Ramirez—welcome to the *real* big leagues.

May 12th

Mr. Kim's headed for Pawtucket, where they say he'll throw only two innings at a time. Supposedly this will help him get back his velocity faster. Theo says BK's shown he can dominate major league hitters, and that that quality doesn't just go away, but it's hard to tell if he truly believes this.

A note in the *Courant's* Sox column says that Trot took BP yesterday and hit some out, and that Nomar knocked a couple over the Monster. It's possible, since the Sox were batting a little before the gates opened. I didn't see Trot until after the game, congratulating the line of guys coming off, but I saw Nomar take around thirty swings, and nothing was close to going out.

The website says right-handed reliever Jamie Brown will be taking Mr. Kim's spot on the roster, making him something like our twentieth pitcher this season. Whatever happened to Bobby Jones? Instead of all these kid relievers, I'd rather see them bring up a big righty stick like perennial triple-A prospect Andy Dominique for late-inning situations. Twelve pitchers seems like a luxury, and I'm not sure we're getting anything out of it. There's such a traffic jam in the pen that Williamson hasn't thrown in six days.

Tonight it's Wake versus Cliff Lee, a young lefthander who's 3-0 with a nifty ERA. It seems every time the Indians have someone on, they take advantage of Wake's slow delivery and steal. Twice Bellhorn lets throws from Mirabelli skip by him into center. The Indians get a run in the second, and the third, and the fifth, and two in the sixth on a Monster shot by Tim Laker. Wake's just not sharp, and Lee is. In the ninth, down four, the crowd rallies. It's louder than it's been all night when Dauber's pinch double scores Bill Mueller. Johnny hits a hopper up the middle; Vizquel and Belliard look at each other, and it rolls into center, scoring Dauber. It's 6–4, and up to the plate steps the tying run in the form of Mark Bellhorn. The count goes 2-0, David Ortiz is on deck and Betancourt is sweating like Calvin Schiraldi. Just last week, Bellhorn hit that two-run shot in the ninth to tie the game against KC—at the same score too, 6–6. He must be thinking the same thing, because he goes fishing for a couple balls well off the plate and Ks to end the game.

So Cleveland takes two out of three from us, and we go 3-3 on the home stand. Now it's off to Toronto for four games—all against righties, mercifully.

Please, please, let the Yankees lose.

May 13th

In the mail, a phantom piece: a pennant with the Sox logo and printed signatures of all the players surrounding WORLD CHAMPIONS 1986. Earlier this week I received a phantom soda cup that would have been sold at Wrigley during the much anticipated Sox-Cubs World Series last year. They're not fakes, just survivors of large runs, the majority of which were destroyed by reality. On eBay I've seen phantom tickets for playoffs and World Series dating back to the sixties, including some years in which we never even came close (say, 1970, 1987). There's a twinge of pain attached to these no-longer-possible futures, but also, by the pieces' existence, a validation of what should have happened.

Unless something weird happens, we're done for the season with Cleveland, and considering that we finished 3-4, that's probably a good thing. "Looks like Wakefield's carriage turned back into a pumpkin, Dad," my son Owen said during last night's postgame call. (Not so fast, kid—Wake's been down before, but he's never been out.) Now we're on to Toronto, and what my *other* son likes to call the CreepyDome, because it's been so empty over the last three or four years . . . and especially now, while playoff hockey is still wending its slow way through the lower intestine of bigga-time sport.* Schilling is starting for us tonight, and since Toronto beat him last time when Schill insisted on holding on to the ball in the late innings, this should be a game worth watching. But first I have to watch *Jeopardy*. This is Political Gasbag Week, and I have to root for Keith Olbermann, himself a recent émigré from the Land of Bigga-Time Sport.

Later: "This one's no masterpiece," Jerry Remy of the TV crew opines in the seventh inning of tonight's tilt, and that's an understatement. Every pitcher seems to have one team he just can't seem to beat, and for Curt Schilling, it's the Jays. He went into this game with only one victory against them in something like half a dozen tries (that one win came in his Diamondback days), and he's not going to improve on that record tonight. The final score is 12–6. Schill struggled, and he'll probably get tagged with the loss, but that's not the real story of this game; he only gave up three runs, and the Sox have already scored twice that many as we play into the eighth.

The story of the game isn't even the Red Sox defense, which has been horrible—a Johnny Damon error in center let in two runs, and Mark Bellhorn's failure to snag Frank Catalanotto's foul pop cost another two (Catalanotto singled on the next pitch). No, the real problem, it seems to me, is that the Sox have turned lackluster in their last five games, playing catch-up in four of them and only successfully in one of those. The Yan-

*Here's what I understand about hockey: Bulky men wearing helmets and carrying sticks in their gauntleted hands skate around for a while on my TV; then some guy comes on and sells trucks. Sometimes chicks come on and sell beer.

kees won earlier today, beating the Angels (Mariano Rivera was shaky, but had just enough gas to survive a bases-loaded jam in the ninth), and if things don't turn around, the Red Sox are going to find themselves with a 5-9 mark for the month of May . . . and in second place. They need a shake-up. This may be where our new manager really starts earning his paycheck . . . assuming he can, of course.

Two final notes (unless the Sox pull it out, that is): Orlando Hudson has scored five of the Jays' runs, tying a team record. (Ask me if I give a shit.) And on the radio, color commentator Jerry Trupiano has been reduced to wondering how the sitcom *Frasier,* which finishes its run tonight, turned out.

It's been that kind of game.

May 14th

7:40 A.M.: Ordinarily I tune in to NESN's morning sports show, which runs on a constant fifteen-minute loop from 5 A.M. to 9 A.M. seven days a week, while I do my push-ups and crunches, but not today. Not even the thought of Jayme Parker, who's blond and *very* good-looking, can motivate me into picking up the remote this morning. The Yankee win and the Red Sox sloppy D, combining to put the Bombers back into first (thank *God* I didn't have to look at the *New York Post* today), is bad enough; that look of lackluster, who-cares sloppiness over the last few games is worse. Last night it even seemed to have gotten to Curt Schilling; I fancied I could read it in his dispirited dugout sprawl after he was lifted.

Dammit, don't you guys know that O'Nan and I are counting on you to win the pennant? I want to shout, "Wake up! It gets late early in this game so *wake the hell up!*"

Grumbling in the paper about Francona going to DiNardo and Malaska with games on the line. Why, *Courant* beat writer David Heuschkel asks, are we relying on our number eleven and twelve pitchers when we've got a stocked pen?

The answer's obvious, and goes back to the off-season. For several years we've been short on lefties, and we haven't had a reliable middle guy since Rich Garces—El Guapo—hurt his elbow. Theo never went out and dealt for a lefty, so in spring training we saw a logjam for the last bullpen spot, won, finally, by retread Bobby Jones, who lasted all of a week. The guy right behind him, Tim Hamulack, hasn't made it up yet, while DiNardo, Malaska and Phil Seibel have all seen work. Theo probably thought the middle relief was covered by Arroyo and Mendoza. Mendoza's on the DL (as always); Arroyo's now part of the starting rotation. Our only major league lefty, Embree, is a situational and setup guy who throws best when going an inning or less. So when Francona needs a lefty in the sixth to hold a game, he *has* to go with the kids.

9:50 P.M.: Once upon a time (and it doesn't seem so long ago), there were no Eastern, Western, and Central Divisions; there was just the American League and the National League, with eight or nine teams each. The bottom four or five of these were known as the *second* division, and the bottom couple of teams were the *cellar-dwellers*. (Red Sox fans from the late fifties and early sixties came to know these terms well.) Last night and tonight, the Red Sox and the Blue Jays have played like second-division teams from 1959—Boston and Washington, let's say, battling it out for a sloppy nine in front of a few thousand dozy afternoon fans (many of them more interested in their newspapers than the game unfolding in front of them) while the Yankees cruised the stratosphere twenty or so games above them both in the standings.

Tonight the Red Sox are leading 9–3 as we go to the bottom of the ninth, but Derek Lowe was once more miles from sharp (it's Alan Embree's game to win, he of the bright blue eyes, scruffy beard, and amazing cheekful o' chaw), and the Sox scored most of their runs in one inning during which the hapless Jays chucked the pill everywhere, including into the stands.

The best things you can say about tonight's performance are that we'll keep pace with the Yankees, who are also winning, and that better days are coming, both defensively and on the mound. Meantime, at least it's a win at SkyDome.

May 15th

It's eighty-nine degrees, a record, and my old car, which I just got back from the shop, breaks down on the commercial strip in town—maybe vapor lock? While I'm outside Party City waiting for the wrecker, a guy pulls up with the game on and waits while his wife runs inside.

"Who's winning?"

"I just turned it on," he says. "I know McCarty has an RBI."

He sees my Fenway 1912 shirt, I see his—from last year's ALCS—and he gets out to talk. In February he went down to the Civic Center to see the Sox Winter Caravan and got autographs from Kevin Millar and Bill Mueller. "I was worried it would be weird, you know, the big-kid thing, but once I got up to the table, I got this smile on my face, and the guys were cool."

We weigh our chances for the season.

"Now there's a rumor Nomar might have a tear," he says, "not just a strain like they've been saying."

He also wonders why Trot's taking so long to come back from a hamstring, and we bat around the possibility of him being on steroids (or off them now).

His wife returns, and they've got to run. "Go Sox!" she calls, and they're gone.

The tow truck comes, finally, and Trudy, to drive me home. It's too hot upstairs, so I go down to the cool basement and watch the rest of the game on her parents' old TV. It's 4–0 Sox, and Arroyo's only given up three hits. He's going after guys with his fastball, dropping his sweeping curve in for strikes. Toronto's a good-hitting club, and the SkyDome's a launching pad, but he's putting down Wells, Delgado and Hinske in order.

There's a grounder to third, and to my surprise, Kevin Youkilis fields it. Bill Mueller's knee is aching, so Francona doesn't want him playing on Toronto's hard turf. When Youkilis comes up to bat, they show him earlier in the game, hitting his first major league home run and then trotting back to the dugout, where the guys give him the silent treatment—a tradition with rookies. Youkilis gets it, giving phantom high fives. Only after he sits down do the guys break up and congratulate him.

Arroyo's making his case to be the number five starter. Yesterday, in Pawtucket, in the first inning of his first start, Kim gave up a three-run homer. Trade rumors are cropping up, the most notable, Kim and Johnny D to Seattle for Freddy Garcia, who we then ship to KC for Carlos Beltran. Beltran's a serious five-tool player, but I'd hate to lose Johnny's laid-back personality. He's a fan favorite, especially with the ladies, and great for the clubhouse. Though I'd love to see Beltran in right and Johnny in center.

But look at the team we have on the field right now: Arroyo and Mirabelli, Youkilis, Crespo, Bellhorn and Ortiz, McCarty, Damon and Millar. And we're winning—on the road.

Arroyo goes eight, giving up 3 hits, walking none and striking out 6. Foulke closes easily (something I'm getting accustomed to), and though my car broke down and I've gotten nothing done today, I'm happy.

In the Bronx, the Yanks are in extra innings against Seattle, tied 7–7. I watch for a couple innings, but not a lot's happening, and there's yardwork to be done. After dinner, when I check ESPN, the final's a lopsided 13–7, Seattle. Once Rivera was gone, the Mariners feasted on Gabe White.

So we're in first again, barely.

SO: And it will forever be known as: The Day of the Youkilis.

SK: The Revenge of Moneyball.

May 16th

And the O's lost again, so we gained ground on them too. I know it's pointless to be scoreboard-watching in May, but I can't help it, just as I can't help looking for the Pirates' score (we beat the Giants again) and seeing if we're still in the cellar.

In their search for a number five starter, the Yankees pick up former Devil Ray Tanyon Sturtze from the Dodgers for a player to be named later. Sturtze's 3-0 for triple-A Las Vegas, but is that really the best Brian Cashman and George can do? Wait till July and the trade deadline.

In Toronto, it's Pedro-Halladay III, a series I'm growing fond of. Pedro won the first two, and Manny gives him a 1–0 lead with an RBI single in the first. Both aces look good, setting the sides down quickly. In the bottom of the fourth, Youkilis misplays a carpet hopper from Vernon Wells. "You can't do that in a close game," I tell him through the TV. "Especially with Carlos up next." Delgado makes my fears a reality, taking a high fastball over the right-field fence. 2–1 Toronto. Besides that one mistake to a quality hitter, Pedro looks good. In the sixth, he gives up another run on a blooper by Reed Johnson that Johnny gets a late jump on.

Halladay's over 120 pitches and finished after seven. Likewise, Pedro's over 100 and done. We have two full innings to go after their relievers. With one out in the eighth, Ortiz doubles. Rather than let Manny tie the game with one swing, Carlos Tosca decides to put him on. It's an easy decision. Dauber goes down looking, Tek goes 0-2 before popping to first, and that's our best chance. Terry Adams works a scoreless ninth and Doc Halladay finally beats us.

It's not disappointing. I'm sure Pedro's not happy, but Roy Boy threw well. It was a good, tight game with Hall of Fame matchups like Halladay-Manny and Pedro-Delgado. Major League Baseball, and you can't gripe about that.

The Yanks play a similar game, but get it done, Kevin Brown going to 5-0 as they beat the M's 2–1 and move back into first.

After a brief return to first place (one day—a cup of coffee, really) the Red Sox gently subside once more to second, half a game behind the Yankees. The most notable event of our final two games in the CreepyDome— which was actually pretty full for the weekend games—was the major league debut of Kevin Youkilis, subbing for Bill Mueller (sore knee). Youkilis hit a home run in his first at-bat and will bear watching if only because he personifies the *Moneyball* mind-set and strategy, which can be defined as a way of thinking that both arises from and revolves around on-base percentage. Youkilis, the so-called "Greek God of Walks," tied a minor-league record, reaching base in *seventy-one straight games,** and it's sort of a wonder it's taken him as long as it has to reach the bigs, especially under the umbrella of Major Theo. It will be interesting to see how he develops, and how much PT he gets as the season heats up.

May 18th

In the mail, a box from Steve with a YANKEES HATER cap in Sox colors. The logo, **yh,** is designed so it looks the same upside-down. "Cool hat," Steph says, and once he puts it on, it's his.

Driving him to his sax lesson, I tell him about another YANKEES HATER cap I saw Steve wearing earlier in the year. It was black with an orange logo, like a Giants cap.

"Do the Giants hate the Yankees?" he asks.

I try to remember if the Yanks ever beat those great early Mays teams

---

*The record he shares, perhaps not so coincidentally, with fellow former Portland Sea Dog Kevin Millar. SO

(just once, in '51, when they were still the New York Giants). It takes me a minute to recall the '62 World Series, when Bobby Richardson snagged Willie McCovey's liner. It was the Yanks' last pre-Steinbrenner championship.

"No," I say, "they're too busy hating the Dodgers."

And then I realize that, though you never hear them bandied about as a cursed or hard-luck club, the San Francisco Giants have never won a World Series.

Although it might have just been my imagination (I've been accused of having an overactive one), I thought I heard cries of "Dead team walking!" tonight in the hollow air-conditioned confines of Tropicana Field. How avidly Lou Piniella, fiery competitor that he is, must be dining upon his own liver these days! The Devil Rays (until further notice to be called the *hapless* Devil Rays in this fan's notes) looked much improved on paper, but as one wit or another has surely pointed out, baseball games aren't played on paper, and the D-Rays—*excusez-moi,* the *hapless* D-Rays—have the worst record in the majors, just 10 wins against 27 losses after tonight's contest, which the Red Sox won, 7–3.

In a game last week, new citizen Manny Ramirez trotted out to his position carrying a small American flag. Tim Wakefield declined to go out to his tonight with a burp-rag over his shoulder, but maybe he should have; it was his first game as a new dad, and what better place to celebrate than the Trop, where he's never been beaten?

As for the Yankees, they're on the West Coast, so I can go to bed safe in the knowledge that we're at least tied for first place.

May 19th

First thing in the morning, I walk down the driveway to the road for the paper, pull it out of the box and unfold the front page. The header's in red—PERFECT GAME FOR RANDY JOHNSON; YANKS LOSE IN 11. I laugh and head back to the house. It's already a good day.

Tonight it's Schilling versus Rob Bell, just brought up from triple-A. Bell's all over the place and Schilling's solid. It's tied 1–1 in the third when Johnny goes deep, and a fan makes a nice barehanded catch of it in the right-field stands. Of course, there's no one near him to interfere. Later Don will announce the paid attendance as 13,690, but the Trop looks even emptier than last night.

Two batters later, Bell is 3-0 to Ortiz and throws too nice of a strike. David has the big green light and doubles, adding to his league-leading total. Bell falls behind Manny with two down and first base open, but Lou decides to pitch to him, even though Manny hit a 390-foot fly to dead center his first time up. After Bell throws one to the backstop *on the fly*, Manny hits a 420-foot homer to dead center, and it's 4–1.

After seven, Schilling gives way to Embree, who gets an out and then a Rocco Baldelli grounder to Bellhorn that should be the second out. Bellhorn bobbles it and throws to first. It's a close play, but the ump calls Baldelli safe. Bellhorn's puzzled; he thought he got him. It's not until we're well into the count on Aubrey Huff that a second replay shows that he did indeed get him. Huff then hits a nubber to the right side that Embree thinks he has a shot at. He doesn't. Ortiz fields it and turns to throw the ball to Embree, but Embree's brain has short-circuited, and he's stopped. Bellhorn races over to cover but it's too late. Tino Martinez flies to center, advancing Baldelli to third, and with runners on the corners and two out, Francona goes to Foulke.

It's one of Bill James's pet theorems that the most important at-bat often isn't in the ninth, so there's no reason to hold off bringing in your closer. In this case, it's a no-brainer: Foulke's a better pitcher than Embree, and all we're asking him for are four outs. On a 3-2 count, Robert Fick hits a smash off Ortiz's chest that ricochets into foul ground. Ortiz scrambles after it, and, unlike Embree, Foulke hustles over to cover and makes the play to end the inning.

Foulke throws a one-two-three ninth, and that's the game, another uneventful win. Besides the two homers, the only play to savor was Pokey ranging to the right-field side of second to steal a hit from Geoff Blum, and Pokey's played so well that we're almost used to that kind of highlight. And used to winning this kind of game: a quality start, just enough hitting for a cushion, then a shaky setup and a solid close. I suppose I shouldn't complain about the lack of drama.

Later, checking my e-mail, I come across a story that says the Yankees are dropping Cracker Jack from their concession stands, going instead with Crunch 'N Munch, which they say tastes better (and still comes in a box). George, you're insane.

May 20th

Yanks won, O's won, so the East remains the same. Lieber looked good, which is a worry. Contreras is iffy, so the Yanks still don't have a real number five guy, but if Brown and Vazquez and Lieber throw as well as they have, they'll stick around. At some point the O's hitters are going to fall into a slump, and their pitching won't carry them.

More injury woes. Williamson, who's been complaining of soreness in his elbow for a few weeks, finally gets it checked out. Bill Mueller's knee was hurting him again last night, so he's flown back to Boston for an MRI. And Manny's at DH again because of "a tender groin." This is turning into the photo negative of last year, when everybody was healthy.

The Sox won last night and so, out on the Left Coast, did the Yankees, so Boston maintains its half-game fingerhold on the top spot. It's far too early to worry about who's in first (although never too early to worry about who's *on* first), but it's important to keep pace, and so far we're doing that. I stand by my belief—or maybe it's an intuition—that the wild-card team won't come out of the AL East this year, but if the race were over today, the Yankees would be that team, beating the White Sox in the Central Division for the spot by a mere half a game. Anaheim—the team the Yankees beat last night, and one the Sox have yet to play—has the best record in baseball, at 26-13.

The Red Sox, not far behind at 24-16, have cobbled together a winning team—and, perhaps just as important, a winning chemistry—out of what amounts to spare parts, and I have to wonder what happens when Trot and Nomar come back (in last night's pregame show, Theo Epstein said they were both getting close). The question isn't whether or not they're good enough to play for the Red Sox; that's a no-brainer. The real question is how quickly they can get up to speed, and who goes where once they do. I think that the original plan was for Pokey Reese to play second and Mark Bellhorn to ride the bench, but Bellhorn has been clutch for the Sox during the first seven weeks of the season. Not spectacular, like Manny Ramirez, who's currently batting something like one point for every day of the year, but clutch just the same. So who rides the pine when Nomar comes back? Probably it *will* be Bellhorn, but I hate to lose his bat (and his discerning eye at the plate). And while I won't miss Kevin Millar a bit in right field—he made another one of those absurd shoestring attempts last night, during Schilling's rocky first inning—I *am* anxious about how quickly Trot and Nomar can ramp up their bats.

No matter. On to the important stuff. Baseball is a great game because you can multitask in so many ways and never miss a single pitch. I find I can read two pages of a book during each commercial break, for instance, which adds up to four an inning—more if there's a pitching change. Thus it's sometimes possible to read as many as forty pages a game, although it's usually less, because there are always bathroom breaks and fridge runs.

Then there's the Face Game. I play this by keeping an eye on the faces of the spectators behind home plate. Some nights I'll run a ten-point Nose-Picking Competition, which can be played solitaire or with a friend (you get the odd innings, your friend the even ones). Ten is a good number to play to in this game, I've found, but when playing Cell Phone, you have to play to at least twenty-one, because these days almost everyone has one of those annoying little puppies. ("Hi, hon, I'm at the ballpark. . . . What? Oh, not much, Rays are down by three . . . I hear people whispering 'Dead team walking' under their breath . . . it's a little spooky . . . Bring home a quart of milk? . . . sure, okay, call you later . . . gotta pick my nose on national TV first . . . okay, love you too . . . bye.") And last night—remember, I never lost the thread of the game during this, that's the beauty of baseball—I had this wonderful idea for a story. What if a guy watches a lot of baseball games on TV, maybe because he's a shut-in or an invalid (or maybe because he's doing a book on the subject, poor schmuck), and one night he sees his best friend from childhood, who was killed in a car crash, sitting in one of the seats behind the backstop? Yow! And the kid is still ten! He never claps or cheers (never picks his nose or talks on his cell phone, for that matter), just sits there and watches the game . . . or maybe he's watching the main character of the story, right through the TV. After that the protagonist sees him every night at every game, sometimes at Fenway, sometimes at Camden Yards, sometimes at the CreepyDome up in Toronto, but every time there are more people the poor freaked-out guy knew, sitting all around him: this guy's dead friends and relatives, all sitting in the background at the ballpark. I could call the story "Spectators." I think it's a very nasty little idea.

Meanwhile, Derek Lowe goes for us tonight, and here is an interesting little factoid: the hapless Devil Rays are almost forty games into the baseball season and haven't yet won two games in a row. Lou Piniella must be finished with his liver and thinking of moving on to his kidneys. It's a shame, but we've got a job to do here, and hopefully Dee-Lowe will do his part.

For the final game in Tampa it's Lowe versus Victor Zambrano, a decent matchup, at least until they take the mound. Zambrano has a weird first, alternately walking and striking out hitters, finally getting Tek looking to leave the bases loaded. Lowe responds by giving up a single through the middle to former option QB Carl Crawford, then letting him steal second and third. With one out, the infield's back, and another grounder scores him.

Both pitchers settle down in the second, but in the third, with one down, Lowe gives up a single to Brook Fordyce. Then, on 0-2, he leaves a pitch up to Crawford, who doubles down the line. With the infield in, Baldelli bounces one through the middle. 3–0 Tampa Bay. Huff nearly skulls Lowe with a line single, then Tino singles on a pitch above the waist. 4–0. Dave Wallace visits, meaning we're going to leave him in. It's a mistake. Jose Cruz Jr., who's hitting under .200, doubles to left-center. 6–0. Lenny DiNardo's warming, but Francona can't get him in quick enough, as little Julio Lugo takes Lowe off the wall in left for the seventh straight hit. 7–0 D-Rays, and that's it for D-Lowe.

Zambrano follows with his own nightmare inning, loading the bases with nobody out and giving up three runs. In the fifth, Tek puts one on a catwalk and Johnny doubles in two more.

That's as close as we get. Timlin and Jamie Brown conspire to give up two runs, putting it out of reach. The D-Rays' pitchers walked 10, but they also struck out 15, including Manny four times, while the only pitcher of ours who had any success was DiNardo. A complete mess, cancelling out Schilling's easy win last night. A bigger worry: Lowe, supposedly the best number three starter in baseball, hasn't won this month.

May 21st

It's the revenge of the header: MUSSINA LEADS YANKS PAST ANGELS, 6–2. We lose ugly to a last-place club while they beat the team with the best record in baseball (and on top of that, beat their ace, Colon). At least the O's lost; otherwise it would be a total wipeout.

I'm trying to be optimistic and look ahead, but tonight it's Arroyo versus

Halladay. Our travel day knocked the two rotations out of sync, so Pedro's facing the lefty Lilly tomorrow. On Sunday, the game we'll be at, we get the far less interesting Wake versus Miguel Batista. We need two out of three from these guys, but right now the pitching matchups are in Toronto's favor. Halladay's stronger than Arroyo, and we have trouble against lefties and historically don't give Pedro much run support. Wake-Batista's a toss-up.

Maybe it's just last night's game that's bothering me. If Arroyo can match Halladay and get us to their pen, we should win, and Pedro's flat-out better than Lilly. Batista's ERA's around 5 and, like Zambrano, he walks a lot of batters. If we hit and Wake has the knuckler fluttering, we could sweep.

The off-field news is that Johnny's shaving his beard for a literacy program at the Boston Public Library. Gillette's sponsoring the event to kick off their new line of razors. A crowd gathers on the plaza by the Prudential Center to watch some hot models lather him up. He sits still while they take the blades to his face, but in the end he finishes the tricky spots himself. He looks younger, baby-faced, and with his long mane he's got the Elvis-as-Indian-brave thing going on.

Dee-Lowe was dee-readful, but tonight the Red Sox are back at the Fens, and for the first time this year I'm in the house. It's a beautiful night for baseball, too, sixty-nine degrees at game time.

Ray Slyman, who works for Commonwealth Limousine and has been driving me and my family to Red Sox games ever since the kids were small, is usually an optimist about Boston's chances, so I'm surprised—no, I'm shocked—to find him sounding downbeat tonight, even though last night's loss coupled with the Yankees' win on the West Coast has left us only half a game out of first. It makes me uneasy, too. Partly because Ray's in the car all day and listens to all the radio sports shows (discounting the crazies who call in as a matter of course); thus he's hip to all the current gossip. Mostly because Ray's one smart cookie. It's from Ray that I first hear the idea that Nomar should be back *right* now, and DH-ing. It's also from Ray that I hear a lot of fans are beginning to lose patience with Nomar; once the season begins, major league baseball quickly becomes a game of what-have-you-done-for-me-lately, and in Boston, cries of "Play him or trade him!" are beginning to be heard.

Coming into the ballpark, lots of folks tell me hi. Most call me Steve.

One woman tells her boyfriend, "Look, there's Steven Spielberg!" This is more common than you might think, and I sometimes wonder if people point at the famous director and tell each other that it's Stephen King. The guy selling programs just outside Gate A pauses just long enough in his spiel to ask me how I'm feeling. I tell him I'm feeling fine. He says, "Do you thank God?" I tell him, "Every day." He says, "Right on, brutha," and goes back to telling people how much they need a program, how much they need a scorecard, just two dollars unless you're a Yankee fan, then you pay four.

Do you thank God?

Every day.

Yes indeed I do. I'm blessed to be alive at all, and have the sense to know it. It's especially easy to give thanks walking into Fenway Park under my own power on a beautiful spring night in May. ("We're inside the TV," I once heard a wondering child say after getting his first look at all that green.) I'm still considering the novel idea of Nomar Garciaparra as the designated hitter when a woman cardiologist throws out the first pitch. She may be a hell of a doc, but she still throws like a girl. We all give her a big hand, and we give the Red Sox a bigger one when they hit the field in their fine white home uniforms. I feel the same thrill I did when I saw them go out there for the first time, at the age of eleven or twelve, on an afternoon when the Tigers were their opponents and Al Kaline was still playing for them, and my arms prickle when John Fogerty starts singing "Centerfield" over the PA. They prickle again at the end when the Red Sox put away the Jays, 11–5, and the crowd starts out with the Standells singing "Dirty Water."

Every ballpark has its eccentricities. One of my Fenway faves—many fans hate it—is the late-inning playing of Neil Diamond's "Sweet Caroline." I have no idea when this started or why fans took it to their hearts (it's such a *forgettable* song), but there you are; it's just a Fenway Thing, like The Wave.* The first *notes* of this song cause great excitement.

---

*There was a time when you could see The Wave going around at almost all baseball parks and football stadiums; to my knowledge, only at Fenway does it survive. Survive? Nay, sir or madam, it *thrives!* Tonight it went around and around in the eighth, when the Sox sent eleven men to the dish and scored six times. I myself refuse to wave unless I am also allowed to scream *Sieg heil!* at the top of my lungs.

When Neil sings *"Sweeeeet* Car-o-*line!"* in the chorus, thirty thousand people respond at once (and with no apparent prompting), *"WHOA-HO-HO!"* at the top of their voices. And when he adds, "Good times never seemed so good!" the crowd responds, *"So good! So good! So good!"* How do these things get started? There's simply no telling, but such things—which occur when the TV-watching world is stuck with yet another "Meet me at Foxwoods" jingle—are very much a part of not just *the* ballpark experience but *your* ballpark experience: what makes home home.

Man, I had a great time tonight. Manny Ramirez hit a moonshot, Mike "The Hardest Workin' Man in Showbiz" Timlin got the win, and I was there to see it all with my friend Ray. Oh, and Kevin Youkilis, aka The Greek God of Walks, was up to his old tricks. In the bottom of the second inning, after getting behind 0-2, he fouled off a bunch of pitches from Roy Halladay, last year's Cy Young winner, and finally worked a walk. He scored. Later, in the eighth, he walked and scored again.

It's an OBPC thing: on-base per centage.

May 22nd

When they don't announce the game-time temperature at Fenway, you know you're in trouble, and tonight they didn't. It was overcast and raw at 7:05 P.M., when the game started; raw and downright cold* when it ended at about ten past ten. I still haven't warmed up. At 10:45, I'm typing this with hands that feel like clubs. *Tingly* clubs. Still, it's all good. We won, the Yankees lost down in Texas, and all at once there's a tiny bit of daylight (a game and a half) between us and second place.

Ted Lilly pitched extremely well for the Blue Jays tonight, and had a two-run lead going into the sixth inning. That was when Manny Ramirez launched his second home run in the last two games over the left-field wall and into the night. It's the big dinger that'll get the ink in the newspapers tomorrow, but the key hit of the inning—and probably the key to the whole game—was Mark Bellhorn's infield single in the sixth, which caromed off Lilly's shin, hurried him from the game, and thus got us into Toronto's less than reliable bullpen. Without Bellhorn on first, no chance for Manny to tie things up; QED. And an inning later, Youkilis, the rookie

---

*48 degrees, according to Channel 4 weather when I got back to my hotel.

with the big on-base-average reputation, led off with a single and scored what proved to be the winning run. Keith Foulke was once more lights-out in the ninth—nine saves in nine opportunities—and I'm two for two this year at Fenway Park.

And my hands are finally starting to warm up. See? It's all good.

May 23rd

It's Vermont Day at Fenway, and we're the first ones in Gate E. Last time out I was discouraged by my net play, and the usher in Section 163 told me not to give up. He's glad to see me back, and I'm glad for the support. Steph thinks I'm nuts.

We get the good spot on the corner, but there's a portable screen set up at third base so only a hooking liner can reach us. And the security guy says I can't go after any balls in fair territory, a rule which seems arbitrary to me.

The only balls I'll have a shot at will be liners that bounce off the Monster and back along the wall, and about ten minutes in, that's exactly what Nomar hits. The ball rolls to a stop twenty feet behind us. No one can reach it from the high wall there, but I should be able to drag it closer and scoop it. I climb over the seats and section dividers until I'm in position above it. I can't quite reach it, and stretch as far as I can with one hand, just nudging and then covering the ball—and drop the net.

It lies ten feet below me across the foul line.

What an idiot. Steph, I'm sure, is pretending he doesn't know me. I figure the security guy will come out and confiscate it; at best, he'll give me a lecture.

Gabe Kapler's witnessed my embarrassment, and saunters over, shaking his head. I think he's going to take the ball from under the net and toss it to someone more deserving to teach me a lesson, but he throws it right to me. Then he takes the net and jogs back out to left with it.

"He could have used it last night," someone says.

For a while Gabe keeps his glove on and holds the net with one hand, but then he says the hell with it and tosses the glove. Manny and Nomar are up, spraying the ball around. When a Manny liner bounces to the side of him, he stabs at it and misses cleanly. See, it's not as easy as it looks. After about five minutes of just standing there with the net, he brings it back over. I get a picture of him—proof for Trudy.

Another guy comes by and asks if that was me he saw up on the Monster a few weeks ago, and I find that I like this minor celebrity. Steph says a Sox photographer just took a picture of me.

We're also visited by Chip Ainsworth, the reporter who interviewed me the first time I brought the net. He says we should see a game together from the press box. I worry a little about that blurry line between journalist and fan, but then I think: man, the press box!

Steve arrives in his YANKEES HATER cap, and I go over to hang out with him and Steph. On the endpages of the John Sandford novel he's reading, he's scored the last two games. It's been a while, and we fall to talking, interrupted from time to time by folks who want to take a picture of him.

We're sitting there discussing Manny's hot streak and Wake's last few starts when one of the Sox comes out and signs along the wall two sections down. From the inch-high brush cut, it can only be Tek. It's his day off, with Mirabelli catching Wake. I excuse myself and climb over the section dividers and then wait in the crush. "Go ahead and take the sweet spot," I tell him. "It's all yours."

Tek's signature is neat and readable. Thanks to eBay, I've seen it dozens of times, both authentic versions and fakes. He never finishes the final kick of the k, so it reads *J Varitel, #33*. On the pearl it looks superclean, and I thank him and carry it by the seams like some weird breaking ball, making sure not to smudge the ink.

"I got a shot of you," Steph says.

"Yeah," Steve says, "we got a picture of you pushing those little kids out of the way."

"Hey, they were pushing *me*."

Wake looks good in the first, striking out his first two batters. Batista looks awful, walking Johnny on four pitches around his ankles. Orlando Hudson doesn't help him, booting Bellhorn's easy grounder, and David Ortiz scorches a ground-rule double into the seats just past the Pesky Pole. 1–0 Sox. Manny Ks chasing a 3-2 pitch, Dauber walks, then Millar walks in a run. Batista's thrown 25 pitches, only 7 for strikes.

After Youkilis strikes out, Mirabelli comes up with bases loaded and fouls one behind him, high off the facade of the .406 Club. Last year, a ball hit in that same spot ricocheted off the glass at an angle and landed in the row behind us. I turn, keeping my eye on it, and here it comes, right at me (Steph thinks I think this about every ball). The sun is blinding, and I'm not wearing shades, so all I see as it falls is a tiny black dot surrounded by white light. It's going to be just short, and I reach above everyone. I feel it hit, then feel nothing, and I think it's gone, that I've missed it—then look down, and there it is in my glove. Maybe because it's the first inning, or because it was a crazy angle, or because the bases are loaded and we're up two runs, but the crowd goes nuts. I hold my glove up and take in the applause—unexpected and exhilarating—and slap hands with Steph and Steve. When I sit down, my heart's pounding and I'm shivery inside my skin. I thought I'd missed it, so it's a guilty thrill—a freak accomplishment I doubt even now.

I don't have time to think about it, because Mirabelli fouls off the next pitch the exact same way—caroming off the same pane of glass and dropping two rows behind Steve. I'm up and ready in case it bounces my way, but it's smothered and picked up.

Batista gets Mirabelli and gets out of it. In the second he has to strike out Dauber to leave them loaded again.

"This guy's terrible," I say. "We should be up at least four nothing."

"We're not hitting with men on," Steve complains, and Mason, a neighbor in the front row, shows us a thirty-page stat sheet that has the season completely broken down. So far with the bases loaded, we've hit two doubles and twelve singles. Johnny and Pokey have the doubles. Johnny and Pokey also have the most hits with bases loaded, three each. Kapler and Bill Mueller are 0-4, Ortiz, Dauber and Crespo 0-3.

Wake throws an easy third, and we finally cash in on Batista, scoring four. Ortiz has the big hit, a two-out, two-run double, making him 3 for 3 with 3 RBIs. It's 6–0 and Batista's thrown 90 pitches.

Now that Wake has a big lead, he gets sloppy, loading the bases with no outs and going 3-0 on Delgado. Delgado singles, bringing in two, before Timmy gets a double-play ball from Phelps and a first-pitch flyout from Hinske.

A sudden roar and wave of applause from the third-base side. It's someone famous climbing the stairs between two grandstand sections. Because it's Vermont Day, I think maybe it's Fisk, a Vermont native, but the tall gray-haired man's surrounded by so much security that I know without even seeing his face that it's John Kerry. As if to prove his loyalty, he's wearing a Sox warm-up jacket. Later, when he comes back from the concession stand, I see he's in the second row, and I think: our seats are better.

We pick up another run in the seventh to make it 7–2, and Timlin and Embree close it with little difficulty, but two things happen that are worth noting. In the eighth, Cesar Crespo, who's turned three double plays today, and missed a fourth only because Bellhorn's throw pulled Ortiz off the bag, makes an error and is loudly booed. Then in the ninth, when Francona puts in the hands team and Pokey's name is announced, the crowd gives him a sustained ovation. It's taken Pokey three years to get here, but now that he is, he's a favorite. Even among skeptics like Steph and Steve and myself, whenever a ball skips through the middle or drops in short center, we say, "Pokey woulda had it."

We win, but on the out-of-town scoreboard, the Yanks are up 7–3 on the Rangers. In the car, it's a final, 8–3 Yanks, so we're still only a game and a half up.

When we get home, I find out that Bill Mueller wasn't even there today. He was out in Arizona, getting a second opinion on his knee. Regardless of the result, it's bad news. Youkilis better take some extra grounders.

My third straight game at Fenway and my third straight win. I'm starting to feel like if I'd been here from the start of the season, we'd be ten games in first (God will get me for saying that). Stewart came with his son, Steph, both of them equipped with gloves. Doug Mirabelli banged a foul off the glass facing of the .406 Club in the first inning; Stew turned, stretched and caught it neatly just as the sun came out. The crowd up the first-base line gave him a spirited ovation. Stew had class enough—and wit enough—to tip his cap. It was a nice moment, and I'm glad his son was there to see it.

So Wakefield gets the win, the Red Sox sweep the Blue Jays, and our bullpen was pretty much untouchable throughout. Kevin Youkilis? Glad you asked. The Greek God of Walks reached base three times (one fielder's choice, two bases on balls) and scored once.

May 24th

Seems like we always have a day off just when we're getting hot. It gives me time to prepare for tomorrow's first meeting with Oakland since last year's Division Series—bound to be loud. It's a sweet matchup: Schilling versus Tim Hudson, who's 5-1 with a 2.90 ERA. It's Foulke's first game against his old club, and Terry Francona's, and of course Scott Hatteberg will get a couple of hits, and maybe Johnny Damon. Mark Bellhorn was also an A once, though a low-profile one. With all the turnover lately (and Dan

Duquette's endless fire sale of our best prospects), it's hard to find a club that doesn't have some Sox connection.

Tonight's the Nomar Bowl in Malden, where dozens of Boston sports celebrities and their fans get together at Town Lanes and roll a couple of strings for charity. My friend Paul's wife Lisa is taking some balls for Nomie to sign, and one of them's for me.

May 25th

It's eighty degrees in Hartford; in Boston it's fifty. I thought I'd be warm enough in a corduroy shirt, but I'm not. Waiting with me outside Gate E is a guy with a giant black wig. I think he's one of Damon's Disciples, but it's a Manny-as-Buckwheat wig, a wild, lopsided 'fro. He and a friend are sitting on the Monster; tomorrow they're in the .406 Club—they shelled out for the very tickets I'd seen on eBay and seriously contemplated buying, just 'cause I've never sat there.

The .406 Club has rules: no jeans, and you have to bring a credit card to buy drinks (there's a free buffet). During the standard tour of Fenway, the guide says when they finished construction, they realized that because of the thickness of the glass, the room is virtually soundproof. They had to install speakers so customers could hear the game. Any other day, I'd say the .406 Club is no place to watch the Sox, but tonight the idea of being inside is tempting.

The gates roll open and I hoof it down to the corner in left. I nab a couple of balls in BP and report my haul to my favorite usher Bob, then stop by Autograph Alley to see who's signing. It's Rich Gale, a pitcher who was with us briefly in '84, then came back to coach in the early nineties. I remember that he pitched in Japan, and ask him to sign his picture with "Ganbatte!"

"You mean 'Ganbatte mas!'" he says.

It turns out he pitched for the Hanshin Tigers.

"The Red Sox of Japan!"

"That's right—and I was there in '85, the first year we won it."

"That must have been pretty wild."

"*Oh* yeah," he says, and stops writing, as if he hasn't thought of that time in a while, and his expression is both ecstatic and guilty, as if he's recalling infinite, ultimate pleasures.

I have him add HANSHIN TIGERS 85–86 and leave him with a loud "Ganbatte!"

Over at the seats, Steve's reading a suspense novel. Our neighbor Mason delivers the bad news: Bill Mueller's having arthroscopic knee surgery and will be out at least six weeks. It's another blow, but Youkilis has done such a good job offensively that there's no panic. If Nomar gets back soon, we can put Pokey at second, as planned, slide Bellhorn over to third, and still have a solid backup.

Again, we're all thinking of that magical day when Trot and Nomar come back, when right now we're playing fine without them.

"Temperature at game time," Carl Beane announces, "forty-eight degrees." It makes me think of spring training, and how happy those Minnesotans were to escape their weather. Here we're proud of it. Forty-eight? It'll get down to forty-two by game's end. Tack on the windchill and we're talking mid-thirties.

It's overcast and *very* chilly tonight—shit, call a spade a spade, it's *cold*. My colleague Stewart O'Nan is undaunted. He shows up apple-cheeked and grinning, toting a bag of scuffed balls he shagged in BP. (Proudest acquisition: a David Ortiz swat.)

The Weston High School Chorus—all nine thousand of them, apparently—line the first- and third-base lines to sing the national anthem, and the sound, which comes bouncing back from the Green Monster in perfect echoes that double each line, is spooky and wonderful. Stewart, meanwhile, is off trying to give Gabe Kapler a photo of Kapler holding Stew's custom fly-shagging net . . . which, some wits might argue, Kapler could put to good use during his tours of duty in right field.

The Red Sox (who will go on to romp in this one) put up just a single run in the bottom of the first—not much, considering that they once again send seven men to the plate. The Sox stats this year with bases loaded and two out are pretty paralyzing: just 12 for 54, only two of those for extra bases (both doubles), all the rest mere singles. This time Kevin "Cowboy Up" Millar is the goat, grounding weakly to first. He leaves two more on base in the third, and leaves 'em loaded again in the fourth. The Sox score three that frame, but Millar has stranded eight men all by himself, and the game isn't half over. I bet his agent won't be bringing *that* stat up at contract time.

Even without Millar doing much (anything, really), it's 9–1 after five, Tim Hudson's gone, Oakland's baked, and I'm on my way to my fourth straight Fenway win. Mark Bellhorn gets 5 RBIs, Manny Ramirez hits another home run, and Kevin Youkilis reaches base four times in five at-bats, scoring twice.

There are lots of things to like about this game in spite of the cold. But maybe the best . . . there's this little kid, okay? Ten, maybe twelve years old. And late in the game, after a lot of people have taken off, he grabs one of the front-row seats, and I spot him and Stewart deep in conversation, cap visor to cap visor. They don't know each other from Adam, and there's got to be thirty years between them, but baseball has turned them into instant old cronies. Anyone looking over their way would take them for father and son. And what's wrong with that?

May 26th

Two number fives on the downward slide: Mr. Kim returns to Korea for unspecified treatment of his back and hip, while the Yankees give Donovan Osborne his outright release. It's late May, and the Yankees haven't figured out their rotation. Having Bronson Arroyo definitely gives us the edge.

Tonight it's the struggling Derek Lowe against Mark Redman, 3-2 with a 3.60 ERA. By comparison, Lowe's ERA is 6.02.

We have Steph's sax recital and then dinner after, and get back in the A's fifth. It's 6–2 Sox with two down and no one on. I figure Lowe must be throwing okay. Kotsay doubles, Byrnes singles him in. Chavez homers off the wall behind Section 34, and it's 6–5.

I wonder if it's me—if I should turn the TV off and come back later.

I'm glad I don't. In our sixth, Johnny's on third with one down. Ortiz can't deliver him, and with two down and first open, Macha has Redman walk Manny. At this point, Redman's thrown 120 pitches. The switch-hitting Tek is coming up, so with his relievers up and warm, Macha can choose which side of the plate he hits from. He lets Redman pitch to him. Tek hits one onto Lansdowne Street and we've got a four-run cushion again.

Anastacio Martinez relieves Lowe, giving up three straight hits and a run before Embree comes on and gets out of it with a double-play ball.

In the A's eighth, they have two on and one out when Billy McMillon stings one down the first-base line. McCarty gloves it behind the bag in foul territory; his momentum takes him halfway to the tarp before he spins and throws to Timlin covering. McMillon slides and gets tangled up with Timlin—he's out! The replay's crazy: I've never seen anyone make that play so far in foul ground, and perfectly. That's exactly why McCarty's on the team. It makes me wish I could send him back to 1986 to spell Billy Buck for an inning.

In the ninth, McCarty shines again, with a sweeping snatch of a bounced throw by Bellhorn, helping Foulke to a one-two-three inning for his tenth straight save.

On the postgame show, Eck tries to figure out Lowe's problem. Of the fifth, Eck says, "It's a mystical inning," and we crack up. Groovy Eck with his Farrah Fawcett wings. But he's right too (right on, Eck!): "When you win a game and your ERA goes up, you know you didn't pitch too good."

May 27th

9 A.M.: Neither Stew nor I made it to the ballyard last night. I had a PEN dinner in Boston's Back Bay and Stewart had his son's saxophone recital—which, he assured me, is nonnegotiable. The Red Sox did not miss us. Derek Lowe was once more far from perfect, but the Sox bats stayed hot and in his start against Oakland, Lowe was just good enough to go six and eke out the win. The Red Sox rolled to their fifth straight, their seventh in their last eight games.

But I watch *SportsDesk* this morning musing on my Yankees essay—the one where I talked about how we hate what we fear—and looking at my new hat, which was sent to me from yankeeshater.com. Because the Yankees have *also* been winning, and while we've been doing it at home, they've been doing it on the road, which is a tougher proposition. They came from behind last night at Camden Yards not just once but *twice*, finally putting the Orioles away 12–9. So in spite of this nifty streak of ours, we're still only a game and a half in front. Two Sox losses combined with just two Yankee wins, and we're back in second place. This is what the Yankees do. They hang around.

Those suckers *lurk*.

10:30 P.M.: The summer's disaster movie, *The Day After Tomorrow*, opens this weekend, but disaster struck tonight at Fenway Park, as Boston's brave little five-game winning streak went bye-bye in a big way. Oakland beat the Red Sox like a drum, pounding out 17 hits on their way to a 15–2 win. Me, I knew it was going to happen. I went to the game with my nephew, Jon, who goes to school in Boston. He came over to my hotel room before the game and tossed my hat on the bed, which everyone knows is just about the worst luck in the world—talk about bad mojo! But I don't blame him; the kid just didn't know.

Also, most (or maybe all) major league teams now insist on a five-man pitching rotation, and our fifth man, Bronson Arroyo, while promising, is still very much a work in progress. That fifth man in the rotation is about stre-et-ching the starting pitching . . . and that, of course, is all about the money. We've been there before in this book, and will undoubtedly be there again. But I can remember a time, children—I believe it was 1959—when the White Sox went to the World Series with what was essentially a *three*-man rotation. Of course, those were the days when a good pitcher still got paid in five figures and a man could take his whole family to the ballyard for twenty bucks, parking included (and smoke a White Owl in the grandstand, if he was so inclined). I'm not saying those were better baseball days . . . but I'm not saying they weren't, either.

In the midst of all this, Kevin Youkilis drew a walk in his last at-bat. He still hasn't played in a major league game where he's failed to reach base.

A final note before I pack it in for the night: I took myself off this afternoon to see *Still, We Believe,* an entertaining documentary which chronicles the star-crossed Red Sox team of 2003, the one that voyaged so far only to tear out its hull (not to mention the hearts of its fans) on those cruel Yankee reefs in the seventh game of the American League Championship Series. This film is currently playing in theaters all over New England, plus a few New York venues (where it is attended largely by sadists in Yankee caps, one would suppose), and probably nowhere else. It's a charming, funny, sweetly poignant film. Its token efforts to explore the Mind of Management—always supposing Management *has* a Mind, a hypothesis with little evidence to support it—aren't very interesting, but when it focuses on the fortunes of four fans, it's a lot more successful. One is a young man who is wheelchair-bound due to an accident; two are semidaffy (but very endearing) young women I kept thinking of as Laverne and Shirley; the fourth is Angry Bill.

Angry Bill is a piece of work: overweight, hypertensive (he suffers persistent nosebleeds during the '03 postseason), full of nervous energy, bursting with cynical pronouncements that barely cover his bruised baseball fan's heart. This guy has lived and died with the Sox for so long (mostly the latter), that he sums up an entire New England mind-set when he states, in effect, that the Sox are *always* gonna lose, he knows they're gonna pull an el foldo in August just as sure as he knows the sun's gonna come up over Boston Haaabaaa in the east, and if they don't pull an el foldo in August they'll pull a tank job in September, just as sure as the sun's gonna go down over Attleboro in the west.

And yet, with Boston ahead during the early going of that climactic Game 7 in October of 2003, Angry Bill briefly allows himself to become Hopeful Bill . . . because the Red Sox do this to us, too: every year at some point they turn into Lucy holding the football, and against all our best intentions (and our knowing that those who do not learn from history are condemned—fucking *CONDEMNED!*—to repeat it) we turn into Charlie Brown running once more to kick it, only to have it snatched away again at the last moment so we land flat on our backs, screaming *"AUGGGH!"* at the top of our lungs.

And when, after Grady Little leaves Pedro in long after even the most casual baseball fan knows he is toasty—fried, broiled, baked, cooked to a turn, stick a fork in 'im, he's done—when the coup de grâce is delivered by Aaron Boone long after Pedro has trudged to the shower, Angry Bill stares with a kind of wondering disbelief into the documentarian's camera (at us in the audience, seven months later, seven weeks into a new season later, us with our tickets to tonight's shellacking by the Oakland A's in our pockets) and delivers what is for me the absolute capper, the jilted Red Sox fan's Final Word: "Don't let your kids grow up to be sports fans," Angry Bill advises, and at this point the movie leaves him—mercifully—to contemplate the Patriots, who will undoubtedly improve matters for his battered psyche by winning the Super Bowl . . . but I'm sure Angry Bill would admit (if not right out loud then in his heart) that winning the Super Bowl isn't the same as winning the World Series. Not even in the same *universe* as winning the World Series.

Meanwhile, the Yankees—the Evil Empire, our old nemesis—have come from behind to beat Baltimore once again, and our lead in the AL East is down to a mere half game. I'm off to bed knowing that the boogeyman has inched a little bit closer to the closet door.

May 28th

It's the big holiday weekend. Once the kids get home from school, we've got to drive down to the Rhode Island shore and help my in-laws open up the beach house, so after lunch I run around town trying to fit in my last errands. I'm at the Stop 'n Shop when I remember the new Reverse the Curse ice cream, and there it is in the freezer section. The carton is boring and generic. I'd hoped for more interesting packaging, maybe a nod to the Monster that I could use for a penny bank. Still, the ice cream should be good.

We poke along I-95 with all the other Memorial Day traffic. Trudy and her parents have been lifting and cleaning all day, and don't feel like cooking, so we go out for dinner. By the time we make it back, the Sox are down 4–1 to Seattle in the fifth. Ichiro's just driven in a run, and steals third on Pedro, who has that dull, long-suffering look he gets when things aren't going right. There's only one out, and Edgar Martinez is up. Pedro gets him swinging, then gets the next guy to pop up.

In our fifth, Millar and Youkilis tag Joel (pronounced Joe-El, as if he's from Krypton) Pineiro for back-to-back doubles, making it 4–2. See, all the Sox needed was us watching. Pokey Ks, but with two gone Pineiro walks Johnny and Mark Bellhorn to load them for Big David. On the first pitch, Ortiz lofts a long fly to right. Ichiro goes back sideways, and keeps going, all the way to the wall, where he leaps. He hangs there, folded over the low wall, only his legs showing. We can't see the ball, but the fans behind the bullpen fence are jumping up and down—it's gone, a grand slam, and we're up 6–4.

In St. Pete, the Yanks have beaten the D-Rays, so we need to hold on to stay in first. Pedro settles down. In the eighth he gives way to Embree, who throws a scoreless inning. J. J. Putz comes on for the M's and gives up a smoked single through the middle to Manny (it makes Putz riverdance) and then, after a long at-bat, a double to Dauber off the bullpen wall. Bob Melvin decides to walk Tek to set up the double play, which Kapler foils by popping up. Putz goes 2-0 on Youkilis and has to come in with a strike; Youkilis slaps it down the right-field line for a double and two more insurance runs, and the PA plays the corny old Hartford Whalers theme, "Brass Bonanza."

Foulke closes, but it's a battle. He throws 30 pitches and leaves runners on second and third for an 8–4 final. A tougher game than expected from the last-place M's, but El Jefe (Big Papi, D.O., David as Goliath) brought us back.

May 29th

It's Saturday of Memorial Day weekend, but I've had all of Boston and Fenway Park I can take for a while—seven games in eight days is plenty, especially given the uniformly shitty quality of the weather.* And that's not all. Hotel living gets creepy after a while, even when you can afford room service (maybe *especially* if you can afford room service). Also, my wife headed back to Maine after the PEN dinner on Wednesday, and I miss her. But as I run north under sunshiny, breezy skies, I keep an eye on the dashboard clock, and when 1 P.M. rolls around, I hit the radio's SEEK button until I find the voices of Joe Castiglione and Jerry Trupiano, comfort food for the ear.

Listening to a baseball game on the radio may be outmoded in this age of computers and satellite television, but it hath its own particular pleasures; with each inning you build your own Fenway of the mind from scrap-heap memories and pure imagination. Today the wind is playing tricks, Wakefield's knuckleball is staying up in the zone, and the usually lackluster Mariner hitters pounce on it right from the git. In the second inning a Seattle batter hits a towering fly foul of first, but the wind pushes it back into fair territory. Mark Bellhorn, today playing second, tries to stay with it, can't. The ball bonks him on the wrist and falls for a double. I see all this quite vividly (along with Manny Ramirez's homer to left, hit so hard it leaves a vapor trail, Troop assures me) as I drive north between Yarmouth and Freeport with that same wind pushing my own car. Since I can't read a page of my current book between innings (the galley of Chuck Hogan's *Prince of Thieves* is now tucked away in my green 1999 All-Star Game souvenir carry-bag), I punch the CD button after each third out and listen to two minutes—timed on my wristwatch—of Larry McMurtry's *The Wandering Hill,* volume two of the Berrybender Narratives. I have found that two minutes gets me back to the game just in time for the first pitch of the next inning.

In this fashion, the 240-mile trip to Bangor passes agreeably enough. One wishes the Red Sox could have won, but it's hard to root against Freddy Garcia, a great pitcher who is this year laboring for a bad ball club

---

*The start of last night's game was held up for an hour and a half in anticipation of rain showers that never came.

in the Mariners. And the worst the Sox can do on the current home stand is 6-4; one may reasonably hope for 8-2.

One may even hope the hapless Devil Rays will beat the Yankees tonight, and we will retain our half-game hold on the top spot a little longer.

Waiting at home in the mail is the Nomar ball from the Nomar Bowl, a nice souvenir of his lost season. My e-mail in-box is sluggish, filled with pictures of Lisa at the Town Lanes with Nomar, with Dauber, with David Ortiz, with Mike Timlin, with Alan Embree, even with Danny Ainge. Everyone's smiling, though I don't see any players actually bowling.

The Yanks beat the Rays 5–3, so they're in first place. I smother my sorrows in a bowl of Reverse the Curse and read the sports page. My Pirates, amazingly, are at .500, thanks to a pair of walk-off homers to take a twin bill from the Cubs. And it says Nomar's scheduled to start his rehab stint at Pawtucket tomorrow—the best news I could hope for.

9:50 P.M.: I take my wife to the crazy-weather movie, which we both enjoy. I walk the dog as soon as we get back, then hit the TV remote and click on Headline News. Weekends, the ticker at the bottom of the screen runs continuous sports scores, and ohhhh, *shit*, the Yankees won *again*. They've regained the top spot in the AL East, one they've held for almost *five consecutive seasons*, leaving me to wonder how in the name of Cobb and Williams you pound a stake through this team's heart and make them lie still. Or if it's even possible.

May 30th

We've got Monster seats and get going early. I'm taking the kids while Trudy's bringing her parents from the shore. The weather's clear, traffic's light on I-84, and a cop stops me for speeding. So the morning, which started so promising, turns bitter even before we hit the Mass Pike. I worry that the feeling will linger and ruin the whole day, but there are enough miles to put it behind us.

We hit Lansdowne Street, where the sausage vendors are open early for the family crowd. A woman Trudy's mother's age has a sweatshirt that says FOULKE THE YANKEES.

• • •

I'm sure that Stew was at the ballpark today for what turned out to be an extraordinary game, and probably in the prime real estate of my second-row seats next to the Red Sox dugout, but I enjoyed it fine at home in my living room with my wife close by, propped up on the couch with the computer on her lap and the dog by her side. I've come down with a fairly heavy cold as a result of my week of chilly carousal at Fenway, and there is something especially satisfying—akin to the pleasures of self-pity, I suppose—about watching a baseball game with the box of Kleenex near one hand and the box of Sucrets near the other, coughing and sneezing your way through the innings as the shadows on both the infield and your living room carpet gradually creep longer.

This game had a little bit of everything. Curt Schilling flirted with perfection into the sixth; Keith Foulke blew his first save of the season (his first blown save in his last twenty-four attempts, it turns out) when Raul Ibanez hit a dramatic three-run home run, putting the Mariners up 7–5 in the eighth inning; the Red Sox came right back to tie it in the bottom of the eighth. Then, in the bottom of the twelfth, Sox sub David McCarty crushed a 3-0 fastball to what is the deepest part of the park to give the Red Sox the win.

And at the risk of sounding like Angry Bill in *Still, We Believe,* I called the shot. Yeah! Me! I'd claim my wife as a witness to this feat of prediction, except she was pretty heavy into the computer solitaire by then and I doubt like hell that she was listening. The Mariners' fourth pitcher of the afternoon, a young man with the unfortunate name of J. J. Putz, entered the game with a reputation for wildness, but was into his third inning of exceptional relief work (he struck out both David Ortiz and Manny Ramirez in the eleventh) when the roof fell in. After getting the first out in the twelfth, he hit Jason Varitek with a soft breaking pitch.* Enter McCarty, inserted into the lineup mostly as a defensive replacement. The count ran to 3-0. Most batters are taking all the way on such a count, but Terry Francona gives most of his guys the automatic green light on 3-0. (I like this strategy as much as I loathe his refusal to bunt runners along in key situations.) I said—mostly to the dog, since my wife was paying el

---

*In truth, Tek—for some reason only known to himself, Stewart O'Nan always calls him Tek Money—did not try very hard to avoid this pitch; it was a classic case of taking one for the team if I ever saw one. And, as a man who got to watch Don Baylor play, I've seen my share.

zilcho attention, "Watch this. Putz is gonna throw it down the middle and McCarty is gonna send everyone home in time for supper." Which is just what happened, and thank God the camera did not linger long on the head-hanging misery of young Mr. J. J. Putz as McCarty went into his home run trot. These are the kind of games you either win or feel really bad about losing, especially at home. I feel badly for Putz (pronounced *Pootz*, thank you very much), but the bottom line? We won it. And the bonus? The Yankees lost to Tampa Bay (who just barely held on), which means we're back in first place.

There are three major milestones in a baseball season: Memorial Day, the Fourth of July, and Labor Day. The first of these milestones in the 2004 season comes tomorrow, when we play a makeup game with Baltimore, and for a team with so many quality players on the disabled list, we're doing pretty damned well going into the first turn. Especially when we can look forward to two of those—Nomar Garciaparra and Trot Nixon—coming back between Memorial Day and the Fourth. A third, Bill Mueller, may return to the club between the Fourth and Labor Day.

That brings us back to Kevin Youkilis, Mueller's replacement, who has now begun to attract so much notice that Terry Francona has had to publicly state that no, Youkilis will *not* be keeping the job at third once Mueller's fit and ready to play no matter *how* well the GGOW* does between now and the happy day of Mueller's return.

A piece in the Portland Sunday *Telegram* today by Kevin Thomas (who knows Youkilis from Youkilis's days with the Portland Sea Dogs, the BoSox double-A affiliate) points out that Youkilis's locker is on the far wall of the clubhouse, the traditional place for players who are just up for a cup of coffee in the bigs . . . as is undoubtedly the case with Andy Dominique, who delivered today's game-tying hit in the bottom of the eighth. Thomas also points to previous Red Sox minor leaguers such as Wilton Veras, who came up to play third with high hopes, only to fade into obscurity.

Obscurity would not seem to be in young Mr. Youkilis's future, however. "I know I'm going to be playing," he told Kevin Thomas in today's interview, speaking with quiet certainty, and with every passing game his on-base percentage seems simultaneously harder to believe for a rookie and less like a fluke. Moved up to the two-hole today, all Youkilis did was go

*Greek God of Walks . . . but you knew that.

three for five, with three runs scored. His batting average is .317, and his OBP is hovering right around .425. The fans know that Bill Mueller may have to battle for his old spot back, no matter what Terry Francona has to say on the subject.

It sounds like they're booing the kid when he walks to the plate, but the grin on Youkilis's face says he knows better; that sound sweeping around the ballpark like a soft wind is the first syllable of his last name: *Youk...* *Youk...Youk...*

Two weeks ago he was playing triple-A ball in Pawtucket; tomorrow, on Memorial Day, he's going to be playing the Orioles before a packed house, for the first-place Boston Red Sox. And I don't want to jinx the kid, but do you know what I think, after having watched him in almost all of those games?

I think a star is born.

After the McCarty walk-off job, Netman learns from fan services that the Sox have decided to ban his net from Fenway. Like the speeding ticket, it could taint the day, but I won't let it. I've had a great run with the net, and it was a wild game today—half a no-hitter topped by a late-inning comeback and then the tension of extra innings released with McCarty's game-winner. The Yanks lost at the Trop, so we're in first place. Happy birthday, Manny.

Hell, I'm better with the glove anyway.

May 31st

In response to flooding on the border of Haiti and the Dominican, David Ortiz, Manny and Pedro are joining with the Sox to collect donations for aid. I send a check, and while this book won't be out for another six months, I'm sure the victims down there will still need the support then. The address is Dominican Relief Effort, Red Sox Foundation, Fenway Park, Boston, MA 02215.

Of Boston's four established starting pitchers—the other three being Pedro Martinez, Tim Wakefield and Curt Schilling—Derek Lowe has been the most obviously troubled. In his last three winning starts, all at home and all shaky, his teammates have been wearing their red jerseys instead of the usual white ones, so it's no surprise that those were the ones they were wearing when they took the field for their makeup game against the Orioles.

It was Lowe's best start in weeks, but this time the red tops didn't help. The real problem today wasn't Lowe so much as it was the middle relief. Like most teams in the wretchedly overstocked major leagues, Boston can't boast a lot in that regard. Yes, there's Timlin and Embree, but Francona doesn't like to throw them in when the Sox are down by more than a couple, and both of them have worked a lot lately and needed the day off. So it was the PawSox Pitching Corps, mostly, and no way were they equal to the task. The Sox were down 9–0 before you could say Lansdowne Street. We've played from behind a lot on this home stand, and have *come* from behind a lot . . . but not from this far behind. Not against Oakland, not against Seattle, and not against Baltimore today.

So now we're off to the West Coast, Nomar's almost ready to come back (always supposing his rehabbed ankle stays rehabbed after some actual game action with the triple-A club, where he went 0 for 3 last night), and the first third of the season is over. The biggest surprise—at least to me— has been how quickly, after the initial scramble, the teams aligned themselves just as they have in previous years. Pick of the first fifty: the Sox taking six of seven from the Bronx Bombers. And in spite of that, we've reached the Memorial Day marker fifty-one games into the season in a dead tie for first with them.

Who woulda thunk it?

Steve calls, and we dissect the game. They came out flat, we agree. But, overall so far, Steve says, we're playing way over our heads. Look at these guys who've been getting it done for us: Youkilis, McCarty, Bellhorn. Nomar's not too far away, and Trot. Sure, we're headed out West and the Yankees are coming home, but historically we do okay out there.

He's more optimistic than I am—a rarity—but he's right too. And yet, after I hang up, I'm still worried about Lowe, whose ERA must be pushing 7.00, and who hasn't made it out of the sixth inning in over a month.

JUNE

The June Swoon

June 1st

Last night in Louisville Nomar went 2 for 3 with a walk, a reason for some optimism. I know he's not going to solve all our problems when he comes back, but having a live righty bat won't hurt.

We're playing late in Anaheim, a 10:05 start. I catch some of the pregame—Jerry the former Angel back where he started—but by game time I'm so busy finishing up everything I didn't get done during the day that I miss the first couple of innings. When I tune in, it's bedtime, 11:30, and it's only the top of the third. We're up 2–1 and Colon has runners on first and second with one out. Millar singles to left, and Sveum sends Manny, but Manny decides not to go. Good thing, because the throw from Jose Guillen is a strike. Youkilis steps up, and I think we're going to break the game open, but the first-base ump calls an obvious check swing a strike and then the home-plate ump rings him up on a pitch well outside. Youkilis swears, and Jerry says the rookie's got to be careful not to get tossed. Colon goes 3-1 on Pokey before unleashing his good stuff, and we come away with nothing. Through three we've left seven men on base.

I'd love to stay up and see how it turns out, but it's almost midnight. It's a defeat, in a way, voluntarily leaving an interesting game in progress. I'll feel disconnected and behind until I read the score in the paper tomorrow morning. For now, I just have to trust Arroyo will hold them and that our big guys will get to Colon.

June 2nd

We lost, 7–6, though only a ninth-inning two-run shot by Dauber off Troy Percival made it look that close. We had a three-run lead at one point, but Arroyo didn't make it out of the sixth. With the score tied, Vladimir Guerrero ripped a two-run double, and we never really threatened after that.

And the Yanks beat the Orioles again, running their record against Baltimore to 1,000–0 over the last couple years, so we're a full game back.

And while the paper agrees that Nomar could join the big club as early as Tuesday against the Padres, it also says that Trot's had yet another setback with his quad and will sit out several extended spring-training games. Fifty games into the season, it's hard to imagine there are that many guys still stuck down in Fort Myers. The facility must be a ghost town, lots of empty parking spots. Even while he's sitting out, Trot will take batting practice; one of the pitchers he'll be facing—Ramiro Mendoza.

SK: We're on the West Coast, graveyard of many great Red Sox teams, and we blew a lead last night while the Yankees were holding on to one. Also holding sole possession of first place. I think that in the steamy depths of July, we may look back on May, when the Yankees kept pace, and shake our heads, and say, "Sheesh, won't _anything_ stop them?"

SO: Hey, don't ascribe them any superpowers. That's what they're going to be saying about us. Already around the league people are wondering how we're doing it with all these supersubs.

Since I missed last night's game, I make a point of staying up for tonight's, even scoring it on a Remy Report sheet. Johnny's not playing; I'd heard his knee is still bothering him from the ball he fouled off it—and that had to have been a month ago. On the mound for the Angels is lefty Jarrod Washburn, who was Cy Young material two years back but hasn't thrown well since. We've got Pedro going. He's said he hasn't been able to throw his curve much because of the cold weather (the grip, I suppose), so I'm discouraged in the first when Vladimir Guerrero yokes a hanging curve over the wall in left for a two-run shot.

Don Orsillo takes this opportunity to inform us that the Yanks have come from being down 5–0 to beat the O's 6–5. I don't know who I hate more, the Yankees for being the Yankees or the O's for rolling over.

Manny gets one back in the second with a solo blast to dead center, and in the third an Ortiz sac fly brings in Bellhorn to tie the game (to a healthy

"Let's go, Red Sox" chant). But in the bottom of the inning Guerrero puts the Angels in the lead again with a two-run double.

Neither starter has anything. The Sox chase Washburn in the fourth with six straight hits, scoring five. We'd have more, but Ramon Ortiz comes on and gets Millar to bounce into an easy 6-4-3 DP. Still, we've come back to take a 7–4 lead on the road, and I'm happy I stayed up to watch this one.

In the bottom of the inning, Guerrero hits a sac fly to score Bengie Molina, making it 7–5. Vladi has all five of their RBIs.

It's midnight, past the Sox's bedtime, and their bats go the way of Cinderella's coach. The rest of the game, they manage just one two-out single.

Pedro's done after David Eckstein's fourth single of the night (the former Sox prospect will go 5 for 5, the Angels' first three batters a preposterous 12 for 13) and a four-pitch walk to Chone (pronounced Shawn) Figgins. I'm glassy, a little pissed off but dull and punchy, fatalistic. Timlin comes on to face Guerrero and ends up facing the left-field fence, watching a three-run shot knock around the rocks out there. It's 8–7 and Guerrero has all eight RBIs. He pops out of the dugout for a well-earned tip of the cap.

The Angels add two more in the seventh, when Foulke, coming in early in hopes of keeping it close, lets two of Timlin's runners score. Guerrero's in the middle of the rally again, knocking in his ninth run of the night.

Sitting there by myself in the dark house, facing the screen, I have nothing to distract myself from the terrible baseball I'm seeing. There's no one to commiserate with or to help absorb the loss; it's all mine. We've hit the ball well enough, and while our outfield isn't close to their cannon-armed trio of Jose Guillen, Raul Mondesi and Vladi Guerrero, we've fielded decently, but our pitching has been horrendous. All three pitchers we ran out there tonight got their butts whipped. By the ninth inning, as Francisco "K-Rod" Rodriguez strikes out David Ortiz and then Manny, I'm in a sour mood, blaming the Sox for my own impatience and irritability. The final's 10–7, the third time in a week we've given up double digits—and we came in with the league's best ERA. It's one o'clock, only a three-hour game, though with all the scoring it feels like four, four and a half. I feel crappy and blue. I feel like I've earned the day off tomorrow.

June 3rd

Boston's on the West Coast, and I hate it. We always seem to do poorly out there during the regular season, and the pennant hopes of more than one

Red Sox team have been buried in places like Anaheim and Oakland. This year is looking like no exception. The Angels have now beaten us twice in a row, and in both cases we've come from behind only to blow the lead again. *Youch.*

And when they go out there, I always feel as if the Olde Town Team (Boston *Globe* writer Dan Shaughnessy's term) has voyaged over the curve of the earth and clean out of sight. News travels faster than it used to, granted—I can get game highlights on NESN instead of just a bare-ass score on the morning radio—but details are still pretty thin unless you actually stay up and watch the game, as O'Nan was threatening to do last night (and gosh, he must have gone to bed grumpy in the wee hours, if he did). What I want most of all is a *box score,* dammit, and there won't be one until tomorrow, by which time last night's game will already be old and cold.

Or maybe Boston's West Coast swing and current three-game losing streak are only cover stories for a deeper malaise. Later, in August and September, I'll dumbly drop my neck and accept the yoke of fan-citizenship in Red Sox Nation, but in June and July I resist a rather distasteful truth: as summer deepens, I find that instead of me gripping the base-ball—apologies to Jim Bouton—the baseball is gripping me. This morning is a perfect case in point. The alarm is set for 7:30 A.M., because I don't really have to get up until quarter of eight. But I find myself wide-awake at 6:15, staring at the ceiling and wondering if the Red Sox managed to come back from a 4–2 deficit, which was where I left them. I'm also wondering if the Yankees, who were playing Baltimore at home, managed to win yet again. I'm thinking that the Orioles, with good hitting and fair pitching, must have managed to beat the Yanks at least *once.* I'm also wondering what Nomar Garciaparra's status is, and if there's any update on Trot Nixon.

By 6:30 I can stand it no longer. I get out of bed (still cursing my own obsessive nature) and switch off the alarm. It will not be needed today. I go to the TV and have only to punch the ON button; it's already on NESN, NESN is right where I left off seven hours ago, NESN is where the electronic Cyclops in my study is gonna be for most of the summer. Just like last summer. (And the summer before.) A moment later I'm sitting there on the rug in my ratty Red Sox workout shorts, hair standing up all over my head ("Your hair is excited," my wife says when it's this way in the morning), looking at Jayme Parker, who is for some incomprehensible reason doing the sports today on location from Foxwoods Casino, and although she's as good-looking as ever (in her pink suit Jayme looks as cool as peppermint ice cream), all the news is butt-ugly: the Sox blew their lead and lost, the Yankees came from behind and won. The Evil Empire now leads the AL East by two games. Even Roger Clemens, the pitcher then-Sox general manager Dan Duquette proclaimed all but washed-up and then traded away, won last night; he's 8-0 for the Astros.

The Red Sox continue their West Coast swing tomorrow night. It's way too early to liken this particular tour of duty to the Bataan Death March (although that simile has done more than cross my mind in other years, on other nightmare visits to Anaheim, Oakland, Seattle, and yes, even Kansas City, where we go next), but not too early to restate my original scripture: on the whole, I'd rather be at Foxwoods.

Francona's talking like Nomar will be back on Tuesday and that he'll be used as a DH for a while, letting Pokey, Marky Mark and Youk stay on the field and in the lineup. Ultimately though, he'll have to sit someone. Pokey's the glove and the glue, Bellhorn's the table-setter, but it's hard to pull Youk after how well he's played. For his .318 average and .446 OBP, he's been named May's AL Rookie of the Month.

A stray stat in the paper: since 2001, the Yankees are 44-17 against the O's.

Make that 45-17, as the O's succumb once again. They're under .500 now. The problem, I think, is that the O's are basically a cheaper version of the Yanks—so-so pitching backed by lots of free-agent bats. Like the Yanks, they're designed to overwhelm mediocre clubs, a wise enough strategy in this post-expansion era (the same strategy the Yanks used in the '50s, when their ace was the lackluster Whitey Ford and they feasted on the second division), but no guarantee of success in the playoffs. As the D-Backs, Angels and Marlins (and 1960 Pirates) have proven, to beat a club that grossly outspends you, you have to bring a whole different *style* of ball. There's no way the O's can match George's payroll, so they'll always be a few bats short.

We're two and a half back for the first time all year. It's not a hole, but it will take a streak to get us back even.

At the high school senior awards assembly, Caitlin's friend Ryan, who we've been giving grief about his Yankees since April, says, "Have you seen the standings?"

"Hey," I say, "you guys'll do fine if you only have to play the O's."

June 5th

It's time to admit it: this is the dreaded Red Sox losing streak.

Worse, it's the dreaded Red Sox losing streak combined with the even more dreaded (and apparently endless) Yankee winning streak.

No Jayme Parker on NESN's *SportsDesk* this morning to ease the pain; it's Saturday and Mike Perlow is subbing. And although I tune in at 7:12 A.M., near the end of the show's fifteen-minute loop and during a story about the Olympic Torch reaching Australia (huh?), I already know the worst. Perlow is one of those late-twenty- or early-thirty-somethings who look about fourteen, and this morning there is no sparkle in the Perlow eye, no lift in the Perlow shoulders. We lost. I'm sure we lost. But of course I hang in there to be sure and of course we did. The unsparkling eye does not lie.

Our pitching staff is having the week from hell. Derek Lowe lost to Baltimore in the Memorial Day makeup game; Bronson Arroyo and Pedro Martinez lost to the Angels; last night Tim Wakefield lost to the Kansas City Royals and Jimmy Gobble (a name at least as unfortunate as that of J. J. Putz). The Yankees again won by a single run—I don't know how many one-run victories they've rung up so far this year, but it seems like a lot—and we once more got half-bucked to death as KC put up a run here and a run there until the game was out of reach. It's the kind of slow bleed that drives managers crazy. Mark Bellhorn did not help the cause any by running into an out between third and home, killing a potential rally.

I think that for serious Sox fans, this sort of losing streak is exacerbated by the fact that the Yankees aren't losing *RIGHT NOW* combined with the sinking feeling that they will *NEVER LOSE AGAIN*. For serious control-freak fans (sigh—that would be me), it's exacerbated even more by the fact that *I CAN'T DO A FUCKING THING ABOUT IT*; all I can do is stand by and watch. Oh, and two other things. One is to remind myself that we owned first place less than a week ago, and are now three games out of it. The other is to try and find that Stephen Crane poem where the guy says he likes what he's eating because it's bitter, and because it is his heart.

Stop that and stay upbeat, I tell myself. This is not impossible or even that hard to do on a beautiful June morning with the grandchildren on the way. It's a long season, after all, and September is the only month where a losing streak can absolutely kill you, and only then if it's combined with the wrong team's winning streak.

Besides, I have to think of Stewart, who stayed up until maybe two in the morning to watch one of those awful games with the Angels where we blew the lead in the late innings. Man, I haven't even dared e-mail him about that. As for tonight, I have my choice: the new *Harry Potter* movie, or the Red Sox. If my older son actually does make the scene with the grandkids, I think I'll let him decide.

Who says I'm a control freak?

Later: The headline of this morning's Sox story in the *Lewiston Daily Sun* reads: GOBBLE FEASTS ON SOX. Hours later, while Peggy Noonan is getting all misty about the passing of Ronald Reagan on CNBC, I think, *GOBBLE FEASTS ON SOX,* and I crack up all over again.

When you're losing, you take your chuckles wherever you can get them.

As I'm cutting the grass, my next-door neighbor Dave waves me over to the fence. Dave's a big Bruins and Sox fan, and we have the occasional bitchfest about the sorry state of the two teams. Dave says the thinness of the roster is starting to show—that we've gone too long playing second-stringers. I say we've got to find a way to protect Manny; Tek and Dauber have struggled, and Millar's been nonexistent. "And where's our friend Mr. Kim?" Dave asks. "I haven't seen hide nor hair of him." I wonder where Mystery Malaska is, whether he's in Pawtucket or on the DL. In the end, I tell Dave that it's early and that we'll turn it around.

But really, do we need to turn it around? Are we really stumbling that badly? Even with this second streak, we're still up there with the league's elite. It's a luxury, worrying about being three and a half back. A lot of clubs are already well out of it.

June 6th

7:30 A.M.: The Red Sox won last night. Schilling (now 7-3, God bless him) stopped the bleeding at four games and the Yankees lost, so for the time being, all's well as it can be.* It's funny, though, how being a fan takes over your life. Ronald Reagan died at 1 P.M. yesterday. At the time he left for that great Oval Office in the sky, he was ninety-three—the oldest living ex-president. And, I realize, he would have been seven the last time the Red Sox won the World Series. *Hmmm,* I think. *That's old enough to have a rooting interest. Wonder if The Gipper was a fan?*

You know what Ole Case would have said, don'tcha? Right. You could look it up.

The latest Pedro worry is that he showed up at the clubhouse yesterday wearing a wrist brace on his pitching arm. When asked why he had it on, he told reporters, "Because it looks good." Lately he hasn't been able to throw his curveball, so this just sets off a wave of speculation that something's physically wrong. We'll find out Tuesday, when he's scheduled to take on David Wells and the Padres.

Nomar should be back for that game. Last night in Toledo he went 2 for 4 with a homer and a two-run double. I expect to be on Lansdowne Street Tuesday afternoon, trying to catch one of his batting practice home runs.

5:30 P.M.: This was a good afternoon for we the faithful. First, the team Nomar Garciaparra is likely to rejoin on June 8th will be ten games over .500, thanks to today's win. Second, Lowe went five respectable innings and then lucked into the win when his teammates scored five runs in the top of the sixth (the only inning in which they managed to score *any* runs). Third, and maybe most important, I finally saw signs that, yes, Derek Lowe cares. After giving up a two-run gopher ball to KC Royals batter Mike Sweeney in the first ("A ball that just screamed 'hit me,'" commentator Sam Horn said in the postgame show), the camera caught a look of weary disgust on Lowe's face that summed up all of his feelings about what must seem a nightmare season to a big-money player in his walk year. *What have I got to do to get out of this?* that look said. Or maybe *What have I got to do to make it stop?*

Work is the answer to both questions, of course, and following the Sweeney home run, Derek Lowe worked quite hard. He's clearly got a

---

*It's true that Smarty Jones lost the Belmont Stakes in the final hundred yards yesterday, but he can't bat cleanup or go to his left on a ground ball hit deep in the hole, so fuck him.

long way to go—and at 5-5, he's not looking like the answer to any team's 2005 prayers—but at least he now looks like he's *awake,* and that's an improvement.

Then there's Mike Timlin, who's old-time tough and has the looks to match, with his red socks pulled up almost to his knees and his no-nonsense low leg-kick and stride delivery. Timlin is, in my humble opinion, worth a Lowe and a half. He came on in relief of Derek, pitching a perfect three innings before turning the ball over to Keith Foulke. And if Mr. Mike wants to give all the credit to the Lord, more power to him.

Oh, and by the way—did I happen to mention that Kevin Youkilis was last week's Pepsi Rookie of the Week? Yep. Yesterday he hit his second home run. Today the Greek God of Walks just . . . walked.

Hey, it's good enough for me.

June 9th

I had a big day yesterday. The sixth of my Dark Tower novels, *Song of Susannah,* was officially published, and I was in New York to do promotion (mostly those morning-radio drive-time shows— not glamorous, and grueling as hell when you pile them up, but they seem to work). The original idea was to fly in from Maine on the evening of the 7th, get a night's sleep, get up early, do my thing, and fly back late the next afternoon. Instead, I rearranged things on the spur of the moment so I could go to Boston instead. The attraction wasn't so much the opening night of interleague play—this year the San Diego Padres are in Fenway for the first time—or Pedro Martinez, who has been less than stellar this year, as it was the bruited return of Nomar Garciaparra.

Funny thing about that bruiting. Not only was Nomar not in the Red Sox lineup, he wasn't even in Boston. He was in Rhode Island, where he played six innings for the PawSox and went 0 for 3. And no one seemed sure just how everyone got so sure he was going to make his major league debut last night in the first place. As I settled into my seat on the third-base line—call last night's locale halfway between Kevin Youkilis and Manny Ramirez—I couldn't even remember where I had gotten the idea. I even played with the notion of skipping the game altogether. I'm really, *really* glad I didn't. Last night's tilt would certainly have to go on my list of Steve's Top Ten Games at Fenway Ever.

The thing is, you *never* know when you're going to be reminded why you love this game, why it turns all your dials so vigorously to the right. I've been at Fenway for three 1–0 shutouts, and the Red Sox have won all three. Wes Gardner, an otherwise forgettable Sox righty, pitched the first under a gorgeous full summer moon one night in the eighties; Roger Clemens pitched the second on a sweltering weekend afternoon in the early nineties; Pedro Martinez and Keith Foulke (who worked a one-two-three ninth) combined on the third last night.

"The Pods," as they are called (as in Pod-people, from *The Invasion of the Body Snatchers*? one wonders), may be strangers to Fenway, but their starter, David Wells, knows it well . . . and we, the Fenway Faithful, know him. Never inarticulate, Boomer has often expressed his distaste for pitching in the Beantown venue. And with good reason. Until last night, fresh off the DL, I'd never seen him pitch well there.*

He made up for that in his first start as a "Pod Person," giving up just four hits, all singles, and working ahead of virtually every batter. This year's Red Sox hitters are a patient bunch, and they usually wear pitchers out. Not Wells, last night; most of our guys just ended up getting in the hole 0-2 or 1-2, and slapping harmless grounders in consequence. If Wells hadn't been lifted so as not to overuse him in his return, the game might still be going on.

I think he was better than Pedro over the first five, and given Pedro's postgame comments ("I want to build on this"), Pedro may have thought so too.† Martinez certainly got great defensive backing from his team-mates, who have at times this season been decidedly . . . shall we say *iffy*? . . . in the field. Johnny Damon made a leaping catch in center, and Mark Bellhorn made a diving, dirt-eating stop between first and second. The stop was good, but what reminded me again—forcibly—of what makes these guys pros was how quickly he was back on his feet again. "Quick as a cat" ain't in it, dear; "if you blinked you missed it" is more like it. But the defensive play of the night once again belonged to Pokey Reese,

---

*Today's newspapers described Wells's latest stint on the DL only as resulting from an "off-field incident." A guy I know who follows the game closely says Wells injured his wrist when he fell off a barstool. I assume that was a joke, but given Wells's declared proclivities, one cannot be entirely sure.

†Although he *was* clearly pleased (at one point during his postgame comments, Pedro called it a "dream game"), and given the outcome—no runs and just two hits in eight innings pitched—he had every right to be.

who has flashed divine leather all season long. I won't bother describing it, other than saying he went to his left at a perfectly absurd speed, and maybe—*maybe*—got a helpful last-second bounce. I *will* tell you that I believe no other infielder except Ozzie Smith could have made the play, and relate two overheard comments from behind me, Charlestown accents and all:

"Do you think Nomah could play right field?" was the first.

"Nomah *who?*" was the second.

And today I complete the experience by driving out of Boston on the first *bona fide* day of summer, temperatures in the mid-nineties, me in a Hertz Rent-A-Car I picked up at Logan Airport, driving up Route 1 as I have after so many games at Fenway Park, since my first one in 1959. There's something just totally balls-to-the-wall about driving north past Kappy's Liquors unhungover at 9:45 in the morning under a gunmetal sky; you've got that almost flawless two-hit, 1–0 win under your belt, and there are almost four more months of baseball to look forward to. I've got a cold Pepsi between my legs, the radio's turned up all the way, there's a U2 rock-block going on, and "Angel of Harlem" is pouring out of the speakers of my little Mercury Something-or-Other. Call me a dope if you want, but I think this is as good as it gets with your clothes on.

June 10th

Last night was #5 Night at Fenway Park; the Return of Nomar. The crowd gave him a vast roar of a standing O, and Nomar, obviously moved, saluted them right back. He took the first baseball to come his way flawlessly, starting a 6-4-3 double play. In his first at-bat, he singled smartly into left field, to the crowd's vast delight. The only problem was the Red Sox lost and the Yankees won, coming back from an early 4–0 deficit in their game with the Colorado Rockies. The Sox are now down three and a half games.

I find this out this morning, having given up on the Sox at 11 P.M., when a rain delay (it eventually clocked in at two hours and fifty minutes) progressed from the merely interminable to the outright absurd. The loss wasn't entirely unexpected, as the Red Sox were down a bunch when the rains came, but the fact that the Yankees won yet *again* came as a rather nasty shock. They are starting to look more and more like those mono-lithic Yankee teams from the mid-to-late fifties that inspired the late Douglas Wallop (a Washington Senators fan) to write *The Year the Yankees Lost the Pennant*, which became the musical *Damn Yankees*.

A final note. In a move that may make sense to manager Terry Francona but seems incomprehensible to lowly fans like me, the Red Sox have sent Brian Daubach down to Pawtucket. Andy Dominique started for the Sox last night at first base. After blanking the Padres for four innings, a provisionally rejuvenated Bronson Arroyo found himself with two men on and two out. Brian Giles hit a grounder deep in the hole, which Garciaparra fielded, going to his right. He then made one of those patented across-the-body throws that have nailed so many surprised runners at first. Not last night. The throw was accurate enough, but a little short. The ball bounced first off the dirt, then off the heel of Dominique's glove. My opinion? Maybe Ortiz doesn't make that play, but David McCarty almost certainly does . . . and so does The Dauber. My question?

What's the guy with Show experience doing in the minors when we're in a pennant race?

With all the network Thursday-night shows over, it's easy to claim the good TV. I've got revisions to do, and settle in. The Yanks have already won, completing their sweep of the Rockies this afternoon, so once again we need to keep pace.

Schilling's pitching, and I'm shocked when leadoff batter Sean Burroughs doubles and scores in the first. Ismael Valdez (a seaworthy name if I ever heard one) throws blanks till he meets Pokey Reese in the bottom of the third. In BP, Pokey has to work to reach the wall, but Valdez finds the perfect spot up and in and Pokey loops it into the first row of M7. The next inning, Valdez hangs a curve to Manny with David on first, and Manny goes over everything and into the parking lot.

Meanwhile, Schilling's throwing 94 with authority, striking out a bunch. In the fifth, Youk's RBI double off the scoreboard chases Valdez.

CUT TO: crazy handheld zooms of heavyset goateed man in familiar Western shirt gorging on bucket of KFC to raucous music. It's Millar, in the same shirt he wore to the movie premiere. EXTREME CLOSE-UP of bucket with SFX of chicken pieces disappearing one by one. "Going, going . . . " Millar says.

When we return, reliever Brandon Puffer intentionally walks Manny to load the bases. Nomar steps in to a standing O and knocks one off the

Monster for a 6–1 lead. Millar follows with a double to the left-center gap—"Chickenman!" me and Steph yell.

It's 8–1, and the rest of the way's uneventful, save a woman being ejected below Don and Jerry. While the camera's not allowed to watch her, the crowd is. She must flash them, because there's a roar, and for the next three minutes Don and Jerry can't stop laughing. "I wonder how that looked on high-definition," Jerry says.

In the ninth, a momentary scare when Nomar bangs his bad foot off second base as he comes across to make a play, but he seems fine. McCarty lets us forget it by making a brilliant diving stop on a hopper down the line, reaching high to snag a bounce that should get over him. Lenny DiNardo's frozen on the mound, so the runner's safe, but it's the kind of play (after Andy Dominique last night) that makes me want to see McCarty play more.

June 11th

In his first two games back, "Nomah" is batting in the five-hole. In last night's game, the Padres elected to intentionally walk Manny Ramirez with one out in order to face Garciaparra with the bases loaded and the force-at-any-base situation in effect. #5 rewarded this strategy (which, the Padres' manager would probably argue this morning, made sense at the time, with Garciaparra having been on the DL for the entire first third of the season) with a double rocketed off the left-field wall. That baseball-battered Monster giveth and taketh away, as Fenway fans well know. Last night it tooketh from Nomar Garciaparra: in parks with lower walls, that ball surely would have carried out for a grand slam. Oh well, we beat the Pods, 9–3.

The Yankees won again, of course. They have now won thirteen straight in interleague play. Damn Yankees is damn right.

June 12th

Baseball's most delicious paradox: although the game never changes, you've never seen everything. Last night's tilt between the Red Sox and the Dodgers is a perfect case in point. With two out in the top of the ninth, it looked as though the Sox were going to win their second 1–0 shutout in the same week. Derek Lowe was superb. Even better, he was lucky. He gave way to Timlin in the eighth, and Timlin gave way to Foulke in the ninth, all just the way it's s'pozed to be. Foulke got the first two batters he faced, and then Cora snuck a ground-ball single past Mark Bellhorn. Still no problem, or so you'd think.

That's when Olmedo Saenz came up and lifted a lazy fly ball toward Manny Ramirez in left field. Saenz flipped his bat in disgust. Cora, meanwhile, was motoring for all he was worth, because that's what they teach you—if the ball's in play, anything can happen. This time it did. Manny Ramirez hesitated, glanced toward the infield, saw no help there, and began to run rapidly in no particular direction. He circled, back-pedaled, reached . . . and the ball returned gently to earth more or less behind him. Cora scored, tying the score and costing Derek Lowe the victory in the best game he's pitched this year. David "Big Papi" Ortiz eventually sent the crowd home happy in the bottom of the ninth, but what about that horrible error by Manny? How could he flub such a routine fly? Here is the Red Sox center fielder, with the ominous explanation:

"I was the one person closest to the action," Johnny Damon said after the game, "and I saw all these weird birds flying around. I think they definitely distracted Manny's attention when he needed it most. That really wasn't an error at all. It was a freak of nature."

As one of the postgame announcers pointed out, this may have been the first use of the "Alfred Hitchcock Defense" in a baseball game.

Manny was even more succinct. "There goes my Gold Glove," he said.

June 13th

A worrisome article in the Sunday paper: Schill has a bone bruise on his right ankle (his push-off foot) and is start-to-start. He's been taking Marcaine shots before throwing and wears a brace on days off. What else can go wrong?

June 14th

Interleague play, my ass—why not call it a marketing ploy, which is what it really is? It fills the stadiums, and I suppose that's a good thing (even the somehow dingy Tropicana Dome was almost filled yesterday, as the temporarily-not-so-hapless Devil Rays won for the eighth time in their last ten games), but let's tell the truth here: fans are paying to see uniforms they're not used to. Many of the players inside of those exotic unis (Shawn Green, for instance, a Blue Jays alum who now plays for L.A.) are very familiar. Or how's this for double vision: In last night's contest (an

8:05 EDT/ESPN-friendly start), you had Pedro Martinez starting for the Red Sox. He used to pitch for the Dodgers. And for the Dodgers, you had Hideo Nomo, who used to pitch for the Red Sox (only before the Red Sox, he used to pitch for the Dodgers). I'm not saying life was better for the players before Curt Flood—it wasn't—but rooting was both simpler and a lot less about the uniform. One of the reasons I'm such a confirmed Tim Wakefield fan (and am sorry his last couple of starts have been disasters) is because he's been with the Sox for ten years now, and has done everything management has asked of him—starting, middle relief, closing—to *stay* with the Sox.

Meanwhile, we won yesterday evening's game, 4–1. Pedro (the one who used to be with the Dodgers and probably *won't* be with the Red Sox next year) got the win, with a little defensive help—a lot of defensive help, actually—from Pokey Reese, who made a jaw-dropping leap to snare a line drive in the seventh inning and save at least one run. "Play of the week" ain't in it, dear; that was a Top Ten Web Gem of the *season*.

Today we have off. We ended up taking two of three from the Pod People and two of three from the Dodgers, and *still* the Yankees mock us. Yesterday the Padres led the Yanks 2–0 going into the bottom of the ninth and blew that lead. Led them 5–2 going into the bottom of the twelfth and blew *that* lead, as well. The Yankees ended up winning, 6–5, to maintain their three-and-a-half-game edge. I looked at that this morning and reacted not with awe but a species of superstitious dread. Because that kind of thing tends to feed on itself.

The rest of the AL East, meanwhile, is bunching up behind the Red Sox in interesting fashion. Baltimore's in third and Tampa Bay's in the cellar; both to be expected. What's *not* to be expected—except maybe I did, sorta—is that at this point, approaching the season's halfway mark, those two teams are only two games apart, Baltimore 11.5 out and Tampa Bay 13.5.

June 16th

When I turned in last night at 11:15, the Red Sox were down a run to Colorado, 4–3, but I had a good feeling about the game, and why not? The Rockies have been horrible this year. Besides, I'd gotten a call from my publisher saying that *Song of Susannah* was going straight to number one on the *New York Times* best-seller list, and that's the sort of day that's supposed to end with your team winning—it's practically a national law.

I wake up this morning at 6:45 and turn on *SportsDesk*, feeling like a kid about to open his Christmas stocking. Unfortunately, what I get in mine is a lump of coal. Red Sox lost; Yankees won.

The Christing Yankees won *again*.

I can hardly believe it. Jayme Parker is telling me these bozos now have the best record in baseball, which is no news to me. I'm thinking they must have the best record in the entire *universe*. The Red Sox aren't doing badly; by my calculations, we would have won the wild-card spot by two full games, had the season ended yesterday. But I am just so *sick* of looking at the Yankees' collective pin-striped butt in the standings each and every day, so sick of realizing that we'll still be in second place even if we sweep them when we see them later this month.

There's nothing better than waking up to find your team won and the other guys lost. Conversely, there's no worse way to start the day than finding out your team lost and the other guys won. It's like taking a big swig of the orange juice straight from the carton and discovering that it's gone over.

June 17th

The Red Sox are now back to full strength, or almost (Pokey Reese is day-to-day with a jammed toe, as a result of that spectacular catch on the thirteenth). Trot Nixon returned to the lineup with a bang last night, stroking a home run to what's almost the deepest part of Coors Field. So all's right with the world, right?

Wrong. The Sox got behind early again and couldn't quite come back, Schilling lost (television viewers were treated to the less than lovely sight of Father Curt, the staff's supposed anchor, pounding the shit out of a defenseless Gatorade cooler after giving up a key two-out hit), and the Yankees won for the 730th time in their last 732 games. Consequently, we've fallen five and a half games out of first place. These will be hard games to make up, assuming they can be made up at all (probably they can), and what hurts the most is that the last two losses have come at the hands of the Rockies, currently major league baseball's worst team. But the Red Sox have a talent for making bad teams look good, I sometimes think; we have done some almighty awful franchises the favor of making them look terrific for their fans, especially during the two or three weeks after Memorial Day.

For this is almost certainly the beginning of that yearly Red Sox rite known as the June Swoon. Longtime fans know it so well they can set their calendars by it, if not their watches; it begins when the NBA finals end. During this year's Lakers-Pistons finals,* the Sox were busy taking two out of three from both the Padres and the Dodgers, who are vying for the top spot in the NL West. Now that the finals are over, they are busy getting their shit handed to them by the lowly Rockies and their lead in the wild-card race—yes, even that—has melted away to a mere single game.

If it *is* the Swoon, I don't think I can bring myself to write about it . . . but I'll be watching it happen. Have to do it, man. It's my duty, and not because of this book, either. It's because that's the difference between being a mere fair-weather fan and being faithful. Besides, July's coming, and the Red Sox always turn it around in July.

Usually always.

I take the Fenway tour in the morning, hoping to catch BK working out. He's not. The grounds crew is doing something to the track in left; they've dug up the corner and pulled some padded panels off the wall. We can't go down to field level—a drag, since I wanted to walk the track and peek in the scoreboard. We hit the press box, then the .406 Club. While we're listening to the guide's spiel, I notice two members of our tour being escorted to the mound far below. A man and a woman. The man goes to one knee. KELLI, WILL YOU MARRY ME? the scoreboard flashes. She kisses him, and the tour applauds.

We cross the Monster for the big view. I'm surprised by how many tours are running at once, and how much activity there is. There are several school groups circling the top of the park the opposite way. Under the bleachers, a crew is setting up a catered job fair; in the right-field grandstand, work-men are replacing old wooden seats.

The last stop is the right-field roof tables, an anticlimax, and we walk back down the ramp to Gate D, looking down on the players' lot. The guard there says BK should be in any minute.

•   •   •

*Go, you Pistons! Stick it *to* 'em! Booya, Shaq! *Double*-booya, Kobe!

Back home, the schedule makers sneak today's game by me. It's a 3:05 start, 1:05 mountain time, and when I tune in to NESN at nine o'clock they're showing Canadian football, complete with the 55-yard line and Labatt's ads painted on the astroturf. I check the website: 11–0 Sox. Lowe threw seven strong, getting 17 ground-ball outs. Ortiz put it out of reach in the sixth with a three-run shot. It figures—the one game I miss.

June 18th

ESPN notes that Lowe's shutout was only the second of the Rockies at Coors in their last four hundred games. And the Yanks lost to the D-backs, so we gained ground.

Francona kept Wake out of the Colorado series, citing knuckleballers' poor history there, so Wake opens against the Giants at Pac Bell (SBC, if you want to be a stickler). As in his start against the Dodgers last Saturday, he's got nothing. The Giants run on him at will, and Marquis Grissom takes him deep twice for a 7–2 lead in the fourth.

I'm at the beach, watching with my nephew Charlie.

"Why don't they take him out?" Charlie asks.

"Because we don't have anyone else." And there's Malaska warming.

With the 10:05 start and all the offense, it's late, and we don't want to keep the rest of the cottage up.

My father-in-law, stumping to the bathroom in his skivvies, asks how we're doing.

"Ah, we're getting crushed," I say.

June 19th

The local edition of the *Providence Journal* only stayed up as late as I did. They have the score 7–2 in the fifth—as if that helps anyone.

"They won," Charlie says, shrugging. "The score was something like eleven to eight."

No one can verify it, so I get on my father-in-law's laptop and hit the website. 14-9 was the final. Ortiz and Manny went back-to-back and Millar had a pinch-hit three-run shot over Barry Bonds—all in the top of the fifth. Son of a bitch. All we had to do was stay up another ten minutes.

"Fair-weather fans," Trudy says.

"No," I say. "It's the opposite. When I watch them, they lose. I turn it off and they win."

June 20th

7:45 A.M.: Today's game against the San Francisco Giants will mark the end of interleague play for the nonce, and I'm glad. I don't like it because I think it's a marketing stunt, but that's secondary. A New England team has no business on the West Coast, that's what I really think.

Still, it should be an interesting contest—the rubber game in a three-game series the Red Sox would dearly love to win. For one thing, it would send them home with a .500 record for the trip. For another, they'd go back to Boston four and a half behind the Yankees, only three and a half if the Dodgers can beat the Yankees again today. And Sox pitching has pretty well muzzled Barry Bonds, who strikes me—admittedly an outsider, but sometimes outsiders see with clearer eyes—as one of the game's more arrogant and conceited players. His fans in left field hang rubber chickens when Bonds is intentionally walked, but they haven't hung many in this series.

Oh, and by the Ray—the *Devil* Ray, that is—those Tampa Bay bad boys have now won a franchise-best *ten straight*. And you know what that makes them, don't you? Right.

Hapless no more.

SO: So where was Foulke yesterday when Alfonzo came to the plate? I know our pen threw five Friday night (tanks, Wake), and that Williamson just got off the DL, but Francona's use of the bullpen's been a real mess lately. We've been behind a fair amount this road trip (just like the last two), but D-Lowe's 11–0 laugher should have given us a breather. Does Theo need to go and get a middle guy to replace Mendoza and Arroyo, or are Mendoza and Kim actually going to come back and contribute? The All-Star break's three weeks away, and all we've gotten out of those two is a single quality start from BK.

Meanwhile, Dauber languishes in Pawtucket, the forgotten Sock. Yesterday he jacked a foul ball out of McCoy Stadium into the middle of the football field next door—thing must have gone 475 feet.

SK: Where's *Francona* been lately? He could have cost us the game on Friday night, playing Bellhorn at third. Wuz just luck it worked out.

The rubbah game today should be good. Did you see the Harvard-prof piece in the *NY Times* about how teams that pitch to Bonds instead of walking him (tentionally or un) do better than those who don't? The Giants score .9 runs an inning when he's walked with none on and no outs, and .6 an inning when he's pitched to in that situation. We pitched to him yesterday, and altho I didn't see the whole game, I think he went 0-fer.

Oh, and by the way—how 'bout those THIRD PLACE Devil Rays?

SO: That just ties in with the Bill James/Moneyball OBP philosophy. Get men on and you get men in. And yeah, Barry was 0-for yesterday and looked asleep out in left.

10 in a row for the D-Rays—Lou must be pumped. And the O's fans must be pissed.

4:00 P.M.: It's Father's Day, and I'm right where I belong, with a blue western-Maine lake just to my left and the Red Sox ready to start on TV in front of me. I've got my book—a really excellent novel by Greg Bear called *Dead Lines*—to read between innings, and all is okey-fine by me. It's Jason Schmidt against Bronson Arroyo, a mismatch on paper, but as pointed out both on ESPN and in these pages, baseball games aren't played on paper but inside TV sets. So we'll see. One of these things we'll see is whether or not Schmidt can strike out ten or more (he struck out twelve Blue Jays in his last start), and whether or not Arroyo (currently 2-5) can keep the ball around the plate.

4:30 P.M.: Bronson Arroyo (whose goatee unfortunately *does* make him look a bit goatlike) finds his way out of a bases-loaded jam in the first, partly by inducing Barry Bonds to pop up. Bonds continues to be an offensive zero-factor in the series. By the way, you have to give it to the people who designed SBC Park; the only ugly thing about it is the name.*

5:00 P.M.: Arroyo settles down, but the Red Sox still don't have a hit. Kevin Millar took Schmidt deep, but Bonds snared that one, flipping it backhand into the crowd in almost the same motion. The gesture is grace-

*And maybe that giant skeletal Coke bottle in left field.

ful and arrogant at the same time. Watching Barry Bonds play makes me remember the late Billy Martin muttering about some rookie, "I'll take the steam out of *that* hot dog." Bonds is no rookie, but I think the principle is the same.

5:30 P.M.: Kevin Youkilis breaks up Jason Schmidt's no-hit bid with a hard double. Arroyo fails to bunt him over, but then Giants catcher A. J. Pierzynski drops strike three. It's just a little dribbler, but *Pierzynski forgets to throw down to first.* A couple of batters later, the Sox find themselves with runners at the corners, two out, and Ortiz at the plate. Big Papi, who leads the AL in runs batted in, stings the ball, but first baseman Damon Minor (who's even bigger than Ortiz) makes a run-saving stab, and Ortiz is out to end the inning.

6:20 P.M.: After a disputed call at third base that goes against the Sox (and gets Terry Francona thrown out for the first time this year), the Giants win the game, 4–0. Edgardo Alfonzo won it yesterday with a two-run shot off Alan Embree; today he gets the grand salami off Mike Timlin. On the whole, I sort of wish Signor Alfonzo had stayed with the Mets. Them we don't play this year. In any case, Bronson Arroyo's best performance of the season was wasted and the Red Sox can finally go home after a disappointing 2-4 road trip.

But hey—it's Father's Day, the first day of summer, and I'm by the lake with my family. Also, there *was* baseball. Ain't nothing wrong with that.

June 22nd

I only have to see three at-bats of this one. Caitlin's birthday dinner eats up the first six innings; it's the bottom of the seventh when I tune in. We're up 3–1, so Schilling must have thrown well. Johnny's on second, Bellhorn's on first, one out, with David Ortiz at the plate. He lines a double off the center-field wall even Torii Hunter can't get to, scoring Johnny. With first open, Ron Gardenhire goes by the book, intentionally walking Manny, except now the number five guy isn't Tek or Dauber or Millar, it's Nomar. Reliever Joe Roa dawdles on the mound, and Nomar steps out. He steps back in. Roa delivers, and Nomar blasts one to center that bounces off the roof of the camera platform and ricochets into Section 34. 8–1 Sox, and Nomar's got his first homer of the season and only our second granny. 9–2's the final, with Foulke leaving them loaded.

And Theo finally picks up some middle relief help, former Royal Curtis

Leskanic, a thirty-six-year-old righty with arm problems. He was 0-3 with an 8.04 ERA this year before KC cut him. Okay, now tell me the *good* news.

June 23rd

The Sox, clearly happy to be back from the West Coast, put a hurtin' on the Minnesota Twins last night. The newly returned Nomar Garciaparra hit a grand salami of his own to dead center field. And NESN, in slavish imitation of its bigger brother, Fox Sports (even the name of the feature's the same—Sounds of the Game), decided to mike a player and pick up some ambient audio. The player they picked was the *also* newly returned Trot Nixon, a wise choice, since Trot, like Mike Timlin, is long on *Praise Jesus* and short on *Y'oughta knock 'is fucking head off for that*. It was a noble experiment, but a failure, I think. When Nomar's home run brought the capacity Fenway crowd to its feet, cheering at the top of its lungs, the TV audience was treated to the sound of a laconic Trot Nixon: "Go, ball. Go on, now. *'At's* right." And, greeting #5 as he crossed the plate, these immortal words: "Good job, Nomie."

Nomie?

Well, everyone has his walk in life, or so 'tis said—the sportswriters have one, the ballplayers another. Maybe that's the point.* And we kept pace with the Yankees. That might also be the point. *And* the hapless-no-more D-Rays won their twelfth straight. *And* Kevin Youkilis sat last night's out while Mark Bellhorn did not do too much at third base. *And* Brian Daubach is still hitting meaningless home runs for the triple-A PawSox. Those things might also be the point. Multiple points *are*, after all, a possibility; even a probability in this increasingly complex world, but—

Git out, ball?

Caitlin's graduation takes place on the high school's baseball field. The stage is just beyond first base, and we're sitting in shallow right. I've brought a pocket radio the Pirates gave away in the early '80s with a single sneaky earbud, and as the speeches drag on, Minnesota loads the bases with no outs in the first. Lowe gets two ground balls, but again, we can't turn either double play, and the Twins go up 2–0 without hitting the ball out of the infield.

Later, at the graduation party at our house, I tune in to find the Twins up

---

*So what the heck does that make me and O'Nan?

4–2 in the eighth. Pokey hurt his thumb and left the game early. It's a worry because it's the same thumb that put him out nearly all of last season.

The Twins hold on to win. I catch the highlights: Torii Hunter hit a two-run shot in the fifth to put them up 4–0. We got solo shots from Trot and Bellhorn, that was it.

Miraculously, the O's beat the Yanks, so we're still four and a half back.

June 24th

We're the first in Gate E for today's businessman's special, and nab the spot in the corner, hauling in five balls during BP. Pokey doesn't hit, but Bill Mueller's here, joking and taking grounders at third. One gets by him and rolls right to me. Thanks, Billy!

I hang around the dugout and get Manny to sign my glove, and Gabe Kapler and new guy Curtis Leskanic to sign my all-purpose pearl. I notice Pokey's wearing a brace on his wrist and hand—another bad sign.

Wake looks better today. He doesn't have that scuffling first inning, and David Ortiz gives us a lead in the bottom with a towering homer down the right-field line that goes over the Pesky Pole. I've poached a seat at the far end of the Sox dugout, right behind the camera well, and I have to look to the first-base ump for a fair call; behind him, Twins first baseman Matthew LeCroy is signaling foul.

The Twins get two on a strikeout and passed ball and a pair of wall-ball doubles to go up 2–1. In the sixth I snag a foul ball from Bellhorn, a two-hop chopper that clears the NESN camera in front of me. It's the easiest play I've made all day, a chest-high backhander, so I'm in an even better mood when David Ortiz brings us back in the seventh, singling in Youk and Johnny.

For some reason, Francona leaves Wake in to pitch the eighth. He gets in trouble, giving up yet another wall double, but Scott Williamson comes on to shut the Twins down. Foulke throws a clean ninth, but we do nothing with our half, and go to extras.

Leading off the tenth, speedy Cristian Guzman hits a roller far to Nomar's left. Nomar gloves it behind second, then spins to get more on his throw. It's wide. Millar lays out but can't keep it from going in the dugout. Jose Offerman bunts Guzman over to third, giving Lew Ford the chance to knock him in with a soft sac fly.

In our half we've got David Ortiz, Manny and Nomar. David flies to right, Manny waves at a third strike a foot outside, Nomar pops foul to the catcher, and we lose 4–3 on an unearned run. Pokey and McCarty make that play. At the very least, the throw doesn't end up in the dugout. Millar also went a very bad-looking 0 for 4. I have no idea what he's doing out there instead of McCarty after the seventh.

June 25th

7:50 A.M.: The Red Sox have won exactly one game in each of their last three series, making them three for their last nine. Pokey Reese is injured. The pitching staff is struggling. Our position *vis-à-vis* the Yankees has for a second time sunk to a season-worst five and a half games out of first place, only this time we've lost our lead in the wild-card race (the Red Sox are currently tied with Oakland for that dubious honor). At the general store where I do my trading during the summer and fall months, people have started asking me "what's wrong with the Red Sox." (Because I have been interviewed on NESN, I am supposed to know.) I am also asked when I'm going to "go on down there and whip those boys into shape." I guess I'd better do it this weekend. I'll write for a couple of hours, then throw some clothes and a fresh can of Whip-Ass in a bag, and leave at 1 P.M. this afternoon. From the lake over here in western Maine, Fenway's a three-and-a-half-hour drive. The weather looks murky, but what the hell; the way the Sox have been playing, a rainout would be almost as good as a win. Besides, Michael Moore's polemic *Fahrenheit 9/11* opens tonight. If all else fails, I can go see that.

The Carlos Beltran trade finally goes down, a three-way deal that sends him to Houston and Astros closer Octavio Dotel to the A's while the Royals pick up three prospects. It's a bad deal for the Sox. Dotel's a hard thrower, and the way things are going we may end up battling Oakland for the wild card.

Friday night and we're in a local pizza place. I see the game all the way across the restaurant on a TV above the bar. I can barely make out the score: 2–0 Sox in the fifth, and Pedro's working. I figure we're in good shape, since he's gotten past the first.

We're talking, and when I look up again, Manny tags one to deep right. It looks out, but Bobby Abreu goes back hard and leaps at the wall, banging into it as the ball lands in his glove. He falls, hanging on to the wall with one arm—he's got it. Manny just smiles and jogs back to the dugout. I notice it's 3–0 now, so I've missed something. Trot walks, Millar singles. New pitcher. Tek singles, knocking in another run. It's 4–0 and we're paying the check.

Driving home, it's still the sixth inning. Youk sends a double off the wall in left-center and takes third on the throw home. 6–0. Bellhorn legs out an infield hit, scoring Youk. New pitcher.

We get home and I click on NESN and it's *still* the sixth. The new pitcher has walked Ortiz (who I discover led off the inning with a solo shot) to load the bases for Manny (who has a home run and an RBI double besides being robbed). Manny slices a liner to right that carries over Abreu into the corner. It takes a hop toward a fan at the wall who whiffs on it with both hands, knocking over his beer in the process. The ball caroms off the wall, still live, and all three runners come in. 10–0 Sox, and this one's done, except for a brilliant diving catch by Manny in the seventh that has Pedro pointing with both hands, giving him props.

Pedro goes seven, giving up two hits. Curtis Leskanic throws his first inning as a Sock, and then in the bottom of the eighth the rains come, and the ump calls it.

In the Bronx, the same rain wiped out the Mets and Yanks, so we pick up a half game to make it five even.

June 26th

It's still wet when the gates open, so there's no batting practice today. I hang around the first-base line and watch the grounds crew roll the tarp off. Mike Timlin signs, and Lenny DiNardo, and just before game time Nomar walks over. I'm in the first row, and the crush is enormous. Little boys scream and plead for an autograph—rock star Nomar. I'm a foot away from him, and think he'll actually sign the pearl I've brought, but he only does a couple before scooting down about twenty feet.

I poach the corner seat at the end of the camera pit—a great spot for foul balls—and am immediately rewarded by David Ortiz, tossing me a warm-up ball. I get the boot early, and go over and join Steve and Owen. Bronson Arroyo's pitched way better than his 2-6 record, but today he's consistently behind hitters. Youk misses a foul pop by the visitors' on-deck circle, then can't handle a throw by Johnny; he chases it down, only to gun it too high for Tek to put a tag on the runner. Jim Thome hits a monster opposite-field shot. Arroyo muffs an easy grounder. Later in the same inning Millar kicks a double-play ball into right field. The Phils score five runs, making it 7–1, and the Phillies fans chant. The Sox are putting the leadoff man on nearly every inning, then stranding him. Late in the game, the stands are half-empty.

"It's not just that they're bad," Owen says. "They're boring."

June 27th

So I cued up some good CDs and made the three-and-a-half-hour run from our little town in western Maine to Boston, pumping up for the drive into the city by playing Elvis's "Baby, Let's Play House" and "Mystery Train" at top volume about nine times, and do I succeed in spraying my fresh can of Whip-Ass on the Red Sox? I do. Sort of. We lose the middle game, 9–2 (the Sox commit a numbing four errors), but Pedro wins on Friday night and Schilling wins on Sunday when the Red Sox bounce back from a 3–0 deficit. Pedro's eighth win; Curt's tenth. The former was a totally righteous 12–1 drubbing shortened by thunder and lightning in the eighth inning.

The best thing about the weekend is that my youngest son came up from New York to share the Sox with me. These were his first Red Sox games of 2004, his first regular-season games in two years. It was great to be with him, swapping the scorebook back and forth just like old times, catching up on what we've been doing. Stewart O'Nan joined us on Saturday and that was good, too—it made an essentially boring game fun—but there was something especially magical about just the two of us. One of the things baseball is made for, I think, is catching up with the people you used to see all the time, the ones you love and now don't see quite enough. In our family, baseball and swapping scorecards—sometimes bought from a vendor outside the park, sometimes from one in the concourse, sometimes a homemade job scrawled on a legal pad—have always been a constant. I've got a drawer with almost thirty years' worth of those things saved up, and I could tell you what they mean, but if you've got kids, you probably know what I'm talking about. When it comes to family, not all the bases you touch are on the field.

The Yankees, thrifty baseball housekeepers for sure, are busily sweeping up the Mets in a Sunday day-night doubleheader, which means we'll go into our final series of the month with the Bombers five and a half games back. Not an enviable position, but one we've been in before.

• • •

A gorgeous Sunday afternoon. It's Visor Day, and they're giving out posters with Tek and Wally promoting reading. Pokey takes BP, a reason for optimism. I'm in my favorite spot for BP, hauling in balls, when Placido Polanco rips a hooking liner our way. "Heads UP!" I bellow, because it's going to be a few rows into the crowd behind me. I expect it to bang into a plastic seatback, like most screamers, but this one hits skin—and not the fat smack of a thigh or biceps, but a spongy, fungolike sound, unmistakable: it nailed somebody in the head. The ball ricochets at a right angle another ten rows into the stands, and a bald guy in his late fifties who was coming down the aisle reels sideways into the seats, still holding his two beers.

He wobbles like a fighter trying to stay upright until people take him under the arms and sit him down. He looks dazed, mumbling that he's all right. I'm already waving to security to get a trainer out here, medical staff, somebody.

Former Sox pitching coach Joe Kerrigan has been pacing the wall all BP, warning kids to keep their eyes on the batters. He gets a ball for the guy, and is standing there talking to me about how dangerous this place is—how Yankee Stadium's the same way down third—when Polanco stings one right at us. It skips once on the track, Joe backs off a step, and I glove it.

When BP ends, I check on the bald guy. He's sitting down, surrounded by security and a couple first-aid guys. On the side of his dome he's got a purplish knot the size of a fried egg. I think he should go to a hospital—at the very least he's got a concussion—but he's talking with them, giving them his information. He wants to stay for the game.

Trudy's over at Steve's seats. She saw all the hubbub; people around her thought it might be a heart attack.

She shows me that the souvenir-cup makers have fixed the SHILLING. "He must have a good agent," she says.

The pregame ceremonies pay tribute to all the middle-aged guys who took part in the Sox's pricey fantasy camp. They fill the baselines, stepping forward and doffing their caps as Carl Beane announces their names. No one except their families is paying attention until two guys on the third-base line unfurl a messily spray-painted bedsheet that says YANKEES SUCK. It gets a big hand, but, in typical Fenway fashion, when the guys walk by us on their way off, someone behind me hollers, "Is that the best you could do with the sign?"

173

June 28th

Both the Sox and Yanks wanted Freddy Garcia, but the White Sox got him, for a second-string catcher and a pair of prospects. Like the A's, even if they don't take their division, they'll be in the wild-card hunt, and they've made themselves stronger. Theo's got another month to cut a deal. One more solid starter would solve a lot of problems. Jeff Suppan, who we let walk after last year, is 6-5 with a 3.75 ERA for the first-place Cards. (And Tony Womack, one of our spring-training invitees, is hitting .300 for them and running all over the place.)

Tomorrow we start a three-game set with the Yankees in the Bronx. Short of a sweep by either team (unlikely), it won't change the standings much, but it could set the tone of the All-Star break. Looking back at the first half of the season, I'd say we've played well with a banged-up club. Ten games over .500 isn't great but it isn't bad either, given the team we're putting out there. And yet they do seem like the same old Sox: a couple of great hitters surrounded by mediocre guys, zero defense, inconsistent pitching, and the usual June swoon. It could be 1987 or 1996 or 2001.

June 29th

Both Lowe and Vazquez have thrown well lately, so the opener's an even matchup. To show how big of a game it is, Vice President Dick Cheney's crawled out of his hidey-hole and is sitting in the front row.

Johnny D sets the tone, leading off with a home run. The Ghost of Tony Clark gets it back in the second with a two-out RBI single. To prove it wasn't a fluke, Johnny hits another out in the third, and we're up 2–1.

In the bottom, Lofton leads off with a ground ball to Millar's right. He drops it, and by the time he recovers, Kenny's beaten Lowe to the bag. Jeter singles, and Lofton scoots to third. On the first pitch, Sheffield flies deep enough to left-center to tie the game. Jeter steals second easily. A-Rod singles off the third-base bag, the ball popping straight up so that Bellhorn has to wait for it, and Jeter holds at second. With Matsui up, Jeter and A-Rod pull the double steal on 2-2—unforgiveable, with a lefty batting. On a full count, Matsui knocks a curveball that's down and in (terrible pitch selection to any lefty, but especially this guy, who cut his teeth on breaking stuff in Japan) into right. It's 4–2, and the rare weeknight sellout crowd is on its feet.

In the Yanks' fourth, with one down, Lowe walks former Cardinal

Miguel Cairo, who, on the very next pitch, steals Tek's sign for a curve and swipes second.

"Does Varitek throw *any* runners out?" my father-in-law asks, and I have to defend him. Like Wake's knuckler, Lowe's sinker is a tough pitch to dig out.

With two down, Nomar kicks a grounder from Jeter that should end the inning, and Sheffield takes Lowe out to left-center for a 7–2 lead.

The next inning, Pokey *(Pokey!)* muffs a double-play ball, and Tony Clark goes long. It's 9–2, and all the runs have come from hired guns: Sheffield, Matsui, Clark. Lenny DiNardo is warming, and short of a miracle, this one's done.

Ortiz homers, and the Yanks tack on a pair for an 11–3 final. It's hard to blame Lowe entirely, when he got enough ground balls to at least keep things close. By now I expect the occasional error by Millar (wherever you put him), and Pokey's got a splint on his thumb, but Nomar's got to do better. And, with credit to Vazquez (another new hire), three runs don't cut it in Yankee Stadium.

It's just one game (just one of those games, like the one against the A's, or the Dodgers, or the Phils), but we're six and a half back and playing badly, and being embarrassed there annoys me even more.

SO: Getting beat by a horse like Matsui is one thing, getting beat by a BALCO Boy and the Ghost of Tony Clark is another.

June 30th

I didn't want to write this down, but after last night's crushing loss to the Yankees, I suppose I really ought to. About five days ago—just before my trip to Boston, anyway—I discovered a nearly perfect crow-shit Yankees logo on the windshield of my truck. This is a true thing I'm telling you.

You're asking do I have photographic proof?

Are you *crazy?*

What the windshield washer wouldn't take care of immediately, I got rid of with a filling-station squeegee just as fast as I could (and it took a distressing amount of elbow grease; those big woods crows shit *hard*). I told myself it wasn't an omen, but look at last night. Dick Cheney shows up in a Yankees hat, the Red Sox commit three more errors, the Yankees hitters are patient, the Red Sox hitters aren't. Derek Lowe, who has lately shown signs of his old craftiness, last night looked like an escapee from that old Spielberg film *The Goonies*.

Any halfway knowledgeable baseball fan will tell you there are three aspects to the game: you have to be able to throw the ball, catch the ball, and hit the ball. Last night, the Red Sox did a bad job on all three. And the Yankees have changed since April; this is Frankenteam. But there is good news, and it isn't that I stayed at a Holiday Inn Express last night. The crow-shit Yankees logo is no longer on my windshield, and at midnight tonight, June is officially over. I'm expecting the Swoon to be over with it. This team is just too good to keep playing as it has over the last dozen games.

I hope.

That's right, *I hope*. Because that's what Red Sox fans do.

Gloom and doom from Sean McAdam in the *Providence Journal*. I can't imagine how hard the *Globe* is riding the team. The Sox need to demonstrate some character, the Sox need to show why they have the second-highest payroll in baseball, you can judge a team by the way it responds to adversity, etc. Hey, Sean, maybe you've forgotten, but we've *had* our adversity, and we responded by leading the division for a couple months.

It's a case of what-have-you-done-for-me-lately, which for the beat reporter means a couple hours ago. We're 6-2 against the Yanks so far, and we've played a big chunk of the season without Nomar, Trot and now Bill Mueller. As long as we stay close, we can pick it up in the second half like we did last year and make the playoffs, and in a short series, with Petey and Mr. Schill and Foulke to close, we've got a shot.

Tonight's Wake-Lieber matchup is in our favor, considering how Timmy's pitched in the Stadium. It goes that way through six, 2–0 Sox on a David Ortiz homer and RBI single. We hit Lieber but leave a lot of men on, while the Yanks can't touch the knuckler.

In the top of the seventh, we load the bases with no outs, and Torre goes to his middle guy, Felix Heredia. He's not a top-of-the-line pitcher, and we've got the top of the order up. With the infield drawn in, Johnny grounds to Tony Clark, who goes home to cut down the run—Kapler, running for Millar. Now, with one down, our man on third is Doug Mirabelli, the slowest guy on the team. Francona must want three more outs from Wake, because he doesn't pinch-run, and Bellhorn's fly to short left does nothing. On 2-2, David Ortiz takes an outside pitch and the ump rings him up. It's a terrible call, and Ortiz stays at the plate, taking off his helmet and batting gloves, muttering, "Motherfucker," while the ump walks away. When Ortiz takes the field, he's still jawing at him.

I'm wondering where Francona is. Managers can't argue balls and strikes, but there's nothing more important, and we just got robbed. I don't care if he gets tossed, he's got to protect his players.

Wake hits Sheffield with his first pitch. After A-Rod Ks, BALCO Boy steals second. On 3-2, Wake walks Matsui on a borderline pitch that gets past Mirabelli. Francona goes to Williamson to get Bernie Williams, and he does, on a splitter down. Posada—so typical—works the walk, loading the bases for the switch-hitting Tony Clark. Clark's a hundred points better lefty. We should have Embree warm, but he's just getting up—and now Williamson's complaining of arm pain, and trainer Jim Rowe, Dave Wallace and Francona converge on the mound. Either it's ridiculous coincidence, or Williamson is acting. It's ruled an injury, so our reliever can take as long as he wants to warm up.

I think it's going to be Embree, but when we come back from commercial it's Timlin. He gets Clark to hit a one-hopper to Ortiz, who stumbles as he bends to glove it, and the ball goes through him into right, and all I can think is, *He pulled a Billy Buck.*

Two runs score, and we're tied.

"Where's McCarty?" I ask the TV.

Ortiz gets a new glove, as if that was the problem.

Cairo grounds out to end the inning, but they get two runs without a hit.

Tom Gordon throws a perfect eighth against Manny, Nomar and Trot, reaching 96 mph.

Lofton leads off their eighth with a grounder to the hole that Nomar backhands. He leaps, twisting, and throws. It's short and to the right-field side, but well in time. Ortiz misses the pick and it ricochets off his arm and into the stands.

"Where is McCarty?" I yell.

Jeter bunts Lofton over to third, then Sheffield fouls off seven fastballs on 0-2 (later Eck will say, "I might think about mixing in a breaking ball there—you know, that's just me") before pulling one past Bellhorn for a 3–2 lead. Embree comes on to face Matsui, even though Matsui's 3 for 8 lifetime against him. Make that 4 for 9, and we're down 4–2.

Mo takes care of the ninth—ironically, McCarty's the last batter, and never puts on his glove—and we lose one we should have won. The loss is on Ortiz, but also on Francona for not having his hands team out there late in a close game. You can always stick David at DH. Instead, he had the hobbling Trot at DH (obviously that quad's still bothering him), Millar in right and Youk on the bench. His use of Timlin and Embree seemed a little whacky, and after Wake left the game, Timlin and Mirabelli had trouble communicating during Sheffield's at-bat, shaking each other off several times before the last pitch. Why not go to Tek, who usually catches Timlin? And what about the philosophy of using your closer for the most important at-bat of the game? We didn't even see Foulke warming. Terrible. If yesterday's loss was embarrassing, this one's humiliating. They didn't win, we actively lost. Now Petey's got to be tough if we're going to avoid the sweep. That we're 6-3 against them is no consolation, seven and a half back.

Turn the Page

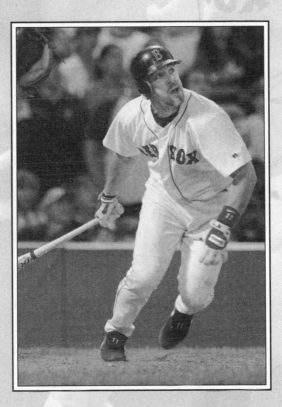

July 1st

"Why did football bring me so to life? I can't say precisely. Part of it was my feeling that football was an island of directness in a world of circumspection. In football a man was asked to do a difficult and brutal job, and he either did it or got out. There was nothing rhetorical or vague about it; I chose to believe that it was not unlike the jobs which all men, in some sunnier past, had been called upon to do. It smacked of something old, something traditional, something unclouded by legerdemain and subterfuge. It had that kind of power over me, drawing me back with the force of something known, scarcely remembered, elusive as integrity—perhaps it was no more than the force of a forgotten childhood. Whatever it was, I gave myself up to the Giants utterly. The recompense I gained was the feeling of being alive."

Frederick Exley, *A Fan's Notes*

Now, if you substitute *baseball* for *football* and *Red Sox* for *Giants*, you have a very fair picture of my rooting geography.

Francona must be feeling the heat, because Ortiz is DHing and McCarty starts at first. Nomar's not playing—to give him a night off, as ridiculous as that sounds. Youk plays, Trot sits, so essentially we're fielding the team we had in May, minus Bill Mueller.

Petey's feisty, plunking Sheffield and then glaring back at him when he takes exception. In the second, he walks Posada, and that damn Tony Clark waits on a change and puts it out. Meanwhile, rookie lefty Brad Halsey is setting us down. In the fifth, Posada takes five straight pitches before fouling off the payoff pitch, then lifts one into the upper deck. 3–0 Yankees, and things look bad.

In the top of the sixth, Ortiz leads off with a slicing fly to left. With the shift on, Matsui can't get there, and the ball hops sideways into the stands for a ground-rule double. Manny steps in and crushes one to dead center—he pauses to admire it a second, watching Halsey as the rookie turns away. It's 3–2 and the Yanks have to go to their middle guys.

In the seventh, Quantrill gives up a deep leadoff fly to right-center by McCarty. Lofton gets there, just short of the track, but one-hands it, and the ball pops out. Youk singles to left, so we've got first and third with no outs, and a big inning's brewing. Pokey hits into an easy 4-6-3 DP, but McCarty scores to tie the game.

Pedro finishes the seventh, and they go to Tom Gordon, who's solid. Foulke throws two innings for us, sneaking out of a one-out bases-loaded jam in the bottom of the ninth. Mo gets us one-two-three in the tenth, while Embree has to battle Bernie with first and third to reach the eleventh.

We load them with no outs. Millar's due up, but we've got Nomar and Trot available. Francona sticks with Millar, who hits into a 5-2 double play. McCarty flies out, and I think this one's over, but Embree gets them one-two-three.

The Yanks go to Tanyon Sturtze, who puts runners on first and third with one out, but Bellhorn pops up (he popped up last night in a similar situation). With two gone, Francona decides to pinch-hit Trot, who flares one to left that Jeter snags on the run, then—weirdly—takes two strides and dives into the seats, banging up his face. On the replay, he's got room to swerve or slide, but there he goes into the stands like a bad stuntman. In Japan they call that a *hotu dogu*.

We're down to Curtis Leskanic, who gives up a leadoff triple to Enrique Wilson when Johnny misplays a hop off the wall. Giambi strikes out, looking bad on three splitters, but Leskanic hits Sheffield (Torre comes out to bitch), and we intentionally walk A-Rod to set up the DP.

We're in the top of the twelfth right now and scratching like mad to salvage one game. The ESPN boys are saying that if we get skunked, we're dunked. I don't believe that, but a win would be nice . . . salvage a little of the ole self-respect. Garciaparra has been dog-bit in the field, and I really think Francona has been a bad choice as manager. Not in Daddy Butch's league (at least not yet), but he's not doing much to turn it around, is he? And if he's looking for a team leader, who is he going to look to? The guys

who've been out all season and just came waltzing back in like they had a free pass? Manny? Don't make me laugh. And Ortiz last night . . . Buckner all over again. Sign me, Just Plain Glum.

Meanwhile, in the game, runners at first and third, one out. As the old gypsy says, "I see handsome men on horseback."

If it has to be anybody, let it be Tony Clark.

And if it has to be anybody else, let it be good old Tom Gordon.

With Millar as a fifth infielder, Bubba Crosby, who pinch-ran for Matsui, takes the count full before grounding to Pokey, who goes home for the force. Bernie Williams falls behind 0-2, and Leskanic gets him with a splitter and we worm out of it.

Manny leads off the thirteenth with a rocket off the camera platform in left-center, and suddenly we're up 4–3. All we have to do is hang on.

Leskanic looks strong, striking out Posada, then making a nice play on a dribbler to the third-base side by Clark. I want him to finish off Ruben Sierra—a guy who strikes out a ton—but Sierra bounces a single up the middle. Now with two out, the outfielders have to play deep so nothing gets through to score the runner. Leskanic gets ahead of Cairo 0-2. His next pitch is on the corner, and I yell, "Got him!" but the ump blows the call. I hold my arms out wide, beseeching the TV. On the next pitch, Cairo hits a fly toward the right-center gap. Millar heads over. He may not have a shot at catching it, but at the last second he veers away from it and toward the wall, trailing it as it hops across the track. Sierra's chugging around third; he's going to score easily.

"What the fuck is Millar doing out there?"

Once again, Francona's fucked up. He pinch-ran Kapler but didn't pull the double switch. Kapler gets to that ball—at the very least he cuts it off.

John Flaherty, a backup catcher who played for us in the '80s, pinch-hits. He's hitting .150, but he lofts a double into the left-field corner, and the game's over.

So we go from embarrassing to humiliating to painful, finding a new, more wrenching way to lose each night. I should have never mentioned the word *sweep*. We're eight and a half back, and the tone of the break is definitely set.

In bed, still pissed off, I revisit the question of what the fuck Millar is doing out there in the thirteenth inning. The answer goes back to spring training, and the last man cut from the squad. Rather than keep Adam Hyzdu as a bona fide backup outfielder, Theo and Francona made the decision to go with Burks, Dauber, McCarty and Millar, understanding that Trot wouldn't be back for a couple of months. None of those four gets to that ball. Hyzdu does. And why is Kapler watching the play from the bench? It's like Francona has to learn the same lesson game after game—and it's common sense: to protect a late lead you want your best defense on the field. It's just fundamental baseball. Numbnut.

July 2nd

SO: Not Tony the Tiger or Flash. It was Miguel Cairo, who kicked Tek on the force at home in the twelfth. In Little League he would have been tossed.

SK: Hate to give you the news, but this is the bigs.

SO: The big leagues, where you can gobble down steroids and not even get suspended. Would you buy a used car from Bud Selig?

SK: You got a point there. Where money talks and bullshit takes a walk on Boardwalk.

Shit.

The Yankees took all three games at the Stadium—swept us out, sent us packing, dropped us eight and a half games back in the AL East, and the second-to-last thing in the world I want to do this morning is write about baseball. The last thing I want to do is write about the Boston Red Sox. Since I have to, maybe the best thing to do is get it out of the way in a hurry.

It was clear from the Yankees' jubilation that they really *wanted* the sweep, probably as payback for the humiliation of being beaten six of seven earlier in the season. For Boston fans, the series was a quick-and-dirty refresher course on how hard being a Red Sox fan can be. It's not the sweep that hurts so much as the fact that we *should* have won last night's game (the Yankees took that one by a score of 5–4 in thirteen innings), we *could* have won the June 30th game, and I would argue that we might even have won the first game of the series, in which we were blown out, if not for the errors (the Sox committed three, two by Garciaparra, who committed three overall in the series—he didn't play last night).

Being a Red Sox fan, particularly when playing the Yankees at crucial junctures of the season, can be such a filthy job. Two nights ago, with the Sox leading 2–0 but in a jam, Tony Clark hit a hard ground ball down to first. It should have been the third out. In the dugout, Tim Wakefield— down for the win, if the Sox could hold on—raised his hands joyfully. But instead of being an out, the ball squirted through David Ortiz's glove and into right field.* Ortiz blamed his glove, claiming the webbing was defective. Boston fans, knowing where God and the Fates stand in regard to our benighted club, did not doubt it.

In last night's game, Manny Ramirez hit a home run in the top of the thirteenth to put the Sox up, 4–3. In the bottom of the inning, the first two Yankees to bat went harmlessly. Then Sierra singled, Cairo doubled, and Flaherty doubled. Ball game. The loss doesn't hurt so much as coming so close to winning. Twice during that nightmare inning we were only a strike away.

And so I found myself doing what I have done after so many Red Sox close-but-no-cigar losses in my lifetime: lying in my bed wide-awake until maybe two or two-thirty in the morning, seeing the key base hit that opened the door skip past the pitcher's mound, then past the shortstop (Pokey Reese in this case) and into center field; seeing the celebrating Yankees; seeing our manager (Terry Francona in this case) hustling out of the dugout and into the clubhouse just as fast as his little legs could possibly carry him. Only this time I lay there *also* thinking that when I got up again after a night of bad rest, I was actually going to have to *write* about this fuckaree, thanks to my friend Stewart O'Nan, who got me into this.

Thanks, Stewart.

But there's one very good thing about July 2nd. The Red Sox are on to

---

*Everyone except Warren Oates has played first base for the Red Sox this year. Manager Francona had Oates down for it one night, but had to scratch him when he found out that Oates had died some time ago.

Atlanta. Atlanta usually kills us, but they're having a down year, and at least I don't need to write about the damn Yankees for a while.

After blowing two we should have won in the Bronx, we head south to take on the Dixie equivalent of the Evil Empire, the Braves. They're not that good this year, having lost most of that nibble-the-corners staff of the '90s, but they play in the worst division in baseball, the NL East, so they're still scrapping. Bill Mueller's back, and to make room for him, the Sox put Crespo on waivers, with an eye toward assigning him to Pawtucket.

Arroyo throws well, as does former Cleveland phenom Jaret Wright. Ortiz goes deep in the first, and Bill Mueller knocks in a run in his first at-bat, but the Braves get solo shots from Chipper Jones and J. D. Drew to tie it at 2.

In the middle of the sixth, Steve calls. He's watching up in Maine. "The Sox are playing like old people fuck." He's worried about the season going down the tubes.

"Hey," I say, "we almost have our starting lineup out there for the first time all year. Bill Mill at third, Nomar at short, Trot in right. The only one missing is Pokey."

"Is that a good thing, though, Stewart? Wouldn't you rather have the other guys playing the way they were playing in April or May? Pokey's not the one who hit .225 and made three errors this week. Nomar cost us a game." (As he says this, Bellhorn whiffs, and a caption says that his 90 strike-outs lead the league.)

"And Francona cost us at least one."

"I hate looking into the dugout and seeing him rocking back and forth."

"Like Danny in *The Shining*. I keep looking for drool."

"Redrum! Redrum!"

Steve says he couldn't sleep after last night's game, that he lay in bed, seeing Sierra's ground ball up the middle. I confess to lying awake as well, as if we're joined by a sickness, and we are.

When he hangs up, I feel like I've lost someone on the suicide hotline. I think I should have been able to cheer him up, but I can't lie; we've looked awful lately. Just have to ride it out.

It's 2–2 in the eighth when the starters give way to a roll call of relievers. It's almost a replay of last night's game, with each team putting runners on and then not being able to drive them in.

In the tenth Manny finally breaks the tie, knocking a single up the middle to score Johnny. In comes Foulke to close, even though he threw two innings last night. Rafael Furcal, who's the second fastest person in the stadium, doubles to left-center, then takes third on what the replay shows to be a foul ball (Francona stands blankly at the dugout rail). Little Nick Green hits a sac fly, and we're tied.

We do nothing in the eleventh or twelfth, and trust the game to Anastacio Martinez, recalled today to fill the spot left by Williamson, back on the DL. Anastacio looks good in the eleventh, but in the twelfth he gets no one out, giving up a single, a single and then a three-run homer to end it. 6–3, and we suck. At least the Mets beat the crap out of the Yanks, 11–2. Go Mets!

July 3rd

SK: I'm not writing in the baseball book until after the All-Star break. After last night's 12-inning heart-wrecker, I just can't. The team has clearly closed up shop until after the break. They need to take a few deep breaths and then just focus on winning game-by-game. The wild card is still possible, but right now losing it looks all too likely. I don't read the newspaper sports pages when we're losing—too depressing—but the screams for Francona's head have surely begun. Yes?

SO: You are correct, sir. Much second-guessing, though I've yet to hear anyone ask for the head of hitting coach Ron Jackson, and it's Papa Jack's boys who are stringing out the pen and making every defensive out crucial. We've scored four or less runs in all of these losses, against decidedly borderline pitching (save for Vazquez, the sole quality arm; last night Jaret "Fat Elvis" Wright was mowing us down like alfalfa). That don't cut it, even in the NL. Bellhorn is stone-cold, and when we do get runners on, we're not moving them around. Tell Theo, and tell John Henry too: it's time to kick some ass.

SK: They've got the bats, they'd argue; where are the *hits* in those bats?

SO: Papa Jack's slogan last year was "Somebody got-ta pay." This year, if we don't start rippin', it could be him.

Walking on the beach this morning, we pass a couple on a towel. The guy spies our Sox hats and says, "How 'bout those Yankees?"

"How 'bout those Marlins?" I ask.

Later, driving on I-95, I'm cheered by the sheer number of Red Sox stickers and license-plate holders, even an official Mass license plate like Trot hawks on NESN. I pass a car that has one of the free BELIEVE stickers Cambridge Soundworks gives out by Autograph Alley, and I think: yes, it's that simple. We may be down now, but this is my team, and I'm going to believe in them, whatever happens. Fuck the Yankees, and fuck their no-showing, front-running, fair-weather fans.

We all have our little strategies for dealing with loss, and right now I'm using all of mine. The Red Sox, who seem to be imploding, lost another heart-wrecker last night, this time in twelve innings, in Atlanta. That's four straight, the last three close ones. Strategies for dealing?

One: Stop reading the sports pages. Right now I won't even read about Wimbledon, lest my eye should stray to a baseball story, or, worse, the standings, on the facing page.

Two: Kill the sound. I watch the game every night on TV, but now with the MUTE function engaged, because I have conceived an active horror of what the announcers may be saying. MUTE doesn't work when the game's on ESPN, because their closed captioning kicks in, and in those cases, I have to turn the volume all the way down to 0.

Three: Change the station when the game is over. Just as soon as the final out is recorded I punch in Channel 262, better known as Soapnet. No way am I waking up to NESN's *SportsDesk* these days, even though I know I may be missing the always fascinating Jayme Parker. No, for the foreseeable future, I'll be catching up on *All My Children* while I shave and do my morning exercises.

Meantime, good news—and it has nothing at all to do with me saving a bunch on my car insurance. It looks like the current BoSox skid is going to end at four—it's the top of the ninth, and Boston's leading Atlanta 6–1. Curt Schilling's on the hill for the Sox, looking for number eleven. He's been our most reliable pitcher, because that sucker's not just good, he's *lucky*. Tonight Doug Mirabelli came up with two outs and the bases juiced, and although the Sox have been horrible all year in that situation, tonight was Mirabelli's night—he put one over the fence to dead center, and that should be lights out for this light-hitting Braves team.

Mr. Tripp, who owns the local general store, gave me a T-shirt today that says RED SOX on the front and I SUPPORT TWO TEAMS, THE RED SOX AND WHOEVER BEATS THE YANKEES on the back. I wore it for tonight's game, and I intend to wear it again tomorrow. And every day until they lose. (I also intend to keep on watching *All My Children* on Soapnet instead of *SportsDesk* on NESN for the foreseeable future. Less stress.)

July 4th

After losing the other night, Anastacio Martinez is shipped back to Paw-tucket, making room for Theo's newest acquisition, former Pirate Jimmy Anderson, a finesse lefty who last pitched for the Iowa Cubs. He's not the solution to our middle-relief problems, and I think Theo's pulling a Dan Duquette, trying to get away with cut-rate band-aids. If he really wants a quality arm, he's going to have to give up something.

I'm reading on the beach when my nephew Charlie says the Sox are winning 4–1. I wander into the house to see for myself and watch as Lowe gives up a walk, an infield single, another walk, a groundout by pitcher Mike Hampton that scores a run, a single, a double, a single. We've all seen how quickly Lowe can melt down, and throughout this sequence we're begging Francona to lift him, yet for most of it there's no one warming up. Francona lets him throw to lefty Chipper Jones, who predictably sticks one in the bleachers. It's 8–4, and everyone around the set is swearing. Francona finally calls on new guy Jimmy Anderson, who walks his first batter on four pitches, then gives up a double to Andruw Jones and a triple to Charles Thomas. I've only been watching for ten minutes and Atlanta's sent ten guys to the plate.

"Can they fire a manager in the middle of the season?" Charlie asks.

SK: Sox getting roasted 10–4. When I snoozed off, it was 4–1 good guyz. This be bad. Another day, another shellacking by a sub-.500 club;

another series lost to same. It's time for Terry to go while there's still a season to save.

Bring back Tollway Joe.

SO: Francona the Terryble. Bet the *Globe* and *Herald* scribes are sharpening their instruments.

At least the Mets sweep the Yankees (their fans chanting, "We're not Boston")—and on a horrible call. Late in a close game, Cairo hits one to the right side that Piazza can't reach. It gets by him and hits Posada. The first base ump rules him safe; the crew chief overturns it. Torre comes out to argue, to no avail. The rule is that if a fielder's had a chance to handle the ball, then the runner's safe. The crew chief decided that Piazza hadn't had a chance in the official sense, and that the second baseman might, and was therefore deprived of the chance to put Cairo out by the ball hitting Posada. Torre protests the game. And while the Yanks were the recipients of dozens of homer calls from the umps during our last series (including the noncall on that 0-2 count to Cairo that would have ended Wednesday night's game), I can't help but be annoyed at the incompetence. Get it right, Blue.

July 5th

The All-Star teams are announced. Schilling, Manny and David Ortiz made it—no surprise. What *is* shocking is that the three players implicated in the BALCO scandal—Bonds, Giambi and Sheffield—are all starting. Nice job, fans. Way to clean up the game.

Is life simpler, as Americans like to believe, down on the farm? We're hoping, driving through a monsoon to see the PawSox, whose ticket office assures us the weather will clear up and they'll get the game in. They almost do. At one point the grounds crew has the tarp off and is raking sawdust into the infield dirt, and Anastacio Martinez and Ramiro Mendoza and Frank Castillo and Mystery Malaska warm up down the third-base line. But by the time we have the ceremonial pitches (it's Latino Day) and Dauber and Adam Hyzdu and Big Andy Dominique come out to stretch, it's misting again, then straight-out raining, and two hours after game time, they call it, to halfhearted boos. So it really is a day off: no baseball at all.

July 6th

Tonight the Sox open a three-game series with Oakland, one of their chief wild-card opponents, and for the time being, at least, Boston's postseason hopes are all about the wild card. Tonight will also be Boston's eighty-first game of the year, which puts them almost exactly at the halfway point of the season.

Any real analysis of the first half will have to wait until the All-Star break, but I think it's fair to say that I have rarely seen the feeling in my little corner of New England turn so quickly, so decisively, and so almost *poisonously* against our only major league club. Who knows, by the time the All-Star break comes around, I may be willing to drop the *almost*. This sea change isn't that hard to understand. What we have here is a team filled with high-priced talent, much of which started the season on the disabled list. The team did well out of the gate nevertheless, contending in rather spectacular fashion in large part with the scrappy hit-'n'-field skills of guys like Bellhorn, Youkilis and Reese to complement the booming bats of Ramirez and Ortiz.* Then, just as the big boys started getting well, the team got sick. If it's going to get better again, the convalescence must begin soon.

How bad is it right now in what sportswriter Dan Shaughnessy has dubbed Red Sox Nation? I peeped in at NESN's *SportsDesk* this morning (I felt I could do this without too much fear of damaging my fragile sports superego because the Sox were idle yesterday) and was horrified to hear Sox-approved commentator Mike Perlow bandying Red Sox–Marlins trade rumors concerning Nomar Garciaparra and Derek Lowe. Of course there will be trade gossip as long as there's pro baseball, but because NESN is a quasi-official arm of the Red Sox organization, one is tempted to sense palsied fingers (perhaps on the hand of Red Sox general manager Theo Epstein) creeping toward that red button marked PANIC.

My decision to tune in NESN (Channel 623 on my satellite hookup) was clearly foolhardiness masquerading as bravery. The thought of Nomar in a Florida Marlins uniform is dismaying, almost nauseating. After no more than five minutes, I made haste to Soapnet and *All My Children*, where Erica is currently enduring the world's longest alcohol inter-

---

*Nor has it hurt that Johnny Damon is off to what may be a career year at the plate.

vention, Babe is in the hospital recovering from something her boyfriend JR (with a nickname like that you know he's a rat) put in her drink, and no one, so far as I can tell, is in danger of getting traded to *General Hospital*. Right now that makes it a safer, comfier world.

Wake versus Barry Zito doesn't sound fair, but in the second, Billy Mueller launches a three-run Monster shot. Zito loads the bases in the fourth and walks in two runs, then, after a smoked liner to third by Nomar, Millar doubles down the left-field line, scoring two more. It's 7–0 and Zito's thrown over 100 pitches. A's reliever Justin Lehr gives up four more in the fifth, and it's a laugher.

SK: Maybe the worst part of the current Red Sox woes is that there's this weary-ass old paper-delivery dude up here who drops off the *Globe* and the *New York Times* to the general store. He's worse about the Red Sox than Angry Bill in *Still, We Believe*. "Those damn *Red Sox!*" he says one day. And this morning it's "That damn *Nomah!*" And every day it's "I been chasin' those bums my *whole life!*" You know, like he's the only fucking sailor on the *Pequod*. Well, it's 11–0 Red Sox tonight in the sixth, and unless things go horribly wrong—and after that last game in Atlanta, I guess anything is possible—I can face the weary-ass old paper dude tomorrow with equaminity (sic). The problem is, it's only *one game*. People are asking me about our chances in the wild card *already*. I mean, it's come to that. I'm telling them "Hold the phone, there's still a division race going on here." But we've got to get the old Magic Streak going, like with the formerly hapless D-Rays.

Could this be the magical night it starts to happen???!!!?

Hold de fone! And git yo FREEK on!!!

SO: Naysayers everywhere. It's too easy. You could damn the chances of every team in the majors and at the end of the year you'd be 29–1. Haven't the Pats taught him anything? Dare to believe.

Speaking of streaks, d'ja see my Bucs reeled off ten straight before losing to the Marlins last night? So it can happen to anybody.

July 7th

Tonight Mark Bellhorn takes Mark Redman deep in the first for a 1–0 lead. Like Zito, Redman struggles. In the second he gives up a solo shot to Nomar, and then a batch of hits, including a big double by Tek and a two-out RBI single by Johnny, and we're up 6–0 and on our way to a rare blowout behind Pedro.

July 8th

It's Game 83, two past the halfway mark, and for the very first time (including spring training) we field our real starting lineup: Schill and Tek; Millar, Pokey, Nomah and Bill Mueller; and Manny, Johnny and Trot, with Big David at DH.

The Schilling-Harden matchup's in our favor, and goes that way early. Ortiz busts out of his slump with a tater over the Sox bullpen in the first, and Harden throws one at Manny's head. In the third, Manny retaliates with a three-run opposite-field shot. By the fifth it's 7–1 and this one looks in the bag.

But the A's don't roll over. Schilling's had a twenty-five-minute wait before the sixth, and they get a pair off him. In the seventh, Timlin gives up a two-out double to Erubiel Durazo and an RBI single to Bobby Crosby, and it's 7–4. Francoma (as the press has been calling him) leaves him in in the eighth; he gives up another run, and with one out, we have to go to Foulke. He gets Byrnes with a change-up for the second out, but on 0-2, Scott Hatteberg slaps another change off the chalk behind third and it's a one-run game. Jermaine Dye, 0 for his last 15, skies one to left-center. Johnny goes back toward the corner where the Monster meets the center-field wall and leaps, but it's off the Monster and bounces across center toward Trot. Hatteberg scores to tie the game. Dye's into third standing up, and Fenway's grumbling. Durazo chases strike three to end the inning, but our six-run lead's history.

Foulke throws a one-two-three ninth. Octavio Dotel looks tough, getting them to the tenth, but the A's pen has thrown too many innings this series. They go to Justin Lehr, who gave up four runs in a single inning Tuesday. He gets Tek and pinch hitter Mark Bellhorn, but Johnny singles to left. The A's move their outfield back so nothing gets through. It's a shrewd move, as Bill Mueller lines one to the left-center gap. Kotsay ranges over from center to cut it off in front of the scoreboard, but bobbles it. Johnny's going to try to score anyway—at home you make them make the play. The crowd's up and loud. The relay's good, Crosby to catcher Damian Miller, but Johnny belly flops and slides a hand across the plate, and David Ortiz is there to call him safe and wrap him in a bear hug. The dugout rushes the field, mobbing Johnny and Bill Mueller, and it's a sweep. We're 46-37 and tied with Oakland for the wild card, and on *Extra Innings*, Eck is pumped. "Oakland's not going to do it," he says. "They're showing me nothing. They're done. Remember, I was the one that said it."

July 9th

Although things are heating up on *All My Children*, I was able to forego Babe's struggles with the evil JR and JR's equally evil (and well-heeled) daddy to relish the highlights of last night's 8–7 Red Sox win over the A's, completing the Sox sweep and returning Boston to a tie in the wild-card race. More important to me at this stage of the season, one three-game series away from the All-Star break, is the fact that we've managed to make up some ground against the Yankees, who have lost five of their last seven.

The papers made much this morning about Oakland's surge in the late innings of last night's game (they pounded out 17 hits, most of them against the bullpen and the key ones against Keith Foulke, who blew the save opportunity), but my take on it is more optimistic. Here's a good Oakland team that gets blown out in the first two contests of a key series, their pitching touched up for 22 runs. Trailing by six runs in the final game, they do what good teams do: fight and scratch and claw their way back into contention, trying to come away with *something*. But in the bottom of the tenth, Johnny Damon singled to left, then scored when A's center fielder Mark Kotsay bobbled Bill Mueller's line shot. It was only the smallest of bobbles—only a step's worth, surely—but Damon was running for all he was worth and that one extra step (and a hard slide across home) was just enough to win the game. It was a thrilling play, bringing the crowd at Fenway (and yours truly at home) to their feet, cheering. In the end, it was the good twin of the game Boston tried so hard to win against the Yankees and lost in thirteen innings.

So that's three. That's your little streak. Tonight we're back to Arroyo. It's up to you, Bronson: keep me away from *All My Children*.

SO: What do you think of the resurgence in Randy Johnson rumors? Could we get him for, say, Arroyo and BK, or is now the time to ship Lowe, before he walks?

And on a lesser note, did you see Ellis Burks had to go back and have surgery on that knee a second time? He'll be out till September. So, since he has three singles and a homer so far, we're paying him roughly two hundred thou a hit.

SK: A lot of talk about "blowing" that lead, but what really happened was Oakland struggling desperately to take one of three . . . and we held 'em off! Now we gotta keep going. As for the Ellis Burks thing . . . well, this is an old Red Sox trick. Next thing you know, we'll be bringing the Hawk out of retirement.

Or the Eck.

SO: Why stop with one Hawk? Bring back Andre Dawson too. Speaking of knees.

Tonight it's Bronson Arroyo versus the Rangers' Joaquin Benoit at Fenway, yet another sellout crowd. In the dugout, the Sox are goofing with an over-sized bobble-head doll of Pedro. The controversy is that Francona's given him permission to go home to the DR, since he doesn't pitch until after the break. "I bet a lot of guys would like to go home early," Jerry grouses, and he's right.

To start, Arroyo gives up a double to Soriano, but Kevin Millar makes a great snag of a liner at first to turn two and bail his pitcher out.

SK: God, but ole Bronson looked shaky in the first inning, didn't he?

I've seen tonight's plate umpire before. He played the World Champion Blind Lady in a revival of *WAIT UNTIL DARK.* Oh well, 1–0 Sox [Johnny scoring on a Manny sac fly in the bottom of the first]. Go Bronson. But shave that goat.

That umpire is a serious Cheez-Dog. Hasn't given pore ole Bronson one *single corner*. The A-man won't live long against a hard-hitting club like this getting calls like that. He's got 3 Ks through 3 2/3; with the same stuff (and the same ump), Pedro would have 7.

Benoit's thrown okay as well, but in the fifth Johnny hooks one around the Pesky Pole, and while Benoit gets the next three guys, they all hit the ball hard. In the sixth, he loads the bases with no outs. Tek Ks on three pitches before Bill Mueller hits a sac fly, and here's Johnny again, poking a wall double to score two more.

SK: Arroyo looks like the real deal tonight, don't he? At least through 7.

SO: Make that 8. [As I'm typing, Johnny hits one into the Rangers' pen.] And Johnny is just smoking. 4 for 5 with 2 dingers, 4 RBIs and 3 runs. I don't know what Papa Jack did before the Oakland series, but it stuck. Come on, D-Rays! (They're finishing the first half with the Yanks, of course.)

We win 7–0, and it's a fast game, as quick as Pedro's two-hitter against the Pods.

SO: And there you have it, a nifty three-hitter, with Curtis the Mechanic throwing a lean and clean ninth.
   So, you think we're really going to try for Randy Jo?

SK: I think we'd be fools not to try for him. Hey, what harm? Throw all the lettuce into the Saladmaster, and let's have some World Series coleslaw.
   We got four, I want some more—

SO: Hey, if John Henry's buying . . .

And in a briefly noted roster move, we send nice kid Lenny DiNardo down to Pawtucket and bring up veteran righty Joe Nelson, who didn't pitch at all last year due to injuries. He's the twenty-second pitcher we've tried in the first half.

July 10th

We're driving the kids to camp in Ohio, a nine-hour jaunt. As darkness falls, we're on I-90 west of Erie when Trudy's cell phone plinks. It's her father, excited about the game: Manny's hit two out and we're up 11–6 *in the third*. Bellhorn's made two errors behind Lowe, but atoned with a homer of his own.

Later, during the Oakland-Cleveland game, we hear an update: Sox 14–6 over Texas in the eighth. Tek's gone deep, and Nomar. Looks like five in a row, our second-longest streak of the season.

July 11th

Coming home, the only game we can pull in on the radio is the Buffalo Bisons and Durham Bulls, and all the way across the Southern Tier we listen to the Indians' and D-Rays' minor leaguers (including old Sock Midre Cummings) pay their dues. During a pitching change, the announcers dump the out-of-town scoreboard on us. "Up at Fenway, it was Texas beating the Red Sox six to five."

"Shit," I say. Notice that the first stage is anger, not denial—that comes later.

"The Yankees outlasted Tampa Bay—"

"Dammit." I sag back in my seat, defeated. I really thought they'd pay the Rangers back with a sweep, maybe even pick up a game, but no, we win two out of three from a first-place team and lose ground.

July 12th

The recap in the paper is weirdly cheery, the writer giving us credit for fighting back, as if that proves the character of the team. We were down 5–2 in the bottom of the seventh when Doug Mirabelli hit a two-run shot and then Johnny D soloed to tie it. In the eighth, Foulke gave up a run, then in the ninth, Pokey, pinch-running, got picked off first. Everyone agrees that the ump blew the call, but they also agree that the ball beat him there, it was just a high tag. Shades of Damian Jackson pinch-running against the Yanks last year and getting picked off second. It's great that we came back, sure, but that makes Foulke's blown hold that much worse. He's been shaky lately, one reason why the only games we win seem to be blowouts.

And Manny, listed on Francona's lineup card, begged off at the last minute, saying his left hamstring felt tight, giving the columnists something to gnaw on.

In the wild-card race we're still a game up on Oakland, with the Angels and Twins only a half back of them.

The Randy Johnson sweepstakes is on. The D-backs have the worst record in the majors, and Randy Jo's forty years old and can't wait for them to retool. The Sox and Yanks are interested, and possibly the Angels. The Unit seems to be having fun with all the attention, saying he can't decide which chowder he likes best, New England or Manhattan. Really, it's a no-brainer; Mr. Schill could tell him that. The guys who bring a title to Fenway will be folk heroes. In New York, he'd be just another hired gun. I mean, seriously, who'll remember Jon Lieber?

Tonight's the All-Star Home Run Derby, and Manny's stepped aside to give David Ortiz his spot. El Jefe's taken batting-practice pitcher Ino Guerrero with him to Houston as his secret weapon, but can't find his groove. He hits a girder beneath the roof, a titanic shot, but it doesn't count. He's got five outs on him before he sticks one into the upper deck and ends up with three, not enough to make the semis. Manny jogs over and sticks a Yankee cap on Ino.

July 13th

Tonight is the All-Star Game, and I find that working on this book has turned me into a kind of ex officio ballplayer in at least one way: because my team isn't playing, I have almost no interest in which show horse wins the make-believe contest.* Like the less stellar ballplayers, I'm just kicking back, watching some VH-1 (also some *All My Children* reruns on Soapnet) and enjoying my three nights off. Chillin'.

I had intended to write some sort of midseason summary, and find I have little to write. That's a good thing. Boston ended the first half winning five out of six and putting all trade rumors (except for that sweetly wistful

---

*The "almost" qualification is easily explained. Manny Ramirez and David Ortiz are playing tonight. I don't want either of them hurt, as Pedro Martinez almost certainly hurt his arm by throwing too hard in the 1999 All-Star Game.

one that has Randy Johnson in a Red Sox uniform) to rest. Their won-lost record is almost exactly what it was at the break a year ago, when they went into postseason as the AL wild-card team, and indeed they lead the wild-card race this year by a game (over the Oakland Moneyball boys).

But still . . . the gloom. Why?

Because that Reverend Dimmesdale–Hester Prynne jazz in *The Scarlet Letter* isn't just romantic bullshit, that's why. There is a very real streak of dour pessimism in the New England character, and it runs right down into the bedrock. We buy new cars expecting them to be lemons. We put in new heating systems and expect them not just to go tits-up but to do it *stealthily,* thereby suffocating the kiddies in their beds (but leaving us, their parents, to grieve and blame ourselves for at least fifty years). We understand we're never going to win the lottery, we know we'll get that unpassable and exquisitely painful gallstone on a hunting or snowmobiling trip far from medical help, and that Robert Frost was fucking-A right when he said that good fences make good neighbors. We expect the snow to turn to freezing rain, rich relatives to die leaving us nothing, and the kids (assuming they escape the Black Furnace Death) to get refused by the college of their choice. And we expect the Red Sox to lose. It's the curse, all right, but it has nothing to do with the Bambino; it's the curse of living *here,* in New England, just up that Christing potholed I-84 deathroad from the goddamn New York Yankees.

With all that at work, it's hard for the head to convince the heart how good this current Red Sox team is—the front three pitchers are solid, the hitting is fearsome from one to seven (I hate that Youkilis, an on-base machine, is sitting on the bench so much, though), and on a good night the defense is adequate. Terry Francona has shown mediocre managerial skills at best in the first half, but he's also shown a willingness to learn. Sure, the Yankees are the elephant in the living room; at 55-31, they are the best team in major league baseball (given their incredible payroll, they *better* be). But let's brush aside a little of our natural Red Sox/New England gloom here long enough to point that at 48-38, the Red Sox are ten games over .500, and that other than the Yankees, only Texas in the AL and St. Louis in the NL have better records*. . . plus we just beat Texas

---

*The Los Angeles Dodgers were also 48-38 at the break, good enough to lead the NL West by half a game.

two out of three. Now that we have our big guys back and starting to hit the ball, I think we'll be in it till the very end, be it bitter or sweet. That's as far as I'm willing to go right now, but I think in mid-July, that's quite far enough. When I get the glooms, I just tell myself things could be a lot worse.

I could be writing a book about Seattle (32-54), for example. Case closed.

It's 1–0 AL in the first inning of the All-Star Game, and Clemens is struggling (Jason Schmidt should have started for the NL, but politics is all). With one aboard, he gets two strikes on Manny. Yankee groupie and chucklehead blabbermouth Tim McCarver hasn't brought up the fact that it was Clemens's high fastball to Manny in the ALCS last year that sparked the Pedro-Zimmer brawl. He doesn't have time now, as Clemens misses his location, serving Manny a thigh-high fastball on the inside of the plate, and Manny lines it into the left-field seats for a two-run shot. And while this is only a silly exhibition game, it's a measure of vindication and revenge. Not a word from McCarver, as if his memory banks have been wiped clean.

Clemens gives up 6 runs in the first, and I wonder if batterymate Mike Piazza is telling the hitters what's coming. Speaking of revenge.

Later, when the AL lead is 7–4, David Ortiz outdoes his amigo, going upper deck on former Sox prospect Carl Pavano for a two-run job, sealing the win. It's the first time AL teammates have gone deep since Cleveland's Al Lopez and Larry Doby in 1954. Not Mantle and Berra or McGwire and Canseco or even Lynn and Rice, but Ramirez and Ortiz. I'm thinking maybe they'll give Manny and David a joint MVP award, but the game's being played in Houston (at old Enron Field, with the elder Bush in the front row), and they give it to Texas's Alfonso Soriano for his three-run shot, which was just padding at the time. Still, I'm proud that we represented, even with Mr. Schill not throwing. And, as I e-mail Steve, after playing on the road throughout the playoffs last year, we can sure use the home-field advantage.

SK: Yep. Otherwise, I don't care. What's the comparison between the Red Sox won/lost record for last year versus this year at the All-Star break?

SO: Last year we were 55-38 at the break and only two games back (compared with 48-38 and 7 back this year). According to the archives on redsox.com, folks were stoked about our surprising offense (and especially impressed with Theo's pickups like Ortiz, Millar, Todd Walker and Bill Mill, and the explosive debut of just-acquired Gabe Kapler), though still worried about our pen. We may have blown some late-inning heartbreakers, but the swoon waited until after we pulled within a game of the Yanks in late July.

July 15th

The newest Randy Johnson rumor has Theo shipping Nomar to Arizona. It's too much, even if we don't think we can re-sign him. The idea's weird: Nomar reunited with his free-swinging pal Shea.

Meanwhile, due to league rules, Mendoza has to be promoted to the big club or released, so to make room for him, Theo and Terry send Kevin Youkilis down to Pawtucket—unfair. Since Bill Mueller's been back, there's no position for him, but it seems a shame not to carry him as a pinch hitter.

Tonight it's Lowe versus Jarrod Washburn out in Anaheim, a 10:05 start. I've been jonesing for some ball since last Friday, and plan on staying up for it. Last time I did this, Vladimir Guerrero had nine RBIs; I figure this has got to be better. The Yanks have already beaten Detroit, so—again—we need this one.

From the start there are problems. Manny's hamstring's bothering him again, so Francona's moved him to DH, Ortiz to first (scratching McCarty) and Millar to left—a shift that leaves us weaker at two positions. Unless his quad's still iffy, Trot's sitting because Washburn's a lefty (weak, since even Dauber was allowed to hit against lefties in 2002), so we've got slightly better defense in right. Kapler proves it in the third, cutting off a ball toward the line, then spinning and gunning speedy Chone Figgins at second. But Millar just can't cover the territory in left. A pop fly down the line falls between him, Bill Mueller and Nomar—just foul. The batter singles on the next pitch, and even though he doesn't score, it means Lowe has to get four outs, and his pitch count is climbing. He's throwing well, though, not walking people, fighting to the end of every at-bat.

In the fourth, with first and second and two down, at the end of a long battle on a full count, Figgins lofts a similar pop-up down the line. Bill

Mueller goes hard, Nomar trailing him. Billy realizes he's not going to get there and looks to Millar, who's pulled up, running at half-speed, and by the time Kevin realizes it's his ball, he can't get there. The ball drops a foot inside the line, and Bengie Molina, who's been jogging home out of sheer habit, crosses the plate, and the runners end up on second and third. The TV shows Millar back at his position. I've been pacing the room, stopping in front of the set for each pitch. Now I lean down and jab at the screen like Lewis Black. "Why do you suck so much?"

Shaken, on the next batter Lowe steps off the back of the rubber with the wrong foot, balking. Mike Scioscia's up and out of the dugout, pointing. It should bring in a run, but the ump doesn't call it, and we sneak out of a jam.

In the top of the fifth, we get the run right back, but in the bottom of the inning, Lowe tires. With Darin Erstad on second, Molina singles to left. Millar has the ball in his glove before Erstad rounds third, and Erstad's just coming off a leg injury, but Millar's a first baseman, and his throw is weak and low, bouncing three times as Erstad slips past Tek. Embree's been up for a while, and Lowe's over 100 pitches, so he's done. He pitched well enough for a quality start. If he has a real left fielder, the game's still 1–1.

Embree should be well rested, but can't muscle a fastball by Adam Kennedy, who singles. Little David Eckstein, who has no home runs, misses one by five feet, doubling off the wall in left-center, scoring Molina. Figgins singles to center, and soon it's 6–1. It's midnight, and I think about going to bed, but hang in, only to see Curtis Leskanic groove one to Erstad for a two-run shot. We're down seven runs and dredging the bottom of the bullpen, while the Angels can always call on twin closers K-Rod and Troy Percival, so good night, nurse.

In bed I'm still pissed off. It's a demoralizing loss, with little good to point to, and against a club that—if we're really contenders—we need to beat. We're now 0-3 against them, and we're plainly a sub-.500 club on the road. We're eight back. I try not to overreact. Part of it is that I'd been waiting so long to see them play, and they played badly. It's just one game, and it's a four-game set. Pedro's going tomorrow. The season's long. Breathe.

July 16th

I must admit the second half of the season got off to an inauspicious start last night in Anaheim. The Red Sox, who rarely do well on the West Coast (at least during the regular season), put on a particularly vile show against the Angels, losing 8–1. Derek Lowe, although victimized by poor defense behind him (not for the first time this year, either), did not exactly cover himself with glory, either. In other news, the Sox sent down the on-base machine known as the Greek God of Walks in favor of a middle reliever whose last name is Martinez. Any resemblance to the Sox starter of the same name simply does not exist.

This could be a long road trip.

SK: And here's how we start the second half: by losing to the Angels (big) and sending on-base machine Kevin Youkilis back to triple-A to make room for a mediocre pitcher. The conventional wisdom once more clamps down. You build an expensive multimillion-dollar racing machine and give it to a clodhopping middle manager with a cheek full o' chaw. This is dopey-ball, not moneyball.

Disgusted in Maine,

Steve

SO: I feared the vengeance of the disappointed fiend. —Franconastein

---

Now the papers have Nomar going to the Cubs for prospects we then ship to Arizona for Randy Jo. Seeing as we're eight games out, all this talk seems frivolous and off-target. We just need to play better. Now.

But the All-Star break is a good time to panic. Houston, right at .500 despite signing Clemens, Pettitte, Jeff Kent and Carlos Beltran, fires ex-Sox skipper Jimy Williams. Seattle, dead last in the West, continues its fire sale of high-priced veterans, tagging John Olerud, one of the best hitters of the era, for reassignment—meaning, essentially, they're cutting him, hoping a contender like the Sox will want his stick (and Gold Glove at first) and pick up his salary.

Tonight's another 10:05 start, and despite my history, I decide to stay up and watch this one to the end. The Yanks have already lost to Detroit, Mike Maroth one-hitting them, so we have a chance to make up a game. Manny's not starting, and—one day too late—Francona's figured out the right lineup: Trot in right, Kapler in left, Ortiz DHing, Millar at first, Pokey at second. It's the same lineup Trudy proposed last night before quitting on the game. "How much is he getting paid?" she asks.

Kelvim Escobar's throwing 95, Pedro 94. Home-plate ump Matt Hollowell is squeezing both of them, and Nomar takes advantage of it, leading off the second with a first-pitch homer to left-center when Escobar tries to get ahead with a fastball down the pipe. Here's how much Hollowell's squeezing them: in the bottom of the inning, Pedro issues back-to-back walks to their number six and seven hitters.

With the tight strike zone, both pitchers' counts are rising. In the bottom of the fourth, Pedro has Guillen 0-2 with two down and decides to challenge him. Guillen catches up to the fastball and sends it to deepest center. Johnny goes back to the wall and leaps. Jerry thinks he has the ball when he comes down, but Johnny takes off his glove and flips it to show it's empty.

Pedro looks tough, despite the umpiring. In one stretch through the middle innings, he strikes out six of his last seven batters (in one cruel at-bat, he throws five straight changes to Jeff DaVanon, then gets him on a 3-2 fastball down Broadway), but with two down in the sixth he walks Guillen, who steals second (that's smallball, running with two out and a decent hitter at the plate) so Erstad's single brings him in. It's a one-run game and Pedro's thrown 115 pitches. This one's down to the pen.

In the top of the seventh, Scot Shields gets a gift third-strike call against David Ortiz on a pitch up and in that's been a ball all night. Ortiz turns on Hollowell—he's not the first to have words with him—and by the time Francona can run out and get between them, Hollowell's tossed him. Ortiz wants a piece of him, and Sveum, bench coach Brad Mills and Papa Jack have to help Francona restrain him. He's still mad when they bull him over to the dugout. He yanks two of his bats out of the rack and flings them in the direction of home plate. They nearly hit two other umps standing on the first-base line. It's a dumb move—he'll probably end up getting suspended, and we need his bat. At the same time, Jerry and Sean agree that Hollowell's been so bad that it was just a matter of who was going to blow up on him.

Curtis Leskanic gets two quick outs in the seventh on two hard-hit balls, then gives up a single to Eckstein before being pulled for Embree. Like last night, Embree gives up a hit to the first guy he sees. It's first and third for Garret Anderson, and I'm having flashbacks. He's 1 for 10 lifetime against Embree, but that doesn't comfort me. He grounds to the hole between first and second, a tough play for a mortal second baseman—an adventure for a Todd Walker—but Pokey makes it look routine, and once again I'm glad we have him. He could go 0 for 200 and I'd still want him out there.

It's a four-game series, and Scioscia wants two innings out of Shields. Shields has his fastball popping, but for some reason tries a curve on 3-2 to Kapler. It hangs belt-high, and Gabe puts it into the third row in left for his second of the season, and we've got some breathing room.

Timlin sets up, with McCarty at first, and gets a brilliant play from Pokey on a chopper, snagging a short-hop a foot from the bag at second and gunning Guillen. Foulke's the recipient of a tumbling shoestring grab by Kapler on his way to a one-two-three ninth. We win, and look good doing it. I'm surprised to see it's 1:17: it's been a tight game all night, well played if poorly umpired, definitely worth staying up for. The Angels are a good club; it took everything we had to win this one, and that's satisfying. Let's come back and play this way tomorrow.

July 17th

Saturday night, and by the time we switch over from the hilariously stiff *They Are Among Us* on the Sci-Fi channel, the resurrected El Duque and the Yanks have beaten Detroit and Wake's given up three runs in the first. Colon walks the bases loaded in the second, but Johnny flies out. Vladimir Guerrero, looking like an MVP candidate, bombs a high knuckler onto the rocks, and it's 4–0. Not only is Manny not playing, Bill Mueller is nowhere to be seen, and because it's Wake throwing, Mirabelli's catching, meaning (with the shift of Bellhorn to third) we've added Kapler, Pokey and Doug to a lineup already struggling to score runs.

A scary play in the fourth, when hefty Jose Molina lines one at Wake's head. He ducks, and it nails him in the back, just above the 9 in 49, and ricochets—still playable—high into the air. Nomar snares it coming across the bag for a pop out, but Tim's still down. On the replay it catches him solidly, and I think he's got to leave the game, but he takes some warm-up tosses and stays in. On his first pitch, Adam Kennedy cranks a flat knuckler into the right-field seats.

In the fifth, Johnny gets one back with a line-drive homer down the short right-field line, but that's it. New guy Joe Nelson relieves. #57, he features "The Vulcan," a breaking ball gripped between his middle and ring fingers so his hand is split like Spock's live-long-and-prosper sign. In the sixth, Nelson loads them, and Francona, considering this one finished, calls on Jimmy Anderson, who throws two straight wild pitches, then gives up a single to Garret Anderson. It's 8–1 and 12:30, and I'm done.

July 18th

The final last night was 8–3. All I missed was a pair of solo shots by Johnny and Big Papi. Today's a 1:05 Pacific time start, meaning I won't have to stay up till one-thirty. And Mr. Schill's on the hill, though I must say I'm getting a little grumpy with the club only winning his and Pedro's starts (they're a combined 13-1 since mid-May). Wake and Lowe have been shaky, sure, but we've also given up 40 unearned runs behind them.

Manny's sitting again, with Kapler filling in in left, McCarty at first and Bellhorn at second. Good news, though: the Tigers have beaten the Yanks, so we can get back to seven with a win.

As the game gets under way, the TV presents us with a mystery. Anaheim's a fine team, we're a marquee club with a large following, and it's a beautiful Sunday afternoon, yet the outfield sections are half-filled and there are empty rows all around the ballpark. Do the Angels fans deserve this team (this day, this game)?

In the first, David Ortiz powers one off the wall in left-center. Mike Scioscia's resting everyday left fielder Jose Guillen, and veteran Tim Salmon can't get over quick enough to back up the carom, giving David a gift triple. Right-hander John Lackey, a number four starter at best, strikes out the side, and comes back in the second to strike out two more.

Schilling's cruising too, and then in the third he hangs a curve to hefty Bengie Molina, who puts it into the left-field stands for a 1–0 lead. Lackey bears down, snapping off a curve that gets lefties like Tek and Trot and Bill Mueller; by the fifth he's struck out a season-high 7.

Entering the sixth, both pitchers have given up two hits, but Schilling's pitch count is rising. With one down, Johnny works a walk. Bellhorn follows with a single through the right side. Maybe Lackey's tired, because his fastball to David Ortiz is knee-high and in, right where David likes them, and Big Papi golfs it over the fence in right.

With his next pitch, Lackey drills Nomar in the elbow. The ump warns both benches, and Scioscia hustles out to argue. It's stupid, since the warning hurts us more than them. Now if Schilling retaliates, he gets tossed. The ump should wait till we even things up, then say, "Okay, boys, that's enough."

Lackey flags. He loads the bases and gets out of it only because McCarty hits a bullet to Figgins at third. For some reason Scioscia leaves him in, and Kapler greets him in the seventh with a leadoff homer on another knee-high, 90 mph fastball. Johnny doubles down the line, and, too late, Scioscia goes to Scot Shields. Ortiz singles Johnny in for his third hit and fourth RBI of the day, then scores when Nomar triples off the scoreboard in right.

With a 6–1 lead, Schilling goes after Guerrero in the seventh, blowing him away with a 94 mph fastball down the pipe. He strikes out the side, like Pedro signing a win. He's up to 100 pitches, so I'm surprised when he comes out in the eighth. He Ks Salmon, then plunks Molina (who hit the home run earlier) right in the ass. Molina looks out at him with both hands open—what's up? Schilling's had great control all day, and there's no doubt this one's payback. With the warning in place, the ump should toss him, but, inexplicably, doesn't. Scioscia storms out of the dugout and plants himself in front of the ump, one hand on his hip, the other jabbing the air as he unleashes a stream of profanity we can easily lip-read. The ump tosses him, and while it's unfair—maybe *because* it's so unfair—we laugh.

Timlin closes—poorly, opening the ninth by giving up back-to-back singles to Figgins and Garret Anderson and a run on a sac fly by Guerrero (about thirty feet short of the rocks), but finally gets out of it with a pair of ground balls, and we're off to Seattle to face the terrible Mariners.

Manny Ramirez is day-to-day with sore hamstrings (any number of sportswriters seem to think he's malingering, but let's see some of those overweight juiceheads get out there and run around left field for a few days) and Tim Wakefield took a fearsome line drive in the back last night, but we split four with Anaheim in their house, and to me that's a great escape. We may even have picked up a game on the Yankees, who continue to struggle—go figure—against the Tigers. Still, the Red Sox look maddeningly lackadaisical, a befogged team of grizzled male Alices in baseball Wonderland.

But Schilling was great again today. As my younger son would no doubt say, he's so money he doesn't *know* he's money. Two more like him and never mind the World Series; the Red Sox would be ready for the Super Bowl.

July 19th

Another 10:05 start, another sleepless night. The Yanks have already lost to Tampa Bay, and when Tek breaks a 1–1 tie with a three-run bomb off J. J. Putz in the eighth, it looks like we'll be six back. Arroyo's thrown brilliantly, striking out 12 (including 11 straight outs by strikeout at one point), and the only run Seattle scored was due to some typical sloppy fielding.

Because Schilling went so deep yesterday, the pen is rested. Embree and Timlin set up and combine to let in a cheapie, abetted by Bill Mueller winging a double-play ball past Bellhorn into right field, but Timlin gets a big strikeout with two in scoring position to end the inning.

Foulke comes in to close. With one down, he gives up a solo shot to Miguel Olivo.

"They sure don't make it easy on us," I tell Steph and my nephews. All the other adults have long since gone to bed.

Edgar Martinez is next. At forty-one, he can't run, so all Foulke has to do is throw him three low changes and he's meat. Instead, Foulke throws him an 88 mph fastball over the heart of the plate. Edgar's been killing this pitch since he was fifteen, and doesn't miss. Johnny and Kapler both leap at the wall in right-center, but it's gone, the M's have gone back-to-back, and the game's tied.

"Unbelievable," I say. The boys are angry and want Francona to take him out, but we don't have anyone else. Embree, Timlin, Foulke—this is our A-team.

Foulke gets the last out on a long fly to right, then struggles so much in the tenth that the boys quit. It's 1:15 in the morning and we have to get up early tomorrow. Overall, Foulke throws 41 pitches. After starting the year 10 for 10 in save opportunities, he's 4 for his next 9, and that shaky streak started against Seattle, that Sunday game when Raul Ibanez took him into the pen and McCarty bailed him out in extras with a walk-off job.

In the eleventh, McCarty, leading off, gets on on an error. Kapler bunts too hard down third, and they get the force at second. Again, we've got no smallball. Kapler takes second anyway on a wild pitch, but Bellhorn looks at a very wide strike three, and Johnny flies to left.

Since Foulke's gone two, we have to bring in Leskanic. He gets behind Olivo 3-1, and Olivo singles through the hole. Dave Hansen wants to bunt him across. Curtis does the job for him, walking him. Then, in what must be seen as team play in Japan, on the very first pitch Ichiro bunts them over. Francona intentionally walks Randy Winn and pulls the infield in for Bret Boone. On 0-1, Boone hits a fly to left-center. It's deep enough to score the run, so the fielders ignore it and jog in as the ball clears the wall for a walk-off grand slam. It's 1:45, and I'm so pissed off that I'm glad they lost, because they suck. (See—it's not *we* now, it's *they*; the loss is so deranging that for a few minutes I have to separate myself from the team.)

They didn't hit or field for Arroyo. The three-run shot by Tek was a gift. All they needed was six outs, against the worst team in the league.

I want to blame someone, and the obvious target is Foulke. But I know that closers blow games. Even Eric Gagne blew one the other day. And while it's true that the pen hasn't looked good lately, Theo hasn't helped matters by picking up retreads like Anderson, Nelson and Leskanic. Mendoza, who should be covering some of these middle innings, is taking up a roster spot but may never pitch another meaningful at-bat in the majors. But Theo didn't give up back-to-back jacks.

It's just a loss, a brutal, late-night, extra-inning loss of a game we should have won, a game we needed (since we need all of them now), and there's nothing to do but eat it and go on.

July 20th

It's also the kind of loss that makes you nervous the next time the game's on the line, and tonight we get a nightmarish rerun of last night when Lowe has to leave early with a blister and Seattle chips away at our 8–1 lead until it's 9–7 in the ninth, with two on and no out and Foulke sweating buckets. Seattle has 18 hits, including 4 from Ichiro (along with 4 stolen bases), but has left 14 on.

Because of last night, I don't believe in Foulke at all. He could give up another walk-off job to Boone here, and I'd just shrug. Because I'm still pissed off at him (at *them*). The Yanks have already won, so a loss would drop us 8 back, and I think, fuck it. 7, 8, 9—it doesn't matter. If we keep losing on the road like this, we don't deserve to be in any race.

Foulke doesn't try to nibble like last night. He leads with his fastball to get ahead, then goes exclusively to the change. He strikes out Boone. Strikes out Edgar. Strikes out Bucky Jacobsen for the game.

For an instant, as the ump rings up Jacobsen, I'm excited, but I cool off just as quickly. We barely squeaked this one out, and it should have been a laugher, after an eight-run fourth (David Ortiz with a three-run bomb, then Manny going back-to-back). Same problem as always: no middle relief. Leskanic let two of Lowe's runners score. In his one inning, Timlin gave up a run. Nelson allowed two runs and only retired one man. Mendoza sat on the bench and watched. Kim was in Columbus with the PawSox. I have no idea where Theo was.

July 21st

SO: Thanks for the tickets for tomorrow and the weekend. This six-game home stand is crucial, after the ugly road trip. A bad time to stumble, since the Yanks are faltering as well. Kevin Brown pitched against the PawSox last night and looked good, so he may be back sooner than we might wish.

SK: Last night's win was just about as ugly as they get. I'll take .500 on the road, especially on the West Coast, but we had a chance to come back 4-2, and in much better shape. I'm reading *Moneyball* now, and it's really a jaw-dropping book. Lewis asserts, with no reservations whatever, that Art Howe is no more than the ventriloquist's dummy on Billy Beane's knee. Which leads me to wonder if that is now true in Boston— i.e., if Terry Francona is the dummy on Theo Epstein's knee. And, if Epstein is following the Beane paradigm, then our team is in middling good shape assuming Theo is planning trades before the deadline. Beane feels good if he can go into the second half of the season six or less back. Still, I don't buy into everything the book suggests, either from the standpoint of strategy, and certainly not from the standpoint of business morality.

SO: My main argument with *Moneyball* is that the modest success of the A's is based on Mulder, Hudson and Zito, and it's pretty much a matter of luck that they came up at the same time and fulfilled the scouts' expectations. So many prospects don't, but these three did. Otherwise, the no-running, no-fielding, big OBP club has trouble scoring when it doesn't hit three-run home runs—hey, just like us! Billy

Beane's always crowing about his genius, but look at the Twins, who've put together a better, steadier club with even less money. They've lost core guys like Eric Milton and A. J. Pierzynski, yet they keep on keepin' on. And for a solid club that knows how to play the game, I'll take the smallball Angels any day, even with their terrible starters.

SK: I disagree. They were a certain *type* of ballplayer, picked for talent and affordability. And in the case of Zito, the scouts hated him. He was Beane's pick.

All that aside, this year's Red Sox team is a sick entity right now, and I hate it. I keep going back in my mind to one of those games versus the Angels. We're down by at least three runs, and maybe five. There are two out, and the Angels pitcher is struck wild. There are two on for us and Pokey at the plate. He puts on a heroic at-bat, finally drawing a walk to load them for Johnny Damon, who swings at the first pitch he sees—*the first motherfucking pitch he sees!*—and lines out to center. The fielder didn't even have to take a step. That's just deer-in-the-headlights baseball. Something going on around here, what it is ain't precisely clear . . . but I'm *not* lovin' it.

SO: It's the twenty-first, meaning Theo's got ten days to close his deals. I think we've got to land a quality arm, probably a starter who lets Arroyo be the middle-relief ace (a huge advantage, since no one out there has a Mendoza-type guy, and Nelson and Anderson are fire-starters). But I'm not holding my breath.

First-pitch hitting is a killer, but Johnny obviously thought the guy was going to groove one to try to get ahead (like Foulke last night—any of those guys swings at that 88 mph double-A-quality fastball and it's "See ya!").

SK: I thought of that, but it's *still* a bonehead move. One of the things Lewis points out in *Moneyball*—courtesy of Bill James and the sabermetrics guys—is that batting average goes up seventy-five points if a batter takes the first pitch and that pitch is a ball. He also reminds the reader of Boggs, who *always* took the first pitch, and Hatteberg, who mostly does.

SO: What hurts is watching all these opportunities go by, and that's also a product of the OBP thing. Speaking of guys who always took one: Roberto Clemente. The Anti-Nomar. [Nomar is a notorious first-pitch hitter, regardless of the game situation, just as the Great One *never* swung at a first pitch.]

Do you believe we're tied for the wild card? Seems impossible, the way we've been playing. Almost wish the D-Rays would reel off another eleven straight to shake things up. Somnambulism, baby, that's where we're at.

At least tonight I won't have to stay up till 1:45 to watch us tank.

No, only till the sixth inning, when Tejada breaks a 3–3 tie with a bases-loaded single to left. Pedro, who's been missing his spots all night, nearly gets out of it, but Johnny's throw on Javy Lopez's short sac fly is weak and up the first-base line, and it's 6–3. Earlier, Johnny misjudged a Tejada liner into a triple, leading to their first three runs, and later, in a whacky play, he relays a David Newhan shot to the wall in center toward Bill Mueller (who started, bizarrely, at second, with Youk at third), but Manny—in another classic Manny move—intercepts it, diving, then relays it to Bellhorn (who started at short), and by the time Mark guns it to Tek, Newhan's in with the easiest inside-the-park homer you'll ever see. It's 8–4 and the Faithful boo. Melvin Mora follows with a single, and Petey's done. Mendoza throws a third of an inning and gives up two hits, and Malaska has to save him. Then Jimmy "I'm the Boss" Anderson comes on and gives up his usual two runs before recording an out. It's a 10–4 final, and with the Yanks stomping Toronto, we drop to 8 back.

The only Sock who comes out of this one looking good is Gabe Kapler, who made a tumbling catch in right in the fourth, then hit a three-run shot onto the Monster to tie it at 3. The rest of the team looked like they'd gotten about three hours of sleep, which they did, since their plane got in at three in the morning (shades of Opening Day).

Meanwhile, lots of roster moves right before game time. Pokey to the DL with a pulled rib-cage muscle, Youkilis up from Pawtucket. Joe Nelson down, Malaska up. And to have a backup for Nomar, Theo picked up journeyman shortstop Ricky Gutierrez from the Iowa Cubs. Ladies and gentlemen, your 2004 Iowa Red Sox!

July 22nd

SK: I'm off to Los Angeles. I'm leaving this crucial home stand to your guidance, and probably a good thing. They looked so mizzable last night, didn't they?

It's a day-night doubleheader today, and since Wake's scheduled to start and the Yanks are coming in tomorrow, we can't shift the rotation to cover the extra game. We don't announce a starter till late morning: Abe Alvarez, a lefty from double-A Portland (Jimmy "I'm the Boss" Anderson is designated for assignment). #59, Abe's pipe-cleaner skinny and looks about seventeen. He wears his cap cocked to the side like C. C. Sabathia, but throws soft—fastball topping out at 88, slow curve, change. He has trouble finding the plate in the first and gives up three runs, two on a Monster shot by Tejada, who is just murdering us this series.

It's hot—sweaty hot, heatstroke hot—and we're in the sun. Over the course of the game I buy ten bottles of water for Steph and the nephews. We squirt them in our hats and down our collars and at each other. "Hey, frozen lemonade!" "Hey, sports bah!"

Ortiz hits two triples, a kind of miracle, but doesn't score either time. Melvin Mora lofts a shot toward the Sox bullpen that Trot has the angle on, but at the last second he gets alligator arms and shies away from the wall, and it goes over. The Faithful boo him—very rare.

We also boo villain Karim Garcia every time he steps in. It's his first visit to Fenway since he jumped the bullpen wall during last year's ALCS to punch and kick a groundskeeper his buddy Jeff Nelson was already assaulting. "You're a goon, Garcia!" we holler. When he strikes out midway through the game, the crowd behind the O's dugout stands and jeers at him—maybe the most satisfying moment of the day.

Abe Alvarez leaves with the score 5–1. He hasn't pitched well, but he's battled, and for a double-A guy the beefed-up O's are a tough assignment. Francona goes to a triple-A guy, Mystery Malaska, who gives up a run. Millar, who's been booed every at-bat since he hit into an early rally-killing DP, crushes a two-run shot to bring us within three, but in the ninth Francona goes to Mendoza (our washed-up guy), and Mora pounds a two-run bomb to put the game out of reach.

All afternoon we've been watching the New York–Toronto score, 0–0 in the third, the fourth, the sixth. It's been stuck in the eighth for more than an hour, as if they're purposely withholding it. Now that we've lost, it changes to a 1–0 Yankees final. We're nine back, the deepest hole we've been in all year, and 2-6 against the O's.

After the game, as we're fighting traffic on Storrow Drive and then 93 and 95, the Sox option Abe to Portland, making room for Ricky Gutierrez. Trudy wonders how much they paid him for the guest spot.

Between games, Bill Mueller, who went 0 for 5, decides to shave his head for luck like Trot and Tek and Gabe.

And the league office informs David Ortiz that he's received a five-game suspension for throwing his bats the other night in Anaheim.

For the nightcap, the O's roll out *their* kid pitcher with a high number, #61, Dave Borkowski. Gutierrez gets the start at short, Youk at third, McCarty in left. McCarty's a revelation. We know he's got a great glove as a first baseman, and an arm that can top 90 mph. In the first, he puts those together, snagging what ought to be an easy sac fly and nailing speedy leadoff man Brian Roberts at home with a perfect one-hop peg. It kills what could be a big inning, and in our half, with two down, he slices a bases-loaded single to right to give us a 3–0 lead.

Wake's crafty tonight, or maybe the O's are tired. Both teams are listless, and it's a quick one. Youk hits a solo shot into the second row of M5. Timlin sets up with a one-two-three eighth, then Embree gets a double-play ball in the ninth, and a strikeout to close it. A neat 4–0 final, and it's only 9:30.

It's a win, but losing two of three to the O's before the Yanks roll in is disheartening. Like Steve said, they're miserable, and I'm miserable, and the rumors that we'll trade Nomar while we can still get something for him are more miserable still.

July 23rd

The crowd around Fenway before game time is typical of a Yankee–Red Sox game: more loudmouth drunks, more shutterbugs and gawkers, more shills handing out free stuff, but at eight and a half back it's hard to muster any showdown spirit. Call this one a grudge match, with the Sox trying to save some face. WEEI's K posters say: SCHILLING IS THRILLING, and we hope he has enough to beat retread Jon Lieber.

Outside Gate E, a guy's wearing a T-shirt that says DAVID ORTIZ FAN CLUB with a picture not of Big Papi but of Esther Rolle as Florida in *Good Times*. On the back it has what I hope is a fictional quote from him: "This is not hot sauce, this is not barbecue sauce, this is the Boston Red Sauce."

Steph and I are the first in and man the corner for BP. A lot of the Sox have their kids with them in the outfield, wearing miniature versions of their uniforms.

Jeter and A-Rod throw, and Jeter backs up till he's right beside me. He's wearing Nike spikes with the logo of the leaping Michael Jordan.

"Now, the way Michael Jordan hit," I ask, "isn't it bad luck to wear his spikes?"

"I wouldn't know," Jeter says dully, as if he doesn't care.

After BP, we roll around to the Sox dugout. It takes a while, since the aisles are clogged with newbies and Yankee fans who can't find their seats. They stop and stare at their expensive eBay tickets and then up at the poles of the grandstands, as if having difficulty reading numbers. "Keep it moving," we say.

We make it to Steve's seats in time for the anthem, which is live and not Memorex (as it has been in the past), the proof being the guest Irish tenor botching the words—"the last twilight's glea-ming," "the rockets' red glares." Nice job, Dermot.

As the game starts, again I have this sense of letdown. It's Friday night, a packed house, Schilling on the mound against the Yanks, but we've played so poorly lately that it's sapped the drama out of the matchup. We still chant "*BAL*-CO" when Sheffield steps in, but halfheartedly.

When he takes Schilling out, hooking a Monster shot, all of that changes. Maybe it's a sense of fair play, honest outrage at Sheffield getting away with his steroid use, or maybe it's just hurt, but for the rest of the game, whenever Sheffield or Giambi come up, we greet them with "LIFE-TIME BAN, LIFE-TIME BAN" and "Mar-i-on Jo-ones! Marrrr-i-ooonnn!"

Lieber's hittable, and in the second Trot doubles in Nomar, then Bill Mueller launches one into the bullpen, and we're up 3–1. Millar tacks on a solo shot in the fourth, and with Schilling only up to 54 pitches, we're looking good.

In the fifth, Mr. Schill gives up a leadoff single to Posada, then another to Matsui. Enrique Wilson flies one to left that looks like trouble, but it quails and Manny hauls it in on the track. Kenny Lofton follows with a ripped single to right. It should score the runner, except the runner's Posada. Trot fires a one-hopper to Tek. Posada beats the throw, but Tek's got the plate blocked. We can hear the plastic clack as Posada knocks into his shin guards. Tek spins and tags Posada's shoulder, and he's out.

No, he's safe—ump Tim Timmons is calling him safe. Tek looks down at the plate openmouthed with shock. Schilling races from his backup position, pointing. Francona trots over from the dugout. The crowd's been booing the whole time, but the argument's quick and civil, Timmons laughing, as if there's no way he could be wrong.

Our neighbor Mason later sees the replay upstairs. "He was out," he says, "but it was a tough call."

"Yeah," I concede, "you'd have to be a professional umpire to make it."

The run throws Schilling off, and he loads them before overpowering Jeter (who looks lost at the plate) and getting a force on Sheffield.

In the sixth, A-Rod takes Schilling to 3-2 and then fouls off a few fastballs before singling up the middle. Giambi goes to 3-2 and fouls a few over the second deck, then walks on a curveball that stays up—terrible pitch selection. Posada goes 3-2, fouls off a couple, then singles through the right side. Bases loaded, nobody out, and Schill's pitch count is in the high 80s. He works deliberately to Matsui and gets a hard hopper to Millar at first. It should be a double play, but Millar's throw to Nomar is high and off the bag to the infield side, and Schilling doesn't get over to first fast enough. Nomar holds the ball rather than risk throwing it away. 4–3 Sox, runners at the corners.

Formerly washed-up Ruben Sierra pinch-hits for Enrique Wilson. Schilling has him 0-2 quickly, and Sierra has to fend off a good inside pitch with a protective swing. It's a nubber down first, a swinging bunt. Millar fields it on the run. It looks like he's got a play right in front of him at home on Giambi, but he glances back at first—Schilling's assumed he'll go home and hasn't covered—and has to eat the ball. The Faithful boo.

When Lofton sneaks a soft double past Millar that McCarty would have stopped, we boo harder.

That's it for Schilling, a frustrating end to a promising start. Usually our defense backs him up better than this, but if he can't get a fastball past the "intestinal parasite"–weakened Giambi, then he didn't have it anyway.

Timlin comes on, and washed-up Bernie Williams rips a double into the right-field corner, scoring two. 7–4 Yankees, and more booing, curses, then a disappointed (disapproving) silence.

When Millar comes up in our sixth, the crowd boos him lustily. "He hit a home run his last at-bat," Steph points out. You can see Millar's pissed off in the on-deck circle, focused, his teeth clenched. He rocks a Paul Quantrill fastball onto the Monster for his second solo shot, and when he crosses the plate, though the kids in the front row do the we're-not-worthy salaam, his expression hasn't changed.

In the seventh, Johnny singles, then scores on Tek's double to left-center when Matsui boots the ball. Ortiz walks, and we've got first and second, nobody out, and Manny up. So far Manny's 0 for 3 with 2 Ks, but we rise and chant his name, expecting deliverance. He grounds into an easy 6-4-3 DP, and the crowd mutters. Formerly washed-up Tom Gordon then hits Nomar in the shoulder, but Trot flies to center.

Curtis Leskanic comes on in the eighth, causing some consternation, and throws a one-two-three inning. Then Millar (cheered now) leads off with a blast onto the Monster to tie the game, his third homer of the night, and the place is louder than it's been since the playoffs. We're watching a great game, fuck the Yankees, fuck the standings. We stand and cheer through half of Bill Mueller's at-bat, but Millar—justifiably—doesn't come out for a curtain call.

Billy singles, and since he'd be the go-ahead run, Kapler pinch-runs for him. With nobody out Bellhorn needs to bunt him over. Is there anyone on the bench who can bunt better? No, not with Ricky already done and Pokey on the DL. Bellhorn fouls off two, then hits a weak grounder and has to hustle to avoid being doubled up.

"Simple fundamental baseball," I say.

"*Little League* baseball," Mason says.

Johnny doubles. Instead of Kapler scoring, Bellhorn is held at third. We still have two shots at getting him in, but Tek—batting second for some crazy reason—chases a slider from Gordon in the dirt on 3-2, as does Ortiz, and we go to the ninth tied at 7.

Foulke's in to hold it. After several questionable ball calls by Timmons (and no argument at all by Francona), Sheffield arcs one toward the Monster that looks gone. A couple fans in the front row reach down, and it hits ten feet from the top for a double. A-Rod singles him in—it's that simple,

217

a poor pitch by Foulke, a good swing by the Mariner shortstop—I mean the Texas shortstop . . . you know what I mean.

It's 8–7 for Mariano Rivera in the ninth. Timmons's blown call at home has been big all game, but it's massive now. Mo has no problem getting Manny, Nomar and Trot, leaving Kevin Millar in the on-deck circle. As he stalks back to the dugout with his bat, I call, "Great game, Kev," but his face is still clenched and he ignores me.

We're nine and a half back and behind the White Sox in the wild card. That's not drama, that's desperation.

July 24th

Together the Sox and Yanks have spent over 300 million dollars on their rosters. Is Bronson Arroyo versus Tanyon Sturtze really the best they can do?

Today's the family picnic, and it's raining at the beach, so all of Trudy's aunts and uncles and cousins and nieces and nephews are crammed into the one main room of the cottage to watch the game. They're lifelong New Englanders from Woonsocket and Westerly, and watching the Sox is like watching home movies—it gives them a chance to remember how Uncle Vernon rooted (optimistic all the way to the last out) or Trudy's grandfather Leonard (watching TV with the sound down because he hated the announcers, a transistor radio pressed to his ear, and he would never go to the games).

We watch Arroyo get behind hitters, and get behind two-zip. I go out to shoot some hoops, and as I'm dribbling around, a shout comes up from the house next door: "Fight! Fight!" My nephew Sam comes tearing out. "Uncle Stew, there's a bench-clearing brawl!"

We run inside just in time to see the replay. Arroyo hits A-Rod on the elbow with a pitch inside—nothing new: Arroyo's second in the league in hit batsmen. A-Rod jaws at him right out of the box, though the pitch wasn't up or behind him; in fact, it hit him on the elbow pad. Tek says something to A-Rod. A-Rod says, "Come on," and Tek shoves him two-handed in the face, then ducks and grabs A-Rod around the upper thigh and lifts him, bulling him backwards. The whole room cheers and laughs. What kind of idiot challenges a guy in a mask and shin pads to a fight? Obviously he's never played hockey.

The benches clear. It's a harmless scrum except for Sturtze getting Gabe Kapler in a headlock from behind—a bad move when you're on the opposing team's side of the scrum. No idea how their starting pitcher ended up by

218

our on-deck circle, but David Ortiz is nearby and won't see his teammate treated this way. He grabs Sturtze and flings him to the ground. In the replay, as they fall, gravity gives Kapler some revenge as his knee lands in Sturtze's crotch. Trot piles on, but by then things have settled, and they're pulled apart.

Tek's ejected, as is A-Rod, and Kapler. Sturtze has a bloody scratch near his ear, but stays in the game. In the dugout, Kapler's pissed. "He grabbed *me*!" he shouts, demonstrating. (Later I discover that Kenny Lofton's been tossed, though only he and the ump know what he did.)

The game's on Fox, and the idiots in the booth say that maybe this will change New Yorkers' minds about A-Rod's lack of toughness. I keep looking for evidence in the replays (because they show it ten times), but all I see is Tek shoving him in the face and lifting him off the ground. They also say this is a case of the Red Sox's frustrations boiling over, except A-Rod started it. They run a montage of Sox-Yanks brawls going back to Fisk slugging Munson after their collision at home. In every clip, the Sox are whipping their asses.

When order's restored, the Sox come back over the next couple innings to take a 4–3 lead. Sturtze's gone and Juan Padilla is on. In the fifth, there's a terrible call on Johnny at second when Enrique Wilson drops a pop-up in short right and throws late to second for the force. Johnny, who's always a gentleman, says, "No!" and he's right. Francona comes out to argue, and no doubt he's arguing about last night's blown call at home too, and Timmons's awful work behind the plate. Francona actually gets excited for once, swearing and spitting at the ump's feet, and gets tossed.

He's in the clubhouse to watch the Yanks come back in the sixth. Wilson slices a spinning Texas leaguer over third. Posada pokes a low wall-ball and is meat at second on a perfect throw by Manny, except Bellhorn sets up too far behind second (not expecting Posada to try it) and waves at the in-between hop. Matsui doubles to put them ahead. Arroyo battles for two outs, but Cairo hits a quail off the end of the bat that floats over Bellhorn, and it's 6–4. Dave Wallace visits the mound. Bernie Williams singles. Brad Mills, as acting manager, pulls Arroyo for Leskanic. Curtis threw well last night. Today he can't find the plate. He walks Jeter (0 for his last million and groveling for a walk) to load them, then walks Sheffield to bring in a run. He goes full on Wilson, who singles to right, scoring two more. 9–4. He walks Posada, and that's it, he's gone (0 IP, 1 H, 1 R, 3 BB), and Mystery Malaska's on to face Matsui. On 3-2 Matsui takes a strike down the middle for the third out. Before this, I considered Matsui the most professional of the Yankees, but what is anyone doing taking a pitch on 3-2 with a five-run lead? That's bush, and even in the bush leagues will earn you some lumps.

Nomar leads off the Sox sixth with a ripped single. When Padilla goes 2-0 on Trot, pitching coach Mel Stottlemyre goes to the mound to calm him down (and stall). Padilla's way off the plate, as if he's afraid of lefties, and walks Trot. On a 1-1 count to Millar, Torre interrupts the flow of the game by bringing in Quantrill. It's the old Cuban slowdown, but even in the Pan-American games, where the umps let you do anything, I can't remember two mound visits on consecutive batters in midcount. After a five-minute delay for warm-ups and commercials, Millar singles to load them. On 3-1 Bill Mueller has a fat pitch to hit but skies it to center for an unsatisfying sac fly. Bellhorn strokes a wall-ball double, and it's 9–6. Johnny singles to left—9–7. Because Tek got ejected, Mirabelli's batting second, and we don't have a backup catcher, so we can't pinch-hit Youkilis for him. Mirabelli Ks, and Torre brings in Felix Heredia, who walks Ortiz to load the bases for Manny. Stottlemyre visits the mound again (their fourth visit this half-inning). Heredia goes 3-2 on Manny, who's hit like crap this series, then misses with a pitch a good foot up and out. 9–8, and Nomar's up, but look, what's this, it's Joe Torre plodding out to the mound. Another five-minute delay while Scott Proctor of the Columbus Clippers warms. Home-plate ump Bruce Froemming, who's built like Violet in *Willy Wonka* after she turns violet and the Oompah-Loompahs roll her away, makes it easy for Proctor, giving him a first strike call on a ball nowhere near the zone, and after all the waiting and screwing around, Nomar's pissed and just swings at anything (hey Joe, the tactic worked!) and strikes out to end what has to be the longest inning I've ever seen. One hour and seven minutes, according to Fox's clock.

While I think the Yankee/Cuban National Team stuff is crap, and definitely unsporting, it's legal. But it's also the home-plate ump's responsibility to control the game, and in the rule book there's a powerful clause that says the umpire can penalize any behavior that he independently deems "makes a mockery of the game." The classic example is running the bases backwards. I would submit to the league office that the slowdown not only makes a mockery of the game, it makes for bad TV, since that's the only thing the league office seems to care about. Steroids, what steroids? (In other sports, not only are players banned, but their teams' victories are retroactively forfeited and their championships taken away, their records expunged. Just a warning, Sheff, in case we ever have a real commissioner again.)

Ruben Sierra (career, what career?) leads off the seventh with a Monster shot off Malaska to make it 10–8. The crowd in the humid room groans. I go out to the beach, where there's a little kid in a Red Sox T-shirt with a Wiffle bat hitting stones into the ocean in the rain. Stone after stone: clack, clack, clack. Finally, some perspective. The game's not about the slowdown, or the TV contract, or the groan, it's about how fun it is to swing a bat and make contact. That clean ping.

Embree, who worked out of a jam in the seventh, is angry in the dugout because Mills pulled him for Mendoza. I'm horrified to see Mendoza myself, since he hasn't thrown a clutch inning since last June, including his season-long stint in the minors. Somehow—physics won't explain it—he does today, and not just one, but two of them.

We go to the ninth down 10–8, facing Mo, as always. He's converted 23 straight save opportunities, the Yanks are 56-0 when leading, blah blah blah. With two strikes, Nomar doubles on a particularly flat cutter. Rivera goes 3-1 on Trot, who crushes the next pitch to right. "Get OUT!" we yell, rising from our chairs. Sheffield goes back sideways, then backwards, crablike, and hauls it in on the track. In any other park it's a game-tying home run. Fenway giveth . . . Nomar moves over, and while we're still talking about Rivera's ineffectiveness, Millar bloops one to right, making it a one-run game. Mo's not Mo. He's missing high, missing wide, all over the place. He goes 3-1 on Bill Mueller, then gives him the same flat pitch he threw Trot, and Billy gets it. "That's gone!" I say, and Sheffield knows it too, turning to show us his number as the ball lands in the glove of Sox bullpen catcher Dana LaVangie. The Sox jump up and down at home, slapping Billy on his shaved head (for some reason he pulls his helmet off just before he touches the plate—maybe he wants to really feel it to remember it forever). In the room, we're all up and shouting, trading high fives and hugging. "I told you!" Steph says. "You did," I admit, because he's been behind Billy all the way, even when he hit into a rally-killing DP early on.

So it's a double win, a TKO by Tek and a walk-off shot by Bill Mueller, enormously satisfying, and just.

And weird, the way Mendoza was suddenly unhittable (where in Pawtucket the Rochester Red Wings were wearing him out), and Mo *so* hit-table—and wild, very much unlike him. The fight's great for ratings too, and reinvigorates the rivalry, after being down nine and a half games. As a novelist, I'd say the plot's too pat, designed for the big finish, like some of the NFL playoff games the last couple years. The more I think of it, the less I like it.

SO: Now I know what you're doing out there: writing scripts for Fox Baseball, a division of the International Roller Derby Association. Today's walk-off sure looked cooked—the same bad pitch to Trot *and* Bill Mill? Talk about a groovy situation. I swear when Trot stepped in he looked out at Rivera apologetically, as if this wasn't his idea (Thou shalt not lie, Christopher Trotman Nixon). But we're so desperate that we'll gladly take it and be thankful. Pay no attention to the man behind the curtain.

July 25th

ESPN's showing the rubber game of the series, meaning it's an 8:05 start. It also means ESPN's built a temporary stage just past the third-base dugout, and the screen that's usually at third has been moved to protect Peter Gammons, Harold Reynolds and John Kruk. When Miguel Cairo smokes a rope right at me in BP, I realize why the screen is there. The ball's hit so on-the-nose that it knuckles, and I have to follow it all the way into my glove. I actually catch it in the pocket with a satisfying smack, getting a hand from the crowd and a few glances from the Yankees gathered at short, but it's hit so hard that my index finger—which sticks through the Holdster opening and is cushioned by at least three layers of leather—is numb and then tingly.

"How's it feel?" a guy behind me jokes.

"Good," I say, and in a way it does. I've played a fair amount at goalie and at third base, and it's the hardest shot I've ever stopped.

Here's how big the game is: instead of the Hood blimp cruising low over us like Friday night, it's the Met Life blimp. We've gone from regional to national.

I get a ball that A-Rod kicks taking grounders, then I'm off to Autograph Alley where Oil Can Boyd is signing, accompanied by a beefy, bleached-blond guy with a bright Hawaiian shirt and ten pounds of gold jewelry, like a wrestler's manager. The Can is gaunt but stylish, fringes of gray in his close-cropped hair.

"Nineteen eighty-six," I say as he's signing my ball, "ALCS Game Six. You were here, I was here. Thanks, Dennis."

The concourse is gridlocked, and I miss the Marine honor guard unfurling a massive American flag that covers the Monster, and then John Kerry throwing out the first pitch. (Kerry/Edwards campaign aides are handing out SOX FANS FOR KERRY signs throughout the park—a by-product of owner Tom Werner's support of the Democrats.)

I reach my seat in time for Derek Lowe's first pitch. Right from the beginning, the ump's squeezing him. Lowe has Kenny Lofton struck out, but there's no call. Lofton grounds a single to left that somehow makes it to the wall and becomes a double. Lofton takes third when Jeter—in a Zoolander-stupid move—bunts him over. Sheffield hits a fly to center that's short enough for an interesting play at the plate, but Johnny waves both arms as if he doesn't see it. Bellhorn's going out, Kapler's streaking in from right. Kapler dives, an instant too late. Lofton scores; Sheffield, jogging, ends up at first. A-Rod nubs one that Bill Mueller has no play on, then Lowe bounces one that just nicks Posada on the foot (Andrew tosses me the traitorous ball). Matsui hits a fly deep enough to get Sheffield home. Bernie Williams flies to Manny—a nice running catch in the corner—but it's 2–0 Yanks, and Lowe is red-cheeked and unhappy.

Jose Contreras's ERA at Fenway this year is over 20.00, and he shows us why. Johnny legs out an infield single, then moves to second when a pick-off throw gets past Tony Clark. Contreras quickly walks Bellhorn and Ortiz, bringing up Manny with bases loaded and no out. Manny rips a grounder to third, and Johnny's off. A-Rod thinks he has a play at home, but he rushes the throw, yanking it to the infield side, and Posada has to lay out to get it, his foot coming off the plate. Johnny's in there—but ump Hunter Wendelstedt punches him out.

What? I'm out of my seat and screaming at him, trying to keep my language clean so I don't get kicked out. Trudy's embarrassed but amused too. Our neighbor Mason laughs, shaking his head. "That's the third horrible call that's gone against us this series."

"And two were for runs!"

Bases are still loaded for Nomar. He jumps all over a Contreras fastball and lines a bullet to Matsui in left, too short to score Bellhorn. Two down, and it looks like we're going to blow another opportunity, but Millar, who's been blazing lately, dumps one into center that Lofton can't quite get to. They should have a play on Manny, but it never materializes, and the game's tied.

Lowe has no problem with the bottom of their order (Bernie, Tony Clark and Enrique Wilson will go a combined 1 for 10), and in our half of the second, Contreras hits Mirabelli, gives up a smoked single to Kapler and then serves up a pretty Pesky Pole shot to Johnny, the ball rising into the night, then hitting the woven metal skirt of the pole and dropping straight down. We're still celebrating when Bellhorn takes one out. It's 6–2 and only the second inning.

Contreras picks up his second hit batsman of the inning when he throws *behind* Millar. The crowd is pissed and loud. After Friday night's game, and how blatant the pitch was, I expect he'll be heaved to keep order, but no, Wendelstedt just issues a warning to both clubs. So the Yanks get two free ones. When a pitch gets through Mirabelli and knocks Wendelstedt's mask off, sending him to one knee, there's a sense of frontier justice.

Torre decides to save the pen and let Contreras hang, and it works for the most part. The unstoppable Millar hits a Coke bottle shot in the fifth, and the two runs we tack on in the sixth are partly reliever Felix Heredia's fault, and partly Matsui's, when he gets fooled by a fly to left. Earlier in the series, he got caught too close to the wall and a ball hopped over his head; now he plays too far off it and David Ortiz's slicing fly hits the padding about five feet off the ground, and a catchable ball becomes a run-scoring double. Millar singles Ortiz in for his fourth RBI. It's 9–2, and the game's turning into a party.

John Kerry's sitting two sections over from us, right by the end of the Sox dugout, along with John Glenn, Joe Biden, Tom Brokaw, Tim Russert, and a gaggle of other Democratic National Convention celebrities. Between innings, the teenage guys sitting in front of us gesture to him with a ball they want signed. Kerry waves it on. The kid's throw is short, hitting Katie Couric. Kerry signs it, and since I'm the only one with a glove, he throws it back to me. When the next half-inning's over, I catch Kerry's eye with the ball I snagged from Miguel Cairo and toss it to him—the right distance, but wide. I think it's going to bounce onto the field, but Kerry reaches over the wall, stretches and makes a sweet one-handed grab. I point to him, surprised; he points back and nods. After he signs, his toss is perfect, head-high, and again we point at each other. Oil Can Boyd and John Kerry in one day!

In the top of the seventh Bellhorn pulls up on a grounder by Kenny Lofton. Lowe gets Jeter ("Zooooooooo-lan-derrrrr!") and Sheffield ("Juice! Juice! Juice!"), but Lofton steals second and A-Rod walks. Lowe's pitch count is around 120, so Francona goes to Timlin, and I go to the bathroom, figuring a six-run lead is safe. It's quiet in the bathroom, too quiet, I think, and then there's a cheer. Then nothing. When I get out of the stall, there are maybe five guys at the long line of urinals, and I know something's wrong.

When I sidle my way up the ramp, I check the scoreboard: Sox 9 Yanks 6.

"What happened?" I ask Trudy. "I go away for five seconds and everything goes to hell."

"Timlin happened," she says. "Matsui hit a grand slam."

So it's a game again, and the newly acquired Terry Adams (yikes) makes it even more torturous in the eighth by walking number nine hitter Enrique Wilson (now batting .215). Lofton spanks a double down the right-field line, and they have second and third with one out. Foulke comes in to face Jeter, who rips the first pitch off Foulke's shin, and in a very un-Red-Sox-like sequence, the ball ricochets directly to the one man who can throw Jeter out: catcher Doug Mirabelli. Mirabelli even has time to glance at third, then guns it to first. The ball hits Jeter in the shoulder and rolls into right.

Wendelstedt is on the play immediately, waving both arms to one side, like a football ref signaling a field-goal try wide right. It's interference: Jeter's out for running to the infield side of the baseline, purposely trying to block the throw. The runners have to return to their bases.

"It's the Ghost of Ed Armbrister," I say, conjuring up another demon to be exorcised.

Joe Torre pads out to argue, but it's pointless. Jeter the Cheater finally got busted; the Sox finally got a call, and just in time too.

Sheffield's up next, and smokes a hooking line drive—right to Manny, and we're out of it.

Foulke throws a quick one-two-three ninth, the crowd on its feet for every pitch. It's another big win, and after last night, maybe the start of the turnaround we've been waiting for. We're 8-4 against the Yanks on the year and back in front in the wild card, with Pedro going tomorrow. Let's go Sox!

July 26th

I rarely in my life wanted to be at Fenway as much as I wanted to be there for the three-game series between the Red Sox and the Yankees that just concluded. Not because John Kerry threw out the ceremonial first pitch in prime time last night; not because there's always a chance the two teams will go at it (as they did, and full-bore, on Saturday); not even because the atmosphere when these two teams play is always crazy-scary-electric, like Victor Frankenstein's lab about twenty seconds before the monster on the slab opens its eyes. I wanted to be there because it was an absolutely crucial series for the Red Sox, if they are to maintain any thin chance of winning the AL East. Lose two, I thought, and the players can probably forget about that part of it; get swept, and the fans can start questioning the team's commitment to winning *anything*.

Well, wish in one hand, shit in the other, see which one fills up first—I think Mahatma Gandhi said that. Instead of being in Boston, I found myself on the West Coast, three thousand miles from Fenway Park, speaking to a bunch of doctors about how it feels to get hit by a small van (not good) and how long it takes to get over it (quite a while).

Still, Red Sox fans can't escape the Red Sox; that is the basic fact of our existence. Even in L.A., I went to bed sick at the 8–7 loss on the night of the 23rd. Distance didn't lessen the pain; it made it worse. With no NESN, I was reduced to the coverage in the Saturday *Los Angeles Times*—which, due to their ridiculous infatuation with the Dodgers, was skimpy. Still, there was enough to make it clear that Curt Schilling and Keith Foulke—our supposed Yankee-killers—both played a part in the loss. It's hard to blame Schilling, who all season has worked like a railway yardman in need of overtime and has been consistently effective. It's also hard to blame Foulke, but easy to be exasperated with him. I think that goes with the role of closer. And of course it had to be Alex Rodriguez, The One Who Got Away, who delivered the game-winning hit.

Ironically, it was also Rodriguez who seems to have galvanized the Red Sox since, and all because he couldn't just put his head down and trot to first. Nope, he had to jaw at Bronson Arroyo, who plunked him on the shoulder pad. Jason Varitek got between pitcher and batter, telling A-Rod in "a few choice words" (Varitek's version) to take his base.* Rodriguez told Tek where he could stick his base, Tek pushed A-Rod's pretty face, and the rumble was on. By the time it was over, Yankee pitcher Tanyon Sturtze had sustained a healthy cut on the side of his face (David Ortiz might have had something to do with that), four or five players had been ejected, and Varitek ended up sitting out Sunday's game. Probably just as well, from a catching standpoint; John Kerry threw out the first pitch, and while he may be a helluva politician, his slider needs serious work. (Can you even trust a politician with a good slider?—just asking.)

Following the rhubarb, the donnybrook, and the ejections, the Sox finally woke from their stupor, winning one of the most thrilling games of the year in the bottom of the ninth on a Bill Mueller walk-off home run. They won Sunday's game 9–6, and are schooling the Orioles tonight behind Pedro: the score is 12–5 in the bottom of the seventh. If this is the place where the season turns around—and stranger things have happened—then you can give Jason Varitek the MVP for getting in Alex Rodriguez's face.

July 27th

Trot's on the DL, I discover, having aggravated the quad. The team makes it sound like a brief stay, just to let him rest, and to make room on what's now a crowded roster. Yesterday in Pawtucket I watched Cesar Crespo play badly, and I wonder if it's the effect of us signing Ricky Gutierrez, knocking Cesar that much further down the depth chart.

My neighbor Dave was at the Saturday brawl game and says one reason why the fight started wasn't shown on TV: after A-Rod started barking, Bronson Arroyo walked toward home plate, tugging at his crotch. Ay, I got ya 252 million right here.

July 28th

Three days from the trading deadline, the papers say the Yanks are close to finalizing a deal for Randy Johnson, and the Twins and Pirates are ready to swap former Rock Cat Doug Mientkiewicz and Kris Benson. Theo so far has

---

*On the replay Varitek appears to be saying either "Take your fucking base" or "Get the fuck to first base."

been quiet. Whether that means he's being secretly effective or coming up empty remains to be seen, but it would not bode well if our big midseason acquisition was Terry Adams.

At 45-54, the Orioles are sleepwalking through another disappointing season. You wouldn't know it by the way they've played against the Red Sox, though. Behind Pedro, and still pumped up from beating the Yankees two out of three, we shellacked them two nights ago, but the O's batters had touched Tim Wakefield for four quick runs last night before the game was washed out. Tonight they got four more against Curt Schilling, and sorry, no rain.

We are 4-7 so far against Baltimore this year, and I'd love to be able to comfort myself by saying we just play lousy against the Birds, but it ain't so, Joe. The fact of the matter is that the Birds play lousy against the rest of the league and like World Champions against us. Schilling (12-4) against Dave Borkowski (1-2) was a mismatch on paper, but for the last time, baseball games aren't played on paper and tonight Borkowski—who we'd already beaten once this year—pitched like Steve Carlton in his prime, setting down the first thirteen Red Sox batters to face him before giving up a single to Nomar in the fifth. He pitched seven strong and left the game with a two-hit shutout. The only Boston run came on an Ortiz dinger with two out in the ninth, and Javy Lopez—a Red Sox nemesis from his Atlanta Braves days—hit a pair off Schilling, getting three of the four Baltimore RBIs.

So we're a game behind Oakland in the wild-card race, and we have the unpleasing prospect of three games against the red-hot Minnesota Twins in the immediate future and *eight* more against the O's before the season is over. And if we finish the season series with them at something like 7-12, and lose the wild card by two games, we can blame the Birds. Hell, it beats blaming the Bambino.

July 29th

Now the papers say Theo might try to piggyback that Twins-Pirates deal, shipping Youkilis to Pittsburgh for Mientkiewicz. Just the idea makes me queasy. Trading Lowe or Nomar would be bad enough, even if we have no intention of signing them, but Youk's the future. After what happened with

Freddy Sanchez (though he's been hurt the last year or so), they ought to know better.

The Sox have a travel day, so to get my daily dose I take Steph and the boys over to Norwich for a doubleheader against the Trenton Thunder. Like New Britain, Norwich has a pretty little park that holds around six thousand, but the food is better here. I get a ball during warm-ups and have former Sox closer and current Norwich pitching coach Bob "The Steamer" Stanley and his former batterymate and current first-base coach Roger LaFrancois sign it.

The Thunder are the Yanks' double-A club. They used to be ours before we acquired Portland from the Marlins, and the Navigators used to be the Yankees', so for long-term fans there are some mixed (if not to say confused) feelings. But it's Camp Day, so most of the fans are too young to care. It's a brilliant blue afternoon, everyone receives a coupon for free ice cream, and as we leave, the ushers hand out flyers telling us Willie Mays is coming next week. Makes me wish I could be here for it.

July 30th

It's the big party for Trudy's parents' fiftieth anniversary, a real production, and I can't get away with the sneaky Pirates radio and earphone. A good half of the guests are New Englanders and diehard Sox fans—the men mostly, with memories of the '46 club, and the old Braves. To a man, they think Francona's just another patsy. "The last manager we had with any spine was Dick Williams. You saw, everywhere he went he was a winner." The women roll their eyes.

After the band's packed up, we have a nightcap downstairs in the bar. The TV's silently playing *Extra Innings,* and Eric Friede and Sam Horn and Jayme Parker are all smiling, so my guess is we won. The Yanks did too, and the Rangers, so we're behind the A's again.

They also list a pair of big trades. The Mets have won the Benson sweepstakes. Not only that, but in a five-team deal, somehow they also picked up Tampa Bay ace Victor Zambrano and put themselves in a position to win the wimpy NL East. The other trade is an eight-player swap between the Marlins and Dodgers, the principals being Brad Penny and Charles Johnson, Guillermo Mota and Paul Lo Duca.

No news from Theo.

July 31st

The Yankees have reversed themselves on Giambi's intestinal parasite and are now saying he has a benign tumor and may be out for the season. Also, during Fox's Yankee Game of the Week, an announcer says that Trot will miss the rest of the year (instead of the week or two the Sox originally reported). If that's true, we're screwed.

All the friends who came to last night's party are here for a day at the beach, and there's a revolving audience for the Yankees-O's game. A-Rod takes home on the back end of a double steal that the Orioles fall for, and for the rest of the day the announcers crow about how A-Rod stole home as if he's Jackie Robinson.

I'm just watching the game for any late trade news, since the deadline's almost upon us. Soon it's past four—no news—and the Yanks are winning, so I go pack my things to drive Steph home for a friend's birthday party.

I get the news from my daughter-in-law, a once-upon-a-time Yankee fan (like once-upon-a-time Protestants who convert to Catholicism, lapsed Yankee fans who become Red Sox partisans are the ones who REALLY MEAN BUSINESS), and she sounds the way I feel: shocked but somehow not all that surprised.

The player most commonly identified with the Boston Red Sox, the one whose number most fans probably expected to see someday up on the wall along with Williams's, Pesky's, and Yaz's, is no longer with the Red Sox. Number Five has been traded, and probably the only consolation to be taken by fans who place tradition and heart above salary and statistics is that he's been traded to the one other team in baseball whose long World Series drought has become not just the stuff of history but that of myth. That's right folks; at game time tomorrow, Nomar Garciaparra—Boston's surviving marquee player from the days of Dan Duquette—will take the field as a Cubbie.

Does the deal make sense? I don't think so; I think that two years from now it will look like a panic move made by a young GM who saw his high-priced (and supposedly high-powered) baseball team treading water eight or nine games behind the monolithic Yankees in the AL East and a game or two behind the Oakland A's in the wild card (but still more advantageously placed than their closest competition). In other words, I think that Theo Epstein probably pulled the pin on a big deal at the trading deadline mostly because everyone in Boston's howling oh-God-my-asshole's-on-fire sports community was yelling for it to happen

!!OH JEEZ!!
!!BEFORE IT'S TOO LATE!!

What exactly did we get for our usually dependable, sometimes brilliant, and (I admit it) at times erratic shortstop, who was batting .321 at the time of the trade? We got two Gold Glove infielders, one with a name that can be both pronounced and spelled—that would be Orlando Cabrera—and the other with a name that can at least be pronounced: Doug Mientkiewicz *(man-KAY-vitch)*. Putting the bat on the little white ball has seemed a little harder than catching it for these gentlemen, at least so far this season. Both are hitting around .250.

According to Red Sox general manager Theo Epstein, the fact that Cabrera and Mientkiewicz currently have batting averages seventy points below Garciaparra's doesn't matter. As a disciple of Billy Beane and a follower of Bill James, he likes these men for their defense and their on base per centage (OBP).* He also likes them because Nomar Garciaparra is in the last year of a contract currently paying him $11 million a year, and re-signing him probably would have been *très* expensive. Stories about how Nomar's feelings were hurt during the failed A-Rod deal are probably no more than the usual baseball bullshit, but here's something that isn't: both Nomar and his agent know that baseball is a business. They also know that an athlete's period of top earning ability is severely limited when compared to, say, that of a corporate CEO (or a best-selling novelist), and I have no doubt that Nomar and his man of business were determined to Make 'Em Pay this fall, whoever 'em turned out to be. Theo Epstein just decided 'em wasn't going to be *us.*

---

*Mientkiewicz did his best to make Epstein look like a genius in his first game as a Red Sox, going 2 for 4, both singles. The second hit came in the top of the ninth against Minnesota— the only pro baseball team he'd ever played for until this evening—in a game which the Twins led by a score of 5–4. He got to second base—into scoring position, in other words—before Kevin Youkilis struck out to end the game. The other new Boston players should join the club tomorrow.

Does that make sense? I'm sure it does to Theo Epstein, and it probably does to those of the Billy Beane bent. It does, in other words, if you see big league baseball as a business . . . *and nothing else.* Who it does *not* make sense to is my five-year-old grandson, who was watching ESPN when SportsCenter announced the trade. Ethan is a big Nomar fan. He always pretends to be Nomar when he's hitting in the backyard, when he's throwing, when he's running the bases.

So it's Ethan I'm thinking about as I write this—not his mother (the converted Yankee fan), not Nomar himself, not even the Red Sox, the putative subject of this book. Nope, I'm just thinking about Ethan.

"Nomar's a Cub," he said, then watched the TV for a while. Then, very softly, he said: "I guess I like the Cubs."

Good call, Ethan.

Very good call.

I've just finished my good-byes when my sister-in-law says I've got a phone call. It's Steve.

"They traded Nomar," he says.

"Aw shit," I say, partly because they fooled me. It's almost five o'clock. I thought I was safe.

"To the Cubs. I think we got their shortstop and maybe a pitcher."

Alex Gonzalez is a decent shortstop, and we've been looking at starter Matt Clement, maybe to take Arroyo's place or to assume the middle role. I relay the news to the boys, and they switch back to the game.

Steph runs in. "We got Cabrera and Mientkiewicz."

"So it was a three-team deal."

"So Nomar's gone to Red Sox West," Steve says. "My five-year-old grandson's been in tears. 'But I still like Nomar,' he says. 'I guess I'm a Cubs fan now.'"

I think we must have gotten Clement, since our real need is middle relief, but Steve can't find anything on the website. Nomar for Mientkiewicz and Orlando Cabrera of the Expos (so it's a four-team deal). It doesn't seem like enough—and we've already got three first basemen and three journeyman shortstops. It must have been a panic move on Theo's part, dumping Nomar before he could walk (it's just like the Yawkeys: not wanting to pay a star top dollar and getting nothing for him).

While I'm still on the phone, Steph tells me the Yanks have gotten last year's Cy Young runner-up Esteban Loaiza from the White Sox for Jose Contreras. It's a steal, even with George's three million thrown in—a panic move on Chicago's part that doubly benefits the Yanks. So we got hosed on both deals.

Steve's off to see *The Village*, I'm off to drive a hundred miles. After I hang up, I feel like the season's over, like we've given up.

On the road we tune into ESPN radio and hear that we got speedster Dave Roberts from the Dodgers for outfielder Henri Stanley, who just signed balls for us in Pawtucket on Monday. It's a good deal, but not large enough to make up for the loss of Nomar.

The Sox without Nomar. It seems like a defeat, whoever's fault it is.

During the pregame, Theo talks about how we needed to fix our defense, as if that's what drove the deal. Then, because we have nowhere else to put him, we start Millar in right even though Kapler's been hot. (Steph notes that the music behind his highlights from last night is Tenacious D's "Wonderboy.")

The game is anticlimactic after the video of Nomar leaving the clubhouse for the airport. The announcers—all of them paid by the Sox—put the best face on the deal they can, picking at Nomar's attitude and his heel. Where's Eck when you need him? (Cooperstown, being inducted.)

Lowe throws okay, so does Radke. The biggest moment is when Doug Mientkiewicz steps to the plate for the first time in a Red Sox uniform. Mientkiewicz is a lifelong Twin, and the Metrodome rises and gives him a noise-meter-worthy ovation. He has to step out to collect himself, and I realize we never had a chance to say good-bye to Nomar (we didn't know it, but that Sunday-night game against the Yanks was his last home game).

It's a close game late, tied in the eighth when Embree comes in with one down and the bases empty to face lefty Jacque Jones. He gets behind him, then aims a fastball. Jones cranks it, flipping his bat away. The ball lands ten rows back.

Joe Nathan, throwing 98, closes with the help of Francona. Mientkiewicz singles to open the inning; Kapler pinch-runs. Millar, who should be bunting, swings away. On an 0-1 count, Kapler goes and Henry Blanco guns him by ten feet. Millar flies out. It's a terrible at-bat on all counts, an embarrassment. Bill Mueller then steps in and pulls a long shot down the line—foul. He singles (it would have easily scored Kapler), then takes second on a wild pitch before Youkilis strikes out.

Overall, just a tough day to be a Red Sox fan. Seems like everywhere we turned we did something stupid and got our asses kicked.

There are sixty games left, and we're pretty much where we were last year. It's time to put a stretch drive together. Or else.

The Hottest August on Record

August 1st

Let the juggling begin. Cabrera reports; to make room we send down Andy Dominique. Since we'll see four lefties over the next five games, David Ortiz drops his appeal and begins serving his suspension for the bat-throwing incident in Anaheim. Millar's at DH, McCarty at first and Kapler in right—or would be, except Johnny tells Francona during BP that he's having trouble picking up the ball because of the afternoon sun further lightening the Metrodome's translucent white roof. So Johnny is the least DH-like DH in Sox history, Kapler's in center and Millar's in right.

Cabrera's batting third, which I think is a mistake, but in the first, in his first at-bat as a Red Sock, he takes Johan Santana deep. Then in the bottom of the inning he can't handle a chop over Pedro's head.

It's a tight game, like last night's. Kapler guns Corey Koskie at home, but Tek bobbles the throw and Koskie steamrolls him. Torii Hunter goes back to the wall and casually robs McCarty of a home run. The next inning, McCarty makes a diving stab of a Hunter shot down the line. Manny hits a solo blast to give us the lead again, but the Twins use smallball to scratch back even.

To lead off the seventh, Santana hits Tek. To get more pop in their lineup, Matthew LeCroy is catching instead of Blanco, and Tek steals on him. LeCroy wings the ball into center—Tek to third. Millar then hits a high, medium fly to right. Center fielder Torii Hunter races over to take it from Jones, since he's got the better arm. He's in position behind him, but somehow they don't communicate, because Jones never yields. He takes it flatfooted and his throw is up the first-base line, and Tek scores standing up.

Pedro's brilliant through seven, striking out 11. Santana goes eight, ringing up 12.

Though Pedro's thrown only 101 pitches, Francona goes by the book, bringing in Timlin to set up. Timlin gives up back-to-back singles and doesn't record an out. On Embree's first batter, the young slugger Justin Morneau, the Twins pull a double steal. Morneau then skies one to deep right-center. It'll tie the game, no doubt. Kapler has to go a long way to make the catch, then fires a no-look throw back toward the infield. It sails over the cutoff man, Bellhorn, and Cabrera runs over from second to corral it. He must look up to check the runner, or maybe he nonchalants it, figuring the play's over, because the ball knocks off his glove, and he kicks it—literally kicks it—toward first base. On a real field, the grass stops the ball, but since we're in the Homerdome, it rolls away across the carpet, and by the time Cabrera chases it down and throws home, Lew Ford's sliding in safely, and we're down 4–3. Welcome to the Red Sox.

Joe Nathan gives us an opening in the ninth, hitting Bellhorn, but we don't bother to bunt him over (hey, why change now). Cabrera strikes out, lunging. Manny hits into an easy 6-4-3 turf job, and we lose a carbon copy of last night's game, wasting another quality start.

On *The Simpsons*, Comic Book Guy—a true loser—has a Red Sox pennant hanging in his shop. I channel him now: worst weekend ever.

August 2nd

When I entered in this diary on July 2nd, we'd just been swept out of the Bronx and had fallen eight and a half games back in the AL East. Now, a month later, we're nine and a half behind the Yankees, who continue on cruise control. The Yanks don't have much in the way of pitching, but it doesn't seem to matter; they simply whale the tar out of almost every team they go against. The Red Sox are one of the rare exceptions, but they can afford to ignore us, at least for the time being. Who knows, they may not have to worry about us even in October. For the first time this season one team—it's the Oakland Athletics—seems to have a solid hold on the wild card.*

We've lost both of the games we've played since the big Garciaparra trade, but I actually don't feel too badly about that, even though both were

---

*But the great thing about the wild card—what I absolutely love about it—is that it is, by its very nature, a slippery beast. If Oakland slides into first place in the AL West—hey, presto!—the Red Sox are wild-card-competitive again, only against a different team. There are baseball purists who hate the innovation for this very reason, but they would be folks who, for the most part, haven't been stuck with George Steinbrenner's bloated wallet for the last twelve years or so.

of the tooth-rattling one-run variety. For one thing, both of our new players contributed to the offensive effort (okay, okay, so Cabrera—who hit a home run in his first Red Sox at-bat—also cost us yesterday's game with an error in the bottom of the eighth). For another, the Twins are very good this year, and I'd expect them to take two out of three in their house, just as I'd expect us to take two out of three from them in ours.

But now we finish the year's longest road-trip playing teams that are either sub-.500 or close to .500, and here I agree with the conventional wisdom: this is probably the season's last decisive turning-point, and I'll be watching these games very, very closely. For the next two weeks it's not going to do to just play .500 baseball on the road. I'm hoping we can win eight of the next dozen, and from now until the middle of the month, I suspect this diary will be hearing from me often.

August 3rd

Mark Bellhorn goes on the DL with a thumb fracture after taking that pitch on the hand, joining Pokey, meaning Francona has more platooning to do. The press is on him about the logjam at first. How is he going to keep all of his players happy? I may not have much confidence in Francona, but at least he has the right answer: "That's not what we're here to do."

Last night Wake won on his birthday, a quiet indoor affair with less than 10,000 guests. For tonight's game with the D-Rays Francona pencils in the most alien infield yet: Youk at third, Cabrera at short, Bill Mueller at second and Mientkiewicz at first. Dave Roberts starts in right for only the fourth time in his life, and leads off, followed by Cabrera and Johnny. The new speed lineup does nothing, but Tek hits a two-run shot and Bill Mueller knocks in three more from the six-spot. Schilling (a new guy himself, not so long ago) goes the distance, but the post-trade face of the Sox is just weird.

August 4th

I didn't know how brave I was, asking the Red Sox to win eight of their next twelve, until Jayme Parker (looking cool and beautiful this morning in off-the-shoulder black) tells me that the Sox haven't won back-to-back road games since June. But they managed the trick last night, and now, instead of needing to win eight out of twelve, they only (only!) need to win six out of their next ten. That means playing .600 ball instead of .666, if you're of a statistical bent.

Although I haven't kept an exact count ("You could look it up," I hear Ole Case whispering), I'd guess we've got in the neighborhood of fifty-five games left to play. *Eleven* of them are with the formerly hapless Devil Rays, and this makes me happy, because the D-Rays, after running off a gaudy string of wins (almost entirely against National League teams) before the All-Star break, seem to be subsiding into their former state of haplessness, and fast. Manager Lou Piniella rode his horses hard during the streak ("ran their dung to water," my wife would say), and now they seem punchless and reeling. Tampa Bay management has done its part to destroy team morale by trading D-Rays' ace and chief workhorse Victor Zambrano to the contending Mets. All of which makes me sorry for them, but not too sorry to take pleasure in Tim Wakefield's win two nights ago and Curt Schilling's complete-game victory last night. Not too sorry to hope that Bronson Arroyo can complete the sweep tonight, either, although I doubt the Rays will let that happen. They ain't quite *that* hapless.

SK: Two in a row! For the first time since June! Schill gets the complete-game win! Manny crashes into the left-field wall! Plays dead! Arises and hugs the reincarnation of the Lizard King! Film at 11!

Go, you old Red Sox! Lou Piniella blew his hosses out in June and July, and we get to ride them spavined old nags eleven more times before the end of the season! I'm hoping (praying, actually) that we can take six of the next ten, to make it eight out of twelve after putting the Twins in our rearview mirror. GO, YOU OLD RED SOX!

SO: After the June Swoon and the July Drive-By, I'm a little leery. Who are these guys anyway? I was just getting used to Ricky Gutierrez at short and here comes Cabrera. I almost feel bad for Francona, having to glue together a lineup from these bits and pieces. Thank God for the Devil Rays. But eventually we're going to have to beat the Twins. And the Angels. And the White Sox.

SK: Francona's a dork. And that's true, but first we're gonna see the Tigers, who are currently 50-56. I'd like to finish these six games at 4-

2 and would LOVE to be 5-1. Wouldn't it be great to get like fourteen or fifteen games over .500?

SO: The Tigers have been revitalized of late. Dmitri Young's back from that broken leg, and their young pitchers have turned in some hellacious games, so we better be ready for a scrap. Let's not look past tonight, though. Francona may not know it, but they all count the same.

SK: I just went to check the game. When I sat down to write this e-mail, everything was okay; we had a three-run lead and Arroyo was cruising. Now we're down 5-4, thanks to a Youkilis error (more damn errors) and a Toby Hall granny.

"Stewart and Stephen," said the old psychic dwarf-lady, "*your* nightmare continues."

SO: And now Dave Roberts just got pegged at home in the ninth with NOBODY OUT, and we lose by a run. Congratulations, Dave, you made the Hall of Sveum on your first try.

August 5th

Still, we *almost* got the sweep. Leading 4–1 in the seventh—and cruising—Bronson Arroyo gave up a single and a walk. A Kevin Youkilis error loaded the bases for Tampa Bay with no outs. Then catcher Toby Hall, 0 for his last 18, parked one. Make that score 5–4 Rays, and it stood up. In the Boston half of the ninth, newly acquired Sox speed merchant Dave Roberts, running for Kevin Millar and egged on by third-base coach Dale Sveum, tried to tie the score from second on a Doug Mientkiewicz single.* The all-or-nothing dash for home is always a thrilling play, but this time it went Tampa Bay's way. Center fielder Rocco Baldelli threw a bullet to catcher (and home-run hitter) Toby Hall, who made it easy for the umpire, not letting the willowy Roberts anywhere near the dish. Mientkiewicz got as far as third, then died there when Johnny Damon popped

---

*The decision to wave Roberts home seemed out of character for the usually cautious Sveum and more like his predecessor, Wendell Kim, known to the Fenway Faithful as "Send 'Em In" Kim.

up to end the game. It was another tooth-rattling loss (especially since both the Yankees and the Rangers, our current wild-card competition, won their games), but Tampa Bay hasn't been swept at home all year, so all you can do is tip your cap to them and move on. In this case to Motown, where the Tigers wait.

We're 2-1 in the current twelve-game stretch, and I'm still hoping to take six of the next nine. I know that sounds steep, but at some point this team just has to start setting some steep goals. And meeting them.

SK: I couldn't tell from the paper (or the game) if Sveum sent him. I guess he did. (My son Owen sez the same.)

SO: Sveum sent him, then said afterward that Rocco Baldelli hasn't made a lot of good throws. Only enough to lead the league in outfield assists last year, Dale.

SK: It was a move reminiscent of Wendell "Send 'Em In" Kim. A moment of desperation? A brain cramp? I mean, we could have had guys on first and third with none out! By the way, how many games has this team lost by one run this year? What we have here is a team that's so _agonizingly_ close to being good enough . . . but not quite. You heard it here first: I don't think we're going anywhere but home come October. How I hope they prove me wrong.

SO: I think he blanked—entirely spaced on the situation. And it wasn't like he was sending Ortiz or the Dauber. Even Roberts's wheels couldn't make up for it.

We're pretty much where we were last year. Just hope the bats come alive, the teams out West knock each other off, and the ChiSox pull their usual swoon.

August 6th

SO: What the hell happened with John Olerud? Seattle was in the cellar and figured they'd dump him and go with a youth movement, I understand that, but I thought they dropped him so they could dangle him in front of teams like the Yanks, hoping George or some other nut would pick up his big salary. Then I read in the paper that the Yanks grabbed him and are paying him the minimum 300K while the M's are eating 7 mil. Wha'? Huh?

And Theo—in his Defense Is Good mode—has been crowing over Mientkiewicz's old Gold Gloves. Olerud's got a closetful of 'em, plus he's one of the purest hitters to ever play the game. So, if we had to have a fourth first baseman (Dauber being condemned to the fifth circle, called Pawtucket), instead of the crummy Nomar deal we swung, we could have had Olerud for 300K and the time it took to sign him, and then could have maybe gotten a middle reliever/setup guy to spell Embree and Timlin, who look tired and beaten out there.

SK: Ah, but Olerud wouldn't have looked as good to the cannibal Boston press, which will never speak to me again after they read the August portion of my diary. AND I DON'T CARE. I mean, do you doubt a bit that Mientkiewicz and Cabrera were, to some extent, PR gestures?

SO: But—and this is where my forehead starts to pulse like *Scanners*—didn't we already have a great defensive first baseman in McCarty? And doesn't getting Mientkiewicz now make him totally expendable? I just don't get it. Unless we're putting together some weird MGM production number where every utility shortstop on the team fields a grounder and throws to a matching first baseman for a grand, ceremonial 6-3.

SK: Amen, brother. I've been thinking this for two weeks. When we get Varitek playing first, it'll be the fooking hat-trick. Orlando Cabrera is actually Cesar Crespo by way of Stepford. Yours ever, Ira Levin.

Ted Williams disliked and distrusted the Boston sportswriters. His appellation for them—"The Knights of the Keyboard"—was sarcastic and contemptuous. This doesn't make the Splendid Splinter an aberration but rather the first in a tradition. In the current era, Carl Everett was sent hence from Boston with his ass on fire and the tag Jurassic Carl hanging from his neck. Manager Butch Hobson (never one of my faves, believe me) became known—sarcastically—as Daddy Butch. Pedro Martinez, a proud and emotional man as well as a wildly talented pitcher, has felt so disrespected by Boston's Knights of the Keyboard that he has on at least two occasions vowed never to speak to the media again (luckily for fans, his natural gregariousness has overcome these resolutions). Dozens of Red Sox players, past and present, could tell horror stories about how they've been treated by Boston's sportswriters, who now serve just two papers (if you exclude such peripheral rags as the *Phoenix* and *Diehard*, that is): the *Globe* and the *Herald*. The *Globe* is the more influential, and by far the more vitriolic. Its most recent acid-bath victim has been Nomar Garciaparra.

The story being disseminated by the writers—Dan Shaughnessy leading the pack—goes something like this: Nomar was never a team player; Nomar was a downer even at the best of times; Nomar had a line in front of his locker to keep the media from getting too close; Nomar told multiple stories about his conversations with Red Sox management before the trade that sent him to the Cubs; Nomar expressed doubts about how much of the regular season he'd be able to play because of the injury to his Achilles tendon. (This last is supposed to help we poor benighted fans understand how Theo Epstein could have traded one of baseball's five premier infielders for what boils down to a pair of journeymen with good defensive skills.)

And yesterday, more dirt: According to the *Globe,* Nomar may have lied about how he came by that sore foot in the first place. In spring training we were told—by Nomar—that the injury was the result of a batted ball. Now, according to the *Globe,* Nomar is supposed to have told somebody or other that the injury cropped up on its own. If so, yesterday's story went on to speculate, he may have confabulated the whole batted-ball story in order to keep his market value from going down in his walk year. Because you can heal from an injury, right? But if your body starts to give out on you . . . that's a different deal altogether. And the source or sources of this story? Do you even have to ask? Not named. Little more than back-fence gossip, in other words, just one more yap of the fox who wants to believe that, oh yeah, those grapes were sour anyway . . . and by the way, that big-deal shortstop all the kids love? What a hoser! What a *busher!*

And if Nomar Garciaparra tells his Chicago teammates not to okay a trade to Boston if they can possibly prevent it, no way, under no circumstances, because in Boston the sportswriters eat the local heroes in print and then shit out the bones on cable TV, who could blame them? I'll bet right now Mr. Garciaparra is feeling especially well-chewed.

And why are the Boston sportswriters this way during baseball season—so angry, so downright cat-dirt *mean*—when they are, by and large, pretty normal during the other three seasons of the sports year (football, basketball, hockey)? I think it goes back to the basic subtext of this book, that the Red Sox—like the Cubs—are the derelicts of major league baseball, ghost ships adrift and winless in the mythic horse latitudes of sports legend. That may sound sweet to the poets and to writers like John "lyric little bandbox" Updike,* but sportswriters want *winners,* sportswriters want their bylines under headlines like **SOX TAKE SERIES IN 6**, and this eighty-six-year dry spell just . . . makes . . . them . . . *FURIOUS*. They won't admit it, not hardheaded Damon Runyon archetypes such as they, but underneath it all they're hurt little boys who have been eating loserdust for much of their professional lives and they just . . . fucking . . . *HATE IT*. Can they take it out on management? On Theo Epstein and mild-mannered, bespectacled John Henry? They cannot. Those fellows do not put on uniforms and swing the lumber. Also—and more importantly—those fellows are responsible for who gets press-box credentials, field credentials, and who gets to belly up to the postgame buffet. So, by and large, management gets a pass.† Except, of course, for the poor unfortunate middle-management schmucks who fill out the lineup cards, guys like Terry Francona, Grady Little, Jimy (family so poor they could only afford a single 'm' in his first name) Williams, "Daddy" Butch Hobson, and "Tollway" Joe Morgan.

---

*Haven't seen him at Fenway all year.

†In this context it does not hurt to remind ourselves that *Globe* ownership, *New York Times* ownership, and Red Sox ownership all overlap. In other words, they're all in it together. Time to put the tinfoil on the windows, line our baseball caps with lead, and check our phones for radioactive bugs.

And Nomar. Him, too.

That selfish guy.

That downer.

That *liar*.

That guy who took the money, ran off to Chicago, and left the kids crying.

It's all bullshit, of course, and in their ink-smudged hearts, the Knights of the Keyboard know it. But Boston sportswriters are for the most part mangy, distempered, sunstruck dogs that can do nothing but bite and bite and bite. In a way you can't even blame them. They are as much at the mercy of the long losing streak as the fans who buy their tickets at the window or pony up for NESN on cable TV. Sooner or later—maybe even this year, I haven't given up hope, even yet I am still faithful—the Sox will win it all, and this infected boil will burst. I think all of us will be happier when it does. Certainly we will be more rational.

Later, after a quiet 4–3 loss to the Tigers:

SK: I admit it: after the third Detroit base runner reached with none out, I left the room. Simply could no longer bear to watch. And—between me and you?—a lot of this really *is* just daffy-horrible luck. Derek Lowe hasn't been the only recipient, but he has surely gotten the biggest helping. Last year, the second two batters are harmless ground outs, and we're up 1–0, Detroit batting with a runner on first and two out.

Oh, this is maddening.

Why why *why* did I ever let you talk me into this?

SO: I watched every dribbling, seeing-eye single. That third base runner was a ball Cabrera couldn't get a handle on. Thank you, Defense Minister Theo. I also have no idea why Francona's got O-Cab batting third. He's hitting something like .100.

You've got to have some luck to win the close ones (and some defense, some speed, a bullpen . . .). In answer to your earlier query as to how we've done in one-run games: we're now 7-15. Wasted a great game from Tek—an honest triple, a mammoth tater and then gunning down Carlos Pena to bail out new guy Mike Myers (really, that's his name) in the eighth. Three runs against Detroit? That's anemic. Come back, Big Papi!

It's worse than maddening, and I apologize for dragging you to the death prom. My lament, as a citizen of the Nation—like an injured lover—is: why why WHY are they doing this to us?

August 7th

I've suggested that the team needed to play .750 ball in its twelve-game stretch against losing opponents; Boston is playing the same old so-so wake-me-when-it's-over road baseball instead. After three matches in Tampa Bay and one in Detroit, the Yankees have sailed over the horizon and even the wild card looks . . . well, it still looks perfectly *possible,* but we look less *deserving* of it, okay? We look about a run short, and I'm not talking about the run we lost by last night, or not *just* that one. I'm talking about the game we lost to Tampa Bay by a run, and the two we lost to the Twins— each also by a single run. That's four one-run losses in a row. This team has played an amazing number of games this season that have been decided by one run: twenty-two so far. The only number more amazing is the number of them we've lost: fifteen. Let me write that in bold strokes so we can both be sure of it: *15 GAMES LOST BY A SINGLE RUN.* At least two of those one-run losses were to the league-leading Yankees.

And we had another one of those bases-loaded-with-two-out night-mares last night. Again and again this year the Red Sox have failed to pro-duce in that situation. Versus the Tigers, Kevin Youkilis *did* manage to snare a walk (he is, after all, the Greek . . . aw, never mind), temporarily tying the score for the tragickal Mr. Lowe. That brought up Orlando Cabrera, one-half of Theo Epstein's replacement for Nomar Garciaparra. Cabrera, who is pressing at the plate and looking more and more like a Stepford Cesar Crespo clone, struck out on three pitches, two of them well out of the strike zone, and that was the end of our one big chance. The Sox went meekly in the top of the ninth, as they have all too often this year, and now taking eight out of twelve means taking six out of eight. It can be done, but I doubt it can be done by *this* team.

SK: The game is looking very shaky into the seventh. I _hate_ the way this season is going.

SO: We did finally pull away from the Tigers tonight, but you're right. The way the season's going seems to be lose, Pedro, lose, Schill, lose. Except when Tim-may throws in the Trop or Arroyo faces the Yanks. Or Lowe's every third start. When are we going to put together a decent streak? At least El Jefe's back (and don't you know, Manny comes down with the flu).

August 9th

It was a good weekend for the Faithful. Pedro Martinez won pretty on Saturday and Tim Wakefield won ugly on Sunday.* In their current important twelve-game stretch against underachieving clubs, Boston now stands at 4-2. Only a churl would point out that they _could_ be 6-0. (I am, of course, that churl.) We have moved into a three-way tie for the wild card with two of the AL Western Division clubs (the Angels and the Rangers), and that is a marked improvement over where we were a week ago. I'll take it.

But any longtime follower of the Red Sox will tell you that when the team's cheek grows rosy, the almost automatic response is for someone, either in the media or in the organization itself, to slap a leech on it. In this case the leeching has to do with Kevin Millar's comments about his playing time and the constantly shifting nature of the team's makeup.

Millar's pique over not being in the lineup for the August 7th game against the Tigers ("Here I am, riding the old benchola") is just silly, especially since he ended up being a last-minute add to Francona's card. But pro athletes aren't known for their statesmanlike qualities, and in other baseball markets such comments usually go unpublished. If they are published, they're apt to be—can you believe this?—_snickered_ at. Not in

---

*How ugly? He was the first pitcher in seventy years to surrender six home runs and still get the win. The Tigers hit seven long taters in all, the last coming off reliever Mike Timlin. The Red Sox hit three, one from David Ortiz and two from Kevin Youkilis.

Boston, though; in Boston, Millar's pregame grousing was treated by postgame commentators Tom Caron and Sam Horn as grave news, indeed; the preachments of Osama Ben Millar.*

The part of Millar's comments which was *not* addressed—either on the Red Sox–authorized NESN broadcast or in the predictably anti-player Boston *Globe*—was his perfectly correct and uncomfortably astute assertion that this year's Red Sox team has no identity, and it's that lack which has so slowed the team's quest for a postseason berth, one we all thought would be a slam dunk at the start of the season. (To be ten and a half games behind the Yankees with a team this talented is just flat-out ridiculous.) The 2004 Boston Red Sox has no *face*. And it's not Nomar Garciaparra I miss in this context. Oddly enough—or perhaps not so oddly at all—it's Trot Nixon I miss, Nixon whose intensity can be seen even in the dog-dumb ads he does for Red Sox/NESN license plates. Every time he stares into the camera with those burning eyes and says, "We think of it as a tag-and-release program . . . so we can keep an eye . . . on *YOU*," I wish to *God* he wasn't on the DL.

Never mind Red Ryder; when ya comin' back, Trotter? We may need you to pull our irons out of the fire yet.

August 10th

The key to every sport—to every endeavor in life, maybe—is consistency, and nowhere is that more apparent than in team defense. Football, soccer, baseball, hockey, basketball—all team defense is based on the premise that each player knows where his or her fellow players are, and can rely on teammates to cover either territory or opposing players he or she can't. In the major leagues this assumes that each player knows his teammates' capabilities and habits, a familiarity that can only come from playing side by side game after game until this knowledge becomes second nature and can be acted on with the speed of reflex.

Example: pop fly down the right-field line. First baseman fades straight back, second baseman angles in from the left, right fielder comes on hard. If the ball's high and deep enough, it's the right fielder's, since the play's in front of him. If it's low and shallow, the first baseman has to make an over-

---

*If the more analytical (and amusing) Dennis Eckersley had been teamed with Caron, he probably would have given this part of the Millar fatwa the horselaugh it deserved.

the-shoulder catch running away from the plate. If it's medium, in no-man's-land, usually the second baseman, having the most speed and the best glove (as well as quarterbacking the in-between play), has to flash across and get it.

Ideally, each fielder has played with the other two enough to know both what they're capable of *and* what they'll do. One right fielder may have difficulty getting in on a ball (Millar, the injured Trot) that another (Kapler, Roberts) should catch easily. Likewise, one second baseman may have no problem making a play in foul ground (Pokey) that another has no shot at (Mark Bellhorn, Bill Mueller), while yet another has maybe a 50% chance (Ricky Gutierrez). Some first basemen don't go back well (Ortiz, Millar) and some do (Mientkiewicz, McCarty); with Andy Dominique, it's hard to say, since he's only played a handful of innings at first, the same way Dauber only played a couple games at first or in the outfield, or Cesar Crespo at second and short, or in right, center, or left. And beyond simple ability, there's the confusing factor of personality. Some fielders are aggressive and dash after every in-between ball whether they can make the play or not (Manny, weirdly), while others hang back till the last second, letting others take charge (Kapler, sadly). Does Doug Mientkiewicz have a good feel for the combination of Bill Mueller and Gabe Kapler as they converge on a dying quail with men on late in a close game? For Ricky Gutierrez and David McCarty? Ricky Gutierrez and Dave Roberts? Bill Mueller and Kevin Millar? Bill Mueller and Dave Roberts?

Impossible, considering how little they've played together. Mientkiewicz is still feeling his way into the defense, the same way Bill Mueller's doing his best to acclimate at second base. At best it's guesswork.

Multiply that uncertainty by the number of odd and new combinations in the field (McCarty in left, Youkilis at third and Orlando Cabrera at short all vying for a ball down the line in Fenway where the stands jut out; or Cabrera and Bill Mueller going back on a flare with Roberts, Johnny or Kapler racing in from center) and add in the memory of the seldom-used Damian Jackson ranging back farther than last year's regular second baseman Todd Walker ever could and knocking Johnny out, and you've got a patchwork defense that lets balls drop.

Part of the problem is injuries, obviously, and part is the pre- and mid-season missteps by upper management (never getting a serious replacement for Trot, loading up on platoon first basemen and shortstops to no apparent purpose), but Francona has to take all of that into account and at least try to put a defense out on the field that can work towards becoming comfortable with each other. Until he does, we'll continue to be inconsistent, and to hurt pitchers like Wake and Lowe, who have to rely on competent glovework behind them to win.

August 11th

The Red Sox and the Devil Rays have split in Boston's first two games back at Fenway, and we're now 5-3 in the twelve-game stretch I've elected to put under the microscope—the twelve games leading up to the stretch drive. Boston hasn't made it easy on itself, losing the first game of the final road series against Detroit and the first game of the home stand against Tampa Bay, but the Sox have managed to win their last two series, and they won again last night.

Bronson Arroyo looks more and more comfortable in his role as a starter (and thank *Christ* he finally shaved off that horrible sand-colored thing on his chin). Tampa Bay's Toby Hall beat Arroyo with an improbable grand slam in his last start, but in last night's game Arroyo mixed his pitches better and got more ground balls. Also, Terry Francona, who is right every once in a while,* lifted him while he was merely toasty instead of completely baked. There *is* a difference.

Today there's a three-way tie for the wild card (Texas, Anaheim, Boston), and tonight the tragickal Mr. Lowe will lug his top-heavy 5.50 ERA to the mound against Tampa Bay's Dewon Brazelton, with a tidy little ERA of 2.56. This may be one of those gut-check games that seem to mean hardly anything at the time and actually mean more when you look for the point where a team either started to kick it into gear . . . or didn't.

August 12th

Boston kicked it into gear, all right. Especially Kevin Millar. Millar seems to have decided that if the Red Sox need identity, he'll supply it. In last night's game against the Devil Rays, he went 4 for 4, with two singles, a double, and a three-run shot into the Monster seats, setting the pace as Boston pounded out 15 hits and routed Tampa Bay 14–4. The man who gave the 2003 Red Sox their late-season slogan—"Cowboy up"—is bat-

---

*A trait he shares with stopped clocks.

ting something ridiculous like .470 for the month of August—31 for his last 66. With numbers like that, he can perhaps be excused for bitching about having to ride "the old benchola."

We have one more game against the tasty Devil Rays—today at one o'clock—before tougher meat comes to town: the Chicago White Sox, currently a game above .500. Boston stands at 6-3 in the current twelve-game stretch, and if we could beat Tampa Bay behind Pedro this afternoon, we'd only have to top the ChiSox once to finish 8-4, as I had hoped we would. Meantime, in the wild-card race . . . chillun, we have sole possession. For today, at least.

Later: After writing that, I shut down the computer and head for southern New Hampshire to visit old friends (he's the physician's assistant who has helped me with medical stuff in a dozen books, most notably *The Stand* and *Pet Sematary,* she's a retired nurse who has reached a hard-won truce in her war with cancer). We have lunch on the patio, a lot of good food and good talk (maybe only horror writers and medical people can reminisce fondly about heart attack patients they have known). We promise we'll stay in closer touch, and maybe we even will.

Starting the 140-mile drive back to western Maine, I remember that the Sox are playing the rare weekday afternoon game. I can't find it on the FM; nothing there but rock music and what a friend of mine calls "macrobiotic talk shows." On the AM, however, I find it crackling through the static on WEEI, the self-proclaimed Red Sox flagship station, and am delighted to discover that Boston is winning handily. My man Kevin Youkilis kicked off the day's festivities, swatting one over everything and into the Manny Zone, aka Lansdowne Street. At the one end of the East Coast, Tampa–St. Pete is girding its loins for the arrival of tropical storm Bonnie and the more dangerous Hurricane Charlie. At this end, the Tampa Bay Devil Rays have run into Hurricane Pedro. He almost always pitches well against the D-Rays, but he hasn't thrown this well in . . . what? Three years? Four?

It's a hot, muggy afternoon in what Mainers sometimes call New Hamster. Due to road construction, the two eastbound lanes of Highway 101 are down to one, and the traffic is bumper-to-bumper. A roadworker points at me, shakes his head, and draws a thumb across his throat. It takes me a minute to realize it's almost certainly my truck he's pointing at—specifically to the bumper sticker on the tailgate reading

SOMEWHERE IN TEXAS A VILLAGE IS MISSING ITS IDIOT. All of this should conspire to put me in a foul mood, but I'm as happy as a kitten in a catnip factory. Pedro goes nine innings and strikes out 10 (in the postgame he admits to Joe Castiglione and Jerry Trupiano that in his old age he's come to appreciate quick ground-ball outs and ten-pitch innings as much as the Ks). We're now 7-3 over the last ten games, we need only to split the next two with Chicago to finish the Dirty Dozen at 8-4, and as of today there's a game's worth of sunshine between us and the Anaheim Angels in the wild-card race.

Best of all, though, the last few innings of the game lightened what otherwise would have been a very tiresome drive through heavy traffic, and I think that's really what baseball is for, especially baseball on the radio . . . which is, as Joe Castiglione says in his book *Broadcast Rites and Sites*, the last bastion of the spoken image.

Or something like that.

As Ole Case used to say, "You could look it up."

August 14th

The Red Sox didn't make it easy (that has *never* been a part of the deal with them), but they managed to finish the twelve-game stretch that began on August 2nd at exactly 8-4. The opener in the current series against the White Sox was another one-run loss, and tonight's game began badly, with Curt Schilling giving up consecutive solo home runs to Timo Perez and Carlos Lee almost before the last notes of the national anthem had died away.

But in this game the Red Sox played flawless defense (the highlight was a sliding, twisting, skidding catch in foul territory by Kevin Youkilis, who almost ended up in the White Sox dugout), and you have to admire Curt Schilling, a pitcher whose face—along with those of Bob Gibson and Sandy Koufax, maybe—ought to grace the cover of the *Old School Baseball Encyclopedia*. Following the home runs, he surrendered only one more hit until the sixth. By then the Red Sox had tied the game on back-to-back solo home runs of their own, one by Manny Ramirez and one by David "Big Papi" Ortiz.

Papi came up again in the bottom of the eighth, after Ramirez had struck out looking on three pitches. By then Schilling was done for the evening, but still eligible for the win if the Red Sox could pull ahead. Ortiz took care of his pitcher, dumping one into the fourth or fifth row of seats beyond the bullpen in right center. It wasn't quite as mighty as his earlier rocket, but there was still no doubt when it left the bat. I have never seen such a big man who is able to generate such sudden power, not even Mo Vaughn. God knows how long it will last, but Red Sox fans have been blessed to watch it over the last two seasons, and Ortiz may be having an MVP year.

Keith Foulke came on in the top of the ninth. My wife had gone to bed by then, and that was probably just as well; when Foulke walked Chicago's leadoff hitter on five pitches, my state of jangled nerves approached real terror. It was all too easy to see this one slipping away. Foulke took the mound with 18 saves, not a lot for a club that's now approaching the 65-win mark, and very few of those saves have come in one-run situations. Tonight, however, just enough of Schilling's tough-man air seemed to linger on the mound to carry Foulke through. After the walk came a pop-up, after the pop-up came two strikeouts, the last on a faltering half-swing at a changeup by Juan Uribe, and presto, "Dirty Water" was playing over the PA system. Pedro Martinez was first out of the dugout, giving high fives with what appeared to be a fungo bat.

One final note: the Yankees beat the Mariners this afternoon, maintaining their bonecrushing ten-and-a-half-game lead in the AL East and winning their 75th game of the year with August not yet half over. They are on a pace to win 110 games, perhaps more. This is more than unreal; this is *surreal*.

August 16th

Ten in the morning and I have no idea who won the game last night. We're at camp, away from TV and computers and even the newspaper. The director usually posts the bare-bones scores on a wall in the dining hall (often with a synopsis of the Pirate game), but today he's bumped them for the Olympics. Yesterday, anticipating this, I shelled out five bucks for the modern equivalent of a transistor radio and listened to the Indians and Twins' afternoon game from the Jake, but last night at bedtime I couldn't catch a round-the-league wrap-up.

We've been gone a week now, and this is the first time I haven't naturally run across a score. While we were at my dad's cottage on Lake Chautauqua, Wake's six-homer win over the D-Rays made the Jamestown paper, complete with a photo of Tim-may. The Buffalo TV news at eleven featured our next game, since a local family threw out the first pitch in memory of their son, a high school star and Sox fan, dead of cancer, who'd dreamed of playing at Fenway.

Most nights I'd get just a score and then have to wait for the morning paper to fill me in, though during one newscast after the Bisons beat Pawtucket, we were treated to the Real Deal Player of the Game going deep twice against a skinny submariner wearing number 15—the elusive Mr. Kim.

A straight score, lumped with others from around the league, is flat and paralyzing. If we win, it's great for about twenty seconds, then I'm pissed that I don't know how we won, or why. A loss is awful—irrefutable, infuriating—and terrible for about a minute, until I realize that I don't know anything about the game, not even who pitched. It's a mindless, uninvolved way to follow baseball, almost zero content, as if the game is just about winning or losing.

We don't watch a lot of TV at Chautauqua (getting only two snowy channels will do that), so inevitably I fell a day behind, picking up the paper and dissecting last night's box score, looking for signs. Manny was finally back; Trot and Pokey and Bellhorn weren't. Cabrera continued to struggle at the plate. Bill Mueller, still playing out of position, made another error. Terrible Terry Adams put men on and Mendoza let them in, while Takatsu, the White Sox reliever, inherited three runners and stranded them. Even uglier, their seven and eight hitters combined for 7 RBIs.

Sometimes it's fun to puzzle out backwards what happened, but even a box score is cold matter, a map to treasure already dug up. Stanley Kubrick, insulated in his compound in the English countryside, used to have an assistant here in the States tape the playoffs and World Series so he could devour them at his leisure, and while I admire Kubrick's taste (and appetite), watching a game that's long been over, and watching alone, seems to leach the immediacy from what is essentially a shared experience. Ideally, I want to be *at* the game, reacting to every pitch and situation as part of the loud, honest-to-God crowd; short of that I'll join the far-flung (and far from imaginary) audience all across New England watching Don and Jerry or listening to Joe and Troop or Uri Berenguer and J. P. Villaman, knowing that when David Ortiz cranks one, citizens of the Nation—from the capital of Fenway to the borderlands of the Northeast Kingdom and the Dominican—are hollering like idiots the same as I am. A box score or even a decent recap can't show me what kind of location Lowe has, or how much of a lead Dave Roberts is getting. I need to see it *now,* before what happens happens.

So this is limbo, not knowing anything until it's already over (and even then not knowing the results from Anaheim or Oakland). All I can say, today, is that in mid-August we're solidly in the wild-card race, and possibly in the lead, and that, from all evidence, as a team we're having the exact same problems we had two months ago—the same problems, really, we had last year.

August 17th

I need to go back to the Garciaparra trade again, and it probably won't be for the last time. It's going to be one of the big Red Sox stories of the year, certainly *the* big story if this wounded, limping, patched-together team* doesn't make postseason (or even if it does but doesn't advance).

When we got Doug Mientkiewicz and Orlando Cabrera in return for Nomar, we were assured by management that this was a lot more than trade-mania, the equivalent of the crazy buying that goes on at the annual Filene's Wedding Sale. We were "plugging defensive holes." In addition to that, Cabrera's .246 batting average was deceiving; he was "a doubles machine."

Right, and we won in Vietnam; mission accomplished in Iraq.

Mientkiewicz, although not used as an everyday player by Terry Francona, has played solid, unflashy baseball for Boston, and no surprise there; as a Minnesota Twin he's played on plenty of contending teams, and he's used to the pressure. Cabrera is a different story. Players who come from forgotten teams (and surely the Montreal Expos are *the* forgotten team) either blossom or shrivel when they come to contending teams and pressure-cooker venues like Boston; Cabrera has so far done the latter. The press has been patient with him, but you'd expect that; in Boston most of those guys shill for management, and while they have no problem making Nomar look bad, they'd love his replacement to look good so they can say, "See? He's great. Toldja."

---

*Latest victim of the injury bug is Kevin Youkilis, who suffered a jammed ankle at home plate after being waved in from second by Dale Sveum in the final game of the Red Sox–White Sox series two days ago (Youkilis was out).

More interesting to me—also more surprising and endearing—has been the fans' patience with Cabrera . . . who probably helped himself enormously by hitting a home run in his first at-bat in the Red Sox uniform. None since, though, and his Montreal batting average of .246 has shrunk to something like .225. Worse, he hasn't looked like anyone's idea of a Gold Glover at shortstop. Last night, in Boston's game against Toronto—the first of a three-game set—Cabrera racked up a pair of RBIs, one on a base hit and one on a sac fly. Then, in an agonizing, rain-soaked seventh inning that seemed to go on forever, he gave them both back plus one to grow on with two box-score errors and a third, mental, error that allowed a run which should have been kept right where it was, at third base.

Cabrera's hitting in the clutch has been nonexistent. In the game previous to last night's—the final game of the Red Sox–White Sox series—Cabrera ended things by grounding softly back to the pitcher, leaving the tying run stranded at third after the Red Sox had battled back from a multi-run deficit. So in last night's game I was a little saddened but not really surprised to hear the first scattered boos in the rain-depleted crowd when Cabrera came up following his seventh-inning follies, which turned a 5–1 Red Sox cruise into a 5–4 nail-biter against the American League's bottom dogs. The crowd wants him to be good, and I have no doubt that he *is*—no doubt that Terry Francona is exactly right when he says that Cabrera (who, unlike Mientkiewicz, plays every day) is pressing at the plate—but I also have no doubt that the Nomar trade has already cost this Red Sox team at least three games it could ill afford to lose, and that it will quite likely cost them more unless Orlando Cabrera quickly finds his stride.

I'm not man enough to predict that the Sox will win eight of the current twelve, but they *could*, with half of the next dozen coming against the abysmal Blue Jays and two more against the only slightly better Tigers. And they *should*, if they are to retain their position as the team to beat in the wild-card race, and perhaps even put some distance between themselves and the other contending teams. But the injury situation continues to grow worse rather than better; with Youkilis down, we were last night treated to the bizarre sight of Doug Mientkiewicz playing second base for the first time in his life. And, aside from getting knocked down once by Carlos Delgado, he did a damned good job.

One final note: as the season wears on, I find it easier and easier to spell Mientkiewicz. People can adjust to just a-damn-bout anything, can't they?

August 18th

Having said all that, let me tell you that no one in all of Red Sox Nation was any happier than I was when Orlando Cabrera finally *did* come through in the clutch, turning on an 86 mph Justin Speier changeup and clanging it off the scoreboard in the bottom of the ninth inning last night, chasing Johnny Damon home with the winning run in the second game of Boston's current series against the Toronto Blue Jays.

Fenway giveth and Fenway taketh away. In the first game of the series, it tooketh away big-time from Mr. Cabrera. Last night, that funky just-right bounce gaveth back, and I went dancing around my living room, singing the Gospel According to K.C. and the Sunshine Band: "That's the way (uh-huh, uh-huh) I like it."

Does this mean I think the Garciaparra trade is suddenly, magically okay? No. But I was rooting for Cabrera to come through—not just for the Red Sox but for Cabrera *as* a Red Sock? You bet your tintype. Because, no matter what I or any other fan might think of the trade, the deal is done and Cabrera's one of us now; he wears the red and white. So, sure, I root for him.

Thus, hooray, Orlando. May you clang a hundred more off that funky old scoreboard. Welcome to Fenway Park. Welcome home.

August 21st

SO: Guess who's back, back again . . .

SK: Considering that the Red Sox have won 11 of their last 16, maybe you ought to go back where you were, and I mean find the EXACT SPOT. It was especially great to see Cabrera connect on that crazy wall-ball carom double—like something out of a psychedelic Pong game—to win the game Monday night. And then there was Big Papi hulking down on L'il Massa Lily White [Toronto starter Ted Lilly, who plunked Ortiz on the hand]. Too much fun!

SO: I've missed so much. A friend tells me that in one game Francona started Mientkiewicz at second. Is he shittin' me?

SK: Nope. And Dougie played genius.

It hasn't been Boston's best week (I firmly believe that this season's best weeks are still ahead of them), but we're riding our fifth four-game winning streak of the season, and if we win again this afternoon, the Red Sox will be proud possessors of their fourth *five*-game winning streak of the season. There's better news: I've lost track of *All My Children* almost completely, and am hoping that when my viewing habits once more regularize on that front, the child of Babe and the odious JR will be in middle school and developing problems of his own (kids on soap operas grow up fast).

August has certainly been the best *month* of the season for the Red Sox, and the team couldn't have picked a better time to get hot. There isn't a lot of wild-card competition on the horizon in the Central Division, but with the exception of the Mariners (now better than twenty games off the pace), the West is a shark tank. For the last week or so, all the sharks—Oakland, Anaheim, and Texas—have been feeding on their weaker Midwestern brothers, and all of them have been winning.* One of these clubs will win the division. The other two—along with the Red Sox—are swimming full-tilt at a door only big enough to admit one of them. I comfort myself with thoughts of the schedule, which will eventually force the sleek sharks of the Western Division to begin dining upon each other.

The Yankees, in the meantime, have finally begun to falter a bit as their pitching arms become more and more suspect (may I note—and not without glee—that their trade for Esteban Loaiza is looking especially doubtful; there are already trade rumors floating around). They've lost three out of their last four—the one win an almost miraculous come-from-behinder against the Twins—and while I don't think anyone among the Red Sox Faithful are counting on a total Yankee el floppo (but how sweet it would

---

*The Texas Rangers have won six in a row and show no sign of their usual August heat prostration.

be), I'd guess that few among us are unaware that the New York lead, which was ten and a half ten days ago, has now shrunk to seven and a half. Still a lot, but on August 21st, seven and a half games doesn't seem like an insurmountable lead.

August 22nd

I'm addicted to the Little League World Series the way a college hoop junkie craves March Madness. Every game is high drama, and you never know what to expect. Tonight we switch back and forth between the Sox and the Lincoln, Rhode Island, team, and after a while, like the end of *Animal Farm*, it's hard to tell where one ends and the other begins. Both survive late scares. The kids' defense falls apart in the sixth. In Chicago, the Sox are up a run in the eighth, thanks to back-to-back jacks by Manny and David, when Manny goes to plant himself under an easy fly, slips on the wet grass, recovers, then slips again, and the ball falls behind him. Timlin gets us out of it and Foulke closes, looking sharp. The Angels have swept the Yanks, and the Rangers finally lost, so we're five and a half back in the East and a game up in the wild card. And the New England kids win.

This is terrific—we beat the White Sox again, making us 5-1 in our last six games. The Rangers also won, but the trade-off is that the Yankees took another drubbing from the Angels (and at the Stadium, hee-hee), meaning that the New York lead is down another full game. Knowing that their team has lost almost half their seemingly insurmountable lead in the space of a week cannot make Yankee fans happy. (That lead probably is insurmountable, but north of Hartford the only thing we love more than seeing the pin-stripers have a bad week is seeing them have *two* bad weeks.)

The Red Sox have scored 20 runs against the White Sox in the last two games. Varitek is thumping the ball, and so is Millar, but I think the big offensive story in Chicago has been Manny Ramirez. He's been sluggish at the plate since the All-Star break, but in the last two games he's shown a return to the batting brilliance that made him such a catch for us in the first place. He hit the 16th grand slam of his career in the second inning of the Friday night game (August 20th) and added a three-run job yesterday. He has a total of 9 RBIs in the two games.

To this you should add in Manny's glovework, especially back home in Boston, where he has become more and more comfortable with the eccentricities of left field at Fenway, a position that has made strong baseball players cry. Manny has gotten a reputation as a bad defensive baseball player and will almost certainly carry it with him for his entire career (the only people less likely than baseball fans to change their minds about a player are other players, coaches and, of course, Ted Williams's "Knights of the Keyboard"), but he has mastered the knack of playing the carom off the Green Monster in such a way as to hold runners at first (the world-famous "wall-ball single"), and he has made some brilliant, fearless catches, especially going to his right, into the Twilight Zone territory beyond third base where the wall is hard and foul territory is measured in mere inches. He's no Yaz, but is he at least the equal of Mike Greenwell, and maybe a little better? Our survey says yes.

And damn, ain't he a likable cuss! That wasn't always the case in Cleveland, where Manny had a reputation for taciturnity (he rarely did interviews), standoffishness and laziness. In Boston, Manny always seems to be smiling, and it is a beautiful smile, boyish and somehow innocent. He hustles, and the camera frequently catches him goofing with his teammates in the dugout (in one beautifully existential contrast, the viewer sees Curt Schilling studiously poring over paperwork while Manny mugs crazily over his shoulder). He has even done a shoe commercial which has its own brand of goofy Manny Ramirez charm.*

Some of the change from Growly Manny to Don't Worry, Be Happy Manny may have to do with the Dominican Mafia that, simply by chance, now surrounds him: cheery-by-nature players like Pedro Martinez and David Ortiz. Some of it may be a kind of weird alchemy in Manny's lungs: he pulls in the baleful, media-poisoned air of Boston and exhales his own brand of nonchalant good cheer in its place. I actually sort of buy this, because not even the trade rumors that swirled around him in the off-season changed Manny as we have come to know him: he comes to work, he does his job, and if the Red Sox win, he gives a postgame interview in which he shakes his head and says, "We gotta jus' keep goin', man, you know? We got another sees wee's in the season and we gotta jus' keep goin'."

One of the reasons I'd like the Red Sox to win the World Series is so I can see if Manny would say *"We gotta jus' keep goin', man"* in his postgame

---

*In it, a dreamy Manny fantasizes about becoming the World Series MVP.

interview, if he's that much on cruise control. Probably not, but I'm sure he'd smile, and that smile is worth a thousand dollars.

SK: Admit it: You stole *The Scream*. It reminded you of how you felt in Game 7 versus the Yankees in last year's ALCS.

SO: I stole it and shipped it to Billy Buck, who's staring at it right now, nailed up on the wall of his shack in deepest Aryan Idaho. Edvard Munch was a Sox fan—a ChiSox fan. Talk about tanking: they were in first on July 26th; since then they've gone 8-19. It's not that the Twins have played great ball, it's just a flat-out collapse. When's the last time we swept them in Comiskey?

SK: Been quite a few years. It's nice to feel happy again about the Red Sox, isn't it? If only for a while.

SO: You were dead right about how nice it would be getting 15 games over .500, but I sure didn't count on the A's, Rangers and Angels ALL streaking alongside of us. There's four cars and the tunnel's only two lanes.

SK: All is well as can be here, and Manny is stroking the shit out of the ball. Check out Chip McGrath's "Lost Cause" piece in today's *New York Times Magazine*. Good for a giggle, I think.
  Or a snort of disgust.

SO: I expect it's about the Yanks' el foldo act the last three (make it four) years running.

SK: Can you believe the Yankees lost *five games in one week*??? I went to bed thinking, "If I was Joe Torre, I'd say, 'This is why you like the big lead—you can go through a tough stretch like this and still be on top.'" I got up this morning and damned if that wasn't just what the Skip said. What *our* Skip said was that when Manny dropped the pop, he swallered half his plug of tobacco. Served him right.

SO: Ol' Joe's got the luxury of a six-man rotation and all the bench support George can buy, so he doesn't have to sweat September. October, though . . . If they choke again, there are going to be some changes. Imagine if the heavily favored Sox blew three consecutive postseasons. Why, there'd be talk of a curse.

I'd like to see a reel with all of Manny's wildlights. He's like Charlie Brown out there—or Pig Pen. And I ain't gonna say it, but you know what that plug o' chaw resembles, half-in and half-out of Terry's mouth? Ayuh.

SK: My last bit in the August section is about Manny—Manny at the bat and Manny in the field, and how his bad fielding is a misperception. I think you'll be amused.

SO: I'm sure it'll be a hoot. Wonder if we'll agree. Manny's about style, and I can dig that, but sometimes that feigned nonchalance leads to real goofs, like not running out pops down the line that end up falling fair, or forgetting how many outs there are. He's got a good arm, but he loves to do that cool no-look throw from the corner so much that often he doesn't get enough zip on the ball and ends up rainbowing one in. And of course my favorite was when he forgot to call time after a double, stepped off second and got tagged out. But hey, it's all part of being Manny.

August 23rd

SK: In the *Times* piece about the Yankees' lost weekend, there is, so help me God, this line: "Meanwhile, the Red Sox loom." So take that, Chip McGrath.

Curt Schilling calls the Lincoln, Rhode Island, Little League team to give them a pep talk before their game tonight. The kids and their coaches are gathered around a speakerphone on a table. Everyone's pumped.

"Are you gonna win it?" Schill asks.

"Yeah!" everyone says.

And then one kid—a skinny little joker—leans over the phone and asks, "Are you?"

Just as the room busts up (there's no more explosive laughter than nervous laughter—Vincent Price *Masque of the Red Death* laughter), the ESPN crawl at the bottom of the screen reads: GARCIAPARRA (CHI-NL) OUT WITH STRAINED WRIST.

The advantage we have in the wild card is that with the unbalanced schedule the teams in the West will be facing one another while we feast on scrubs like the Jays and D-Rays. Tonight we plan to cash in, throwing Pedro against Ted Lilly in the mostly empty SkyDome. Reed Johnson leads off the Toronto first with a home run. Orlando Hudson follows with a triple. Again, Pedro's come out like his brother Ramon, as if he's not warmed up to game speed. He settles down after that and throws a great game, only giving up two more hits, but Lilly's on, and with our lack of righty power (and Tek serving his suspension for shoving A-Rod), he shuts us down, 3–0, a three-hit complete game—only the second shutout against us (Jason Schmidt's is the other). The Yanks beat Cleveland on a Sterry Sheffield home run, and the Angels won to pull even with us. And the kids from Rhode Island lost.

August 24th

This is a true adventure in surrealism: I'm in Boston (exploring possibilities for a musical play with John Mellencamp) and the Red Sox are in Toronto (exploring possibilities for extending their season into October). Tim Wakefield, the pitcher who's closest to the center of this Red Sox fan's heart, is on the hill, and I keep running out to check with Ray, my longtime limo driver, who's parked in a loading zone and listening to the game on the radio. At first things don't go well; for most of the season Wakefield's had problems with the gopher ball, and he gives up another in the first. The Jays keep pecking and are leading 3–0 when the Red Sox begin to crawl back, courtesy of Manny "We gotta jus' keep goin', man" Ramirez, who plates a couple with a base hit to center. Then Doug Mirabelli, who regularly catches Wakefield (and will be standing in for Jason Varitek this week while Tek finishes serving his four-game suspension for the brawl with Alex Rodriguez), hits a monster three-run homer to left center, putting the Sox up, 5–3.

I'm headed back to my hotel with Ray when Wake leaves the game. At that point the Red Sox still lead by two, but the Blue Jays have loaded the bases with nobody out. Enter Mike Timlin, who strikes out two . . . and then we lose WEEI's AM signal amid the tall buildings. Ray and I sit, not speaking, at a seemingly endless red light, listening to static. When we get rolling again and the static finally clears, I hear the merry voices of the Giant Glass singers ("Who do you call when your windshield's *bus*-ted?"), and know that Timlin either gave up a disastrous multibase hit and is being replaced—the barn door securely locked by Terry Francona after the horse has been stolen—or he actually wriggled out of it. When the game comes back on, the Red Sox are batting. It turns out that Timlin coaxed Alex Rios, the third batter to face him, into hitting a mild ground ball. Ray and I slap hands, and we're back at the Boston Harbor Hotel before the Red Sox have finished batting.

I rush upstairs, ready to watch the final inning of what turns out to be another one-run nail-biter on TV . . . only to discover that the Boston Harbor may be the only hotel in the Boston metro area that *doesn't* carry NESN. No Red Sox on TV, in other words. I try the radio. Nothing on the FM but opera and Aerosmith, nothing on the AM band but one constant blat of static. I do the only reasonable thing, under the circumstances; I call my son in New Hampshire and have him call the final three batters Joe Castiglione–style over the phone. It feels like bad mojo—the Red Sox *always* seem to lose when I watch or listen with my kids—but this time the Sox hold on, and I go to bed happy even though the Yankees have turned relentless again. We're now 7-2 over the last nine games, and it's hard to be unhappy with that.

Top of the sixth, down 3–2 with two on and one out for Doug Mirabelli against a tiring Miguel Batista. Doug's the slowest guy on the team, a real double-play threat. The book here is to pinch-hit a lefty, and we've got a whole bench full. Problem is, with Tek still out, and Theo and Francona not wanting to waste a roster spot on Andy Dominique, our backup catcher is Doug Mientkiewicz. Mirabelli stands in and crashes a three-run bomb off the scoreboard in left-center. How does that proverb go: some have greatness thrust upon them?

Same thing in the bottom of the inning, when the Jays load the bases with none out. Embree's arm is dead from overwork, and Leskanic and Adams have had control problems. Mike Timlin's thrown way too many innings lately, but Francona's got no one else. Timlin goes to the slider and whiffs Reed Johnson and Orlando Hudson, then gets Alex Rios on a force-out. He gives one back in the seventh, but Mendoza (another unlikely hero) gets two outs in the eighth, and Foulke handles things from there. So, thanks to some clutch play from the shallow end of the depth chart, we keep pace.

August 25th

With Nomar gone and Trot possibly lost for the season, we don't have a true number five hitter to protect Manny and David. Francona's tried a number of guys there lately—just as he tried Dauber and Tek early in the season. When he posts the lineup for our nineteenth and final game of the season against Toronto, Bellhorn sees that Bill Mueller's in the number five slot and jokes, "Are we trying tonight?"

Dave Wallace likes to say that if your eight best pitchers throw 80% of your innings, you'll be in good shape. That's great if you have eight good pitchers. Toronto has two. Kid righty Josh Towers implodes in the fifth, giving up back-to-back jobs to Manny and David, and then, two batters later, a two-run shot to Cabrera on a hanging curve. Schilling goes 6 1/3 and leaves with the score a comfortable 10–1, giving Francona a chance to use some of our worst arms (Terry Adams, Mike Myers, Mendoza—who actually throws well) and rest the real pen for one night.

The Yanks and Rangers lose, but the Angels put up 21 runs against the Royals to stay even in the wild card. Next Tuesday we start a nine-game stretch against the Angels, Rangers and A's. If we can go 6-3 or better, we're looking at the playoffs.

August 26th

You never take the field expecting to lose, but when your number five starter is on the mound, you know you've got to work a little harder. Number five guys can be kids on their way up (Clemens, early on; Aaron Sele; Casey Fossum), vets on the way down (the execrable Matt Young; the puzzling Ramon Martinez; the scuffling Frank Castillo; the iffy John Burkett), or guys in the middle just trying to hold on (usually junkballers like Al Nipper or Wake). The recent number five fad is the converted closer (Derek

Lowe, Anaheim's Kelvim Escobar), which makes more sense, giving a shot to a guy who actually has good stuff—as opposed to the normal borderline number five guy stuff—and hoping he develops into a number two or three.

All number five guys have promise, otherwise they wouldn't be in the majors, but it's rare to see one over the age of thirty bloom into a solid starter, the way ex-Sock Jamie Moyer did in Seattle. More often, the number five who exceeds expectations isn't the vet or the phenom (he's already a number one or two, like the Cubs' Kerry Wood or Mark Prior) but a guy in his mid-to-late twenties getting his second shot and putting it all together, the way Bronson Arroyo does tonight.

Arroyo's skinny as a stick, but he's no kid. At twenty-seven, he's been a pro for ten years, signing with Pittsburgh out of high school and rising through their farm system, seeing limited action with the big club for parts of three seasons until they waived him before spring training last year. He pitched brilliantly for Pawtucket, earning a September call-up, and threw so well—especially against the Yankees—that we made room for him on our playoff roster. This year, with Kim out, by default he became our number five guy, and though his record's only 7-9 (partly due to lack of run support, partly to our weak middle relievers), his ERA is 4.07, a full run better than Lowe's, just .29 behind Pedro—better, in fact, than all the Yankee starters except Kevin Brown. Tonight he has his curve working and shuts down the Tigers for 7 1/3, giving up only an unearned run in a clutch 4–1 win. On the mound he's contained but assured, then almost cocky, sauntering off after striking out the side, as slow as Pedro. It's the kind of performance that makes you wonder if he'll turn into a number one someday.

August 27th

As previously noted, the Boston baseball writers are masters of the bad vibe, maestros of dark karma. If cast away on a cannibal isle, I have no doubt they would soon be kings . . . at least until reduced to dining upon each other. Hardly anything seems to knock them off-stride—how could it, when they cover a team which has been denied the ultimate brass ring for eighty-six years?—but one thing that does give them pause is a protracted winning streak. When Bronson Arroyo notched last night's win over the Detroit Tigers, he helped make the Boston Red Sox nine for their last ten, and the Hub sports pages were flooded with sunshine, most of it thin enough to . . . well, thin enough to read a newspaper through.

Leave it to Dan Shaughnessy to find a reassuring dark spot; just the right familiar note of negativity. In today's *Globe* column (untrustworthily titled "Dark Days Appear to Be Long Gone"), Shaughnessy says, in effect: "Does all this winning upset you? Does it leave you with a feeling of vertigo to get up in the morning and discover the Sox have won yet again? *BLAME NOMAR!*" That's right; blame Number 5, now living it up in Chicago under a different number. Shaughnessy dates the current roll of distressing good times (ooh, my tummy hurts, somebody pass the Dramamine) from July 31st, the day of the Big Trade. Never mind the two horrible losses that followed on its heels, or Orlando Cabrera's terrible struggle to find his feet in the field and his stroke at the plate as he plays for the first time in years in front of a live audience. No, it's Garciaparra's fault, and why? Two reasons. First, because management pulled the trigger and management has to be right. Second, because we have just got to find the dark lining inside this silver cloud. How else can we define ourselves as Cursed, for God's sake? I think George Orwell said it best in his classic allegory, *Baseball Animal Farm Team*: "Orlando good, Nomar bad."

Now—have all you little piggies got that straight?

SO: You know how fantasists talk about the willing suspension of disbelief? After tonight's win over the Tigers (the 10th in our last 11 games, the 16th out of the last 20), I'm experiencing an INVOLUNTARY suspension of disbelief. Knock wood.

And yet, the Angels won their ninth straight to stay a half game back. Seems like we never have room to catch our breath.

SK: Yow! Given the first four months of the season, and the continuing injuries, who would have BELIEVED the August this team has turned in? It is un-fucking-real. September *could* be a fade, but we at least have a tame sked in the second half. Meanwhile, the series with the Angels (don't touch 'em, you'll blister your frogging fingers) is shaping up to be mini-Armageddon. I repeat: ***Yow!!***

Stew—do you believe this shit? It is ***TOO FUCKING GOOD TO LAST*** and ***TOO FUCKING GOOD NOT TO***.

THE HOTTEST AUGUST ON RECORD

SO: I was thinking yesterday that the team has shown a lot of character, and I can't remember when there was as sweet and wild a chase as
the one shaping up. Some real scoreboard-watching. Way it's been
going, I just assume the other three are winning out West. The A's are
just as hot as the Angels. Damn you, Billy Beane!

August 29th

I recently read an interesting note from a sports psychologist—can't
remember who or where, or I'd be happy to attribute it. Anyway, this guy
said that when the local team wins, they're *we,* as in *we* beat the Tigers last
night for the third time straight. When the locals lose, they're *they,* as in
can you believe how lousy *they* were in July?

You can call Boston's recent spectacular run—eleven Ws in the last thirteen games, if my math is right—as a lesson in just how great the disparity
is between the haves and the have-nots in the American League, but that
would ignore the so-so way *they* played against the same clubs earlier in
the season.* It also ignores the fact that *we're* doing it now with many players either on the DL or going out there hurt.

It's a great run, and probably Stewart's and my e-mails show this best.
I hope he'll lay a couple of those daffy suckers in here. (*"Waaba-waaba-
waaba, do you beleeeve this shit, Steve?"* and I'm back with *"Waaacka-
waaacka-waaacka, no fuckin' WAY!"*) And, to top things off, Anaheim
finally *lost* a game yesterday. That means that when the Red Sox/Angels
showdown—mini-Armageddon—starts on Tuesday at the Fens, we're
guaranteed the wild-card lead, and if things go the way I've got them
planned, that lead will be up to two and a half games.

Even the folks at Scribner, who commissioned this book (at no small
cost, either, hee-hee), have stopped crying doom. For the time being, at
least.

SO: You going for the sweep today? Wakey-wakey, eggs and bakey.

---

*Back then, of course, it was Nomar's fault; even while on the DL he was sticking pins in his
Terry Francona voodoo doll.

SK: Shhhh, no Wakey-wakey. Just Tim-MAY.
No wakey them Tigers.

We won again yesterday behind a strong outing by Pedro, and this afternoon there's a carnival mood around Fenway. Manny, who fouled a ball off his knee and missed last night's game, comes out for batting practice wearing coach Ino Guerrero's #65. In the field Manny's manic, flashing how many outs there are to Johnny, to the family section, to the Monster. In the fifth, down 1–0, he comes up with bases loaded and two out, and the crowd rises, chanting, "MANN-y, MANN-y." First pitch, he drills a single to give us the lead. Ortiz rips another, then Millar. Wake throws eight strong, and the party doesn't stop.

It's strange, this high from winning—a straight drug, uncut. Faithful as the Faithful are, we tend to nitpick, even after a win. Not today. Everything's clicking, and, sure, it's only Detroit, but we've won 20 games this month. The underachieving Red Sox have become overachievers, and no one is happier than the Faithful.

SO: It was good and breezy and Wake had his knuckler dancing. Just like yesterday, the Tigers hung in till the fifth, when their starter faltered, and then their reliever totally imploded. Yanks were losing last I heard. Could we be only four and a half back?

SK: Indeed we could! And 1.5 ahead in the wild card!

SO: Supersweet. Now, I don't want to throw cold water on the party, but the Yanks have a cake schedule the rest of the way. They're home 20 of their last 32, and we're the only winning team they face (okay, and three against the Twins, but by then Minnesota will be resting starters for the playoffs). In any case, it's time to square off with the Angels. Some very large games.

August 30th

The last time Tim Wakefield pitched against the Tigers, he gave up six home runs and still got the win, a feat only accomplished once since the days when most big-league teams rode to their away contests on trains.* Yesterday, though, on a day so hot the pitchers in the bullpen used a groundskeeper's hose to spray the fans in the lower right-field bleachers to keep them cool, Wakefield beat the Tigers again, this time more tidily, going eight strong innings and giving up only three hits. No one was any happier than me. I hate to sound like Annie Wilkes here, but I've got to be one of Wake's biggest fans.†

And why not? Look at all we have in common. Wakefield stands 6'2"; I stand 6'3". Wakefield weighs 210; I weigh 195 (and used to weigh 210). Wakefield's middle name is Stephen; my first name is Stephen. Wakefield got hit by a car while jogging in 1997; I got hit by a van while walking in 1999. When Wakefield started against the Braves in the 1992 National League Championship Series, he was the first rookie to do so in nine years. When I started for the Boston Red Sox in the 1986 ALCS, I was the first rookie to do so in *ten* years.‡

More importantly, Wakefield is the sort of player George Will was talking about in his overidealized book-length essay *Men at Work*, one who really *is* a man at work. There is . . . well, I was going to write there's *little* star-time ego about him, but in fact there seems to be *no* star-time ego at all about him. He comes to the ballpark not full of prime-time flash like Jose Canseco did, not wearing the ostentatious earring like Barry Bonds does, or with the panhandle-sized chip on his shoulder as Roger Clemens still seems to do (the Rocket still wants everyone to know they climb when he walks, by God).

Tim Wakefield comes almost the way a man would come to a factory, not plodding but not strutting, just walking steady, with his shirt tucked in all the way around, his belt buckled neatly in front, his hair (what's left

---

*The last time it happened was September 1940, to George Caster of the Philadelphia Athletics, who beat us despite six dingers.

†For reasons he probably could not explain (it's a fan thing), Stewart O'Nan calls the Red Sox knuckler not Wake but Tim-*MAY*. Hey, I don't make the news, I just report it.

‡Call this a lie if you want to; I prefer to think of it as a part of my rich and continuing fantasy life.

of it) trimmed close, his time card in his hand. You almost expect to see him deposit his lunch pail on the bench before going out to the mound.

He is the egoless workhorse* who signed with Boston in 1995, after being let go by the Pirates, and promptly won sixteen straight for the Sox. He gave them innings, innings, innings . . . including one harrowing stint as the club's closer. (He was successful in the role—as he has been in almost all of his roles—but he was also almost impossible to watch.) He became a free agent in November of 2000 and re-signed with Boston a month later, taking a $1.5 million pay cut to stay with the big club (following his heroics in the 2003 postseason, when he came within five outs of being named the League Championship Series MVP, his salary went back to where it had been in 2002). Since then he has again given the big club innings and more innings, keeping his mouth shut while he does it.

Now, after various stints in long relief and that one scary two- or three-week turn as the closer a couple of years ago, Wake is back where he belongs, starting games for the team of which he is the longest-standing member. He's run his '04 record to a respectable 11-7, seems to be rounding into stretch-drive form, and if he doesn't garner the sort of fan adulation the Pedro Martinezes and Curt Schillings receive (not too many people come to the ballpark with *49 WAKEFIELD* on their backs), that's probably to be expected. Working joes—guys who keep their heads down and their mouths shut, guys who just do the job—rarely do. In fact, some guy once quipped, "No great thing was ever done by a man named Tim." *Our* Tim could prove himself the exception to that rule.

August 31st

My wife's gone to see her parents for the night and she even took the dog 'cause I'm going to Boston, so I feel it's perfectly okay to give a yell of triumph when the Sox close out the month at 10:07 P.M. with their twenty-first win and their seventh straight, beating the Angels 10–7. The end of

---

*In a 1993 game against Atlanta, Wakefield went ten innings for the Pirates and threw 172 pitches. In 1996, while pitching for the Red Sox, he threw 162 pitches in a game against the White Sox. Don't dismiss these numbers by saying, "Yeah, but he's just a knuckleball pitcher," until you yourself have tried to throw 150 or so pitches, even soft tosses, the regulation distance of sixty feet and six inches from the pitcher's rubber to home plate on a hot afternoon. I think by number 90 or so, your shoulder's going to be feeling like a turkey drumstick on Thanksgiving day.

this one wasn't pretty, with Sox reliever Mike Myers giving up four straight hits—the last a grand slam by a late-game sub—but in the end we prevail (tonight the Sox can be *we*), and even if Anaheim should get up off the mat and take the next two, they'd still leave trailing in the wild-card race.

And what puts the icing on the cake, the absolute perfect cherry on the banana split? The Yankees lost. Oh, wait—did I say *lost*? With a final score of 22–0, I think it would be fair to say that Cleveland administered a pants-down butt-whuppin'. Pricey midseason acquisition Esteban Loaiza gave up not one but two three-run homers in the ninth inning. The question, of course, is where the Yankees go from here. When the Houston Astros no-hit them by committee a year ago, it served as a wake-up call . . . but that was earlier in the season, before their bullpen had taken such a severe pounding (Yankee starters have recorded just one win in the team's last sixteen victories). Baseball has seen plenty of amazing late-season chokes; this could be the beginning of yet another.

But the Red Sox players would undoubtedly say they can do nothing about the Yankees. They have thirty-two more games of their own to play, and the next eight are going to be very tough. I hope to be at Fenway for as many of them as I can.

Hangin' Tough

September 1st

SK: "The Yanks have a cake schedule the rest of the way . . ." And they start off by getting beat by Cleveland, 22–0. That's some cake.

SO: There ain't no steroids in humble pie (and that was a BIG pie).

I haven't been to Fenway since this terrific Red Sox run began (eight in a row now; 21-7 for the month of August), and I'm astonished by how radically the atmosphere of the old park has changed. The glums and glooms of July are gone, replaced by a giddy nervousness that's not quite a playoff atmosphere. Seconds before Bronson Arroyo throws his first pitch, the PA announcer informs the sellout crowd that it's seventy-seven degrees—the exact temperature of perfect childhood summer evenings, if I remember correctly. New England's First Church of the Baseball Unfulfilled is once more ready to rock, my son and three-year-old grandson are with me (the latter more fascinated by the Hood blimp cruising overhead than anything happening on the field), and the Yankees are now almost close enough to touch.

For the second night in a row I wait for Anaheim's pitching, which has been largely responsible for taking them to eighteen games over .500 in the fiercely competitive AL West, to show up, and for the second night in a row it never does. For the second night in a row Boston puts a four-spot on the board in its half of the first. The difference is that we've got Bronson Arroyo going instead of Curt Schilling, and Arroyo is still years away from Curt Schilling's craftiness. Also, for some reason the kid just

277

doesn't pitch well in Fenway. Tonight the Angels come back from what sportscasters like to call "the early deficit" and briefly make a game of it; after three innings the score is tied 5–5 and Arroyo is gone. In the end, it makes no difference; the final score is 12–7 Boston, and my scorecard suggests there are going to be some very tired Anaheim outfielders tomorrow. I see fourteen fly-ball outs and five strikeouts through eight innings. Add in the sixteen or eighteen hits that had to be chased down, and that's an awful lot of running for the, ahem, Angels in the outfield.

Anaheim came into Fenway on fire. After two consecutive poundings, I'd have to guess that the fire is out, and that when Bartolo Colon takes the mound tomorrow, he'd better have his best stuff working if he wants to help his team avoid a clean sweep. As for the Red Sox, it's now a nice balance: the team is three and a half back in the division and three and a half ahead in the wild card. The stretch drive has begun, and right now it looks as if we could go either way. Of course, I know what I'd like to see: the Yankees scrambling madly for that wild-card berth. And losing it on the last day of the season. I *am* a Red Sox fan, after all.

Tonight we're on the Monster, switching between two single seats and two standing rooms. The matchup of Arroyo versus former Sock Aaron Sele seems to be in the Angels' favor, but Sele comes out shaky and slow. Our guys are hacking at every pitch, and banjo hitters like Bellhorn are swinging for the fences. We score four in the first. The ump is squeezing Arroyo, and he gives two back in the second. We add another in our second, but the Angels tie it at five in the third, and Arroyo's history. Francona calls on Mike Myers to get lefty Darin Erstad. The crowd groans; the PA plays the theme from *Halloween*. Myers comes in . . . and gets it done.

Mike Scioscia gives Sele an extra inning to find his bearings. Instead, he gives up three straight hits and we take the lead.

Like Mike Myers, Terry Adams has had his problems, but, like Myers, he comes in with two down and gets his man, then settles in for two scoreless innings of work (one, I must say, belongs to Tek, who throws out *two* runners in the fifth).

Scot Shields is their crummy middle reliever. We beat him like a rock, Millar sealing the win with a three-run Coke-bottle shot. And to cap it, after Johnny catches the last out on the warning track directly beneath us, he throws the ball up to me. The game's on ESPN, and when we get home I've got e-mails from people who saw it. There I was, filling the screen, point-ing and hollering thank-you, letting Johnny know—once more—that he is still The Man.

September 2nd

Improbable or not, the Sox Express keeps rolling along—this makes nine in a row and we are rapidly leaving the land of the unusual and enter-ing that of the out-and-out, please-pass-the-happy-gas unreal. No ques-tion tonight's game is the toughest of the lot, with Bartolo Colon throwing in the mid-nineties and the Angels offense struggling hard to sal-vage at least one game of the three. It is important that they do, of course, because of "the swing" that comes into play when the clubs in first and sec-ond play each other*; there's a hell of a big difference between leaving Fen-way two and a half games out and leaving it four and a half out. The Halos end up leaving it four and a half out mostly because baseball is also a game of luck and Boston's still running. It would have to be, wouldn't you say, for the Sox to go 2 for 14 with runners in scoring position . . . and still manage to eke out the win?

The tragickal Mr. Lowe, who has been snakebit most of the year (there have been innings when he's been forced to get not just four outs but sometimes even six), only has to endure a couple of miscues tonight, and Adam Kennedy is the beneficiary of both. One is an error by right fielder Dave Roberts; the other is a triple that center fielder Johnny Damon should have caught, and in neither case does the speedy Kennedy end up scoring.

Lowe settles down after giving up single runs in each of the first three. The Red Sox are only able to touch up Colon for four, also in the first three (tonight the Angel bullpen is superb), but four is enough. Between the first of April and the end of July the Red Sox made losing one-run games an art, but now they have turned that around. By the time Keith Foulke faces the last Anaheim batter of the series, thirty-five thou-sand or so of the Fenway Faithful—Stewart O'Nan and myself among them—are on their feet, screaming, *"SWEEP! SWEEP! SWEEP!"*

Foulke induces a harmless fly ball to Orlando Cabrera at shortstop and the Standells launch into "Dirty Water." Stewart and I (not to mention

*In this case, first and second place in the wild-card standings.

the rest of the Faithful) have what we came for. It's unbelievable, but we have swept the Angels. Bring on Texas.

And *can* I say *we*? I think I can, and in a wider context than just my Fenway friends on this clear and slightly fallish-feeling Boston night. According to the New England Sports Network (NESN), the first of the three-game series against the Angels drew the biggest ratings of any regular-season baseball game in the network's history. Seen in 18.5 million homes from Canada to Connecticut, it blew away all the big-network competition. Said color commentator Jerry Remy, "I don't even know how to think about numbers like that." (Only Remy, a Massachusetts native, cannot seem to say *numbers*; he says *numbizz*.)* In any case, the *numbizz* only underline the meaning of the ninth-inning Fenway Thunder I've now heard at the ballpark two nights in a row. This team has caught the imagination of New England. This year it took a while to happen, but it finally did.

And the team has caught mine, as well. This time they—and *we*—could go all the way. Not saying they will; the odds are still against it. But *some* team will become the 2004 World Champions, and yes, this *could* be that team. They certainly have the tools.

Christ, I hope I haven't jinxed them, saying that.

We've won eight in a row and tonight we're going for the sweep against the Angels, a very good club, yet when Derek Lowe stumbles out of the gate, the Faithful grumble. Not this Lowe, not again. The Lowe who just misses his location and gets frustrated, puts runners on and gets distracted, gets ahead of batters and then throws too nice of a strike. The Lowe who kicks absently at the air like a bummed Little Leaguer after an RBI single.

Colon is having an even worse night. It seems we have two on or bases loaded every inning, but he slows the pace of the game (doing a whole lot of yardwork on the mound), and manages to weasel out of what should be big innings. After three, it's 4–3 Sox, and at the rate the game's going, we'll be here till midnight.

With one down in the Angels' fourth, Adam Kennedy flies one to Dave Roberts in right. Roberts isn't a right fielder by trade, and he tracks this one awkwardly, as if he doesn't quite see it, freezing and then waving at the ball

*And to Jerry the Detroit Tigers are always the Tigizz.

as if it's suddenly reappeared out of the lights. It hits his glove, then his leg, then the grass. *Booooooooo!*

It's tough to hear, since Roberts is an eloquent and genuinely nice guy and a recent addition, and he's playing out of position, but it's an important game, and the ball should have been caught. Still, I can't help reflecting that, even in the best of times, the Faithful are a hanging jury.

Lowe walks the next guy. He's struggling, and in even more trouble when Chone Figgins pokes a shallow liner to right-center that should drop. The one real tool Roberts has is speed. He reads this ball perfectly, flashing in and diving, picking it cleanly with a nifty backhand. The runner on second is halfway home, and Roberts doubles him up easily to end the threat. A huge, deafening standing O, and gratifying as hell to see a good guy go from goat to hero in a matter of a few pitches.

Lowe seems to take the lesson to heart, and battles into the eighth, when he leaves to a standing O from the same folks (including me) who were shaking their heads a couple hours ago. We hang on for the sweep, knocking the Angels to four and a half back. The turnaround's complete. Like Dave Roberts and Derek Lowe, with the August it's had, this team has redeemed itself, and the Faithful are more than grateful, we're wild with hope.

September 3rd

Tonight's starter for Texas once pitched for Boston. Red Sox fans remember him well, and not with affection; because of all the home runs he gave up, mostly in a relief role, he became known as John "Way Back" Wasdin. Since then he's been around, and he's improved. Not a lot, mind you, but enough to return to the show after a stint in triple-A and land a starting gig with the Rangers, who have performed above expectations all season long and are only now beginning to fade a little in the wild-card race.

We have Pedro Martinez on the mound, and on paper this game looks like a ridiculous mismatch, but I enter Fenway feeling really nervous for the first time since getting here for the second game of the Angels series. Yes, Wasdin is only 2-2, and yes, his current ERA is an unremarkable 7.01, but he remembers perfectly well what the fans here used to call him and he'd really like to be the guy who ends the Red Sox streak. Also, Texas has a formidable hitting lineup. Guys like Michael Young, Kevin Mench, Hank Blalock, and Alfonso Soriano (who came to Texas in the A-Rod trade and has lit it up at Arlington) seem made for Fenway.

All my worries about "Way Back" Wasdin turn out to be justified, and it doesn't help that two *more* Red Sox players are sitting wounded on the bench: David Ortiz (shoulder) and Johnny Damon (ankle). Wasdin is throwing some kind of heavy shit* that has our makeshift lineup popping up all night, and when Wasdin finally departs, he has given up less than a handful of hits. Luckily for us, one is a home run to Manny and another is a home run to Bill Mueller.

Pedro strikes out nine, and faces only one serious threat, in the seventh. With runners on first and third and two out, Gary Matthews Jr. tests Jason Varitek's arm by trying to steal second. Varitek passes the test. Orlando Cabrera slaps the tag on Matthews, and that takes care of that. Timlin and Embree tag-team-pitch the eighth and Foulke closes out the ninth. The Standells are singing "Dirty Water" no later than ten past ten and the crowd goes insane. The Sox have won their tenth straight, and I find myself doing the Funky Chicken in the aisle with a seventysomething woman I don't know from the Lady Eve. She's wearing a Curt Schilling T-shirt, and that's good enough for me.

Did I say the crowd *goes* insane? That's wrong. They already went. It happened at approximately 9:50 P.M., when the scoreboard showed the Orioles beat the Yankees in the Bronx by a score of 3–1, reducing the Yankees' lead in the AL East to a mere two and a half games. We've gained eight in the East since the middle of August, a stretch of less than three weeks. Later, in my hotel room, I learn that Kevin Brown, who started that game for the Yankees, broke his hand after being pulled. He punched the clubhouse wall in frustration. As so often happens in such battles, he fought the wall and the wall won. At least it was his nonpitching hand, and he's vowed not to miss a start, but I wonder. For one thing, how's he gonna wear a glove on that baby?

I never expected to see John Wasdin starting again in Fenway, but with the expanded roster, he gets another chance. And as the Sox complete their fifteenth shutout of the season, and their tenth straight win, Adam Hyzdu, the twenty-sixth man, the last one cut in spring training, makes his 2004 debut as a replacement right fielder. Like Wasdin, he's made his way back to the show, and if it's only for a short stay, still, he's here, playing under the bright lights.

*A technical baseball term.

September 4th

Sarah McKenna, a Red Sox media rep, calls me while I'm still doing my morning workout and flummoxes me by asking if I'll throw out the first pitch before this afternoon's game. The Farrelly brothers, she says, creators of such amusing (if not quite family-friendly) movies as *Dumb and Dumber* and *There's Something About Mary*, are making a romantic comedy called *Fever Pitch* with a Red Sox background, and they want to re-create Opening Day, complete with sellout crowd and giant flag unfurling across the Green Monster.* I guess neither Ben Affleck nor Matt Damon is in town, and of course native son John Kerry is otherwise occupied this Labor Day weekend.

I want to do it—hell *yes*—but I'm still slow about agreeing. Some of my reasons are purely superstitious. Some, although pragmatic, are *about* superstition. The purely superstitious reasons stem from having thrown out the first pitch at Fenway once before, around the time I published a book called *The Girl Who Loved Tom Gordon*. That was a work of fiction, but in 1998, the year before it was published, Gordon was brilliant—that was a fact.

We lost the game at which I threw out that ceremonial first pitch, and not long after (my memory wants me to believe it was *at that very game*, but surely that can't be right), we lost Gordon to an arm injury for the rest of the season. When the 2004 version of Tom Gordon shows up in these pages, he is, of course, wearing the uniform of the hated New York Yankees. And, only a month later, I was struck by a van while walking at the side of the road and badly hurt. Certainly if I had been a baseball player instead of a writer, my career would have been over.

So the last time I threw out a first pitch, bad things happened—for the

---

Fever Pitch, based on a nonfiction book by Nick Hornby, describes a romantic triangle in which a young man must choose between his girl and his baseball team. He loves both madly, deeply, truly. That the baseball team turns out to be the Red Sox should come as no surprise. As pointed out elsewhere in these pages, the Red Sox is the team of choice for romantics. Can you imagine a poet writing an ode to the Yankees? As for *lovers* and the Yankees . . . good God, you might as well plight your troth in the lobby of the Marine Midland Bank as at Yankee Stadium, that symbol of baseball commerce. No, when it comes to romance and baseball, you pretty much have to have Fenway Park. Wrigley Field has its ivied outfield wall and a certain rusty exterior charm, but I think Fenway remains America's true Field of Dreams.

team, for my favorite player on the team, and for me. Those are the superstitious reasons I'm slow about agreeing to Sarah McKenna's proposal. The pragmatic reasons *about* superstition? Well, look. I know how superstitious the ballplayers themselves are, and the fans put them to shame. I mean, some guy actually risked his life to change that Storrow Drive overpass sign from REVERSE CURVE to REVERSE THE CURSE. And the press only eggs them on. Lately there's been a story on several TV stations about a local Massachusetts teenager who got two of his front teeth knocked out by a foul line drive off the bat of Manny Ramirez. Because this kid just *happens* to live in the house where Babe Ruth once lived, the curse is now supposed to be broken. Broken teeth, broken curse. Geddit? This is the sort of numbnuts story you kind of expect from the local "If it bleeds it leads" TV in the doldrums of summer . . . but then, holy shit, the local papers pick it up too. So of course some people actually believe it. Why not? There are still people out there who think Fidel Castro had JFK shot and that cell phones cause brain cancer.

So one thing I know: if I throw out the first pitch and the Red Sox *lose*, if their ten-game streak ends this afternoon, I will get some of the blame. Because I'm not only a Red Sox fan, I'm (creepy music here) *NEW ENGLAND'S HORRORMEISTER!!!* And worse—what if someone gets hurt (someone *else* to go along with Trot, Pokey, and Johnny Damon), or the game ends with a bum call, or—God forbid—there's some sort of accident in the stands? Or what if the Red Sox go on to *lose* ten straight, end up nine back of the Yankees again, and four behind Anaheim in the wild card? Nor is this an entirely unbelievable scenario, with three coming up against Oakland (on their turf) and then three more in Seattle, who has suddenly gotten hot. *I'LL GET BLAMED FOR THAT TOO! THEY'LL SAY IT ALL STARTED WHEN THAT BASTARD KING THREW OUT THE FIRST PITCH ON SEPTEMBER 4TH!*

So of course I say yes.

1 P.M.: It's stifling hot behind the gigantic American flag, and I'm scared out of my mind. I can't believe I've agreed to do this. On my previous pitching adventure, I only had to walk from the Red Sox dugout to the mound, a matter of twenty-five or thirty steps. Now I'll be walking in from the deepest part of the park. I am, in fact, positioned just beneath CLE in the out-of-town section of the left-field scoreboard.

My introduction finishes. Marty, my Red Sox minder, lifts the flag for me. I step out into brilliant sunshine and off the warning track, onto green grass. The crowd roars, and I have to remind myself that the PA announcer has cued them to go batshit, has told them that the cameras are rolling, and that they should make as much noise as possible. Still, that forty-second walk is a remarkable period of time for me, every second crystal clear, and as I approach the rusty red dirt of the infield, the exact color of old bricks in a factory wall (I cross at shortstop, where Orlando Cabrera will soon be standing and where Nomar Garciaparra stood for so many years before him), I remember that I promised my daughter-in-law that I'd give the crowd the Manny Salute. I do so without delay, cocking my free hand and glove hand like guns, and the crowd roars louder, laughing and delighted, giving me a verbal high five. It's probably the best moment, even better than toeing the blinding white strip of the pitcher's rubber and looking in at Jason Varitek, squatting behind home plate.

Except maybe the moment before I throw is the best moment, because I can see him so clearly (there's no batter, of course, and he's not wearing the mask). His face is grave, as if he actually expects me to throw a sixty-foot strike in front of thirty-five thousand people—me, who does his best work in an empty room with a cup of lukewarm tea for company.

And I almost do. My pitch dips at the last second and hits that red-brick dirt just in front of home plate. Varitek catches the ball easily and trots out to give it to me (it's beside me as I write this, a little red scuff on one curve) as the crowd roars its approval. Varitek is kind, calling it first a sinker, then a "Hideo Nomo strike three." Too cool.

I try to shake his hand with my glove. That's how dazed I am.

3:45 P.M.: The good times have rolled and now my darker fears are coming true. Tim Wakefield—my *current* favorite Red Sox player—is on the mound, and he's getting lit up. When Terry Francona finally comes out and takes the ball, the score is 8–1, Texas.

4:25 P.M.: The Sox make a game of it, at least—Mark Bellhorn hits a grand slam, and David Ortiz follows with a bases-empty round-tripper—but in the end Boston falls two runs short. There is even that bum call I obsessed about, a phantom tag on Dave Roberts the second-base ump sees as one-half of the game-ending double play. Manny Ramirez is left in the on-deck circle, and the Sox streak ends at ten. I am 0-2 in games where I throw out the first pitch, and tomorrow the newspapers will blame me. I just know it.

SK: I got a LARGE charge out of throwing the first pitch today. Broke off a slider that hit the dirt in front of home plate. Varitek, laughing, called it a "Nomo strike three." And then we lost. Shit. But still a great game.

SO: Saw you on the tube joking with Tek—v.v. cool. Taped it if you want it. Wake looked awful. What's his record in day games? Because I've seen him at least twice get shelled on beautiful Saturday afternoons. I called the Bellhorn granny, and had a feeling Big Papi would solo right after that. If Bill Mill's shot up the middle gets through in the eighth, Tek pinch-hits with one out, but that galoot made a skate save. Least the Yanks lost. One more and The Stand's over. Be sweet to bury the Rangers right here right now. Mr. Schill on the hill.

September 5th

Bob Hohler's Boston *Globe* piece on yesterday's game leads like this: "Searching for scapegoats? Try horrormeister Stephen King, who tossed out a ceremonial first pitch."

Blame the horrormeister. What did I tell you?

Please, baseball gods, let Curt Schilling win today.

A weird, glancing Sox experience today. We drive the two hours from Avon to Boston, and around game time we deliver Caitlin and all her stuff to her dorm at B.U., then go over to Beacon Street for a farewell lunch. Fenway's less than a block from us, and fans headed for the rubber game against Texas stream past, decked out in their Red Sox best. So not only do we feel lost, losing Caitlin, it feels like we're going the wrong way, or doing the wrong thing, as in some unsettling, ominous dream.

On the way home, three now instead of four, we listen to the game unfolding farther and farther behind us. Schilling throws well, and we hold a 4–1 lead until the seventh, when Gabe Kapler adds two more with a bases-loaded single. It turns out that we need them, as Francona unwisely gives Schilling a chance at a complete game. Michael Young—again!— hits a Monster shot, and it's 6–3 with one down when Foulke comes in. He gets an out with his first pitch, then gives up a single, a double, a single that makes it 6–5, until, finally, as we're just pulling into the driveway, Bellhorn snares a knee-high bullet to save the game. Yi yi yi.

9:45 P.M.: It was closer than it should have been—the Rangers turned a 6–1 laugher into a 6–5 nail-biter in the top of the ninth—but in the end, Father Curt and the Red Sox prevailed. The Yankees also won (on a bases-loaded walk), and the Angels are winning, but for tonight, at least, I don't care about the other guys. My personal curse has been lifted. Of course all that superstition stuff is the bunk, anyway, and we all know it. And with that said, I can take off my lucky shirt, turn my pillow lucky side up, and go to bed.

SK: D'ja see today's *Globe*? I took the hit for the loss—I knew I would. Superstitious ijits. That's twice I've tossed out the first pitch and twice they lost. Think I'll get the call in Game 7 of the World Series? Steve "Just Call Me Hideo" King

SO: Hey, Hideo, YOU didn't give up the three-run dinger to Michael Young. And Bellhorn's comeback granny was some kind of magic. For a game we were basically out of, it was damn close. The way today's was for Texas. Yeesh! Foulke had absolutely nothing. We'll take the W and plant it on their grave. On to Chokeland!

September 6th

While some of the Faithful grouse that we've become more and more like the Yankees—signing free agents rather than developing our prospects—the team we most consciously resemble is Oakland. Theo and Bill James tend to follow the tenets of Moneyball, valuing on-base percentage above other indicators, and in our two seasons under their reign, we've approached the playoff chase like the A's, staying close until the All-Star break, making a few deals and then charging. Beyond absorbing Billy Beane's philosophy, we also appear to be importing players he's already poached from other teams. Mark Bellhorn, Johnny Damon, David McCarty and Keith Foulke are all recent A's, as is manager Terry Francona, Oakland's bench coach in 2003.

So it's no surprise that the A's are our constant competition, and that the games we play with them are tight—a situation that ironically does *not* benefit a Moneyball club (since defense, speed and a closer are less highly prized in Billy Beane's universe), but a smallball team like the Angels or a more traditional slugging club like the Yankees.

Tonight out by the East Bay, Mark Kotsay (who lost the last Sox-A's game with his bobble of a Bill Mueller double on the track) solos twice off Arroyo early, but Bronson settles down, retiring eleven in a row. In the fourth Manny and David go back-to-back against Barry Zito to tie it. The game stays that way till the seventh, when Bill Mueller and Dave Roberts hit RBI doubles. The A's rally to make it 4–3 after a terrible call in the eighth—Manny clearly traps a line drive by Kotsay, yet the ump calls him out—but in the ninth their lack of a pen shows, as Chad Bradford and the ever-unreliable Arthur Rhodes combine to give up four runs, three of them on a David Ortiz bases-clearing double, and we win 8–3. Thank you, Moneyball!

The Yankees, meanwhile, were scheduled to play a doubleheader against Tampa Bay in the Bronx, but due to Hurricane Frances the D-Rays were late getting to the Stadium and missed the first game. Yanks general manager Brian Cashman immediately lobbied the league office for a forfeit (the league turned him down, I'd hope with a look of disbelief). So while in Florida the storm has torn people's homes and lives apart, the Yankees' only thought was to use it to pick up an unearned win. Now that's class.

September 7th

It wasn't that long ago—at the end of this season's fantasy August, in fact—that Red Sox writers and commentators (not to mention your run-of-the-mill bleacher creatures) were saying that Boston's postseason chances might hinge on how well they could do in the upcoming nine-game stretch against the big fish of the AL West, before leaving those sharks to swim—and hopefully to bite one another as seriously as possible—in their own tank. Most hoped for six wins at most, two against the Angels, two against the Rangers, and *maybe* two against the Oakland Athletics. Many partisans would have been satisfied with five. Few, I think, would have guessed at our current position: six wins and one loss with two of the nine-game set left to play.

When the Red Sox last visited Oakland, during the playoff series against the Athletics in the fall of 2003, they left a bunch of pissed-off A's and A's fans behind. The same was true following last night's rematch, the only difference being that we have to play them again tonight instead of next year, and tonight the chief object of the A's ire will be on the mound. That would be the tragickal Mr. Lowe, who supposedly made an obscene gesture toward the Oakland bench after striking out the final player of the game.

The animus of last night's Oakland Coliseum attendees was directed not at any Red Sox player so much as it was at the ump who ruled Mark Kotsay out after Manny Ramirez appeared—from the ump's perspective—to have made a rolling, tumbling catch of Kotsay's dying-quail line drive. Manny actually caught it on what's known as "the trap-hop," a fact his diving body obscured from the umpire, who fearlessly made the call, anyway. Manny himself acknowledged this in the locker room, after the game. "I knew I din' catch the ball," he said, "but the umpire say I catch the ball, so the guy's out." He then shrugged, as if to add, *Tough luck, Mark . . . but we gotta jus' keep goin'.*

To add insult to injury, Kotsay made almost exactly the same play on a Red Sox dying quail of a liner later on in the game, only this time the ump saw the ball hit the ground and ruled the batter safe. Kotsay raised his arms in frustrated body English even a baby could read: *Aw, come on! Gimme a makeup call here, Blue!*

No makeup calls for Oakland (not last night, anyway), and it probably wouldn't have helped; in the end, the game just wasn't that close. That didn't stop the angry Oakland fans from hurling their trash into the outfield, however. It was a sight that filled me—I admit it—with childish glee. I had zero sympathy for their outrage, given the ump's honest effort to make an honest call; not so soon after the blown call on Dave Roberts that ended our game against Texas three days ago, and probably, if I'm to be honest, in no case.* Blown calls are, after all, a part of the game, and the fans' rage somehow made this one even tastier. *That's right, ya babies!* I thought, watching the hot-dog cartons and empty beer cups rain down. *The umps are relaxing in the Officials' Room, probably soaking*

---

*With this one utterly unforgivable exception: don't ever let me hear of an official (or a player) who takes money to tip a game in which millions have invested their hopes and the energy of their collective imagination.

their tired feet, so take it out on your grounds crew! Go on and chuck that shit, why not?

Are Oakland fans coming to hate us the way we hate the Yankees? *There's* an interesting thought.

Trot comes off the DL today, and Pokey, and Johnny, who's been out with a strained pinkie (when in doubt, pinkie out), is back in the lineup. Scott Williamson, who's been gone a long time, throws batting practice to Trot and may be ready soon. Mr. Kim, however, appears done for the year. The PawSox finished their season yesterday (as did Cesar Crespo and Brian Daubach, who both contributed to the big club early on), and Theo says they're putting together a conditioning program so the $10 million man (and his eleven innings of work this year) will be ready in the spring.

Of course, there's nowhere to put all these guys. The roster, like the dugout, is overflowing. Youk hasn't seen action in weeks, or McCarty, or Ricky Gutierrez.

No one's going to rock the boat, though. The team's doing too well. Tonight Johnny celebrates being back in action by leading off the game with a home run. It's Derek Lowe's first appearance in Oakland since his alleged crotch-tugging in the direction of the A's bench after clinching last year's divisional playoffs, and the crowd lets him know it. He scuffles early (as usual), but Gabe Kapler clocks a two-run shot for a 3–0 cushion, Billy Mueller makes three highlight-reel stops at third, and once again we bulldoze their number four starter Mark Redman for a 7–1 win, making us 7-1 in our gut-check stretch against Anaheim, Texas and Oakland.

September 8th

I'm primed to stay up late and watch the Pedro–Tim Hudson series finale, hoping for the sweep, but Hudson can't find the plate, and after three it's 7–0 Sox and he's gone, and we haven't really even hit the ball yet. What do you do when the one strength of your club fails you? You lose. We sweep the A's at home after sweeping them in Fenway in July.

Even better, the Angels lose, so we're five up in the wild card. And the rain left over from Hurricane Frances—in a fitting revenge—wipes out the Yanks-D-Rays doubleheader, so we're only two back in the East, and with the makeups, their rotation's a mess.

September 9th

The Red Sox offense didn't beat Tim Hudson last night, and Pedro Martinez can't exactly take credit, either. After walking the first three batters of the game (four in the first inning) and giving up a double to David Ortiz and a single to Jason Varitek, Hudson pretty much did the job on himself.

Meanwhile, the Yankees' current series with the Tampa Bay Devil Rays,* a seemingly endless exercise in baseball existentialism during which the D-Rays never win and the Yankees never seem to gain ground in the standings, is continuing this afternoon, with the New Yorkers leading in the first game of a doubleheader by a score of quite a bunch to one. I could check and get an exact score, but it hardly seems worth it. Based on my last peek I can tell you that a.) there's hardly anyone in the stands at the Stadium, and b.) Rocco Baldelli looks like he wishes he were playing for the Tokyo Sunflowers, assuming there is such a team. After last night's rainout and the Red Sox win in Oakland, the gap in the AL East shrank to a mere two games for the first time since early June, and reading the sports pages of the New York tabs has become a wonderfully cheering pastime for Red Sox fans; the *Post* and *Daily News* baseball columnists, used to a steady diet of Yankee triumphs down the stretch, have started to sound like holy-rolling revival-show ministers, warning that the Horsemen of the Apocalypse are on the horizon: *Behold, I saw a pale horse, and on him was Manny, and he spake, saying, "Hey man, we gotta jus' keep goin'."*

Meanwhile, on other fronts:

The hapless Devil Rays will be more hapless still if Ivan, third and worst hurricane to menace Florida in the last thirty days, blows away their JuiceDome down there in Tampa; like a certain unlucky Jew, they may be doomed to simply wander, dragging their dusty equipment bags behind them, playing everywhere and always batting in the top of the first. *"We once had a home,"* they'll tell those who will listen. *"It wasn't very full, and most of the folks who showed up were old, many equipped with shunts and pee bags, but by God it was ours."*

---

*The once more hapless Devil Rays, and please God may they (or the troublesome El Bird-Os) not poke a stick in our spokes as we race down this season's home stretch.

In Foxboro, the New England Patriots, proud winner of exactly one preseason game, prepare to defend their Super Bowl title.

And on I-95, just north of Augusta, Maine, at a little past noon and in a driving downpour (the remains of Hurricane Frances, or so the radio assured me), I saw an oak tree blazing with orange leaves.

Football, autumn colors, hurricanes: omens of the end. Hurry up and finish your four games with Seattle, Red Sox. Hurry up and come home. It's almost time to deal with the Yankees.

SO: Maybe because all this is happening late at night way out West there isn't the crazy celebrating like last week, but it almost seems too easy, too calm. It's quiet . . . too quiet.

SK: It's like people are getting used to it. If so, **bad** people. **Bad** people. **Ungrateful, BAD** people. Or maybe, who knows, they're just not as crazy as we are. Also, they ARE away. And some people DO have to get up and go to work. Not us, I mean, but SOME people.

Tonight in the top-left corner of the country, Seattle throws a rookie lefty I've never heard of—Bobby Madritsch, whose route to the bigs included time in the independent leagues, the outlaws of the minors—while Tim Wakefield takes the hill for us. Wake came out flat in his last start (our last loss), so he's due for a solid game. Wrong. The Mariners score early and often, and when a fly to the track goes off Manny's glove in the fifth for a two-run error, this one's done. We lose 7–1 while the Yanks sweep a doubleheader from the D-Rays, the first game of which has an officially reported attendance of zero. Zero, as in no one. Zero, as in one less than the guy sitting at his desk writing this. If the Yankees win and no one sees it, does it still count?

September 10th

SO: I'm definitely making the Tuesday game next week versus Tampa, and if you're not using the tix, I could see myself there Wednesday and Thursday too. There just aren't that many games left. Here on Monday I went to the Rock Cats' last game of the year; after they won, the players tossed their hats and batting gloves and all the balls in the dugout and even the leftover bubble gum to the crowd, and I realized that once the season's over, that's it, it's fall and then winter. I didn't like the feeling one bit, and I guess I'm doing what I can to stave it off.

SK: You're so right. Winter's coming. I felt a change in the weather the day after Labor Day.

Losing two straight to the last-place M's, with Schilling going, isn't likely, and I'm uncharacteristically certain of this one from the start. Seattle keeps it close till the fifth, when David Ortiz sneaks a line-drive homer over the wall, and then, after an error by backup second baseman Jose Lopez, with two outs, Bill Mueller singles, Dave Roberts doubles, Johnny Damon triples and Mark Bellhorn singles. The next inning, Manny, who started our scoring with a solo shot, piles it on with his 17th career grand slam, and Schilling cruises to become the majors' first 19-game-winner.

Meanwhile in Baltimore, Javier Vazquez melts down, walking and hitting batters with the bases loaded, and the Yanks go down hard, so we're two and a half back. Anaheim wins and the A's lose again, so the Angels are a mere game off the pace in the West. With the unbalanced schedule, the Angels have six games remaining against the A's and a chance to make them our wild-card rivals.

September 11th

Manny Ramirez hit home runs 39 and 40 last night to amble past Boston's Dwight Evans on the all-time list and further enhance his MVP chances (although for that to happen Boston will almost certainly have to win the American League flag). Boston didn't look particularly good against Seattle's collection of battered veterans and freshly called-up farmhands in the first of the teams' four-game series and Tim Wakefield suffered for it, but the whole *team* appeared to be ambling in that game, probably a natural enough result of having just finished an 8-1 tour of duty against Oakland, Texas, and Anaheim. Father Curt took matters in hand last night, thank God (he "righted the ship," as the Sports Cannibals like to say), and bagged his 19th win in the process.

The Angels, currently five back in the wild-card race, are now the only other contender for that ticket to the postseason dance.* They have nineteen games left, two against the so-so ChiSox, seven against the shlubby Seattle Mariners, and ten against good teams, including six against Oakland. We, on the other hand, have six games left against the Yankees, and *eight* against Baltimore, who has played us tough all year. The moral of this story is simple—we gotta jus' keep goin', man.

SK: We kicked their ass, all right . . . another granny for Manny, and it was one inning after I went to bed. As for Being There, Owen has talked me into going down to at least one game and then driving back afterward. Meantime, another day off the schedule, another day closer to the Yankees.

SO: If you're going to catch just one game, make it Thursday's, Curt's first crack at 20 wins.

Arroyo threw well against the Mariners in his other start against them and got screwed out of a W when the pen fell apart. Tonight he's wearing some of the ugliest dirty-blond white-boy cornrows I've ever seen, but he pitches beautifully, that hard curve of his dropping off the outside corner, making hitters lunge. Manny homers again, and Mark Bellhorn. Kevin Youkilis

---

*That could change if Oakland loses its hold on first place in Outer Weird Pacifica, but even if the A's do drop to second, our position *vis-à-vis* the wild card won't change much. For the record, I think Oakland *will* hold on and win the West.

starts at third to give Bill Mueller a breather, and by the late innings Pokey Reese, David McCarty and Ricky Gutierrez all get some playing time.

In the ninth we're up 7–0 when Adam Hyzdu sees his first at-bat as a Red Sock. He looks anxious—and awful, chasing pitches away. He's down 1-2, and I think how much that would suck, striking out in your one at-bat all year. Hyzdu lines a double to the wall in left, knocking in a run. So he's batting a thousand and slugging two.

When the Sox have to declare their playoff roster (knock wood), some of these guys aren't going to be on it. We keep having to make room on the expanded roster for people coming off the DL—like Scott Williamson last night—and with all the guys we added in midseason, I wonder if guys like McCarty and Pokey won't be going to the party. And can we keep Dave Roberts, Trot *and* Kapler as backups? Someone's going to be left out the way Dauber and Cesar Crespo have already been left behind.

September 12th

SO: Did I tell you my theory that *Napoleon Dynamite* is about the Sox pitching staff? Eck is Uncle Rico, wanting to time-travel back to 1982, while Napoleon is the lost and tragickal Derek Lowe.

SK: Who is the nerdy older brother? Bronson Arroyo would be my guess. "Peace out, Napoleon." Cornrows, indeed.

SO: I was actually thinking of Wake for the brother, but you're right, Arroyo's cornrows might win him the role (who did 'em—Manny? Pokey?). And I did see a VOTE FOR PEDRO T-shirt at the park the other day.

Speaking of voting: Mr. Schill should have the inside track on the Cy Young, and Manny sure as heck looks like the MVP.

My "too quiet" prediction comes true, as righty Gil Meche scatters five Red Sox hits for a complete-game 2–0 shutout. Manny sabotages our best scoring chance in the first: with one out and two on, he forgets how many outs there are and gets doubled up off second on what should be an easy sac fly. Derek Lowe's only mistake is a two-run shot to Raul Ibanez. Time of game: two hours, twenty-two minutes.

SK: What can you say? Guy pitched a great game and Manny ran us out of an inning. Oh, that crazy Manny. At least it'll take more than this one game to cost us our dream. But 3.5 back of the Yankees. And how's by the Angels? "White Hot Colon" (as per the Angels website) over Chicago, 11–0. Back to five up in the WC. And do you know what? I think the D-Rays might put a hurtin' on us.

SO: D-Lowe deserved better (and be sure the GM of the O's has taken note of his last seven starts). So we're where we were on Friday, just two games closer to the finish line. With Petey and Mr. Schill slated to go against the D-Rays, I'm optimistic. Just gotta hit.

I wonder how much Manny's little fugue states will hurt his MVP chances. What a weird series he had. He clouts a bunch of big dingers, including that granny, makes a great flying karate-kick, give-up-the-body grab in the corner, then muffs that can of corn on the track, and today he forgets how many outs there are. It's like Sun Ra said: space is the place.

Somewhere I'm missing a game—our record says we have 20 left but I only count 19 on the sked. Must be a rain date in there somewhere. Ah, found it: we've got a doubleheader in Baltimore on the next-to-last day of the season. So that means of the 20 games we have left, 8 are with the pain-in-the-ass O's. And 6 are with the Yanks. So we had better beat the D-Rays.

SK: I doan like the sound of tha', man. Too easy to see the headline: ANGELS IN AS WILD CARD, TEJADA SINKS SOX.

You think? Say "Nahhh . . ."

SO: Nahhh. They'll be meaningless. Our starters will be Abe Alvarez and Frank Castillo. Or whoever needs the innings for his bonus. But you're right, Tejada will hit four homers. (Talk about some fans who should (continue to) be pissed—the new and improved O's didn't even make .500.)

Plus I'm looking for the Angels to knock off the A's. Be nice to see a team with real fundamentals overcome their injuries and eliminate the Moneyball guys.

September 13th

In the mail, a gift from Steve: *The Year of the Gerbil,* by Con Chapman, a chronicle of the 1978 pennant race. The Gerbil, of course, was just part of Bill "Spaceman" Lee's nickname for then Sox manager Don Zimmer. The whole name was The Mad Gerbil. On the cover is a shot from the TV feed from the one-game playoff, the center-field camera keying on Bucky Dent just after his fateful swing, Mike Torrez starting to follow the ball up and to his right. Torrez, I'm surprised to see, is wearing Roger Clemens's #21. Another good reason to retire it.

SO: Thanks, man. The title alone had me laughing (though you know by the end I'll be grim-lipped, bumming once again at Mike F****** Torrez and Bucky F****** Dent). And this year sure looks like a photo negative of '78. We just have to catch the Yanks at the wire and let Mark Bellhorn do the rest.

SK: I saw the cover of this week's *Sports Illustrated* and my heart sank into my boots. If you don't know why—and I'm sure you do—Google *Sports Illustrated Curse.*

SO: I believe Tommy Brady and the Pats survived it, so maybe Mr. Schill can too. At least it's not the Chunky Soup curse; that's a career-ender (Terrell Davis, Kurt Warner). Keep your eye on Donovan McNabb!

If we gather all these curses (*Titanic*, Bambino, *SI*) and STILL win, will folks shut up about them already? And will we get extra points for degree of difficulty (like overcoming all our injuries)?

September 14th

The Yankees got roughed up again last night, roughed up bad, this time by lowly Kansas City. The final score of that game was 17–8, and this morning the New York sportswriters will once more be eating their gizzards out about the pinstripes' lack of pitching—lovely. The Red Sox, meanwhile, only split with cellar-dwelling Seattle, which is a long way from wonderful, but the road trip is over, four more games are off the schedule, and we're coming back to Fenway Park almost exactly where we were in the standings when we left: three games behind the Yankees in the East, four and a half ahead of the Angels in the wild card. Furthermore, we're looking at three with the hapless Devil Rays, and the Sox have been strong against them this year. So, at least until we meet the Yankees on the seventeenth, all's okay with the world, right?

Wrong. There's a problem. A *big* one. Father Curt is on the cover of *Sports Illustrated* this week, *that's* the *problem*. He's standing on the mound at Fenway with his arms spread and every letter on the front of his uniform clearly visible.

How *could* they?

With all the other stuff we have to worry about, how damn *could* they? Because while there's no evidence of the Curse of the Bambino other than the failure of the Red Sox to win the World Series since 1918 (and they are not alone in that), there's *plenty* of evidence that the *Sports Illustrated* Curse actually exists.*

Two games after his cover appearance on *SI*, Kurt Warner suffered an injury that sidelined him for five games (although in Warner's case I'm at least willing to admit the *possibility* that Campbell's Soup may have been a contributing factor). One day after Anna Kournikova appeared on the *SI* cover, she was bounced from the French Open, her earliest exit from a Grand Slam event in three years. In his first *Monday Night Football* game after *his* cover shot, Howard Cosell went from hero to zero by referring to a Redskins wide receiver as "that little monkey." After Dale Murphy of the Atlanta Braves appeared on the cover, the Braves dropped fourteen of their

---

*Unlike, let us say, the supposed Campbell's Chunky Soup Curse, where I can only find four football players—Terrell Davis, Kurt Warner, Jerome Bettis and Donovan McNabb—who actually suffered injuries after appearing in the ads, despite all the rumors.

next fifteen games. Other sufferers of the *SI* Jinx have included Tom Watson, Kirk Gibson, George Brett, Pedro Martinez's brother, Ramon . . . and ex–Red Sox franchise player Nomar Garciaparra. After Nomar, stripped to the waist and looking most righteously buff, appeared on the cover, he went down with a popped wrist tendon and played hardly at all during the first half of the season.

And now, in addition to all our injuries and our far-from-secure lead in the wild card, in addition to a three-game bulge for the Yankees that won't seem to shrink any lower than two games, I have to cope with the near certainty that Curt Schilling will *not* manage to win twenty games in the regular season, but will remain stuck on nineteen instead. Martinez, Wakefield, Arroyo, and the tragickal Mr. Lowe will have to take up the slack.

Thanks, *Sports Illustrated.*

Thanks a pantload.

You guys suck.

Behind Fenway, at the corner of Yawkey Way and Van Ness Street, sits the players' parking lot. Four hours before game time the Sox take over Van Ness, barricading both ends and evicting any parked cars. By then a sizable clump of autograph hunters is already waiting. There's no way you can get close enough to the players' Mercedeses and Volvos and Range Rovers as they pull in (or Gabe Kapler's and Kevin Millar's chromed-out hogs), and the tall fence surrounding the lot is lined with a heavy green tarp so you can't see in, but a hundred feet down Van Ness there are three horizontal slots cut into the fence about thigh-high, and as the players walk from their rides to the clubhouse entrance, some will stop to sign.

The slots are uncomfortably close to glory holes, with all that that implies. The only way to tell who's coming is to kneel on the concrete, press your cheek against the metal edge and peer sideways through the slot like the opening of a pillbox.

Today I'm the first one there, and stake out a spot at the end of the first slot. Position is everything: some guys will sign just a few and then break off, leaving fans at slots two and three grumbling. I've also chosen a weekday for my hunting because weekends people are packed six and seven deep, and I'd feel like a heel claiming a spot before some little kid (little kids also have no qualms about stepping on you or crawling over your back).

As the other hunters show up, I realize that compared to them, I *am* a little kid, a rank amateur. They're mostly pros, dealers who owe each other money and merchandise. They bring bat-bags full of Big Sticks, boxes of balls, albums of eight-by-ten glossies—high-ticket items they can sell on eBay. As we stand there waiting for the Sox to arrive, they're cutting deals and boasting of recent acquisitions, trading information about upcoming shows.

"What are you working there?" one asks me. "Hat? Couple a balls?"

I try explaining that the hat's for me—to wear—but it's impossible for him to understand that I'm just a fan.

The coaches arrive first, together. No one wants them but me. No one seems to know who Ino Guerrero is, or care. I'm psyched to get Adam Hyzdu's autograph on his PawSox card, while they just shrug. Likewise, when the middling Devil Rays players come walking right past us on Van Ness, the pros let them pass ("Damian Rhodes," one calls Damian Rolls, "used to play for Baltimore"—mixing him up with old closer Arthur Rhodes).

When Jason Varitek signs, everyone behind me mobs the slot, crushing me down against the fence, reaching their merchandise over my shoulders and past my ears. Because all Tek can see of us are our hands, the pros get a first autograph, bounce out and grab a second bat or ball from their arsenal, shove in again and snag another. Double-dipping, it's called, and while frowned upon (especially when not everyone gets even one autograph), it's the pros' bread and butter.

"How many Variteks you get?"

"Three."

"Ha, I got four."

I get one and I'm happy. Thanks, Tek.

Johnny Damon signs for a long time. Like Tek, he always tries to sign for everyone, and is always polite and nice. For a guy who looks like a wild man, he's surprisingly soft-spoken, and has impeccable manners, even with the pushiest fans; his parents should be proud. Pokey signs (he doesn't always), and Mark Bellhorn. The pros gripe about some other players who blow us off—Schilling and Wake especially (though Wake, I've heard, only signs for charities, and you have to respect that). They say Pedro and Manny are almost impossible to get out here, and that they hardly ever even *see* Orlando Cabrera.

Doug Mientkiewicz takes the time to sign, and Doug Mirabelli, Dave

McCarty, Ricky Gutierrez, Billy Mueller, Dave Roberts. The hat looks great—silver Sharpie on black. By four o'clock I've got half the club. If I came tomorrow and Thursday as well, I'd be able to get most everyone. And even after three hours of being squashed and elbowed and having to listen to the dealers brag and haggle, I know I'll be coming back. Because while most of these guys are pros, and hustling hard, there's still something kid-like and hopeful about them. The rumor is that next year when the team enlarges the clubhouse the slots in the fence will be no more. I hope that's not true, because for a fan like me, this is as close to the players as I'll ever get.

September 15th

Pedro Martinez has pretty much owned Tampa Bay, the Red Sox have pretty much owned *everyone* while at Fenway Park, and the hapless Devil Rays were sending a twenty-year-old rookie named Scott Kazmir to the mound last night. The result, of course, was a comfy Tampa Bay win. At one point Kazmir struck out five in a row, and the only bright spot for the Faithful was an eighth-inning home run from the newly returned Trot Nixon. We have fallen a game further behind the Yankees (the Mariners beat the Angels, at least, there is that much joy in Mudville), and I find myself doing two things this morning to start the day. One is marking another game off the schedule. The other is wondering why, why, *why* Father Curt ever agreed to be on the cover of *Sports Illustrated*.

SO: Thanks for the use of the seats. Let me just warn you: when the sun goes down, it's fall. Couldn't have been more than fifty degrees out there. I had to buy a pricey sweatshirt to keep from shivering. The offense didn't create much heat either. Mason says it's the return of the pre–July 31st Sox. I think it's the usual we-don't-have-to-hit-for-Pedro virus. Funny how that works. We didn't hit for Clemens either; he was always leaving in the seventh tied 2–2.

SK: 1) It *is* a return to the July Sox.
2) It *is* the Curse of *Sports Illustrated* at work.

3) It _was_ Cabrera (not Nomah) who ended the game first-pitch swinging in the bottom of the ninth.

Sign me,

      Toldja-So Boy

SO: Hey, if we're expecting to win that game down three with two gone in the ninth, we truly are some cockeyed optimists. Ain't no curse when you lose and deserve to, and we did. The only reliever who stopped the bleeding was Leskanic, and by then it was too late. It's not just saves we're missing, it's HOLDS. Our middle guys, like the Yanks' the last three years, are our biggest weakness, and have been since spring training.

SK: Not WIN it, TIE it.

SO: True: play for the tie at home. Still, we were losing from the very first batter.

Tim Wakefield has struggled—to be generous—in his last few starts. Tonight he gives up a run right out of the gate. Mark Bellhorn's two-run shot off D-Rays starter Dewon Brazelton in the bottom of the first gives us the lead, only to have Wake give it back. In the fourth we scrap for two more, but Wake immediately surrenders a pair. It's not that they're shelling him, it's just the usual fallout from the knuckler: some walks, a wild pitch, _five_ stolen bases. That's it: when Kevin Millar's two-run Monster shot gives us a 6–4 lead in the fifth, Francona turns to Curtis Leskanic (he threw okay last night, right?). Three batters later, Tampa triple-A call-up Jorge Cantu ties the game with a blast high off the Sports Authority sign. Not to be outdone, in the bottom of the inning Lou Piniella counters by using four pitchers to worm out of a bases-loaded no-out jam. It almost works—all we get is one on a Manny sac fly. We tack on another in the seventh when Trot's grounder goes through shortstop Julio Lugo's legs and pinch runner Dave Roberts motors around. We're leaving men on all over the place, but Timlin sets up and Foulke closes neatly, and we bag a long, ugly 8–6 win. Since the streak we've been playing terrible ball, splitting the last six with cellar dwellers, and yet, with the Angels and A's losing once again, we're now five and a half up in the wild card, our biggest lead yet, with only eighteen games to go. In other words: we're closer to the postseason than we've been all year.

September 16th

SK: They're talking about taking Tim out of the postseason rotation. That's okay. If we keep playing this way, postseason won't be a problem. I have never—_NEVER_—gone to bed feeling so depressed after a win. They hit everything we threw at them. And they ran our Sox off. Blah.

SO: Maybe this'll cheer you up: before this year, Tim-may was 5-2 lifetime in the Metrodome, 5-2 at the Coliseum, and 5-3 with a 3.32 ERA at Angel Stadium. I wouldn't pull him just yet. You know how streaky he can be. If he gets unhittable after October 1, we could be wearing some big rings. Have hope.

Tonight's the kind of game we've overlooked in the past: the last home game with a patsy before heading down to the Stadium. Before the advent of Curt Schilling, we'd be scrambling to get our rotation in order for the Yanks, try to throw a number four or five guy and get burned. With Schilling going tonight, we're confident of a quality start and can rest assured that Petey will be going Sunday.

So this one's the mismatch we want (the one we've paid for). We jump on D-Rays starter Mark Hendrickson for three quick runs. Lou's going to play us tough though: with one down in the first he's got a guy warming. It's pointless; Schill wants his 20th. His splitter's nasty and his location is spot-on. We're up 6–0 when Kevin Millar hits a Monster shot to spark a five-run seventh, and we're set for the big (but probably hurricane-rainy) weekend in the Bronx.

September 17th

Two more games off the schedule. Boston's three-game series with the hapless Devil Rays—the last time the Red Sox will see them at home this year—is concluded. The Sox won games two and three. Father Curt stood

up to the Curse of *Sports Illustrated* last night by remaining in the game until the eighth (with a three-hit shutout until a Rocco Baldelli home run in the sixth) and becoming the first pitcher in the majors this year to win twenty games. The man is a horse, no doubt about it, but he's also had the kind of run support he almost never saw in his Diamondback days, and there's no doubt about that, either. His teammates, who have provided him with a staggering number of runs per start,* last night staked him to three in the first and eight more by the time he left to a standing O.

Wakefield's start two nights ago was a smellier kettle of fish. I purposely stayed away from this manuscript when it was over, because any words I wrote would have begun harshly: *"This team is almost ready for postseason, where they will become some better club's stepping-stone."* Tim Wakefield did not figure in the decision, and looked terrible for the third outing in a row. The talking heads have begun to speculate that Terry Francona may go to a four-man rotation in postseason, and that if he does, Wake will be the odd man out.

This may or may not happen, but the simple fact of Boston's 8–6 win over Tampa Bay on the evening of September 15th was that almost every pitcher Francona sent to the mound in Wakefield's wake (with the sole exception of Keith Foulke, who pitched a one-two-three ninth) looked terrible. There may not be a Curse of *Sports Illustrated* (I'll wait and see on that one), but there certainly is a Curse of Middle Relief in the big leagues, and once you get past Mike Timlin (and—*maybe*—Alan Embree), the Red Sox also suffer from the disease.

I've rarely gone to bed after a win feeling as unhappy and unsettled as I did after that game on the fifteenth. Usually when I can't sleep, what I see are key plays that went against my team (Jorge Posada's flare of a single against Pedro in Game 7 of the 2003 ALCS, for instance). What I kept seeing after that second game against Tampa Bay—a game we probably deserved to lose—was Curtis "The Mechanic" Leskanic shaking his head after giving up the two-run dinger that allowed the hapless D-Rays to pull even, 6–6, late in the game. *Why are you shaking your head?* I wanted to scream at him. *This is a team filled with weak hitters, Punch and Judy hitters, but they're still major league hitters, my friend, and*

*Nine is the number that comes to mind, but you know what Ole Case said: "You could look it up."

if you hang one, it's going out of the yard. What's so hard to figure out about that?

Never mind, I tell myself; that night's ugly piece of work and Father Curt's thing of beauty last night are both going to look the same in the win column at the end of the year.

Meanwhile, we're just three and a half games out of first, and tonight it's Yankees–Red Sox.

I really don't expect to get this one in, with the train of Hurricane Ivan due, but there's been such hype (and that rarity—an actual capacity crowd at the Stadium, not just a paper sellout, thanks to us) that George will do whatever it takes to play it. In the third there's a rain delay. From their cozy NESN studios, Tom Caron and Eck gush over highlights from the last Yankee series in Fenway. Here's the Tek–A-Rod tiff, and Bill Mueller's walk-off shot against Mo—tape we've seen hundreds of times already.

In fifteen minutes we're back, though it still seems to be spitting. And then a few outs later, it's pouring, and here comes the tarp.

TC and Eck babble for a good twenty minutes before resorting to canned stuff. And what canned stuff should they run first but Steve himself, dispelling the curse and telling us where he was in '78 and '86 and '03 when the roof caved in. In '86 he's in his car outside his place in western Maine because that's the only reception he can get; he's sitting there with the door open and an unopened bottle of champagne on the seat beside him. Now *that's* a storyteller, putting you right there with just the right details.

You know it's a serious rain delay when NESN cuts to the nature shows. At least it's not Canadian football.

And so, like Yeats's great rough beast, The Rivalry has once more come round at last.* The Red Sox are in New York for three. I'm here for the middle game, and so is Stewart O'Nan. Between publicity for *Faithful* (not to mention work on the book itself, which I am now doing) and more publicity for the children's version of *The Girl Who Loved Tom Gordon*, I

---

*I am allowed to say stuff like this, because according to John Cheever, the belles lettres version of Ole Case, "all literary men must be Red Sox fans." My reputation as a literary man is actually in some dispute, but I *am* a man, a Red Sox fan and a writer, so . . . fuggit. I think Norman Mailer said that, in *The Naked and the Dead*.

expect to be immured in hardball until I go back to Maine on Monday night.

With that in mind, I decided I would take Friday night off entirely, and give my nerves a rest. I decided to go to a movie—something with subtitles, the sort of thing that never plays at the North Conway Sixplex or the Bethel Station Fourplex back home—and then return to my hotel, where I'd go straight to bed without even checking the score, lest I be sucked in. I thought the Sox would probably lose the opener, anyway (with the exception of the August streak, they have made a *career* of losing openers this season, it seems) and I could read about it in the *New York Times* the following day—not the *Post,* the *Post* is simply too gloaty when the hometown teams win.

Well, I didn't exactly give my nerves a rest; I saw an *extremely* nervous-making French suspenser called *Red Lights,* but my plan remained on course until I got back to my hotel at around 10 P.M. Then everything fell down. And why, you ask? Because the Yankees–Red Sox rivalry is simply in the air if you happen to be in one of those two cities, and especially if you happen to be in the one where the games are being played. Oh, it's maybe not a big deal among the sort of people who flock to see French suspense movies (with white subtitles that are almost impossible to read when superimposed on white backgrounds, as at least 60 percent of these seemed to be), but when I got back to the hotel, the doorman took a look at my T-shirt (a gift from Stewart O'Nan, it features a picture of David Ortiz and reads I LOVE IT WHEN YOU CALL ME BIG PAPI) and greeted me with "Hey, Mr. King! Welcome back! Your Sox are up one-zip in the third!"

One of the car-park guys joined us at that moment, favored me with a rather loathsome smile—if it was supposed to project sympathy, it failed miserably—and said, "Nah, it's tied, one to one."

Then the house detective, for whom I'd signed a book earlier, came out through the revolving doors. "Nope," he said. "It's two to one, Yanks. Olerud just homered."

So much for my resolution. Five minutes later—no, three—I was sitting in my room with my Red Sox cap out of my suitcase and on my head, watching the game.

Now, the players—some of them, at least—will try to tell you that a match like this is just another game, and that if it *is* more important, it's because of the lateness of the season and "the swing"—first playing second. Few if any of them actually believe such nonsense. You can see it in their eyes during their locker-room interviews, and you can *certainly* see it in the level of play they bring to the field.* Yankees–Red Sox is a classic rivalry, last night's game was one of the best in it I've ever seen . . . *and I only saw it from the fifth inning on!* If not for two rain delays totaling almost an hour and a half (almost exactly the length of my foreign film), I probably would have missed the whole damned thing, and I'm so glad I didn't miss all the excitement in an effort to spare my nerves another jolt of what I was sure they would have to endure: Rivera successful, Yankees triumphant.

The part I did miss was Johnny Damon's upper-deck shot to put the Red Sox ahead 1–0 (I also missed chortling gleefully over how George Steinbrenner must hate all that hair flying gaily in the wind as Damon rounds the bases) and the Ramirez Show: first the Shakespearian non-homer (fair was foul after all) and then the sensational Air Manny catch that robbed Miguel Cairo of his own home run. The fun of that one, of course, every bit as good on the replays, was watching Cairo run the bases in absolute surety that he'd hit the ball out, and his blank look of amazement when he was informed—after slapping the bemused third-base coach's hand on his way home—that he'd been out during his whole tour of the base paths.

I was there, however, by then in my underwear (but still wearing my David Ortiz T-shirt and my Red Sox hat) when Mariano Rivera came in to seal the deal with the Yankees leading, 2–1, in the top of the ninth. That he's one of the great ones there can be no doubt (Johnny Damon says flatly that Rivera is the greatest closer of all time), but he has problems with the Red Sox. Bill Mueller touched him—hard—for a two-run walk-off home run in the July rhubarb game at Fenway, and last night Rivera blew the save with one out and then blew the game with two out. You didn't have to be a lip-reader to see what he was yelling at center fielder Kenny Lofton when Damon's broken-bat flare (another of those dying-quail shots that seem to have decided so many games between these two clubs) dropped ten or twelve feet in front of Lofton on the wet grass:

*Tanyon Sturtze, for instance, lately miserable in middle relief for the Yankees (he went two-thirds of an inning in his last appearance), was utterly brilliant last night.

Catch the ball! But in fact, Rivera had no one to blame but himself . . . or the Red Sox, who simply wouldn't quit and let Rivera pick up his fiftieth save in peace.

The Yankee closer walked Trot Nixon, who was replaced by the speedy Dave Roberts. Then he hit Kevin Millar, who was replaced by the *fairly* speedy Gabe Kapler. With two on and one out, I expected a game-ending double play. Instead, Orlando Cabrera singled through the hole into right. Kevin Youkilis followed with a strikeout (I love Youk, but he was simply overmatched in the ninth last night). Then came Damon, and . . . ball game.

You would say that tomorrow's game—assuming the remains of Hurricane Ivan don't wash it out—couldn't possibly measure up. But with these two teams, I'm afraid to say anything but this: it's going to be another game off the schedule, and last night we maintained our good hold on the wild card. The gap between us and the Yankees for the top spot in the AL East has, meanwhile, once more shrunk to a mere two and a half games.

Like happy families, all blown saves are alike. You overthrow and leave the ball up and out and walk the leadoff guy. Get behind the second guy and hit him. Miss your location and a .260 hitter goes the other way on you, and your right fielder with the best arm on the team throws one up the line so their speedy pinch runner scores. Next guy bloops one that your center fielder usually gets, but this time—for no other reason than things are going to hell—he pulls up and the ball drops, another run scores, and you've just blown another save.

Closers blow saves; that's just a fact of baseball. Yankee fans will say that Mariano Rivera doesn't, but here's proof—again—that it doesn't matter if you're Mo or John "Way Back" Wasdin or the old Derek Lowe or Eric Gagne or Eck in his prime. Closers blow saves. You just hope they aren't important ones. Like Game 7 of the World Series. Oh, sorry, Mo.

September 18th

For our publicity mission to Yankee Stadium (where the only sellouts are the players), I wear my Bill Mazeroski jersey. On the train down, I sit beside an older Yankee fan wearing a Yogi Berra cap. As you'll remember, Yogi was playing left that fateful October day in Forbes Field and watched the Yanks' hopes fly over his head and over the wall. The guy next to me doesn't recognize the jersey, and I think—perhaps uncharitably—that being oblivious of history is a luxury we, as Sox fans, can't afford.

Later, at the Stadium, in response to the chant "Nineteen eighteen," I turn around and bellow "Nineteen sixty."

And—I swear to God—one kid says, "What happened in 1960?"

September 19th

The first game of this series was a pulse-pounder which the Red Sox won in their last at-bat. In yesterday's, played under swag-bellied gray skies and in a drizzle that had become a steady rain by the seventh, the Yankees really won it in the first, when they tacked a five-spot on the tragickal Mr. Lowe, to the joy of the not-quite-full Stadium. (Not to say the relief.) They added four more in the second and were off to the races. By then Mr. Lowe was gone, suffering from a tragickal blowe to the ankle, inflicted by ye olde horsehide sphere. It was, we are told, his earliest exit from a game in five years. I wasn't terribly surprised at how poorly he performed. Mr. Lowe is simply having one of Those Years.

As for the Yankees . . . well, they seem to be making a kind of goal-line stand: *This close and no closer,* with the *this close* part being two games. At one point in yesterday's game it was 13–0 bad guys, and the mostly unremarkable Yankee hurler Jon Lieber took a no-no deep into the game, before David "I Love It When You Call Me Big Papi" Ortiz hit a home run to break up *that* nonsense.

Worst of all, Scribner, who plans to publish this book, had set up an interview with Bob Minzesheimer of *USA Today* at the ballpark, along with a photographer who took pictures of Stewart and me until every Yankee fan in our immediate vicinity* had gotten a good gawk and a chance to boo. I have decided that hell is probably an endless photo op at an opposing team's ballpark where your club is getting its fudge packed most righteously, to the great glee of the sellout crowd where you are not being allowed to hide like the microbe you would dearly love to be.

At last we were allowed to escape, and could I have written all that yesterday? Technically, yes. It was a Saturday-afternoon game, and I had plenty of time later on to jot these fan's notes. Emotionally, no. I was too

---

*That would be roughly seventy-five hundred, most of them equipped with Yankee hats, Derek Jeter T-shirts, and upturned middle fingers for people wearing Red Sox gear.

bummed out. And the bottom line? The *ironic* bottom line? After all the emotional highs and lows of the last two games, the Boston Red Sox are *exactly where they were before coming to New York*. Yes! We're three and a half behind in the AL East, and thanks to an Angels loss to Texas yesterday, we are five and a half ahead in the wild card. So in the end, it's just two more games off the ever-diminishing schedule.

Ah, but this afternoon comes the cherry on the banana split: Martinez versus Mussina. 1:05 P.M., at the Stadium. Wonder if I could scalp myself a little ticket to that game?

Hmmmm.

Later: I did, and Pedro was awful. The Red Sox were awful. The New York fans were loathsomely jubilant. I paid $350 for a box seat and watched the Yanks put an 11–1 pounding on my Sox. This afternoon, even the *sunshine* was awful. It was, in many ways, the apotheosis of the Dark Side Red Sox fan experience: the Red Sox fan not as Fearless Booster of the Underdog but as Beaten Loser, slinking from the park with his head down, eager to put the sound of those cheering fans behind him and clinging to the twin tenets of the Manny Ramirez Credo for comfort: *Turn the page* and *We gotta jus' keep goin', man*.

Tomorrow, Wakefield faces the Birds at Fenway Park. I hope, because I am faithful. I fear, because I know that when you're going bad, you usually get more of the same.

The best news is quiet news from the West Coast: the Angels are also weekend losers, and we're still five and a half games up in the wild-card race. On that side of the dance card, it's just two more games off the schedule. But yes, I fear the Orioles, with whom we have gone 1-4 so far this season at Fenway, where we have won so many against other teams.

Today we get our asses kicked again, 11–1, with most of the damage done in an eight-run fifth, as the Yanks chase Pedro. It's humiliating, the kind of loss your friends at school will taunt you about tomorrow.

It's also strangely unreal. The Yankees aren't this good (even with performance-enhancing drugs), and we're not this bad, and I have a creeping suspicion that this is payback for Friday night. We—Sox fans, I mean—get the thrilling comeback win, and their fans get the revenge blowouts. Looking back at how Mo blew the save Friday night (walk, hit batsman, missed location (and Sheffield's bad throw), bloop that Lofton for some reason pulls up on), I suspect (at the risk of being labeled paranoid) this is all being orchestrated to ramp up interest on both sides. When a team does nothing to win and still wins, you have to wonder. Of course, 1986's Game 6 is a classic example of that: walk, hit batsman, muffed grounder.

Mo also blew the Tek–A-Rod game with a gopher ball to Bill Mueller after throwing one to Trot that he just missed.

And Mo blew Game 7 of the 2001 series. This fan's got to wonder.

The goal would be the dullest but most important of goals—financial security. Obscene TV ratings lead to obscene TV contracts. And who could blame the league? TV money floats the whole show. Just look at the NHL (if you can find them) for the flip side.

September 20th

Wake tonight against Baltimore, and there's a sense of letdown, as if these games mean less. It's not true, of course; it's just a by-product of all the hype, and the fact that it's Monday. (It's no coincidence that of the six series we play against the Yanks, all but one straddle a weekend.)

Wake's lost three straight and has looked awful. Tonight he's sharp until the fourth, when he walks a batter, gives up a ground-ball single, hits a guy, walks a run in, then surrenders a grand slam to B. J. Surhoff. The O's add three more in the fifth, walking and stealing bases, taking advantage of a passed ball and a blown rundown, and while we chip away late to make the final 8–6, this one was in reach only for one or two at-bats.

The Angels win so they're four and a half back. Most of the Faithful think the wild card's in the bag, but we have problems with the O's, and face them seven times in our last thirteen games. Honestly, I'd rather play the Yankees.

September 21st

SK: My son Joe says that Derek Lowe (and a number of other Red Sox) were out partying hearty on Friday night (and into the wee hours of Saturday morning) under the assumption that the Saturday game (i.e., *our* game) would be a rainout. Have you heard this? Is it a Sons of Sam Horn thing?

SO: That Lowe rumor (stumbling in at 4 A.M. from the China Club)—true or not—points to how unprepared and spacey he looked in the first. I can see the logic: only someone still half-drunk would have made that throw to third behind Bernie. But look how we played last night after a good night's sleep. That hot streak seems long ago and faraway.

Dear Red Sox,

It's my birthday, and I'd like you to give me a present. After three straight losses, I'd like a win tonight, and with Father Curt on the mound, I think I have a chance of getting one. Even more than a win, I'd like you guys to take stock of your current situation—do you think you could do that for me?

First, since the splendid (and cattily crafty) win over the Yankees on the 17th, when Red Sox pitching gave up just two runs, the Boston staff has given up an average of *eleven runs per game*. The starters, so good during the August run, have been horrible.

Second, Baltimore continues their absolute dominance of the Red Sox, and this had better change. The regular season has now dwindled to a mere thirteen games, and seven of them—the majority, in other words—are with these perennial Red Sox killers.

Third, the Angels show signs of snapping out of their funk. They won last night, shaving a full game off your wild-card lead. You guys had better realize that wild-card deal isn't sealed yet. Yes, the Angels have six games left against the A's . . . but we have three left against the Yanks. It's time to start winning some damn games against Baltimore. It's been a long time since a sellout Fenway crowd was as quiet as the one last night (especially with the Yankees losing). I think they sense you guys going bad and are waiting, hoping, for you to shake it off. So am I. So start tonight with a win, okay? Because, after the glory of the last six weeks, a September choke would be dismal, indeed.

Thanking you in advance,
Stephen King

10:35 P.M.: Baseball's a funny damn game. I got my birthday present, but it was Red Sox second baseman Mark Bellhorn who gave it to me after the home-plate umpire tried to snatch it away (and after he *did* snatch away Curt Schilling's twenty-first win of the season).

After seven and a half innings of scoreless baseball, during which Father Curt bagged fourteen Birds by way of the K, the Red Sox—who have had to struggle *far* too hard for the five or so wins they've managed against the O's this year—manufactured a single skinny run. On came Keith Foulke, the Boston closer. He got the first two guys, then surrendered a base hit. This brought Sox-wrecker Javy Lopez to the plate. Foulke, who had never surrendered a hit to Mr. Lopez before tonight, massaged the count to 0-2. Then, twice, he threw clear strikes* which the umpire called balls. Finally Foulke hung a 2-2 slider that Lopez lost, high and gone, into the night.

In the bottom of the ninth, Boston put runners on second and third with nobody out (my man Kevin Youkilis led the inning with a walk). Then David McCarty popped up and Johnny Damon struck out. Just when I was absolutely convinced that the Sox were going to scuffle to their fourth loss in as many games, this time squandering a brilliant pitching performance in the process, Bellhorn laced a double to right, winning the game and bringing the Sox out of the dugout in a joyous mob of red-and-white uniforms while the Standells played and the crowd went bonkers: a little touch of Fenway magic on my birthday, not bad.

And even a little something extra: tonight we have a magic number in the wild-card race. It's eight. Any combination of Boston wins and Anaheim losses adding up to that number puts us in the postseason.

September 22nd

NESN, in a strange late-season move, changes the format of their morning *SportsDesk* to thirty minutes and replaces beloved girl-next-door anchor Jayme Parker with heavily coiffed and tailored Hazel Mae, formerly a postgame analyst (read: talking head) with the Toronto Blue Jays. In an introductory guest spot between innings with Don and Jerry, she lays down a swinging patter, trying to be chummy and knowledgeable, but comes off as slick and insincere as a game-show host, without a touch of irony. She's a pro, no doubt, but her style is wrong for dumpy, low-budget NESN: we New Englanders distrust fast-talking outsiders. And she's talk-

---

*Sorry, Blue, but that slo-mo replay has no mercy.

ing mighty fast now, flying out ahead of herself as if she's nervous—as if she suddenly realizes what she's gotten herself into. I can smell the flop sweat through the TV. Don tries to help, feeding her cues to lighten and redirect her spiel. Jerry just stands there, giving her enough rope.

SO: What have they done with our Jayme? And with our 15-minute quick-repeating *SportsDesk*? Is nothing sacred?

SK: Hazel Mae? What kind of name is that? And, to misquote Bob Dylan, "Hazel, you look so HARD!!"

Foulked again. For the second straight night, he gives up a bomb in the ninth to tie the game, this time to the literally hobbling Rafael Palmeiro. We go to extras, where Curtis Leskanic makes us hold our breath before getting out of a bases-loaded jam with an improbable 3-2-4 DP (Pokey alertly covering first), and then Orlando Cabrera, who had a chance to win it in the ninth but ducked a pitch that would have hit him with bases juiced, knocks one onto the Monster for a walk-off and another bouncing celebration at home.

SO: Yi yi yi.

SK: All's welle that endes welle.

September 23rd

The Birds are making it outrageously hard, and Keith Foulke has blown a pair of saves (one with the help of outrageously bad home-plate umpiring, 'tis true), but the Red Sox pulled out another one last night (walk-off home run in the bottom of the twelfth, advantage Mr. Cabrera), and the Angels dropped another one. The magic number thus drops to five, and with the Yankees' loss to Toronto and New York's impending weekend visit to *our* house, even the AL East gold ring seems within our reach. This September still ain't a patch on August . . . but I'd have to say it's improving.

SK: **5**

This magic number brought to you courtesy of the Seattle M's. And by the way, have you checked dem crazy Tejas Rangers lately?

SO: Baby, can you dig your Rangers? Dead and buried last week, but after winning four straight (and going for the sweep of the A's tonight), they're a mere three back in the West, and the A's and Angels still have to tangle six times. It would be sweet to see the one truly surprising club of this season sneak in on the final weekend.

And I'm sure you noticed the milestones last night: El Jefe's 40th homer and Bellhorn's 163rd K. Just numbers. Like 5.

Grady Little is no longer the Red Sox manager, ostensibly for his mistrust of the bullpen in an important game. Tonight new manager Terry Francona shows his faith by resting the hard-ridden Mike Timlin and Keith Foulke and letting lefty specialist and submariner Mike Myers pitch to a right-handed hitter with bases loaded and the score tied in the eighth. Then in the ninth, he lets righty specialist and submariner Byung-Hyun Kim (no, that's not a typo) pitch to a left-handed batter with two on. Bill James—hell, any Strat-O-Matic junkie—could have told you these were low-percentage moves. Francona's trust in his idiotic luck costs us four runs, and, when Manny gets two of those back in the ninth and David Ortiz's two-out, two-strike blast to right settles into David Newhan's glove, proves to cost us the game. Wake up the talk-radio cranks, it's Grady time!

(A side note: Ellis Burks, who'll be retiring after the season, pinch-hits in the ninth for what may be his last major league at-bat. When he first came up from Pawtucket in 1987, he was a reedy outfielder just beginning to develop power. Since then he's ripped over 2,000 hits and 350 home runs (nifty trivia: he's homered against every club in the majors). This year he was hurt and wasn't really part of the on-field effort, but he's a clubhouse presence and sentimental favorite. After receiving a warm standing O, Ellis fights

B. J. Ryan deep into the count before blooping a single to center. At forty, on creaky knees, he's still a professional hitter. We applaud long and loud as he's lifted for a pinch runner, and he goes into the dugout with a smile. Thanks, Ellis.)

SK: We almost took three of four. Papi came up four yards short. Mr. Kim still with the bad karma. My daughter-in-law calls me to ask if it would be all right for her to have ORLANDO tattooed on her ass (I said sure). And consider, S2: THEY COULDA SWEPT US! Baltimore's the only team in the AL with the nuts to leave Fenway feeling bad about "just a split." Holy shit, I'm so *glad* to see the Birds hoppin' somewhere else, and I feel so *bad* about having to finish the season back where we started. The Great Wheel of Ka turns . . .

SO: If Francoma uses the pen by the book tonight we probably win and take three of four. Seems like he wrote this one off in the seventh with the score tied at 5. What good is the forty-man roster if you don't take advantage of it?

Rangers sweep the A's and we've got a wild-ass race in the West.

The Magic Number remains Nomar.

September 25th

Was there the slightest hitch in Terry Francona's walk last night in the eighth inning when he finally went out to take the ball from Pedro Martinez's hand, and the boos began raining down from the Fenway Faithful? I was sitting in my usual place, just a row up from foul territory between home and first on the Sox side of the field—just about the best seat in the house—and I say there was. If so, such a hitch would indicate surprise. And if Francona was surprised, it would indicate that not even a full season at the helm of this team has taught him the most fundamental thing about the clientele it and he serves: this is no ordinary hardball fan-base. The New Englanders who follow the Red Sox are as deeply scarred by loss, particularly loss to the Yankees, as they are loyal to their club. But it's more specific than that. They are especially scarred—*traumatized* would not be too strong a word—by loss to the Yankees in the late innings, with Pedro Martinez, long regarded as the team's ace, on the hill. If Francona cannot grasp that, he cannot succeed in Boston.

The Red Sox lost to New York last night 6–4, in spite of home runs by Manny Ramirez, Johnny Damon, and the fiery, not-to-be-denied Trot Nixon. That they played otherwise with remarkable dullness for a team facing its archrival in a last-ditch effort to capture the divisional flag hardly matters, even when you add in the fact that they did it in front of the fans that have loved them so long and so well (if fruitlessly). Love is blind, and most of them will either be back in the park (that would include me and Stewart) or in front of their televisions tonight, rooting for David Ortiz to hit a couple of bombs, and for Orlando Cabrera to make a few more sparkling plays (my scorebook says he made a six-pack of them last night, although he went only 1 for 4 at the plate). We'll find something to cheer, you may depend on it. To a lover, even a smallpox scar is a beauty mark.

What we *won't* forget—and what the newspapers are full of this morning—is Terry Francona leaving Pedro Martinez too long at the fair, in a gruesome replay of the 2003 ALCS Game 7. We came into the eighth leading the Yankees, 4–3. I think everyone in the park, including Yankee skipper Joe Torre, expected to see Timlin and Embree tag-team that frame while Pedro took his well-earned rest on the bench. But Francona, who apparently never read that thing about how the coach who doesn't learn from the past is condemned to repeat Remedial Baseball, sent Martinez trudging back out, although the little guy's pitch count was well over a hundred by then. The result was what everybody who wasn't asleep expected. Hideki Matsui lost the second pitch he saw, tying the game.

Francona, then giving a perfect demonstration of why we stayed in Vietnam as long as we did, left Martinez in to prove he had not made the mistake he had in fact made. Williams doubled. Francona still left Martinez in, taking him out only after he had fanned Posada and then given up the go-ahead RBI single to Ruben Sierra. My theory is that if Martinez hadn't gotten at least one out to prove Terry Francona hadn't made a mistake, Martinez might still be in there at 10:30 A.M. the following day, with the score Yanks 949, Sox 4, and blood trickling down from Pedro's burst biceps.

But in my fury I jest.

I have serious doubts about Terry Francona's thinking processes and have all year (there are times when I've thought there's nothing but a bowling alley up there between his ears), but Pedro Martinez is as brilliant as he is brave. After the game he said, in effect, "I can only tip my cap to the Yankees. They've proved they're my Daddy." Meaning, in baseball vernacular, *they're better than me; they have my number.* Martinez knows the chances are quite good that he may not be done with the Yankees even yet, and that if he sees them again, the next game will be exponentially more important than this one. His remark was a way of resetting all the dials to zero. If he *does* have to face them again, he's lifted a lot of the internal pressure by publicly stating that they can somehow get over, under, or around the best he can do. When (and if) he takes the mound against the Yankees in postseason—probably in the Bronx—he will be able to tell himself that, based on what he's told the world, *he* is not the one with something to prove; *they* are.

None of which solves the riddle of why a manager would deliberately go out and replicate a course of action which has already visited defeat and unhappiness on so many in the very recent past. When you think about it, being a Red Sox fan may have quite a lot to teach about what we're doing in Iraq.

At Starfleet Academy, every cadet has to confront the problem of the *Kobayashi Maru.* The *Maru* is a freighter caught in a gravitic rift in the Neutral Zone. Cadets naturally respond to its distress calls, but once their starship enters the Neutral Zone, three Klingon cruisers surround and attack it. The Klingons have overwhelming resources and show no mercy, and the cadet needs to realize he or she is in a no-win situation—that, as Kirk says, there are times when a commander doesn't have the luxury of winning.

Red Sox fans don't want to hear that. For all our gloom-and-doom reputation, we expect to win, and we expect our manager to make the right moves to make that happen. And because we're knowledgeable fans, we know what those moves are *before they should take place.*

Last night Terry Francona took the Grady test—the Red Sox version of the *Kobayashi Maru*—and from his solution, it appears he was peeking at Grady's paper. Since the mid-eighties, the standard sequence has been: get seven strong from your starter, setup, close. Simple stuff, and the night before Francona sacrificed a tie game to rest his setup guy and his closer. So there's no excuse for Pedro starting the eighth, or continuing to pitch after Matsui's home run, and we all know it. Once again, the only one who didn't pass the test was the Red Sox manager.

And the Angels and Rangers both won, so our magic number remains 5—it's the Curse of Nomar!

September 26th

When Yankee starting pitching goes south, as Roger Clemens replacement Javier Vazquez did last night in the fifth inning, Joe Torre now has essentially two choices in the matter of middle relief: Tom Gordon (whose loss from the Red Sox I understand and accept but still lament in my heart) and the Bronx Delicatessen Brigade. Having used Gordon to get to Rivera in the first game of this late-season Yanks-Sox series, Torre was stuck with the Deli Brigade last night. After Vazquez came Tanyon Sturtze; after Sturtze came Heredia. And lo, Heredia begat Quantrill and Quantrill begat Nitkowski; so too did Nitkowski begat Proctor, also called Scott. By that time the Yankees were pretty well baked, and the usually crafty Quantrill—left in far too long last night*—took the loss by default.

This was a good night to be at the ballpark and a good game for the Red Sox to win. Although the Angels and the Rangers, now tied for wild-card runners-up (and nipping at the heels of the Athletics in the AL West), both won their games, we reduced our magic number for clinching a play-off berth to three. Better yet, we have made it impossible for the Yankees to clinch this year's AL East flag on ground taxed by the State of Massachusetts. Best of all, at least for the head sitting beneath the bright red YANKEES HATER hat I see in the mirror, is this: no matter how we do against our long-time nemesis this Sunday afternoon, in 2004's last regular-season game at Fenway Park, we will have won the nineteen-game season series. The worst we can do is 10-9, and if Father Curt is on his game, it will be 11-8. This isn't as good as it could have been—especially for a team that was at one point 6-1 against the pinstripers—but when it comes to the Yankees, we take our satisfactions where we can get them.

7:00 P.M.: It's by no means a sure thing that the Red Sox and Yankees

---

*Ah, but under the circumstances, the *always* crafty Joe Torre really had little choice; by then it was a fool's mate.

will meet in the ALCS for the second year in a row—I am sure that base-ball stat wizards like Bill James will tell you it's odds against, given the fact that the opening postseason series are nasty, brutish, and short*—but given the level of competition between the two clubs this season, I have to believe that such an American League Championship Series would be a boon to that larger faithful that loves not just the Red Sox or the Yankees but the game itself.

Last weekend at Yankee Stadium, the Sox won a close one Friday night and then endured two shellackings, to the glee of packed Stadium crowds. At the Fens this weekend, it was the Yankees winning a close one Friday night and the Red Sox winning the two weekend games by lopsided scores, today's final being 11–4, with a woefully unready-for-prime-time Kevin Brown taking the loss (and not escaping the first inning). At Yankee Stadium, the joint resounded to sarcastic choral cries of *PEDRO! PEDRO!* as Martinez left his game on the mound; today at Fenway Park, the cry was *JEE-TER! JEE-TER!* as the New York shortstop flubbed a potential double play and then made way for a pinch hitter in the eighth after going one for a dozen (.083) over the three games.

In the end, Boston took the season, 11-8, but in the crucial runs-scored category, there was in the end almost no difference: 106 for the Sox, 104 for the Yanks. When you think about 171 innings of baseball (excluding games that may have gone beyond the regulation nine), that's an amaz-ingly small margin; hardly more than a coat of paint.

In terms of playing into October, the team's job is now clear-cut (if slightly complicated by Jeanne, the fourth hurricane to strike Florida in the last five weeks). Of the seven games remaining on the regular-season schedule, the Red Sox need to win only a pair to assure themselves of a postseason berth. Another (and more meaningful) meeting with the Yankees may or may not lie ahead; in the meantime, let Trot Nixon, Boston's rejuvenated right fielder, have the final word on this exhaustive (and exhausting) regular-season slate of Red Sox/Yankees matchups. "Nineteen is too many," he said flatly in a postgame interview this after-noon. "We've seen everything they've got, and they've seen what we've got. I don't mind playing them . . . but nineteen is just too many."

• • •

*Three out of five rather than four out of seven.

Ladies and gentlemen, boys and girls, welcome once again to Super Pro Wrestling! For no other reason than he doesn't like the way Doug Mientkiewicz is standing on the bag at first (or might it have something to do with Lofton's mysterious ejection during the Tek–A-Rod brawl?), Kenny Lofton deliberately elbows him as he goes by—on a play that isn't close, in a game that's a runaway. Maybe Kenny's frustrated, or just dumb, because he seems surprised—nay, outraged—when reliever Pedro Astacio throws behind him late in the game. The next inning, the Yanks' kid reliever throws at Dave Roberts's head. Uncool, and Roberts is justifiably pissed.

There's a huge difference between throwing behind a guy and throwing at his head, and everyone in the game knows it. Likewise, if you purposely elbow someone, you had better expect to be thrown at. In both cases, the Yankees broke the unwritten code. If there's any justice (and wrestling is all about poetic justice), the game will make them pay.

Side note: Today's sellout was our 81st of the year. Only three other clubs in the history of baseball have sold out their entire home season. All three were playing in brand-new stadiums.*

September 27th

Hurricane Jeanne has knocked out the electricity in the Tampa Bay area, and for a while it looks as if the game may not be played. The juice is restored, but someone seems to have neglected to tell the Boston bats. Or maybe it's just young Scott Kazmir, exerting the sort of limited but malign influence certain pitchers seem able to cast over certain teams. When Kazmir faced Martinez two weeks ago, you'll recall, he won easily. He seems well on his way to a second win tonight, striking out batter after batter (Kevin Millar on egregiously high cheese), so when my youngest son—up on a wonderful extended visit from New York—suggests we turn off the game and go to a movie, I agree at once, even though the Sox technically have a chance to clinch a playoff berth. I now believe they *will* clinch; I just don't believe it will be tonight.

The code is absolute, and beyond partisanship. Tonight Bronson Arroyo hits Aubrey Huff unintentionally with a curve that breaks down and in too

---

*The Indians at Jacobs Field, the Rockies at Coors, and the Giants at Pac Bell.

sharply. No big deal, even though it puts Huff out of the game with a bruised shin, but then, a batter later, with men on second and third and first base open, Bronson drills Tino Martinez in the back, and Tino rightfully has some things to say.

Former Mets phenom Scott Kazmir, who has yet to give up a hit, retaliates, hitting Manny low. And Manny's cool, Manny understands, and hoofs it down to first without a word. Now that things are evened up, the ump warns both dugouts. Any more of this and both the pitcher and the manager are going. But Kazmir—maybe on Lou Piniella's orders—isn't done. He hits the *very next batter*, Millar, in the ribs. Millar takes exception and the benches clear briefly. Good-bye, unhittable Kazmir. Good-bye, Lou.

It's a foolish move. We jump all over reliever Jorge Sosa for five runs, including a drive to dead center by Manny that lands on the roof of the fancy restaurant out there, and go on to win 7–3 and clinch the wild card. See? That's what happens when you go against the code.

And, ironically, since being on the same team overrides the code, during the locker-room celebration Manny hugs Terry Adams, who he came close to charging back in April after a little chin music.

It's the late show of *The Forgotten* we go to, and in Bethel Station on a Monday night, my son and I are two of just six attendees. As we're leaving, the guy cleaning up behind the candy counter tells me—casually—that the Red Sox were leading Tampa Bay by a score of 7–2 and he thinks that might be a final. Owen and I look at each other in delighted amazement, then hurry to his car and tune the radio to WOXO, Norway–South Paris (which advertises itself as Everybody's Country . . . when, that is, they're not broadcasting NASCAR racing, Boston Red Sox baseball, or Oxford Hills High School football). We discover that the game has indeed ended, and that the final score was 7–3. Bronson Arroyo hit a couple of batters (he leads the American League in that category), and Scott Kazmir retaliated. The umpires let him get away with drilling Manny Ramirez in the knee, but when Kazmir whacked Kevin "I Brake for High Cheese" Millar in the ribs, the kid was gone, taking an incipient no-hitter with him.* Three or four home runs later (Manny hit number 43), the 2004 Red Sox

---

*For the record, I think that hitting Millar was an accident. But, accident or on purpose, Kazmir did the Boston batters one hell of a favor by dealing himself out.

Party Boys are in a clubhouse so wrapped in plastic it looks like a condom, laughing and shouting and pouring beer on each other.

They all acknowledge that the regular season isn't over as long as catching the Yankees remains a technical possibility (by winning, the Red Sox cut the lead of the idle Yanks to three games, and in that light the two we lost to the awful El Birdos during the last home stand look bigger than ever), but in their raucous celebrating, there is an undeniable sense that they feel the real work is now done. Given their lackluster level of play in June and July, that is understandable. In some ways, they are lucky to be here at all.

SO: The Sox are sudsing Manny with champagne. I'm toasting them with ginger ale. I've got a bottle of bubbly downstairs, but I'm saving it for something bigger. Still, to make the playoffs with the injuries we've had, I'm proud of this club. They gave us a great summer. (The punch line: now for a great fall.)

Looks like Minnesota and the great Santana. I'd match him up with Schilling, just go after him. Too bad those games will be on the road.

SK: Mathematically, it was the weirdest clinch ever. [What Steve means is that we didn't whittle our magic number down to zero. We're still at 1, but because our competition for the wild card is Anaheim, that 1 assumes they win the rest of their games, three of which are against Oakland, who they're only one game behind now, and if they do that, they win the West and Oakland becomes our already-defeated competition. So our wish from a few months ago has come true: the A's and Angels knock each other off without even playing the games. Thank you, unbalanced schedule (and unbalanced schedule-makers).]

SO: The rest of our games are most likely meaningless, but . . . it's like Jim Carrey says in *Dumb & Dumber* when Lauren Holly tells him the odds of them being together are more like a million to one: "So you're telling me there's a chance."

Start carving your playoff roster, we're going to the show!

September 28th

Tonight's game against Tampa Bay is an audition for pitchers on the bubble. Derek Lowe pitches dreadfully, scuttling his chance to be the number three starter in the playoffs (Bronson Arroyo seems to have won that spot with his strong second half). Terry Adams throws two-plus ugly innings, so count him out. By the time Alan Embree comes in to throw one shutout inning, it's 8–8. Scott Williamson, who's been injured, walks one guy in his stint, but his velocity is still down around 89, so I doubt he'll make the roster. Pedro Astacio's just getting some work in before he starts half of Saturday's doubleheader in Baltimore. Ramiro Mendoza, though, nails his assignment, pitching a perfect ninth and tenth, striking out two and giving us a chance to win it when Kevin Millar cranks a two-run shot off fireballing closer Danys Baez, who Lou has left out there throwing 96 (and then 94, 93, 92) for three innings. Foulke crafts a one-two-three eleventh and we're two and a half back of the Yanks with five to go.

Much more exciting is the West, where the Angels and A's are now in a dead heat with a three-game showdown looming on the season's final weekend, the results of which will determine the playoff matchups. Right now the Central champs the Twins have a better record (by a mere one win) than Oakland and Anaheim, meaning they'd play us and have home-field advantage, and the Yankees would host whoever won the West (an easier task, given the Twins' brilliant lefty Johan Santana). The Yanks have some control over the situation: tomorrow they start a three-game series against the Twins. They can avoid Santana by rolling over for them, but that's a risk: if they lose too many, we have a shot at catching them. Slim, sure, but a shot.

September 29th

SK: Today is a big day. If we win and Minnesota sweeps . . .
It _could_ happen. One chance in four.
Meet me at Foxwoods.

SO: I know, I'm thinking the same way, but I read in the paper this morning that Francona and Wallace have decided not to change the playoff rotation to go after the division (that is, they'll still throw Asta-cio versus the O's in that doubleheader). The Coma himself: "At the chance of sounding like I don't care, because I do, I'm sort of going to be stubborn about screwing our pitching up. I love the idea of having home-field advantage. I also think that you win with pitching. We're going to somewhat try to remember that."

And as things shape up, it appears Pedro's slated for Game 1 (and therefore Game 5) and Schill for Game 2 (and thus Game 1 of the ALCS). So forget that dream matchup of Schilling-Santana. I guess Terry thinks we can split with Santana and take Schill's start, or maybe he's hoping we'll outslug them at home for our #3 and #4?

Call me the tum-ba-lin di-ee-iice.

SK: "I guess Terry thinks"—You're giving him too much credit.

Your news is unbelievable. The scenario you describe is idiotic. All I can hope is that Francona will change his mind and see reason if Minnesota sweeps New York (they lead in the first game, 3–1, in the middle innings) and we beat Tampa Bay again. Given the last couple of weeks, his plan to start Pedro in Game 1 is also foolish. His inexperience is showing. Not to mention a certain ocher tinge running up the center of his back.

I'm disgustipated, to quote Sylvester the Cat. Could these be orders from Above?—**Sigh**—Probably not.

SO: Since we're two and a half back with five to go, I can almost understand the thinking. Almost. Last year we could have run the table if we'd had home advantage.

And did you see who's sitting behind home plate at Yankee Stadium right now, scouting both the Yanks and Twins for the Cubbies? That's right: Mr. Grady Little.

I'm back in Maine rather than at Fenway Park or at Yankee Stadium, where a sparse crowd is watching the rare afternoon game, but I'm once more wearing my bright red YANKEES HATER cap, and for a perfectly good reason: the sparse Stadium crowd is in attendance at the first of this year's last three really important games, two between the

Twins and the Yankees, one between the hapless Devil Rays and the Red Sox.

The Minnesota Twins, represented on the mound in the first of these crucial tilts by Johan Santana, who will almost certainly win this year's Cy Young Award in the American League, are leading 3–1 in the fifth inning. *If* the Twins go on to win this game (Santana hasn't lost since the All-Star break) plus the nightcap of this hurricane-induced doubleheader, and if the Red Sox can win tonight in Tampa,* the Yankees' lead in the AL East would drop to a single scrawny game. I'm not saying this will happen, but if it *did*, considering the fact that Boston and New York have a combined total of eight games left to play . . . well, in a case like that, all bets would be off.

Maybe it doesn't matter. *Probably* it doesn't matter, in terms of what comes next; once you get to postseason, *all* the matchups are tough. But I want that home-field advantage. Even more, I'd like to see the Yankees humbled. So come on, you Twins! Go, you Johan!

It's weird: here we have the Yanks' ace Moose against Johan Santana in a rematch of last year's ALDS, in a game with playoff implications, yet when I tune in during the second inning I discover the Stadium is a sea of blue seats. There can't be more than two thousand people there—less than the number of folks who turn out for BP at Fenway. Later, the Yankees will list the official attendance as N/A—not available. Hey George, I hear Montreal's looking for a team.

10:15 P.M.: One doesn't like to believe God is a Yankees fan—it's a terrifying idea—but days like this make me wonder. I thought that, with New York playing two against a strong Minnesota team and the Red Sox playing one against the hapless Rays, we really had a chance to pull within a breath of first place. At worst, I thought, New York would split their twin bill with Santana taking the opener.

But no. Santana left after five with a 3–1 lead, pulled by the Twins' skipper, who quite naturally wants to protect his young ace with the playoffs looming. The Yankees then scored a bazillion runs and the camera

*It would be their fifth win in a row.

caught the aforementioned young ace in the dugout, hucking helmets at the cement floor. Getting quite a bounce, too. The Yankees went on to win the second game, 5–4.

In Tampa, Tino Martinez hit a three-run bomb to put the game out of reach in the eighth, but the really disturbing development was how mortal Pedro Martinez looked in his last start of the regular season—how downright *lousy*. The hapless D-Rays won that one, 9–4, and instead of picking up a game and a half, we *lost* a game and a half. The Yankees' margin is now four games, and given that the Red Sox have just four to play, I think that pretty well cooks us in the AL East, don't you? The bottom line is simply that when the pressure got really intense, the Yankees refused to buckle. The Red Sox—aided by the Baltimore Orioles and at times by Terry Francona, who has a tendency to freeze at critical moments like Captain Queeg in *The Caine Mutiny*—did. Now we turn our eyes— ever hopeful, ever faithful—to the playoffs, where we can only hope the script will change.

SK: Santana comes out of the game, the Yanks score four and win. And I saw Santana in the dugout, heaving helmets. It ain't nothing to Gardenhire; he's got a lock.

If we finish second, I have no problem with Tito's doubleheader pitching roster. But what's with this playoff sked? Are we conceding the games Santana pitches, or what? Saving Curt for "winnable" games? Give me your thinking on this. What am I not seeing here?

SO: I thought the Yanks might tank it to make sure we'd get the Twins, but now it appears the Twins tanked it, pulling Santana after five. The playoffs don't start for another six days, so it's not like a starter should be on a pitch count around 70. Boo!

I have no idea what's up with T Franc's playoff rotation. It sounds like he's going with a four-man squad, meaning Curt will start *only* Game 2 of the ALDS. I guess he's assuming that's a W, and he'll have his #3 and #4 guys set for Games 3 and 4 at Fenway. If the 3 and 4 guys and the home bats can't get it done, then he's hoping—someday, some way—for a split between Pedro and Santana. Problem is, Arroyo, who should be our #3, has thrown far better on the road, and at this point we don't have a reliable #4. I think it's cavalier of Francona to assume we don't need two from Father Curt in the first round. Sure, it would be nice to start the ALCS with a fresh ace, but there's not much margin for error in this plan. Minnesota's a good team that's been there before.

September 30th

SO: So was the Coma's initial rotation just smoke? Because now Pedro's saying he's starting Game 2 and Schill's taking Games 1 and 5. And the Angels, now leading the West by one, have the exact same record as the Twins. I have to wonder, is the switch due to the possibility of missing Santana? It's all up in the air for now, and probably will be until the outcome of that juicy Angels-at-A's series this weekend.

SK: I don't know about the rotation. All I know for sure is that I'm considering a petition to the Great High Ayatollah, suggesting a fatwa on the Yankees would be a good idea.

October 1st

As a Red Sox fan, I am of course aware that there is another baseball league, but my grasp of it is vague, like a European's grasp of the New World in the seventeenth century or an American's grasp of the solar system in the nineteenth. Yes, somewhere in the American Midwest there lives a fearsome wand-wielding wizard named Pujols, and I know that in California there be Giants, for my Red Sox did truly visit them once in the season which is now almost over. But like most Red Sox fans, my focus will remain fiercely fixed on what is sometimes called "the junior circuit" until—and if—we have to play one of those quasi-mythological Others in the World Series. And that's okay, because in this final weekend of regular-season baseball, I find plenty to occupy me within the familiar geography of the American League.

Three of the four AL postseason teams have now been decided: the Yankees (AL East champs), the Twins (AL Central champs) and the Red Sox (AL wild card). The winner in the AL West will be decided this weekend, in Oakland, when the A's and Angels, with identical 90-69 records, go head-to-head. It will be, in effect, a mini-playoff, one the Red Sox and their fans will be watching with great interest. We'll play the team out of our division with the best record, but as I write this on Friday afternoon, Minnesota's record is also 90-69. That means we could wind up facing any one of those three. All I know for sure is that I'm hoping Cleveland will put a hurtin' on Minnesota this weekend, because we have to start by playing two away games no matter *who* our opponent is. Given that, I would prefer to steer clear of the Metrodome as long as possible.

Not to mention young Mr. Santana.

The Sox had last night off, ceding center stage (at least here in the East) to the Yankees, who clinched the division with their 100th win (so that's what— 16 against Tampa, 15 against Baltimore, 14 against Toronto . . .), beating the Twins' second-line relievers late after Ron Gardenhire pulled starter Brad Radke in the fifth. By resting, in effect the Twins rolled over this whole series, handing the Yanks the sweep. With the Angels losing and the A's winning, the West is knotted again, and the Twins, Angels and A's all share the same record. Because the Angels and A's play each other this weekend, the winner of the West will have at least 92 wins. The Twins lost their season series with both clubs, so to face the Sox they have to sweep their last three. I have to wonder: By losing this series, are the Twins purposely shooting for a rematch with the Yanks?

October 2nd

Last night the Angels humbled the A's 10–0 at home, and today they come back late against setup guy Ricardo Rincon and new closer Octavio Dotel to win the West. Chokeland has done it again. Billy Beane, you are *not* a genius. With no defense, no smallball and no pen, and ace Mark Mulder denying an obvious hip problem, the A's went into a September-long swoon that their fans will taste for the entire off-season. The Angels, missing Adam Kennedy with a knee injury, and suspending Jose Guillen for throwing his helmet and dissing manager Mike Scioscia, overcame everything to beat their rivals at the wire.

The Cubs, who had a two-game lead in the NL wild card a week ago, eliminate themselves by losing their sixth in seven games (including three blown saves by high-priced free-agent closer LaTroy Hawkins and crucial home losses to cellar dwellers the Mets and the Reds).

On the home front, the Sox sweep a meaningless doubleheader from the O's—something we could never do when the games really counted. Mr. Kim picks up a garbage win. Ellis Burks plays in his 2,000th and most likely last game, adding a single to his career stats.

Afterward, Terry Francona announces that Arroyo and Wake will start in the playoffs and that Lowe won't. Lowe leaves the clubhouse without a comment, and in the postgame, Eck says, "Will Derek Lowe be back next year? Who cares?"

And we still don't know who we're playing in the division series.

I continue to believe that it was our play against Baltimore—identified in my game notes from July on as the LEBs*—that cost us the AL East. Now that *that* little matter has been decided, we're doing all right against the LEBs, having already guaranteed ourselves at least a split in the season's final, meaningless four-game series (please note that *they* has once again become *we*, and will now likely stay that way, for better or worse, until the season ends).

On the West Coast, the Athletics have suddenly—and rather shockingly—come unglued. Anaheim beat them last night, 10–0, and came from behind to beat them again today, 5–4. So the Angels win the West, and all the AL postseason teams are now decided. The only remaining question is who the Red Sox will draw in the first round—the Angels or the Twins. Today's game between Minnesota and Cleveland would have settled that issue if Cleveland had won, but the game was suspended in the eleventh with the score tied, 5–5, so the groundskeepers could prepare the field for a University of Minnesota football game.

Say *what?*

*Loathsome El Birdos.

SK: Regular season's most surreal touch: Minnesota-Cleveland game, which would have nailed down the final playoff locale, suspended for a college football game.

Beautiful.

SO: Go Golden Gophers! Shades of last year's All-Star Game. Imagine if you were in the crowd at the Metrodome. Come back tomorrow? Hell no.

October 3rd

It's the last day of the regular season, and in the majors, the last few games are being played out by the subs, scrubs, and—in a few cases—the stars of tomorrow.

In Chicago, disconsolate Cubs fans are telling each other—without much real hope—that next season may be better (on the South Side, the ChiSox fans gave up on this season long ago).

In Tampa, Lou Piniella has packed away his horrible snot-green pullover for another season and bid his hapless Devil Rays *adieu*.

In Baltimore, the baseball writers have already begun beating the MVP tom-tom on behalf of Miguel Tejada, but given what Gary Sheffield's done for the Yankees and what Manny Ramirez has done for the Red Sox, I don't give them much of a chance.

In Texas, the plotting has already begun to turn this year's AL West dark horse into next year's favorite.

In Oakland, wunderkind Billy Beane may, like Lucy Arnaz, have some 'splainin' to do.

In Toronto, the wunderkind disciples of Billy Beane have probably left their offices for the year only after dropping their cell phones into their shredders.

And in Minnesota, the last playoff question was answered late this afternoon, when the Indians came up with two insurance runs in the top of the ninth and beat the Twins, 5–2. Thus it's Minnesota opening against New York on the East Coast and Boston opening against Anaheim on the West, both the day after tomorrow. I'll be at Fenway for the third game of the Sox-Angels series, and for the fourth, if needed (it probably will be). My heart beats a little faster, just writing that. At this point everything gets magnified, because when the second season ends, it does so either with shocking suddenness or—could it be?—with the sort of success of which Red Sox fans hardly dare dream.

The Twins win the resumption of their suspended game, but then lose to the Indians, making the last Angels-A's game meaningless (though no less painful to those A's fans who bothered to show up).

We lose our last game to the O's (McCarty throws two scoreless, striking out three) and finish 98-64, our best record since 1978. Manny wins the home run and slugging crowns, Schilling has the best won-loss, though it appears the MVP will now go to Vladimir Guerrero for his big September, while Santana should take the Cy Young. Ichiro breaks George Sisler's all-time record for hits in a season, but, coming for a last-place club, and most of them being singles, it doesn't wow serious fans; he's just the new Rod Carew. And the Astros win their final game, snatching the NL wild card from Barry Bonds and the Giants. It's still possible we'll see Roger Clemens in the World Series.

SO: So we've got Anaheim, and the Twins get their wish. I really think they orchestrated the last week (tanking all three to the Yanks, losing to Cleveland today) to get a rematch with the Yanks in the short series, figuring it's easier to get them here than in the ALCS. Gardenhire's no dummy.*

October 4th

SK: If we can get past the Angels, I think the world (series) may be ours.

*NAH—it's just a common sports malady: choking disease. SK

SO: I'm having the same grandiose, bubbles-in-the-blood thoughts, and rightfully: it's a whole new season. Hope springs eternal.

So who's going to be left off the playoff roster? It's like spring training—all these guys vying for the very last spots. For the pitchers, I'd take Mendoza over Leskanic, Williamson and Adams; he's been more consistent, Leskanic can get wild, Williamson's not 100% and Adams stinks. And who gets the nod for the last position player, McCarty or Mientkiewicz? I'm for McCarty: more pop, just as good a glove, and he's got the arm to play the outfield in a pinch. I think we've got to keep Kapler, Roberts and Pokey for D and speed, and Youk for a stick off the bench, but management might surprise me.

As a Rock Cats fan, I want to believe in the Twins. I like that they're going right after them, but if the Yanks can beat Santana just once (or closer Joe Nathan in one of those starts), they're cooked. My hope is they split in the Stadium, then turn on that Metrodome jet-stream air-conditioning and let thermodynamics do the rest.

SK: I'm for Mientkiewicz, mostly because I've finally learned how to spell his name (actually because he's just gotten hot at the plate). I like Curtis "The Mechanic" because I think he's clutch and I don't think Mendoza is . . . and in the end, in the pen, it's gonna come down to the tragickal Mr. Lowe. I hope we don't have to depend on him too much! The guy I really want to see on that roster—but may not—is the Greek God of Walks.

SO: Yup, as in last year's division series, our fate may rest in the shaky hands of Mr. Lowe. But that's the playoffs: maximum stress finding the weakest link.

Somebody Got-ta Pay

October 5th/ALDS Game 1

Twenty minutes before game time, the Sox announce their ALDS roster. Youk, Mientkiewicz and Leskanic made the squad. Mendoza and McCarty didn't.

I try to take a nap before the 4:09 EDT start of the first Division Series game out in Anaheim and can't do it. I'm not really surprised. Too many butterflies. That may sound stupid, but I'd argue there's nothing stupid about it at all. The hell of spectating—a thing I've had to rediscover during several Octobers (although never enough)—is that when it comes to baseball, spectating is all I can do. The script is out of my hands.

Instead of a nap I settle for a brisk walk. I've got a bad hip as a result of an accident, but I ignore its protests of this unwonted late-afternoon exercise. My youngest son rescues me before it can really start to bellow, picking me up in his Jetta and taking me back to the house, where we settle with sodas, pizza, cookies and a homemade scorecard. Owen also has a crossword puzzle in which he tries (with varying degrees of success) to bury himself, admitting he can barely bring himself to watch the Angels bat, especially after the Red Sox secure a slim one-run lead on a suspect Manny Ramirez double (an *E-5 Figgins* on my pizza-besmirched scorecard) followed by a scratch David Ortiz single.

As it turned out, Owen and I didn't have to worry,* although the game remained close until the top of the fourth, and twice in the early going the Angels jockeyed the tying run into scoring position. Then, in the aforementioned fourth inning, Boston staged one of those multirun outbursts that characterized so many of their wins in August and September.

*But of course, as Red Sox fans, we can no more *not* worry—even with a six- or seven-run lead—than we could not blink if you were suddenly to jab your fingers at our open eyes.

Ortiz walked; Millar hit him home with a moonshot to left; Varitek singled; Orlando "I Know Every Team Handshake in the Universe" Cabrera walked; after Bill Mueller struck out, Gabe Kapler hit a single to short left field. Bases juiced, one out, Johnny Damon at the plate. And here's your play of the game, brought to you by Charles Scribner's, the publisher that made New York famous.

Johnny Damon, who hits Angels starter Jarrod Washburn about as well as toads do algebra, directs a seemingly harmless ground ball to Chone Figgins, a utility fielder today playing third for the Halos. Figgins double-pumps, then throws the ball to a location somewhere between home plate and the guy selling Sports Bars in the box seats to the left of the Angels' dugout. Varitek and Cabrera score. One batter later, Manny Ramirez goes *pega luna* for the first time in the Series (but not, one hopes, for the last). It's great, but by then the game is essentially over.

Father Curt was far from his best today, but the Angels—pretty much stuck with Washburn as a result of having clinched on the second-to-last day of the season—were not able to steal Game 1, as I'm sure they hoped to. The question, I think, is whether they are now blown out from their gallop to the divisional title, or if they will bounce back with Bartolo (as in Colon) tomorrow night. My son says they'll bounce. If they're going to, they had better get to Pedro fast or hope Terry Francona repeats the past and leaves him in too long. If neither of those things happen, then—to quote my collaborator, Mr. O'Nan—the Anaheim Angels are very likely going to be gone like Enron, toast on the coast.

SO: So we're guaranteed the split. And if Petey takes care of business, we could be sitting pretty.

When's the last time you saw the Sox squeeze in a run? Nice timing by Mientkiewicz (though McCarty, with his wingspan, might snag that errant toss by Mr. Schill). Is Curt's ankle okay? When he grabbed for it after that play, I thought, "Oh man, there's our season."

SK: Schilling will bull through. He's the kind of guy who's gonna think, "I got all winter to heal this ankle up." And now . . . with any luck . . . we won't need him until the ALCS. I knocked wood when I said it, and the Twins are just three outs away. Accourse against the Yankees that means nada.

SO: That's a final: Twins 2–0 over the Yanks. Looks like the Santana gambit's working . . . so far.

SK: Hopefully the trend of the last few years, where the eventual winners lose the first (or first and second) game, will be reversed. God knows it's time for a statistical correction in that matter.

SO: I hear the Yanks will start Kevin Brown in Game 3. So they had better win tomorrow night.

October 6th

They do, though it's as fishy as Jonah's old clothes—to my nose. The Twins are leading by one in the bottom of the twelfth with one out and closer Joe Nathan toiling through his unheard-of third inning of work. Nathan throws ten straight balls to put men on first and second, then grooves one to A-Rod. It's hit deep to the left-center gap, and the whole Yankee dugout leaps up—except A-Rod's missed it, and the ball barely makes the track (so why leap up when you've seen hundreds of flies to the track there and never moved an inch before?). Left fielder Shannon Stewart, playing back so nothing can get through, should have a bead on it but is uncharacteristically slow getting over and then doesn't even make an attempt. It hits the track, and should win the game anyway, but bounces over the wall for a ground rule double, meaning the trail runner, Jeter, has to go back to third. So with a tie game and one out, Matsui steps in. He's not patient, and ends up hitting a soft liner to right. Jacque Jones is playing in to cut down the run at the plate, and right field in Yankee Stadium is the smallest in all of baseball. Jones, with a decent if not spectacular arm, should have an excellent shot at getting Jeter. It's a situation an outfielder dreams of: there's no other play, no contingency. It can't be more than 180 feet, and he's got time to make sure he gets it there in the air so his catcher doesn't have to deal with a hop. As long as he's not way off-line to the first-base side, he should have Jeter by five steps, easy.

Instead, he *flips* the ball flat-footed to first baseman Matthew LeCroy, who relays it, late, and the Yankees win. ESPN's commentators make no comment on this, which is just as bizarre. So the Yankees split.

SO: Man, *I* could have thrown out Jeter from there. What the hell was Jacque Jones thinking? Fix! Fix!

SK: Say it ain't so, Stew! Next you'll be telling me Jacque Jones was on the grassy knoll.

October 7th

The stuff between my ears feels more like peanut butter than brains this morning, and with good reason; the Red Sox–Angels contest that started last night at 10 P.M. East Coast time didn't go final until five to two in the morning. That's just shy of a four-hour baseball game. A *nine-inning* baseball game.

Part of the reason is national TV coverage—the breaks between half-innings are longer to allow for a few more of those all-important beer commercials—but in truth that isn't the largest part. I'll bet you could count the number of postseason games under three hours during the last seven years on the fingers of your hands, not because of the extra ads but because the style of baseball changes radically once the regular season is over. It becomes more about the pitching, because most managers believe the aphorism which states that in seven games out of every ten, good pitching will beat good hitting.* Games about the pitching become games about the defense. And games about defense and pitching in the field often become, for the offense, games about what is now called by the needlessly deprecating name of "smallball." Few twenty-first century baseball teams are good at smallball, and their efforts to bunt the runner over are often painful to watch (although Doug Mientkiewicz of the Sox

---

*For the record, so do I—I grew up watching Bob Gibson pitch in the World Series, and listening to Sandy Koufax on my transistor radio earphone. Those were the days when the games were still played in the afternoon and pitching the batter high and tight was considered standard operating procedure.

put down a beauty in Game 1, and it resulted in a run), but smallball certainly does burn up the hours. I bet they sold a sea of beer in Anaheim last night, and the hopeful fans had plenty of time to twirl their Rally Monkeys and beat their annoying Thunder Sticks, but in the end neither the monkeys or the sticks did any good. The Angels must now come to our park down 0-2, and their fans have only this consolation: for them, the game was over before 11 P.M., and they won't have to spend much of this lovely fall day feeling like what Ed Sanders of the Fugs so memorably called "homemade shit."

Pedro Martinez got the win in last night's/this morning's game, leaving with a 4–3 lead after seven innings, mostly thanks to a two-run Jason Varitek dinger and a scratch run provided by Johnny Damon. The invaluable Damon stole second after reaching on a fielder's choice, took third when loser Francisco "K-Rod" Rodriguez (who bears a weird resemblance to movieland's Napoleon Dynamite) uncorked a wild pitch, then scored on a Manny Ramirez sac fly. It turned out to be the winning run, because a relay of Boston relievers—Timlin to Myers, Myers to Foulke—were lights-out.

My reward for staying up long past my usual bedtime was watching Orlando Cabrera make the Angels pay for disrespecting him. With two on and two out in the top of the ninth, Brendan Donnelly, the final Angels pitcher of the night, walked Jason Varitek, loading the bases in order to get to Cabrera, who came to the Red Sox touted not only as a Gold Glove but as a "doubles machine." He cranked one of those to left-center in the wee hours of the morning, taking third on a throw home that didn't come close to nailing Varitek.

And essentially, that was your ball game. Foulke ended it by striking out Curtis Pride approximately one hour after the Yankees came up off the mat to put Minnesota away in the twelfth, and now the Red Sox come back to Fenway, hoping to hear "Dirty Water" tomorrow night.

And finally, from our Department of the Late Night Surreal, we have Angels manager Mike Scioscia, on the umpiring in last night's game (by Jerry "I Ain't Missed Many" Meals):

"I think as far as the strike zone, you know, if you are a good team,
if you are a good team, you, is that my throat or is it a thing, I know
I am hoarse, but you know, when you go through a . . . if you are a

team and you are a good team, then you absorb things like maybe a break bad, a line drive and doesn't fall in or an umpire strike zone."

Thus spake Zarathustra.

SO: You said exactly what I'm feeling today. I'm getting too old to be staying up that late. Let's hope that's the last time we'll have to (barring a Dodger resurgence, which I'd accept).

October 8th

It's a brilliant day and the leaves are turning along the Mass Pike, a New England idyll worthy of a coffee-table book. It doesn't hurt that we're up two games to none and I've got tickets to Game 3. It would be our first playoff clincher at home since '86 against these same Angels, and our first sweep since taking the A's in the '75 ALCS. Both years are good omens, and the fact that we have Bronson Arroyo going is even more comforting. In his last nine starts we're 9-0.

In Kenmore Square, the *Globe* comes with a GO SOX poster and red and blue Mardi Gras beads. On Lansdowne, Puma is handing out posters of Johnny sitting on the ground by home plate, flashing a smile and a peace sign. Back at the players' lot, the mood is loose and goofy. Manny shows up in a Michael Vick jersey, which we give him grief for, and then El Jefe arrives in his badass Cadillac roadster with the retractable roof (El Monstro is its name) and is wearing—incredibly—a Tennessee Titans cap. "Let's go Pats!" we holler.

In BP, David usually spoons the first few pitches down the line in left before pulling a bunch of rainbows over the bullpens or hooking them around the Pesky Pole. Today he keeps working on going the other way, poking shots to the hole between third and short, dropping doubles into the garage-door corner. The scouting report must say the Angels will try to work him away, the same way we've worked Guerrero.

As closer Troy Percival saunters out to warm up, I say we haven't seen much of him.

"I know," he says. "I wish I was in there."

"You guys are a better team than you've shown the first two games, but much respect for beating Oakland. Maybe we'll see you tonight, huh?"

"I hope so," he says.

A nice guy, and I'm also thinking ahead to the off-season, when he becomes a free agent. His 96 mph cheese would be a nice complement to Foulkie's 74 mph change.

Our scalped seats are in back of the Sox bullpen, giving me and Caitlin a prime view of Bronson warming up. Dave Wallace stands behind him, clicking off each pitch on a handheld counter. Bronson works from the windup, with that high leg kick. He throws his two pitches, his fastball and his curve, until sweat's dripping off his chin. He stops and towels off, then works from the stretch, popping Tek's glove. He's still throwing when the Dropkick Murphys take the portable stage right behind him to play the anthem. When they finish and start in on their Red Sox anthem, "Tessie," he takes a couple more, and that's it, he's ready.

And he is. He's got the curve working, and the ump's giving him a nice wide zone. We pick up some runs early, then some more. The only mistake Bronson makes is trying to sneak a fastball by Troy Glaus, who sticks it on the Monster, but by then we're up 5–1, 6–1. It's a party.

And then, in the seventh, Bronson walks the leadoff guy. Myers relieves and walks the only guy he faces. Timlin comes in and gives up a single to Eckstein, then with bases loaded nibbles at Darin Erstad and ends up walking in a run, bringing up . . . Vladimir Guerrero.

In batting practice, Guerrero hits the ball so hard that everybody stops to watch him. Today before the game, he blasted one high off the Volvo sign on the Monster, hitting the very top so that the steel beam behind it chimed like a bell and the ball ricocheted back past the outfielders shagging flies in left-center.

Timlin nibbled at Erstad. Now on 0-1 he throws Guerrero a fastball up in the zone, and Vladi jumps on it, driving the ball toward right-center. It arcs through the darkness above the .406 Club straight for us like a crashing satellite. No doubt about it, it's going to make the bullpen easily. Trot's angling over, trailing the play. Trot's an active Christian—he has a cross hanging from the rearview mirror of his Mini Cooper—but as the ball clears the wall, he loudly mouths: "God *dammit!*" You can almost hear it except for the overwhelming groan. Grand slam. It's 6–6. The party's over.

Not again. With the shaky Wake going tomorrow, this could be crucial. We don't want to go back to Anaheim.

Now comes the nail-biting. Johnny has to flash back to the track in deepest center to make a great leaping catch. Foulke works through bases-loaded jams in the eighth and ninth, and then Lowe has to battle with men on first and third in the tenth. We're standing and screaming with every pitch, hoping, wishing. K-Rod is on for the Angels, with Troy Percival warming. This is their one great strength. With apologies to Eric Gagne and Darren Dreifort of the Dodgers, Anaheim's the only team in the majors with two bona fide closers. It looks like it's going to be a long night.

The Red Sox won 8–6 in ten, and this series is over. The Angels are done for the season, and the 2004 baseball version of Woodstock Nation is going to play for the American League pennant. Is it great? Yes. Is it wonderful? You bet. Is it pretty suh-veet, as William H. Macy's car salesman character in *Fargo* was wont to say? That is *such* a big ten-four.

There are all sorts of reasons why this sweep feels so good. Being able to rest Schilling and Martinez, the big pitching arms, is only a strategic reason, valid but cold. The fact that the Red Sox hadn't clinched *any* postseason series in their home park since 1986 (when they beat these same Angels and then went on to play the Mets) is warmer, a soothing of the psyche. For me, the emotional payoff is that, although I wasn't able to bring my mother—an ardent Red Sox fan who died in 1974—I was able to bring my mother-in-law, who is now eighty-one and not in the best of health.*

A Red Sox Customer Service rep met us at Gate D with a wheelchair and escorted us—along with Sarah Jane's oxygen bottle and a backup—to our seats, just to the left of the Red Sox dugout and only a row from the field, a perfect location for a lady who's no longer up to much jumping around. I checked her oxy level before the game started, and the dial on top of the tank said three-quarters, deep in the green, very cool. She was good to go right through the eighth, but as the game neared the four-hour mark (we have discussed the grinding, defensive nature of postseason baseball games) and extra innings loomed, it seemed wise to switch

---

*Earlier in the season she threatened to write the team a letter saying, "You better do it this year, or I can't promise to be around." I don't know if she carried through on that or not.

her over to the spare tank, and she agreed to my suggestion that we leave after the tenth, if the score was still tied. With t he fireballing K-Rod on the mound, that seemed likely, especially after he got Manny on a called strike three, with Pokey Reese (running for Bellhorn) still languishing on first.

Instead of leaving Rodriguez in to face David Ortiz, Scioscia elected to go with Jarrod Washburn, setting up the lefty-lefty match of which the conventional wisdom so approves. What followed was, quite simply, baseball history. I can't report it here to any reader's satisfaction because, although I saw it, my forebrain still doesn't really *believe* I saw it. Part of this is because Big Papi so rarely hits with power to left; *right* field is usually his porch. Most of it, though, is simply that the man's swing was so damn *quick*. The ball seemed to be off his bat and gone into the night before my ears even registered the crack of wood on horsehide.

The place went absolutely giddy-bonkers. "Dirty Water" was playing, but you could hear nothing but the bass line pumping out of the speakers. The rest was lost in the delirious chant of the crowd, not *Papi, Papi* but *Da-VEED! Da-VEED!* The cops in their riot gear, who came out to protect the sanctity of the field from marauding fans in their YANKEES SUCK T-shirts, tried to hold on to their stern don't-tread-on-me frowns, but most of them couldn't do it for long; they broke into delighted winner grins, smothered them, then had to do the smothering all over again as fresh grins broke out. Best of all, I turned around and saw the woman who's been my mom since my own mom died, hands clasped below her chin, beaming like an eighty-one-year-old cherub. I had some doubts about taking her and her oxygen tanks to a potential clinch game with thirty-five thousand rabid Red Sox fans in attendance (and when I checked that second tank later, I saw that she used as much oxygen in the half an hour following Big David's home run as she had during the entire previous four hours of the game), but now, an hour later, there's not a doubt in my mind that tonight I did her a mitzvah. And she did me one. And the team did one for both of us and all of Red Sox Nation. There's more work to do, but tonight there are plenty of mitzvahs to go around.

After El Jefe's walk-off we hang around, dancing on our seats, singing along with "Shout" and "Joy to the World" and "Glory Days" as the locker-room celebration plays on the JumboTron. *WHY NOT US?* Pedro's T-shirt reads.

Euky Rojas empties the bullpen ballbag, tossing its contents to our suddenly lucky section. Thanks, Euky!

Down at the dugout, Ellis Burks does the same. We've moved to the tarp along the first-base line to get closer to the celebration. Dave McCarty (not even on the roster!) comes out and sprays us with beer. Gabe "The Babe" Kapler gives us some skin. Manny and Kevin Millar jog past, slapping hands, and Mike Myers, in a Dominican flag do-rag. Johnny sits in the passenger seat of a groundskeeper's cart while David Ortiz rides in back, kicking his legs and waving to us as they go all the way around the track to the garage door in left. It's a good hour since the game ended, and there are only a couple hundred of us diehards. Unforgettable.

In quiet counterpoint, the Angels, in their street clothes, walk in broken single file across the grass behind short, across right field and out a gate beside their bullpen, headed for the team bus and their hotel, maybe even the airport. We wave to Vladi and David Eckstein, and give them a polite hand. It's true what I told Percival: they're a much better club than they showed in this series, and deserving of much respect.

Outside, at the players' lot, an even rowdier crowd presses against the barriers to watch the Sox leave. With each car, a new wave of screaming, pushing, a galaxy of cameras flashing. There are riot cops in helmets everywhere, and people literally falling down drunk. Pedro comes out and shoots us Manny's gunslinger fingers, and we go nuts.

After he leaves, a man holding a baby on his shoulder shoves by me, then sets the baby down, *and the baby stands and walks away*. It's a little person with the wizened face of Scatman Crothers in *The Shining*—it's Pedro's good-luck buddy Nelson de la Rosa, two feet tall and waddling up Yawkey Way like a hobbit.

But the best is Tek. He comes out in his uniform, carrying a plate of food from the postgame spread. Some relatives of his are leaving in an SUV, and he wants to catch them to say a final good-bye. "VAR-i-tek, VAR-i tek!" we cheer. Security stops them and Jason gives the woman driver (maybe his aunt?) a kiss on the cheek to Jerry Springer cheers ("Kiss *her*! Kiss *her*!"), then pads back towards the clubhouse with his plate, and I think, it's just like Little League when we'd go to the Dairy Queen, still wearing our cleats. It's the same game.

October 9th

SO: Jefe say: Somebody got-ta pay. That's why he's the chief.

I'm hoarse, my hands are swollen from clapping, and my mitt smells like beer. I'm a most happy fella.

SK: It was a great game.

And yes, we're getting a shot at redemption, because the Yankees beat the Twins, though "beat" is maybe too strong a word. In Game 4, down 2–1, Ron Gardenhire throws Santana on three days' rest. With the score 5–1 Twins after five, he inexplicably pulls Santana, meaning—like in that last regular-season series in the Bronx—the Yanks have four innings to get to the Twins' pen. It's totally incoherent, given Gardenhire's now-or-never strategy. Santana's around 85 pitches and has been sharp, and the Twins' pen is thin and tired. Predictably, the Yanks come back against instant goat Juan Rincon and then win in extras, ensuring Major League Baseball and Fox of their greatest ratings ever. Is it a tank job? I sure get a whiff, but who except a Twins (or Rock Cats) fan would complain? Finally we've got our cage match, our Thunderdome. Two teams enter, one team leaves.

Beyond Thunderdome

October 10th

SK: My feeling about having to face the Yankees is extremely conflicted. I heard twenty fat cats (not to mention a very grizzled toll-taker on the N.H. turnpike today) say "Ayyy, Stevie! We got the Yankees, just like we wanted!"

Did we want them?

The fan in me sort of wanted Minnesota, especially after Santana had been bent, folded, stapled and mutilated by the patient Yankee hitters.

The sibyl in me says the Yankees have been our Daddy and will continue to be our Daddy; that we are the _Pequod_, they the great white whale.

The commercial writer in me says this is just the matchup we need to sell the book; that after this, the World Series would be so much wavy gravy.

SO: All we've got to do is go 8-6. Can Mr. Schill, Petey and B-yo with the curve working go 8-6? I dare say they can, with some run support. Will they? Only the baseball tiki gods know for sure.

Santana had very little trouble with the Yanks: 1 earned run in 12 innings, with 12 Ks. No idea why Gardenhire removed him yesterday after only 85 pitches and still looking fine like cherry wine. The commercial writer in you is right: it's the matchup MLB needs, and they got it. It's like Hollywood—you need stars to sell a picture, and, sorry, Jacque Jones and Corey Koskie, but you Rock Cats grads just don't have the wattage (or the superagents).

And if you look closely at our series, there are some wild hairs there

351

too: Figgins's glove leading to six runs in Game 1; the absolutely horrible plate umpire in Game 2; and the sudden appearance (and disappearance) of Jarrod Washburn to end Game 3, when all-time Angels save leader Troy Percival was rested and ready.

I'll hold the league to the same rules I apply to Hollywood: it's cool as long as it's entertaining and believable. So far it's been entertaining.

The 2004 numbers say we do better against the Yanks than against the Twins (or the O's, Cleveland, Texas . . .), but you can't go by that—just by himself, Santana warps the curve. That's how tough he was.

One chance in four. One chance in two would be more than wavy gravy. It'd be Destiny.

October 11th

"It's like déjà vu all over again." Yogi said that—not the one from Jellystone National Park, but the one who hung out in New York and swung a productive bat at many bad pitches back in the good old days when men were men and baseball players still smoked Camels.* Once more the Red Sox have entered postseason via the wild card. Once more they have faced the West Coast team and beaten them (this time quite a bit more tidily, 'tis true). Once more it was Mr. Lowe—magickal rather than tragickal—who was the Last Pitcher Standing, this time notching the win instead of the save. And once more the Yankees have beaten the Minnesota Twins after spotting them the opening victory. It is our ancient enemy—now routinely called the Evil Empire almost everywhere north of Hartford—that we will have to face, and vanquish, if we are to go to the World Series.

I spent most of the weekend in Boston, although this book did not precisely demand it; the Boston-Anaheim series was over, and the Boston–New York series wouldn't start for another four days. Mostly what I wanted was to sample the atmosphere, and what I found myself breathing in was

---

*Yogi Berra was a Yankee, but how could you not love a man who said, "When you come to a fork in the road, take it"? My favorite Yogi Berra story features Hank Aaron. Yogi was a catcher, of course, and when he was crouched behind the plate, he'd always talk to distract the hitter. During the 1958 World Series, he kept telling Henry Aaron to "hit with the label up, Hank, you don't want to do it that way, hit with the label *up*." Finally Hammerin' Hank looked back over his shoulder and said—not unkindly—"I came up here to hit, not to read."

disturbing, bad for sleep.* I would describe it as a kind of nervy bravado—think of all the old gangster movies you've seen where the bad-guy hero is driven into a final blind alley, draws both automatics from the waistband of his gabardine pants, and then screams, *"Come and get me coppers! But I'm gonna take a buncha youse wit' me!"*

Doormen, taxi drivers, a guy from Boston Public Works, a driver on the Boston Duck Tour, a clerk at Brentano's, two homeys at the mall with their hats turned around backwards (Homey A in a METALLICA RULES T-shirt, Homey B wearing one showing Albert Einstein in the audience at a Ramones concert), a woman on the Boston Common walking her little white furball, even a grizzled old two-tooth toll-taker on New Hampshire's Spaulding Turnpike—all these hailed me with variations on the same theme: "Yo, Stevie! We got just who we wanted, right?"

I'm back with a sick smile and a little wave, like *Whatever, dude.* Because I'm thinking of that old saying, the one that goes *Be careful what you wish for.* And when you get right down to where the rubber hits the road, does it even matter? When you get right down to where the rubber meets the road, the Yankees just seem to be our fate, our ka, our name written on the bottom of the stone.

Or maybe that's just so much literary bullshit. *Probably* is. God knows the Boston Red Sox have generated enough to fill two or three hundred Mass Pike Port-o-Sans. It's déjà vu all over again, that much is a pure fact. We can only hope that this time Act II will be different, allowing us still to be onstage, and in uniform, when the curtain goes up on Act III.

Odd news: two relatives of Yanks closer Mariano Rivera were killed over the weekend in a freak accident at his house and he has to fly down to Panama for the funeral, meaning he'll have to jet back just in time for Game 1. And former NL MVP Ken Caminiti, who admitted his steroid use and became a baseball pariah, dies of heart failure at age forty-one (a cautionary tale for anyone on the juice, not just Gary Sheffield).

We also declare our ALCS roster, making only one change.

---

*On the night after the final game against Anaheim, I dreamed that Johnny Damon and I were digging through mounds of discarded equipment—gloves, pads, shin guards—in some filthy, forgotten equipment shed, looking for a magic pitching machine. I think that hitting a few balls thrown by this machine turned you into Mark McGwire. We never found it.

SO: So Youk's out and Mendoza's in. I guess we're hoping he has the book on his old club. And that Billy Mueller doesn't need a breather at third.

And dunno if you've looked this far ahead, but do you know what night Game 7 of the World Series falls on? That's right: Halloween.

October 12th/ALCS Game 1

The hype leading up to Game 1 is typical and idiotic. The game's on Fox, and they've prepared a five-minute *Star Wars* intro, complete with Johnny as Chewbacca. If that's not enough, they play the theme from *The Odd Couple* over and over. The announcers are desperate to tell us what the story lines are, and the personal dramas. This is one reason I hate playoff baseball—the national networks think the viewers have just tuned in. On NESN, Jerry and Don have no need to fill us in on "The Rivalry," they just call the game. They also don't call Bronson Arroyo "Brandon" (McCarver—the true inspiration behind the mute button) or compare A-Rod's and Jeter's mediocre years to Manny's and David's MVP-type seasons.

The game itself is dull and disappointing from the very first. Schilling can't push off on the ankle and gives up runs in bunches (later, Dr. Bill Morgan will describe the injury as a tear in a sheath covering a tendon—shades of Nomar!), while the Orioles' Mike Mussina is spot-on. After three, it's 6–0 Yanks, through six, 8–0, and the only drama is whether Moose will keep his no-hitter. And then, just as news time is rolling around, and viewers naturally think of bailing, the Sox explode for seven runs, and who should be called in to save the game but plucky Mariano Rivera, who just arrived in the fourth inning from the funeral of blah blah blah native Panama. What an astonishing twist! Why, who could have foreseen such etc., etc.! The announcers play it up for all it's worth, and if there's a more egregious use of a human-interest story in sports, please, don't show it to me. Rivera even gets to start the game-ending DP against his nemesis Bill Mueller. It's like watching a cheesy movie, every step feels utterly false and plotted. I mean, come on, who writes this stuff?

October 13th

Last night's game against the Yankees was a good-news/bad-news kind of thing. You know, like in all the jokes you've heard. Doctor comes bopping into his patient's examination room and says, "Mr. Shlub, I've got some good news and I've got some bad news. Which do you want first?"

"Gimme the bad news first," Mr. Shlub says. "Save the good news."

"The bad news is that you're going to die of a horribly painful disease in six weeks or so, your blood's going to boil and your skin's going to creep right off your body, and there's nothing we can do to stop it," the doctor says. "Now do you want the good news?"

Mr. Shlub starts to blubber. "What good news can there be after something like that?" he asks the doctor, when he can speak coherently.

"Well," the doctor says in a confidential tone of voice, "I'm dating a nurse from Pediatrics, and she is *so* hot!"

The worst news to come out of last night's ALCS Game 1 is, of course, that we lost it. The good news is that the Red Sox made a game of it after being no-hit by Mike Mussina into the seventh. Starting with Mark Bellhorn's one-out double in the top of that inning, Boston smacked a total of 10 hits and scored 7 runs, coming back from what was an 8–0 deficit (with the tying run on third in the eighth, the camera caught father-son Yankee fans exchanging caps in some arcane but endearing good-luck ritual). The Sox gave the Yankees a scare; the Sox silenced the Yankee fans; the Sox even gave their own fans something to go to bed at quarter to midnight feeling good about.

The good news about Curt Schilling's *head* is that it's on straight. Father Curt says he doesn't believe in the so-called Curse of the Bambino. "I'm a Christian," he says fearlessly. The bad news about Father Curt's *ankle* is that it's not on straight. He couldn't push off on his right foot last night, threw only two fastballs at speeds greater than 90 mph, and the Yankees made him pay, pounding out 6 hits and 6 runs over three innings.*

---

*It needs to be pointed out that, due to Boston's ferocious late-inning assault, not even those 6 runs were enough to assure the Yankees of the win. Due to the baseball scoring system—and we could argue about whether or not it's fair to Father Curt in this case; there are points to be made either way—Schilling takes the loss, but the runs which really sank us were the two driven in by Bernie Williams, against Mike Timlin, with two out in the bottom of the eighth.

The bad news is that this ankle injury happened at a *cursedly* bad time. The good news is that Father Curt—who doesn't believe in that publicity-stunt curse, anyway—threw only 58 pitches in last night's mortar attack, and if the ankle gets better, he should be more than ready for Game 5, always assuming there is one.

The bad news is that the Yankees scored 6 of their 10 runs after two were out. The good news is that the Red Sox scored *all 7* of their runs after two were out, and stranded only two runners all night.

The bad news is that the Red Sox don't win when Johnny Damon doesn't hit—2004 baseball history pretty well proves this—and last night Johnny wore that fabled golden sombrero, striking out four times and looking more lost each time. The good news is that Jason Varitek socked a two-run dinger over the center-field wall, ending a personal 0-for-36 drought at Yankee Stadium, and followed the dinger with a single against Mariano Rivera to open the ninth when the Red Sox once again—splendidly, against all probability—brought the tying run to the plate. Before the game, Curt Schilling said he couldn't think of anything better than "making fifty thousand or so Yankee fans shut up." He wasn't able to do that, but in the seventh, eighth, and ninth innings last night, Boston batters *were*.

The bad news is that if this series goes more than four games, Moose Mussina will be back. The good news is that the Boston batters who brought the late-inning thunder last night will *also* be back, and in each and every remaining game.

The bad news is that Boston is a game in the hole. The good news is that at this point in the season they don't make you turn in your uniform and condemn you to spend the winter playing golf unless you lose three more.

And finally, there's the most fascinating bad-news/good-news matchup of them all, and the best reason I know to tune in to baseball rather than to the third presidential debate tonight: Pedro will be starting for the Red Sox. The Yankees have hammered him this year, and Pedro has publicly proclaimed them his Daddy. That's the bad news.

But no one has more heart than Pedro Martinez, and no one will try any harder to send the Red Sox back to Fenway Park with a split. That's the good news.

Let's see what news they lead with on the sports page tomorrow.

SO: What a horribly convoluted endgame to get Rivera a save and exorcise the Ghost of Billy Mueller. At 8–0 there's no reason for him to come in, so in the seventh Matsui has *two* balls go off his glove, Bernie commits the worst error on a ground-ball single I've ever seen, and Tek hits a homer, something he hasn't done in the Stadium in years. In the ninth, down three, I knew we couldn't go in order so I wasn't surprised that we got the two guys on to reach Mueller. And wasn't surprised by the double-play ending. The only consolation is that the powers that be have to give us a win to make up for this train wreck.

You'll notice, though, that in all the hubbub they made sure Moose kept his win.

SK: Hey, I thought Moose _deserved_ that win. And when the hurly-burly's done, when the game is lost and won, who gets the blame? Wakefield, for serving up a pair? Timlin, for serving it up to Bernie? Meanwhile, I think Father Curt's done for the year. Maybe there really _is_ a curse. Looks like the tragickal Mr. Lowe in Game 5 (if there is a Game 5; I presume there will be, and the way the weather looks, it'll be about October 25th). Meanwhile, who's your Daddy? Jon Lieber or Pedro Martinez? Or is it . . . Hideous Hideki? Is _he_ your Daddy?

Go Sox!

Wear that hair!

SO: No blame, just an ugly game. But look at it this way: we've already got half of the split (just the wrong half—a-huh a-huh). Let's see what the tiki gods decree tonite. Pedro's got to have it, and we've got to hit early.

Jon Lieber: Pittsburgh Pirate. Bronson Arroyo: Pittsburgh Pirate.

Yeah, the weather's going to test us—scattered showers all weekend, and we're talking three night games, with the temp down around forty-five. Add a little wind and wetness and we'll be sitting in deck chairs on the SS *Fenway*.

October 14th/ALCS Game 2

I could continue with the good-news/bad-news thing, there's plenty of material for it,* but with the Sox headed back to Boston down two games to none, I don't have the heart for it. It's been thirteen years since a team has climbed out of an 0-2 hole in an LCS, and the Red Sox have *never* done so.

I blame some of this on numb bad luck. I think most Red Sox fans (certainly this Red Sox fan) were counting on Father Curt to bring the team back from Yankee Stadium with a split. Now it turns out that Schilling's ankle problem is not a mere tweak, not even a strain, but (oh *shit*) a probable season-ending injury that will need surgery.

We all know both from gospel music and basic first-year anatomy that the knee-bone connected to the leg-bone and the leg-bone connected to the ankle-bone. The problem here, as I understand it, has to do with the peroneal tendon, where the ankle-bone connected to the foot-bone, can you give me hallelujah. In Schilling's case, this tendon has come free of its sheath. When pushing off on his right leg during Game 1, Father Curt said he could actually hear the tendon snapping as it rubbed against the bone. Later, when speaking to the press, Sox doc Bill Morgan said additional pitching wouldn't put Schilling's leg at risk, and I'm thinking: *He can hear that thing snapping like a garter every time he hucks the pill and you say he's not risking his leg? Jeezis, Doctor Bill, I'm sorta glad you don't make house calls in* my *neighborhood.*

Well, let it pass. What it boiled down to was a piece of rotten luck (*not* a curse—I may not be a conventional Christian, but I was raised a Methodist) for the appetizer. The main course was a mostly excellent pitching performance by Pedro Martinez in which his teammates provided exactly two hits (the second by David Ortiz, who was promptly erased on a double play). After the game, Pedro shrugged and said: "If my team doesn't get the hits, I can't do nothing." He said it softly, without rancor. I thought he showed remarkable restraint, considering the fact that

---

*The good news: by the bottom of the fourth inning, all but the most abysmally drunk Yankee fans—the twenty-year-old naked-to-the-waist males with large blue-black entwined NYs painted on their chests, in other words—had given up on the mocking "Who's your Daddy?" chant. The bad news: Pedro was behind 1–0 from the first inning (Derek Jeter, the first batter he faced, scored), left trailing 3–0, and eventually took the loss, 3–1.

he has been in this position in most of the games he's pitched this year. Schilling—even in the ALCS game he left trailing 6–0—gets run support. For some reason Martinez does not.

A downcast Johnny Damon echoed the erstwhile Dominican Dominator in a locker-room interview, saying that Red Sox pitching hasn't been the problem in the ALCS; the problem has been lack of offense. No one is better qualified to speak to this issue than Johnny D, who has gone 0 for 8 in the two games. In my mind it is at this point the crucial difference between the two clubs.

And two points have to be made about the Yankees. First, their much maligned pitching has so far been exceptional. Second, their hitting has been as advertised . . . or perhaps I should say as expected. The Yanks could almost be renicknamed The American League Hoodoo. National League teams are less impressed by their mystique (witness the success of the Florida Marlins against them last year), but while they remain on their own little patch, the Yankees are awesome in the month of October.

What impresses me most is how balanced their attack is. Of the thirteen runs the Yankees have scored (playing exactly the same lineup both nights), Jeter has two, A-Rod has two, Sheffield has four, Matsui has two, Posada has one, Olerud has one (his two-run bomb last night won the game), and Lofton has one. Only Miguel Cairo and Bernie Williams have failed to score for the Yankees—this is just two games.

It's true that all but two of the Red Sox players (Cabrera and Damon) have also scored, but Bellhorn, Ortiz, Millar, Varitek and Mueller have each only scored once, and in a single run-through of the batting order (during innings seven and eight of Game 1). Only Trot Nixon, who *always* seems to step his game up to Yankee levels during the postseason, scored for the Sox in both games.

Meantime, we're done with Yankee Stadium for a while,* and we have the day off to regroup. Compared to those things, there *is* no bad news.

Yep, Pedro made a quality start (on the forty-fourth anniversary of Maz's home run). He had some Ramon-like struggles early, but wriggled out of

---

*The fact that we had to open there at all is something I blame on the LEBs—Loathsome El Birdos.

them and settled down nicely. The high-priced, steroid-pumped, for-mer–All-Star, -MVP, -Japanese national hero heart of the Yankee order did as much as our own vaunted Mark Bellhorn, Kevin Millar and Orlando Cabrera, which was nothing. The home run Pedro gave up was to border-line Hall of Famer John Olerud (yet another midseason pickup, not truly a Yankee at all), with his pitch count above 100, to the short part of a shrunken ballpark. We just didn't hit. Score one run in the AL, you're going to lose; it doesn't matter if you're playing the Yanks or the D-Rays.

So we didn't get the split. It may be demoralizing, but it shouldn't be a huge surprise. George paid dearly for the Yankees to have the best home record in all of baseball. But guess who had the second best? We'll have to win throwing Bronson, Wake and Lowe, but we haven't taken the easy way all year—and that includes overcoming injuries to key players. We just have to stay hopeful and throw everything we've got at them Friday night (weather permitting), win that, battle on Saturday, and even the series. We could even lose a game up at Fenway and win this thing, we've just got to hit. Keep the Faith.

SK: Poor Father Curt. Go you Lowe!

SO: Down 2–0 to our evil nemesis, with our best arms gone, I feel like we're Batman and Robin stuck in that giant snow cone, with the Joker (George) and his dumb-as-mud henchmen in their striped shirts (Yankee fans) laughing their asses off and then leaving us for dead. But you know what happens then . . . that's right, Batman goes to his super-utility belt. It's time for us to pull something out.

October 15th/ALCS Game 3

Stewart and I meet for dinner before the game, and although he agrees to split a BLT pizza on honey wheat crust, he expresses strong doubts about a pizza that comes with a topping of mayonnaise-dressed lettuce. Still, he eats his share. I guess that after some fifty games at Fenway between us, we've had our fill of hot dogs. As we munch, we talk about—what else?—baseball. Of that we have not had our fill. Specifically we discuss which team will be most apt to benefit from a rainout, which seems likely; the Massachusetts weather on this October evening is pretty awful.

We agree, reluctantly, that the Yankees would probably be better served by an extra day of rest, because they could bring Mussina back sooner. The stars seem to be aligning themselves, and the horoscope doesn't look favorable if you happen to be a Sox fan.

When we walk into California Pizza at 5:45 P.M., a light mist is hanging in the air. When we walk back out again at 6:45, the mist has thickened to a drizzle. By the time we've raised our arms to be frisked and have given our game bags over for examination outside Fenway Park's Gate D (it's just how things are done in twenty-first-century America, where the citizenry now live on Osama Mean Time), the drizzle has become a light rain.

Before clearing around midnight, the forecast calls for heavy downpours accompanied by strong winds. During the regular season, the fate of the game would be in the hands of the Red Sox up until the instant play started, and with the umps thereafter. In postseason, however, these contests are in the hands of Major League Baseball, an organization that seems to care a great deal more about TV revenue (witness the 8 P.M. starts, which ace out millions of little kids who have to get up for school on weekdays) than they do the fans, the players or the game itself. Last night, in the Houston–St. Louis game, play went on through a steady downpour. Base hits spun up wheels of water as they rolled into the outfield. I don't mind getting wet, but I really don't want to see Manny Ramirez, Trot Nixon or Bernie Williams leave his career on the outfield grass of Fenway Park.

I don't have to worry about that for long. An usher I know is leaning nonchalantly against the counter of the Legal Seafood kiosk, chattering away into his walkie-talkie, as Stew and I walk by. He drops it into the pocket of his yellow rain-slicker and waves us over. "Go on home, you guys," he says. "Game's gonna be called at seven thirty."

I ask him if he's sure. He says he is.

We hang in a little while, anyway—long enough to soak up the rainy atmosphere of Fenway Park (*soak it up*, geddit?), where the game still hasn't been officially called. The tarp remains on the infield at 7:58 P.M., however, and that pretty much tells the tale. The news and TV guys are huddled under canvas mini-pavilions, reduced to taking pictures of and doing interviews with each other. Peter Gammons comes bopping busily along, looking like some strange but amiable human crow in his black trousers and long black raincoat. Stewart and I pass a few words with him, mostly about the possibility of Father Curt pitching again this year (unlikely but not impossible, given Schilling's fierce competitive drive), and then we leave. I am actually back in my hotel room, drying my hair, before Major League Baseball can finally bring itself to unloose its clenched and rain-puckered fingers enough to let this one go.

October 16th

I open the curtains at 8 A.M. on cloudless blue skies. Tonight the Yankees and Red Sox will play baseball.

I'm bringing the whole famn damily to this one, so I have to buy tickets from a broker, and end up paying through the nose so we can watch what turns out to be the worst game of the year, maybe of my life—worse even than Mr. Lowe's rainy debacle at Yankee Stadium. It's fifty degrees, but the wind is gusting up to 40 mph, and we're sitting in the very last row of the grandstand. Gales blow through the wire fence, around the mercifully insulating standing-room crowds at our backs and into our collars. Caitlin's shivering, so I break down and sign up for a credit card just to get a free MLB blanket.

Bronson's got nothing, but Kevin Brown's equally ineffective. "*Kevin,*" we chant. Jeter makes an error that leads to a run, and it's "*Jeeeee-*ter, *Jeeeee-*ter." (He's been terrible in the field, just as distracted as last year, fodder for critics who say A-Rod should play short; but Jeter doesn't have the reactions or the gun for third, and probably won't accept a demotion to second.) After Bronson we throw the dregs of our pen, as if the Coma is conceding the game—as if he's okay with being down 0-3. Weird.

Matsui drives in five. After Sheffield powers out a steroid shot, the standing-room crowd disperses and the wind cuts through us. In Little League, there's a ten-run mercy rule, but not here, and to save our real pen, Wake volunteers to soak up some innings, meaning Lowe will be starting tomorrow (far better, I think, considering how Wake has thrown this season). But instead of holding the Yanks so we can get back in the game, Wake lets a runner inherited from Leskanic score, then gives up five runs of his own, putting the game *way* out of reach. Embree looks bad, and then Francona leaves poor Mike Myers out there to face righties in the ninth, something that should never happen. Myers sucks it up and ultimately gets it done, but by then it's 19–8.

It's ugly, and humbling, but the worst thing that happens is that the Faithful (if these really *are* the Faithful) turn on Mark Bellhorn, booing him mercilessly when he makes an error that leads to a run, and then with each successive strikeout. It's as if they don't remember the Marky Mark who stepped up and kept us in first place through April and May. It's wrong, and it pisses me off even more than the Yankees taking walks late in the game, or Matsui swinging for the fences with a ten-run lead.

October 17th

The Yankees played. The Sox got shelled.

I slouched into my hotel room well after midnight and jotted only a brief game-related note in my journal (*Red Sox lost. Horrible*) before falling into bed, where I got roughly six hours of shallow, dream-infested sleep.*
I got up at 7 A.M. this morning, pulled on a pair of exercise shorts and my new Kevin Youkilis shirt (a gift from Stewart O'Nan, bless him) and went around to Au Bon Pain for orange juice and a croissant. I did not buy a Boston *Globe* in the hotel newsstand, and I certainly did not turn on *SportsDesk* when I got back to my room. I turned on the headline news program with the ticker across the bottom of the screen instead, and only long enough to confirm the final score of last night's abortion. Then I shut the damned thing off and did my morning exercises for once without the benefit of media: no scores, no polls, no reports of suicide bombings in Baghdad.

19–8. That was the final score. Replace the hyphen with a 1 and you have the last year the Red Sox won the World Series. Maybe there's a curse after all. Or a Curse, if you prefer. Until the third inning of this train wreck, there was actually some semblance of a game. After that, the Yankees simply piled it on. Jason Varitek had a good offensive night for the Red Sox; Hideki Matsui, unfortunately, had a sublime night for the Yankees, the

---

*In the only one I can remember, I was trying to work some kind of trade with George Steinbrenner, who was laughing at me and telling me—this is probably the only interesting part, and surely the most significant—that I needed a haircut.

kind of night baseball players dream about and have maybe once, and only then if they're lucky.

19–8, and I'm sure that Dan Shaughnessy, Boston's Number One Cursemonger, will make hay of that in today's unread newspaper, but the fault, dear Brutus, has lain not in our stars but our stats—especially those of our mediocre relief corps, which this series against the Yankees has mercilessly exposed. Arroyo didn't have much, but Arroyo can only be held responsible for the first half dozen runs or so (ow, it hurts to write that). Leskanic came on and gave up a three-run homer to Gary Sheffield; Wakefield lasted three and a third largely ineffective innings; Embree followed Wakefield and was worse; then came Mike Myers and the song remains the same. There may have been others. "You could look it up," Ole Case used to say, and he was right, but for that I'd have to buy a Boston *Globe,* and while I might be able to avoid Dan Shaughnessy's cursemongering, my eye would surely fall on the hairy, downcast mugs of the Red Sox players.

Coming back from New York, already down two games to none thanks to Schilling's bad ankle and Olerud's home run, the Sox players kept telling reporters they were loose. And so they were; last night they were so loose all four wheels fell off their little red wagon. It's true that Ramirez, Mueller, Cabrera and especially Jason Varitek found their offensive strokes, but putting eight runs on the board means little when you could double that and still lose by three.

Yet still we are faithful; to steal the title of the movie that played in New England this past spring (a spring that now seems impossibly distant and hopeful), still we believe. Tonight we'll once again fill the old green church of baseball on Lansdowne Street, in some part because it's the only church of baseball we have; in large part because—even on mornings like this, when the clean-shaven Yankee Corporate Creed seems to rule the hardball universe—it's still the only church of baseball we can really love. No baseball team has ever come back from a three-games-to-none deficit to win a postseason series, but a couple of hockey teams have done it, and we tell ourselves it has to happen sooner or later for a baseball team, it just has to.

We tell ourselves Derek Lowe has one more chance to turn 2004 from tragickal to magickal.

We tell ourselves it's just one game at a time.

We tell ourselves the impossible can start tonight.

• • •

During BP, a liner dings off the photographers' well in front of me and bounces out into the shallow outfield grass. Don Mattingly's walking back from the cages under the center-field bleachers with a balding guy in a champagne-colored suit, and as they near the ball, I realize it's Reggie Jackson. "Reggie," I holler, "hit the mitt," and hold out my glove, and he does— maybe for the first time as an outfielder.

I hustle over to Steve to show him the ball. I can rationalize my excitement because Reggie, in my mind, will always be an A—and one of those hairy, wild A's from a team much like this year's Sox, kind of goofy and out of control, full of personality. I'm jazzed, just watching the parade of celebrity sportscasters when Steve hands the ball back. On it, he's written: *The curse is off*, and then on the sweet spot has signed it: *Babe Ruth*.

Later, another piece of luck: in the tenth inning, in an incredibly tight and great game, Bernie Williams fouls one high off the roof facing, and the ball plummets directly toward me. All I have to do is raise my arm and the ball hits dead center in the pocket of my glove. The next inning I'm on the Jumbo-Tron with my mitt, and my particles are beamed out across the nation to friends and relatives everywhere—and I have enough sense left (or maybe I'm just too tired) not to point at myself and go, "Look, I'm on the Jumbo-Tron!"

And this is just the beginning. From here the night just gets better.

October 18th/ALCS Game 4

It turned out that Mr. Lowe was pretty magickal, and so we live to fight another day. Today, in fact. This afternoon, at 5:10 P.M., when Pedro Martinez and Mike Mussina match up in the year's last American League game at Fenway Park.

Last night's twelve-inning tilt was the longest game in postseason history, clocking in at five hours and two minutes. I went with my daughter-in-law, and we finally left when Boston failed to score in the bottom of the eleventh. My reasoning was simple enough: if Boston won, I'd be back the next day (make that the same day; it was ten past one when we finally made our way out of the park). If Boston lost, I didn't want to be there to see the Yankees dancing on the carefully manicured pair of green sox decorating the infield.

As things turned out, our final (and winning) pitcher of the night—

Curtis "The Mechanic" Leskanic—was superb in relief after being just one more slice of bullpen salami in the Game 3 blowout. He gave up one of those dying-quail singles to Posada to open the twelfth (this we heard on the radio, heading back to the hotel on eerily deserted streets), then got Ruben Sierra to ground out and Tony Clark to fly out.* Miguel Cairo fanned, setting the stage for the dramatic Red Sox finish, which I arrived back in my hotel room just in time to see.

By then Paul Quantrill was pitching for the Yankees. Joe Torre rolled the dice by bringing Mo Rivera on to pitch two innings and try to close out the series. Rivera is the game's premier closer, but he has occasional problems with the Red Sox, and last night he blew the Yankees' one-run lead in the ninth, giving up a single to Bill Mueller with speedy Dave Roberts, pinch-running for Kevin Millar, on second.† Gordon replaced Rivera and went two scoreless. Quantrill—not exactly chopped liver—was what was left. He never got an out. After yielding a single to Manny Ramirez, he threw David Ortiz what looked to me like either a fastball or a slider. Whatever it was, it was in Ortiz's wheelhouse, and Big Papi crushed it.

Like every other Red Sox fan, I'm delighted that this isn't going to be a sweep, like most postseason series that start off 3–0. As a contributor to this book, I'm even more delighted to have a victory to write about before the ultimate sign-off. But one who loves the Boston Red Sox is also one who loathes the New York Yankees; it's as true as saying night follows day. So it pleases me most of all to point out we are now 12-11 overall this year against George Steinbrenner's team of limousine longballers, and that last night's victory, combined with the ALCS best-of-seven format, ensures an odd and wistfully wonderful statistical certainty: the Yankees can't beat us this year. Not overall. They can go on to the World Series (and probably

---

*Clark, a Red Sox castoff who specialized in strikeouts and earnest postgame interviews while with Boston—which sounds snottier than Clark, one of the game's truly nice guys, probably deserves—played first for John Olerud last night. Olerud was struck by a bat during the Saturday Night Massacre and showed up at the park Sunday on crutches.

†On second because Roberts flat out stole it off Rivera and Posada, both of whom knew he was going but could do nothing to stop him from getting into scoring position. Without this steal, our season's over, and Roberts made it look easy. Theo's very last trade before the deadline—Roberts straight-up for PawSock outfielder Henri Stanley—may have been his best of the year. SO

will, although I still harbor faint hopes we can prevent that), but the best they can do against us for the season is a tie . . . and they can only do that by winning today. That will not matter a single whit to them, of course, but when you're a Red Sox fan, you take consolation wherever it is available.

Last night after the game, I hung around the dugout to shout "Je-feeeeeeeeeeee!" to David Ortiz and chant "*Who's* your *Pa*-pi?" with the rest of the diehard Faithful. When I finally got out onto Yawkey Way it was two o'clock, and most of the players had left. On Brookline Ave, the riot cops were standing in close formation on the bridge to Kenmore Square, forcing us stragglers to walk down Lansdowne and then along the scuzzy streets bordering the Mass Pike. I didn't mind. There were a couple other fans in sight, and we were all ditzy from the win and just how very late it was. The street I was on curved up to Boylston, and as I reached the intersection, a motorcycle cop came wailing up on his Electra Glide and stopped in the middle of the street. He hopped off and started pointing to the oncoming cars, waving them to the side of the road, and as it dawned on me what was happening, here came the Yankees' team bus—appropriately from Yankee Bus Lines, and appropriately yellow—and my legs found a strength and a spring I thought I'd lost back in the fifth inning, carrying me to the exact spot I needed to be in, the right place at the right time. I watched heads inside turn toward me, bleary faces puzzled by this apparition in black in a PawSox hat standing in the vacant other lane, lit like a devil by the red stoplight, proudly holding up his middle finger.

Today the guys show up at the parking lot before Game 5 wearing their very best suits and wheeling luggage like it's any other travel day—a good sign, I think. Yesterday when Mark Bellhorn walked by, a few people booed, and he didn't look over. Today I holler, "Hey Mahk, don't let the bastards get you down!" and he smiles and nods. Johnny's had an adhesive Ace bandage on the meaty flat of his right hand (his lead hand) for a couple of weeks now, and I wonder if he can grip the bat correctly. Every day I ask, "How's the hand, John?" and he says it's okay, but without conviction, as if it's still bothering him. These are the guys we need to set the table for Manny and David. If they don't pick it up, we're going nowhere.

Just before game time, I visit with Bob the usher over in Section 32. We chat and then say good-bye, shake hands. It's our last home game of the ALCS, and there's a fall feeling of the season being over, things being packed away, but I can't let it stand.

"I'll see you for the Series," I say.

"I hope so," he says.

"I *know* so," I say, full of false bravado. "Right here, baby."

October 19th/ALCS Game 5

It probably wasn't the greatest game in postseason history—I'd still pick Game 6 of the 1975 World Series, the one where Red Sox catcher Carlton Fisk waved his extra-inning walk-off home run fair, for that honor—but it was almost certainly the greatest game to be played since the major leagues went to the League Championship format. At five hours forty-nine minutes it was the longest, and the teams who engaged in the struggle were surely the most evenly matched. When it ended, the Red Sox had scored one more run (five to the Yankees' four) and managed one more hit (thirteen to the Yankees' twelve). Each team used seven pitchers, and each committed a single error. The game, which began in broad daylight at 5:20 in the afternoon, ended just an hour shy of midnight, in the bottom of the fourteenth. I have never been so simultaneously drained and exalted at the conclusion of a sporting event; would have believed, prior to last night, the two states of emotional being were mutually exclusive.

According to this morning's box score, there were 35,120 in attendance, but if the Red Sox pull off the ultimate miracle of St. Fenway and go on to the World Series—unlikely, especially with the ALCS now returning to Yankee Stadium,* but no longer *wildly* improbable—ten years from now there'll be a million New Englanders, most of them from Massachusetts, telling their children, grandchildren, bar buddies and anyone else who will listen that they were there on the night the Sox beat the Yanks in fourteen.

Both managers used up almost every damned reliever they had once the starters (Martinez for Boston, Mussina for New York) were gone. Boston finished up with Tim Wakefield, the goat in last year's ALCS Game 7 (the Boone home run), the hero last night . . . in spite of Jason Varitek's miseries with the knuckleball behind the plate. The Yankees finished with Esteban

*Thanks a pantload, Baltimore.

Loaiza, who barely made the New York playoff roster. Loaiza, nothing short of horrible for the Yankees during the regular season, was terrific last night until the fourteenth . . . and even then he did not beat himself. David Ortiz, who has pretty much carried the Red Sox offensively this postseason, beat Loaiza and necessitated Game 6; if the Yankees win the ALCS and then lose the World Series, it may be Ortiz who they will blame.

Mark Bellhorn led the bottom of the fourteenth doing what he has, unfortunately, done best offensively for his team in the postseason: he struck out. Then Johnny Damon, who had a good ALDS and is having a hideous ALCS (in his previous at-bat, he popped out weakly to Jorge Posada while trying to bunt, effectively killing what might have been a game-winning rally in the eleventh), worked Loaiza for a walk. Cabrera struck out. Manny Ramirez coaxed a second walk from Loaiza, and that set the stage for Papi.

Ortiz, who won Game 3 against the Angels with a walk-off home run and beat the Yankees in the twelfth the same way two nights ago, has been little short of Jacksonian this October (that would be Reggie, not Andrew). All he did last night was get the first RBI of the game, scoring Cabrera with a single, and then plated the second run himself (bases-loaded walk to Varitek). In the eighth, he struck a solo home run to left-center, meaning that of the four runs Boston scored in the first nine innings, Ortiz was involved in three.

What I remember most clearly about his last at-bat are the fans to the right of the backstop as I looked toward home plate. They were leaning over the low railing and pounding on the padded face of the backstop, *screaming* for a hit. Everyone in the park was on their feet. The kids in front of me were wearing their hats on backwards, and turned inside-out for good measure. For the first time since I've known him, Stewart O'Nan turned *his* hat around backwards and inside-out. I don't do that; for me, the rally-cap thing has never worked. I took mine off instead and held it with the bowl up to the sky, shaking it in that ancient rainmaking gesture. Two guys in the row behind me started doing the same thing.

Ortiz put on an incredible ten-pitch at-bat. Loaiza must have made a couple of bad pitches in there, because the count eventually ran to 2-2, but I barely remember them. What I remember are those people to the right of the backstop, leaning over and pounding, pounding, pounding on the green. What I remember is Stew in his rally cap, looking weirdly like some

Le Mans race-car driver from 1937. What I remember is thirty-five thousand people screaming and screaming under the lights as Big Papi fouled off pitch after pitch, one to the backstop, one to the glass of the .406 Club, one up the left-field foul line, one screaming down the right-field line, just on the wrong side of the Pesky Pole.

Finally, on the tenth pitch of the at-bat, he hit one fair. The sound of the bat was spongy rather than sharp, not the authoritative crack of good wood, but Ortiz still got all of his broad back into it. The ball flew between Derek Jeter and Miguel Cairo, and well out of reach of either man. Damon was off and running at contact, and the mob was waiting for him at home plate.

"I thought I was gonna be the first one to get to [Ortiz]," Doug Mientkiewicz is quoted as saying in today's paper, "but Johnny Damon's hair was already in my face."

So tonight Father Curt Schilling will get what he probably never thought he would: a second chance to shut up those fifty thousand Yankee fans. He's got a special boot, they tell us, and several million faithful Red Sox fans—in New England and scattered all across the country—will be praying for that boot. Not to mention the ankle inside it.

The big chant last night was Gary Sheffield's "*Who's* your *deal*-er?"

The big pitch was Pedro going up and in and putting Matsui—who's been lunging across the plate all series and hitting .500—on his big Ultraman ass.

The big run—besides the game-winner—was pinch runner Dave Roberts (once again) scoring on a sac fly to tie the game in the eighth.

The big hit could have easily been Tony Clark's. In the ninth, with the score tied at 4, two out, and Ruben Sierra on first, he fought off Keith Foulke with two strikes and laced a ball down the right-field line. It hopped off the track, struck the top of the low wall along the corner and popped almost straight up, into the very first row of the stands, for a ground rule double. Sierra, who would have scored easily, had to go back to third, giving Foulke one more chance to work out of the jam, which he did, getting number nine hitter Miguel Cairo on a pop-up. So the Yanks lost this one, literally, by an inch. It's the kind of break—like El Jefe's humpback single—we never get, and the kind of break the Yankees always seem to, and I gotta say, it feels good.

And the big stats: our pen threw eight scoreless, and the Yanks left 18 on base. So don't feel too bad for them, they had every chance to win.

Driving home late this rainy morning, I flash on a usually blank Mass Pike message board on an overpass just before the tollbooths at Newton. There, for every westbound traveler to appreciate, including the several hundred New York fans who'd hoped to drink champagne in our ballpark, instead of a construction or accident report, is a simple message, easily decipherable by our would-be alien invaders:

RED SOX 5

YANKEES 4

No team in major league history has ever come back from an 0-3 hole to win a postseason series (no team in an 0-3 hole has even forced a Game 7), but it's been done twice in the NHL. The last time it was done, it was done to my team. I was a Pittsburgh Penguins fan in 1975 (I'm *still* a Penguins fan, dammit) when the New York Islanders came roaring back from 0-3 to shame us, winning by the slimmest of margins game after game, several of those in overtime. I was at Game 6 at the Civic Arena, and there was a dispiriting sense in the crowd that we were doomed to lose even though we had a 3-2 lead in games and were playing the last two on home ice. It was like a nightmare, knowing the horrible thing was going to happen but being powerless to stop it. Once we'd lost Game 6, there was hardly any point in playing Game 7, and everyone knew it. We were cooked, broken, useless. We barely showed up, and the Isles push-broomed us into the dustbin of history. Now, granted, the New York Yankees aren't the Pittsburgh Penguins, but I must say that these Red Sox are as hungry as those young Islanders—a team, you might remember, that matured and went on to win four straight Stanley Cups.

SK: Almost game time. Will they play? I think maybe they will. And Mr. Schill? Father Curt? I think maybe _he_ will. And if the Red Sox do instead of die, I've made arrangements to be in Yanqui Stadium tomorrow night for the kill. Drive those _banderillas_ home, boys! One from Arroyo! Two more from the magickal Mr. Lowe! And one more—in the ninth—the killer—from Pedro, the Closer from Hell.

SO: It's on. Gotta hit, and gotta field behind whoever's on the hill. We've overcome big injuries all year, so why change now? I hope to hell you *are* there tomorrow, and the boys bring it home. And if not, we made 'em sweat blood.

Billy Mueller in the #2 slot—good move. Bellhorn and Cabrera weren't getting it done. Billy Mueller, Yankee Killer!

October 20th/ALCS Game 6

At Fenway Park this morning, the groundskeepers will continue their little field-grooming chores instead of embarking on the larger chores that go with making a major league baseball field ready for winter. The concessionaires remain on standby, and the spectator gates will still be up on Yawkey Way. Incredibly, long after the baseball pundits on ESPN's SportsCenter and the sports cannibals in the Boston media had given them up for dead, the Boston Red Sox remain alive; in the words of the immortal Huey Lewis, the heart of rock 'n' roll is still beating.

Terry Francona kept Mark Bellhorn on the field and in the lineup even though the abovementioned pundits and cannibals* were by yesterday morning all but screaming for the manager to slot Reese in at second base, and Bellhorn responded with a three-run home run in the fourth inning. The rest of the night belonged to Father Curt, who dominated the Yankees for seven innings (his only mistake was a fat 3-1 pitch to Bernie Williams, who made him pay by stroking his 22nd postseason home run), and to Red Sox relievers Bronson Arroyo and Keith Foulke. The former ran into trouble when he gave up a double to Miguel Cairo and a single to Derek Jeter; the latter nearly gave me heart failure by walking Matsui and Sierra in the bottom of the ninth. In the end, however, Tony Clark ended the game by doing what he did so many times for the Red Sox in clutch situations—he struck out. Last night, and in the season's most crucial situation, the Yankees stranded their comeback on first base.

---

*Not to mention one cannibalette. That would be Jackie MacMullan of the Boston *Globe*, who spanked Manny Ramirez for keeping the bat on his shoulder too much after Boston's twelve-inning 6–4 victory in Game 4. In that game all Manny did was reach base five times in six at-bats, including the walk which preceded Big Papi's walk-off.

The worst moment for Sox fans came during A-Rod's at-bat in the eighth, following the Jeter single. Rodriguez hit a squibber between the pitcher's mound and first. Arroyo fielded it, saw that his first baseman (Mientkiewicz, at that point) was out of position, and went to put the tag on A-Rod himself. Rodriguez* slapped the ball from Arroyo's mitt, and Jeter raced all the way around to make it 4–3.

After Sox manager Terry Francona came out to protest, the umpires put their heads together and reversed the original decision, which had Rodriguez safe at first, and ruled him out on interference, instead. A sulky Derek Jeter (who slapped a phantom tag on David Ortiz and got an out call in Game 5 at Fenway) was forced to return to first base. He was still there when Gary Sheffield fouled out, ending the inning. Fans pelted the field with various objects; police in riot gear lined the foul lines in the top of the ninth; eventually the Red Sox did what no team has ever done before, which is to come back from a 3-0 deficit to tie a postseason best-of-seven series.

Whether or not they can go all the way and win Game 7 tonight is very much in question, but I intend to be there and see for myself—I called around and wangled a ticket to the game. Yankee Stadium is a horrible place for a Red Sox fan to be at the very best of times, if not Hell itself, then surely the very lowest cellar of purgatory, but I think it must still beat television. After three cold nights at Fenway and one warm one in front of Harlan Ellison's glass teat (when the Bronx fans were clearly freezing), I am prepared to testify in any court of law that being there is better. I think that if Fox had shown me one more shot of Curt Schilling's bloody ankle last night I would have screamed—not in horror or pity, but in rage. And anyone with a lick of sense watches such big-money games only with the volume turned all the way down. Listening to the endlessly blathering announcers always makes me think of what my mother used to say about the village idiot when she was growing up in Prout's Neck back in the late 1920s: "He'd talk about moonlight on a sunny afternoon."

But never mind. That sounds bilious, and I'm not in a bilious mood this morning. Far from it. Now that the Red Sox have come so far, I find it nearly impossible to believe they will come all the way . . . yet not

---

*I have an acquaintance from Brooklyn who says that he and his friends call Rodriguez "Show Pony," because of the seemingly ostentatious way he runs.

completely impossible. I know this much: if there's to be a miracle, I intend to see it with my own eyes.

Time to hit save, eject the disc, and shut this machine down.

Ruth King's boy is going to New York City.

SO: Marky Mark made those boo-birds from the other night eat their words.

A-Rod slapping Bronson's glove off was a weird counterpoint to B-yo hitting him to start the brawl in July. What a bald-faced cheater.

And, man, Joe West has to be the worst umpire in the league—the 2-1 to Sierra was down the pipe.

But the person at Yankee Stadium I feel sorriest for is the fan who had Bellhorn's homer in his hands and dropped it. Come on, dude! Nice that the umps finally got that one right.

Overfuckingjoyed,

Stew

SK: Thank God Tony Clark still owed us a couple of Special Ks.

Off to NYC.

SO: The rule book calls what A-Rod did "an unsportsmanlike act." Fans everywhere are calling it an un*man*like act. So our 340K pitcher once again beat their 252M hitter. Justice prevails . . . for now. Just remember: the price of freedom is eternal vigilance. And cheaters never win.

ALCS Game 7

I'm not planning on going to Game 7. I don't have a ticket, I'm exhausted from four straight late nights and rock-hard hotel beds, and the last time I was at Yankee Stadium we didn't do so well. I figure I'll watch Steve on TV from my warm comfy couch. Then at three our Fenway neighbor Mason calls. If he can swing me a ticket, do I want to go? Because he just might be able to, but he needs to know right now.

I'm thoroughly burnt from the weekend. I mean, I've got nothing left—

no voice, no energy. But if we're going to win tonight, I'm going to be there. I don't care if we lose—I do, but I think the way we've battled, we've got nothing to be ashamed of one way or the other. And if the guys *don't* do it, I'd like to be there to applaud them for the great run they've given us, and the great year. I don't want them to hear nothing but silence or, worse, ugly catcalls.

"Yeah," I tell Mason. "Come on, how can I *not* go?"

"I've got a good feeling," he says.

I do too. We really do have nothing to lose. If we lose, so what? Could it be as bad as 1986? I don't think so. But if we win . . . If we win it will be one of the greatest wins in Red Sox history. In baseball history. And those are the only two possible outcomes: win or lose. I'll take those odds.

"Let me check and I'll call you back," Mason says, and then when he does, it's a go. I toss my stuff in a plastic bag, kiss Trudy good-bye ("Be careful!" she urges, sure the Yankee fans will beat me senseless), hop in the car and zoom off to the Bronx. Last year I didn't go to Game 7, and I was glad. This year, one way or the other, I'm not going to miss history.

I get into the Stadium a half hour before game time, and it's oddly quiet. I expected a seething full house, but here and there are empty seats, and the Yankee fans—though decked out in some of the ugliest team gear I've ever seen—are muttering to each other. Where's the crude, in-your-face stupidity? The 1918 banners? The guys with paint all over them? The crowd seems wary, tight. I see far more Sox hats and shirts than I did last month. It's like we're taking over.

David, the Yankee fan I sit beside, is incredibly polite and well-versed in the game—he's a baseball fan first, and only then a Yankee fan (he began as a Giants fan, and still owes some allegiance to them). It's an unexpected pleasure to sit with him and swap lore.

The Yanks call on Bucky "Fucking" Dent to throw out the first pitch, hoping to stir up old ghosts. Yogi Berra, who watched Maz's homer go over the wall in Forbes Field, catches for him.

Maybe they should have let Bucky start, because Kevin Brown has nothing. In the first, after Johnny is thrown out at the plate on a Manny single—on the very next pitch!—Brown tries to sneak an 88 mph fastball past David Ortiz. Never happen. El Jefe lines it into the short porch (in Fenway it either falls for a single or Sheffield catches it racing *in*) for a 2–0 lead, and the Yanks never dig themselves out of that hole. With bases juiced in the second, Johnny Damon greets Javier Vazquez with a line-drive grand slam into the same short porch that has padded so many Yankees' power stats over the years,* and the thousand or so Faithful drown out the rest of the Stadium.

And that's basically it. Tonight Derek Lowe, who was supposed to be the best number three pitcher in the majors, is just that.[†] He gives up one hit in six innings. I'll say that again: he gives up one hit in six innings. As in Game 4, D-Lowe rhymes with hero. Johnny hits a second dinger off Vazquez, just like he did on June 29th, and we're up 8–1 and chanting "*Reg*-gie *Da*-mon!" The crowd is totally poleaxed, as if they've shown up on the wrong night. They revive only when Pedro comes on for a vanity appearance in the seventh and gives up two runs, one of which Mark Bellhorn (from now until eternity Mark "Fucking" Bellhorn to Yankee fans) immediately gets back with a towering blast off the right-field foul pole. Another garbage run on a sac fly, and yes, finally, that is it.

I'm behind home with Steve as we nail down the last outs. We don't even need our closer. It's 10–3, and no one can hit a seven-run homer. Jeter looks sick. A-Rod and Sheffield have both gone 0-for—complete and total justice. It's as if the Sox have walked through the Stadium driving stakes through every single ghost's, vampire's and Yankee fan's rotten, cobwebby heart. It's quiet and the upper deck is half-empty. The Yankees are cooked, and their fans can't believe it. In the biggest game ever played in this rivalry, the Red Sox have beaten the Yankees *at home*, by a touchdown, on Mickey Mantle's birthday. At one minute after midnight, the start of a new day, when Sierra grounds weakly to Pokey Reese, and Pokey flips to Doug Mientkiewicz (so simple!), the most expensive baseball team in history is history.

And we're sorry, George, but that's more than half a billion dollars you've spent . . . for nothing.

Come on now: *Who's* your Daddy?

Diamondbacks. Angels. Marlins. Red Sox.

---

*And for all of you Hanshin Tigers fans out there, a measure of revenge: Johnny's granny, like Jefe's two-run shot, goes over a sign on the wall touting the Yomiuri Corporation. *Ganbatte!*

†And monster props to Terry Francona for engineering this matchup. It's like Bill Belichick drawing up a play that isolates our hot receiver on their weakest corner. It's a flat-out mismatch, and at an absolutely crucial time. After Game 3, Francona's consistently outmanaged Joe Torre, whether it's using the pen, changing the lineup around, or bringing in pinch runners and defensive replacements. Every move seems to have worked out for Tito, while Joe, with a deeper bench and pen, keeps fucking up. George, are you watching? Are you taking notes?

It's like Papa Jack says: ain't nuthin' for free. SOMEBODY got-ta pay. And, Yankee fans, the one you just bought has a lifetime guarantee.

October 21st

Last night, in a game that was never supposed to happen, the Boston Red Sox completed the greatest comeback in the history of American professional sports. In light of that accomplishment, an inning-by-inning post-mortem would be pretty anticlimactic stuff, and not very helpful in understanding the magnitude of the event. You might as well try to describe a camel by describing a camel's eyeball.

Is winning the American League pennant an event of magnitude? We are, after all, fighting some kind of screwed-up war in Iraq where over eleven hundred American soldiers have already died, not to mention at least two hundred American civilians. We are fighting (or trying to fight) a war on terrorism. We are electing a president in less than two weeks, and the dialogue between the candidates has never been hotter. In light of those things, does winning the pennant even matter?

My answer: you bet your sweet ass it does.

One of the eeriest things about this year's just-concluded Boston–New York baseball tussle is the way it mimicked this year's ongoing political contest. John Kerry, a Massachusetts resident, was nominated in Boston and threw out the first pitch at a crucial Red Sox–Yankees game. George Bush was nominated in New York City, and Dick Cheney attended a Yankee–Red Sox game, wearing a Yankees cap over the old solar sex-panel while snipers stood posted high above the fans. As with the Red Sox in the ALCS, Kerry started far behind, then pulled even in the polls. (Whether or not he can win his own Game 7 remains very much open to question, and even if he does, it probably won't be by the electoral college equivalent of seven runs.)

The four playoff games in New York transcended mere sport for another reason. Except for the Irish tenor warbling his way through "God Bless America" during the seventh-inning stretch—now a tradition at most or all parks, I think—there was little or no sign of 9/11 trauma at Yankee Stadium. The Yanks have had their trials and travails this year (poor pitching chief among them), but the need to provide therapy for their hurt and grieving city by winning the American League pennant was thankfully not one of them.

Yet a comfy tradition of winning leaves one—whether that one be an individual or a sociological overset combined of several million fans—unprepared for loss, especially when the loss is so shocking and unexpected. The headlines in this morning's three New York papers express that shock better than any man- or woman-on-the-street interview ever could.

From the *New York Times*: *RED SOX TO YANKEES: WAIT TILL NEXT YEAR* and *MONUMENTAL COLLAPSE.*

From the *Daily News*: *THE CHOKE'S ON US* and (this is a classic, I think) *HELL FREEZES OVER.* Accompanying the latter is a picture of Pedro with his hands upraised and the caption: "Pedro Martinez celebrates in his daddy's house."

From the *New York Post*, sad and succinct: *DAMNED YANKEES.*

After the game, out by the gigantic bat in front of Gate 4, most Yankee fans were downcast but magnanimous, considering the fact that the Red Sox fans—there were plenty of them—were delirious with joy, pounding each other on the back, giving and receiving high fives, pogo-ing up and down. One large, hairy man grabbed me around the waist and whirled me around thrice, screaming, *"Stephen! Stephen! We won, ya scary sonofabitch! I LOVE YA!"*

"GO, RED SOX!" I screamed back. It seemed safe enough, and besides, it was what I felt.

"GO, RED SOX!" the large, hairy man screamed. *"GO, JOHNNY DAMON! GO, MANNY! GO, YOU LONGHAIRED SONSABITCHES!"* Then he was gone.

From behind me there came a dissenting note—three Yankee fans, teenagers by the sound (I did not turn around to see), who wanted me to know that "Red Sox suck, and you suck too, Steve."

A mounted cop clopped by, leaned down, and said, "Tell 'em to blow it out their asses. Tell 'em you been waitin' eighteen years."

I might just have done that little thing, but he clopped on, magnificent on his steed and in his riot gear.

Such memories are like raisins in some fabulous dream cake. There are others—the churlish, childish failure of the Yankees to congratulate the Red Sox on their electronic scoreboard; the downcast Yankee fan who hugged me and said he hoped the Red Sox would go all the way this time; two crying children, a boy and a girl, slowly mounting the steps and dragging their big foam Number One fingers disconsolately behind them on the concrete, headed out of Yankee Stadium hand in hand—but mostly what I remember this morning are the lights, the noise, the sheer unreality of watching Johnny Damon's grand slam going into the right-field stands, and being wrapped in a big Stewart O'Nan bear hug while he screamed, *"We're going to the World Series!"* in my ear.

And that's a fact: we are indeed going to the World Series. Right now, after coming back from the dead to beat the Yankees four straight, it almost seems like a postscript . . . but yes. We're going to the World Series. It starts in Boston. And it matters. It's part of an American life, and that matters a lot.

SO: We DID IT! And it was great to be there with you to see it. It's a win no one can ever take away from us. History, baby.

The starting pitchers in tonight's NLCS Game 7 are both products of the Red Sox: Roger Clemens and Jeff Suppan, who started with the PawSox ten-plus years ago and then returned for the last half of last season. In this one Suppan outpitches *and* outhits Clemens, executing a beautiful suicide squeeze that scores—of all people—Red Sock spring training hopeful Tony Womack.

SO: So it's gonna be the Cards. Welcome to 1967. Except this time it's the Possible Dream.

SK: Somebody play me the Lullaby of Birdland. We got fucked over by the *Orioles*. We did "okay" against the *Jays*. How you feeling about the *Cardinals*?

SO: Don't bring the O's into this. Just don't. Miguel Te-hater.

And I'm glad it's the Cards, winners of 105 games and by far the best and most consistent team in the majors this year. If we're going to finally win it all, I don't want it to be against a patsy like the Braves or Padres or Mets. Degree of difficulty counts, and whatever we achieve (or fail to achieve) the Cards will make us earn it.

Within hours of last night's win, our e-mail in-box began filling with satirical Yankee-bashing pages. The classic was an advisory from the Red Cross informing us that the international signal for choking (a man holding his throat with both hands) would now be replaced by this more recognizable symbol (the intertwined *N* and *Y*). Marky Mark's head was cut-and-pasted into a cast picture of *Saved by the Bellhorn*, and a shot of Derek Jeter and A-Rod glumly watching from the dugout rail bore the caption: "Not Going Anywhere for a While?" and a Snickers logo. And, God help me, until they started repeating, I laughed at every single one.

October 22nd

There will be baseball tomorrow night under the lights at Fenway Park. In the meantime, these intermission notes:

One—Dan Shaughnessy, Boston *Globe* columnist and author of *The Curse of the Bambino,* has been in full damage-control mode since Boston did its Rocky Balboa thing to win the pennant. Shaughnessy's trying to convince joyful New Englanders that the Curse of the Bambino (largely created by Boston *Globe* columnist Dan Shaughnessy, who has book royalties to protect) is still in full force; beating the Yankees is not enough. "Now Wait Just a Minute: Series Still Must Be Won" is the heading of today's column, which begins, "Let's get one thing straight: the Curse of the Bambino has not been lifted. The job is not yet done."

I happened to catch Shaughnessy on one of the cable news channels last night not long after I arrived home from New York, spinning pretty much the same line. He was on the phone; Red Sox–Yankees highlights were playing on the screen. When he paused for breath, the newscaster asked him what he and Boston baseball fans would talk about *vis-à-vis* the Red Sox next year if Boston *did* happen to win the World Series.

Either the query or the concept behind it seemed to catch Shaughnessy by surprise. There was an uncharacteristic pause, and then he said, "You know, that's an interesting question." Which to my mind is always an interesting *response,* meaning the person to whom the question has been directed has no freakin' idea. Sure enough, Shaughnessy never did really respond to the newscaster's question.

Without the curse to fall back on (or the Curse, if you prefer), they might have to actually write about the *games?* You think? I know some of the Boston sports cannibals would find that a daunting proposition at the outset, but most of them (their taste for the golden flesh of athletes to one side) are pretty damned good writers, and I'm sure they'd rise to the challenge in short order.

Two—During the wee-hours postgame celebration outside Fenway Park, a twenty-one-year-old Emerson College student named Victoria Snelgrove was killed when she was struck by a plastic ball filled with pepper spray. Boston police commissioner Kathleen O'Toole accepted responsibility for the young woman's death (handsome, and no doubt of great comfort to her family), and in the next breath condemned the "punks" who seized upon the Red Sox victory over the Yankees as "an opportunity for violence and destruction." Running beside this story is a picture of the late Ms. Snelgrove, looking not like a punk but a Madonna.

Boston mayor Thomas Menino says the city is considering a ban of liquor sales during the World Series (think how proud his Puritan predecessors would be of *that*), and also of banning live TV coverage of the games in bars and restaurants, because it incites fans.* This is causing the predictable howls of outrage from bar and restaurant *owners,* and they may have a point, especially since Menino failed to mention the sale of beer within Fenway Park itself while the games are going on.

Three—It's going to be St. Louis rather than Houston when the Series convenes tomorrow for another of those hateful (perhaps even beerless?) night games. The Rocket gave it his best shot last night in Game 7 of the NLCS, and the Astros even led for a while, but in the end the Roger Clemens tradition of just not being able to win the big game again held true.

Red Sox rooters looking for additional reasons to believe—and surely any would come in handy, considering that the 2004 Cardinals won more games than any other pro baseball team—might consider this: in the

---

*No word yet on whether or not Menino is considering a ban on pepper-spray-filled plastic balls, which seem to incite Boston police.

NLCS, the home team won every game. And in this World Series, the Red Sox have the home field advantage.

And have it thanks to Manny Ramirez's first-inning home run in the All-Star Game off of . . . Roger Clemens.

The Possible Dream

October 23rd/World Series Game 1

SK: I think Wake is a GREAT choice for Game 1. Sure he's a risk, but he'd be MY choice; he might tie those big thumpas in knots. Even if he doesn't, I give Francona kudos for giving Timmy the ball. And for God's sake, he's gonna put Mirabelli behind the plate, right? Right.

Seeya 5:30,

Steve "I Still Believe" King

I'd violently disagree with Steve—Wake is his boy as much as Dave McCarty is mine, and Wake's been plain awful this year, besides the few usual wins in Tampa; the best thing he did was volunteer to mop up in Game 3 against the Yanks and give Lowe his spot in the rotation* —but I'm out the door and sailing across I-84 before Steve's e-mail reaches me. It's been a long time since I've been to a World Series, and I aim to get my fill.

The souvenir shops around the park don't open until noon. At eleven-thirty, lines of eager buyers stretch far down the block. The amount of free junk people are handing out is astounding—papers, posters, buttons, stickers, pictures, temporary tattoos, Krispy Kreme doughnuts. Fans are staggering around with bags of the crap, in total material overload. When the stores open, barkers with bullhorns herd customers into switchbacked ropes—"This line only for World Series and AL Champion merchandise—this line only!"

---

*All right, I'm no ingrate: he saved our bacon in extras in Game 5, holding the Yanks scoreless for three nervous, passed-ball-filled innings and picking up the win.

385

Hanging out by the parking lot eight hours before game time, the autograph hunters are treated to an impromptu concert by Steven Tyler as he runs his sound check for tonight's anthem. Steven doesn't actually sing the song, he just blows an A on his harmonica and runs through an ascending series of bluesy scales, and sounds great—a cool reminder that Aerosmith started out as an electric blues band influenced by the early Stones, the Yardbirds and Muddy Waters.

After that, PA announcer Carl Beane warms his pipes, rumbling: "Ladies and gentlemen, please welcome . . . the National League Champion, St. Louis Cardinals," over and over, as if he might have trouble with it later. He goes through a fantastical lineup: "Batting first, number one . . . Carl . . . Beane." A minute later, "Batting fourth, number nine . . . Ted . . . Williams," and the crowd outside applauds. "Batting fifth, number six . . . Stan . . . Musial."

And speaking of old-timers, rumor is that Yaz is throwing out the first pitch, a sentimental touch, and overdue, since it's said that Yaz and the club haven't had the best of relationships since he retired. The new owners may be trying to patch things over. We also witness—well in advance—the return of Lenny DiNardo and Adam Hyzdu, two guys who spent time with the club early in the year. It's nice to see the Sox are giving them a taste of the big show (though, of course, the guy we really want to see is Dauber).

Two other early arrivals of note: team physician Dr. Bill Morgan and, fifteen minutes later, wearing a brace on his right leg and no shoe in the cold, Curt Schilling. Before Game 6, Dr. Morgan sutured Schill's tendon to his skin, a procedure he practiced first on a cadaver. Rumor (again, rumor, the outsider's substitute for information) is that he's going to stitch him up again for tomorrow's start in Game 2. On those few threads, our whole season may depend.

Inside, there are more banners than I've seen all year—a lifting of the normal ban, for TV's sake, I expect. It's cold, with a wind whipping in from straight center, which should give Wake's knuckler more flutter. Even the stiff wind isn't enough to keep David Ortiz in the park tonight. In the first, in his very first World Series at-bat, El Jefe busts out with a three-run golf shot OVER the Pesky Pole. We chase Woody Williams early, giving Wake a 7–2 lead going into the fourth.

Beside me, Steve is smiling. Kevin, the usher who comes down between innings with a camp chair to keep people off the wall, is overjoyed with how things are going. "No," I say, glum, "just watch: Wake'll start walking people. He always does when we give him a big lead." And I don't say this to jinx anything, I say it because I've seen Wake all year long, and that's just what he does.

And that's just what he does—walking four in the fourth to break a World Series record, and soon after he's gone it's 7–7. It's like they used to say about Fenway when it was a launching pad: no lead is safe here.

"Man, that was ogly," Orlando Cabrera said in a postgame interview. He paused, then added, "But we won." *Ogly* pretty well sums up the first game of this year's World Series, which ended with a thing of beauty: Keith Foulke striking out Roger Cedeno a few minutes after midnight.

Speaking of ogly, Orlando wasn't looking so good himself in that interview, and he seemed uncharacteristically solemn. A Woody Williams pitch hit him on the shoulder in the first inning, then bounced up into his face, leaving him with a bruised chin, a fat lip, and a temporary inability to smile—which, under ordinary circumstances, Mr. Garciaparra's replacement does often. Pain or no pain, Cabrera must have been at least tempted to test that smile when the Red Sox finally escaped with an ogly but serviceable 11–9 win in spite of four errors (one by Bronson Arroyo—starter Tim Wakefield's fourth-inning relief—one by Kevin Millar, and two by Manny Ramirez). Every one of those errors led to runs, leading me to wonder if any of the Red Sox players felt tempted to visit the Cardinals' clubhouse after the game and assure them on behalf of the home team that Boston doesn't play that way *every* night.

Cabrera might have been even more tempted to test his swollen lip if informed of this statistic: in World Series history, the team drawing first blood has gone on to win the Fall Classic 60 percent of the time. Still, there's that other 40 percent . . . and the fact that the Cards have yet to lose during this postseason on their home field. But—fingers crossed, now—you've got to like the Red Sox going into Game 2. They're nice and loose (what could be looser than four errors and four walks issued by Red Sox pitching?), their demonic archrivals are behind them and they're riding a nifty five-game winning streak.

Last night's game began with a moment of silence for Victoria Snelgrove, the young woman killed by a pepper-gas ball during riot-control operations outside Fenway following Boston's final victory over New York, and while it was both decent and brave of the current ownership to remember her (one is tempted to believe that the previous bunch of care-takers would have swept Ms. Snelgrove under the rug as fast and as far as possible), it was also a reminder of what is *truly* ogly in our brave new world, where all game bags are searched and the clocks tick on Osama Mean Time.

There were lines of Boston police, looking like puffy Michelin Men in their riot gear, watching impassively as the happy and largely well-behaved crowd left the old green First New England Church of Baseball with the strains of "Dirty Water" still ringing in their ears and the memory of Mark Bellhorn's game-winning, foul-pole-banging home run still vivid in their minds. To me those dark lines of armed men outside such a place of ancient and innocent pleasure are a lot harder to look at than the mark on Orlando Cabrera's face, or his swelled lower lip.

11–9 is a crazy score for a World Series game; so is a total of 24 hits and 5 errors. But the bottom line is that we won, Father Curt takes the mound tomorrow night on home turf with his freshly restitched ankle, and that's a beautiful thing. (A remarkable one, anyway.)

I only wish Torie Snelgrove was around to see it.

The most surprising thing to me about Game 1 was how the Faithful booed Dale Sveum during the pregame introductions. I suppose it's a delayed (or should I say sustained?) reaction to Johnny being thrown out at home in the first inning of Game 7 of the ALCS. Whatever it is, I don't like it.

And despite the win, I don't like the way Kevin Millar played, leaving ten men on, making essentially two errors on the same play (double-clutching that cutoff, then throwing the ball into the dugout), and later not getting anywhere near a ball hit down the line that both Mientkiewicz and McCarty handle easily.

By contrast, the Cards' Larry Walker took to the big stage in a big way, making two great catches in right (a Manny liner down into the corner with men on, and a windblown pop he had to run a long way and then lunge for at the last second), and hitting a double, a homer, a single and another double. This is Walker's first World Series, after a long and brilliant career in the hinterlands of Montreal and Colorado, and it was heartening to see him show the world his A game. If Pujols, Rolen and Edmonds had done anything to help him out, we'd be down 0-1.

Mark Bellhorn, meanwhile, seems determined to enforce the curse of the ex-Cubs (that is, the team with more ex-Cubs is bound to lose the Series—the Cards have five while we only have two, Marky Mark and Billy Mueller). Before his home run off Julian Tavarez, he was 2 for 3 against him lifetime, so his success didn't surprise me, only the magnitude of it. It was no fluke. Tavarez didn't fool him at all. Marky Mark ripped the pitch before his Pesky Pole shot high and deep down the line in right, but foul. All he had to do was reload and straighten it out, making him one of a very rarefied club—players who've homered in three straight postseason games.

October 24th/World Series Game 2

On the street outside the players' lot I run into Andrew on his way out to buy some salads for the guys. We're surrounded by a crowd of tourists hoping to catch a glimpse of the stars. Camera crews, cops. Andrew still can't believe this is all happening—a common reaction among the Nation, even those deep inside it. I ask him about Schill's ankle, and tell him about seeing Dr. Morgan yesterday. Yeah, he says, they had him on the table, but he tried to stay away from there.

"How's he look?" I ask.

Andrew just shrugs. "We'll have to see."

Inside, I catch Tony Womack along the left-field wall, joking with an old friend in the stands about beating him at golf next week. When he gets a break, I ask him how his collarbone feels after taking that David Ortiz smash off it last night.

"I'm fine," he says, and I tell him how much I'd been rooting for him in spring training.

"You ran great, bunted great, stole bases. I wish you could have played the field."

"Man," he says, shaking his head, "they didn't want me."

We shake hands, and a minute later he calls Larry Walker over.

Walker looks puzzled until he sees Tony's friend.

"You know this guy?" Tony asks.

"Know this guy?" Walker says. "This guy owes me eight grand!"

It's Sunday, and in the concourse crowds are gathered around the wall-mounted TVs watching the Patriots beat the Jets for their twenty-first consecutive win. If the Pats can win twenty-one straight, the logic goes, why can't we win eight?

Our seats are down in the corner where I normally post up for BP—better seats than I'm used to. How good? Above us in the Monster seats is Jimmy Fallon, and two rows in front of us, so close I could lean forward and tap his shoulder, is Eagles QB Donovan McNabb. He played an outstanding game today in Cleveland, his long scramble setting up an overtime win. He must have showered and gotten right on the plane. He's so tired that the only time he stands up during the game is to go to the restroom, but, like us, he stays for every drizzly, windswept pitch.

October 25th

One summer night in the mid-1960s, right around the time the Beatles were ruling the American music charts, a young music producer named Ed Cobb happened to be walking with his girlfriend beside the Charles River in the quaint old city of Boston, Massachusetts . . . or so the story goes. Out of the shadows came a thief who tried to mug him out of his wallet (or maybe it was out of her purse; on that the story is not entirely clear). In any case, the musically inclined Mr. Cobb foiled the thief and got an idea for a song as a bonus. The song, "Dirty Water," was eventually recorded by a group of Boston proto-punks called the Standells and released by Capitol, who wanted a record Cobb had produced for Ketty ("Anyone Who Had a Heart") Lester. No one expected much from the raw and raunchy* "Dirty Water," but it went to #11 on the *Billboard* pop charts and has remained a standard on the Boston club scene ever since.

It was revived by the new Red Sox management and has become the good-time signature of Boston wins. For the Fenway Faithful, there's nothing better than seeing the final out go up on the scoreboard and hearing that six-note intro with the familiar first-note slide leading into the verse: *Down by the riiiiver* . . . And so it seemed a particularly good omen to see the resurrected Standells in deep center field before the game last night, a lot grayer and a little thinner on top but still loud and proud, singing about that dirty water down by the banks of the River Charles.

A great many things about baseball in general and the Red Sox in particular are about the bridges between past and present—this was just one more provided by a current Yawkey Way administration that seems pleas-

---

*In my high school, the phrase "lovers, muggers and thieves" was routinely construed to be either "lovers, junkies and thieves" or "lovers, fuckers and thieves."

antly aware of tradition without becoming enslaved to it. And when the Red Sox had put this one away in the cold mists of a late Sunday evening, the sounds of "Dirty Water" rang out again, this time with the tempo a little faster and the tones a little truer. And why not? This was the one recorded when the Standells were young. This is the version that hit the charts four months before Curt Schilling was born.

He was awesome last night. The word is tired, clapped-out from overuse, but I've had a 170-mile drive to try and think of a better one, and I cannot. The crowd of just over thirty-five thousand in the old green Church of Baseball knew what it was seeing; many of them may have been in Fenway Park for the first time last night (these Series-only fans are what *Globe* writer Dan Shaughnessy so rightly calls the "Nouveau Nation"), but even they knew. The galaxy of flashbulbs that went off in the stadium, from the plum dugout seats to the skyviews to the distant bleachers to those now perched atop the Green Monster, was chilling in its cold and commemorative brilliance, declaring by silent light that the men and women who came to the ballpark last night had never seen anything quite like it for sheer guts and never expected to see anything quite like it again. Not, certainly, with their own eyes.

Edgar Renteria, the Cardinals' leadoff hitter, battled Schilling fiercely— first six pitches, then ten, then a dozen, running the count full and then spilling off foul after foul.* He might have been the game's key batter, and not the ones Schilling had to face following more Boston miscues (another four) that allowed the Cardinals extra chances upon which they could not capitalize.

Before finally hitting sharply to shortstop (and the often-maligned Kevin Millar made a fine pick at first to complete the play), Renteria tried every trick in the book. Every trick, that is, save one. He never attempted to lay down a bunt. In three starts on his bad peg—two against the Yankees and now one against the Cardinals—no one has tried to make Curt Schilling field his position. I'm sure the Red Sox infielders have discussed this possibility and know exactly how they would handle it . . . but it has simply never come up. And when this thing is over, when the hurly-burly's done, all the battles lost and won, someone needs to ask the Yankee and

---

*To prolong or deepen this drama, the pitch-speed display above the wall in left-center was tantalizingly blank for this half-inning. Who knew what Schill had? Only Tek and the hitters. SO

Cardinal hitters *why* they did not bunt. Of course I can imagine the boos that would rain down on a successful bunter against Father Curt at Fenway, but is it beyond the scope of belief to think that even Yankee or Cardinal fans might find it hard to cheer such a ploy for reaching first (well . . . maybe not Yankee fans)?

Could it have been—don't laugh—actual *sportsmanship*?

Whatever the reason, the Cards played him straight up last night—I salute them for it—and for the most part, Father Curt mowed them right down. Tony Womack and Mike Matheny had singles; Albert Pujols had a pair of doubles. And, as far as hits against Schilling went, that was it. He finished his night's work by striking out the side in the sixth.

For the Red Sox, it was a continuing case of two-run, two-out thunder. Two runs scored after two were out in the first; two more after two were out in the fourth; two more in the sixth, the same way.* By the end of the game (Mike Matheny, groundout), the deep green grass of the field and the bright white of the Red Sox home uniforms had grown slightly diffuse in the thickening mizzle. The departing fans, damp but hardly dampened, were all but delirious with joy. One held up a poster depicting a Christlike Johnny Damon walking on water with the words JOHNNY SAVES beneath his sandaled feet.

I heard one fan—surely part of Mr. Shaughnessy's Nouveau Nation—actually saying he hoped the Red Sox would *lose* a couple in St. Louis, so the team could clinch back on its home soil (yes, Beavis, he actually said "home soil"). I had to restrain myself from laying hands on this fellow and asking him if he remembered 1986, when we *also* won the first two, only to lose four of the next five. And when a team is going this well (RED HOT RED SOX, trumpets this morning's *USA Today*), one loss can lead to others. Winning two at home, within a sniff of the River Charles, may have been vital, considering the fact that the Cardinals have yet to lose a single postseason game in their own house.

Tomorrow night, Pedro Martinez will face the Cards near the dirty water of a much larger river, in a much larger stadium. It will be his first World Series start, and given that no team has ever climbed out of an

---

*Respectively: Tek with a triple to the triangle that's out if the wind isn't blowing straight in; Marky Mark with a similar bomb off the wall in dead center; and O-Cab, who was uncharacteristically ahead in the count all night, bonking one off the Monster. SO

0-3 World Series hole (and surely that sort of thing can't happen twice in the same postseason . . . can it?), I think it's going to be the most important start by a Red Sox pitcher in a long, long time. Certainly since 1986.

October 26th/World Series Game 3

SK: Dear Stewart-Under-the-Arch: Here's my idea of the doomsday scenario, also known as the Novelist's Ending. The BoSox win **one** game in SaintLoo. Come back to Boston up **three games to two.** Lose **Game 6.** And . . . have to start Father Curt for all the marbles in Game 7.

Stewart, this could _actually_ happen.

SO: I'm hoping we can steal one out there, and hey, if we get two, I won't be crying about eating my Game 6 tickets. It's just like the Yankee series: we just have to win one game—the game we're playing.

SK: All lookin' good. Now, if Pedro can only do his part.

You know, I think he will.

SO: Pedro remains inscrutable. We can't hit like it's a regular Pedro game; we have to pretend it's John Burkett out there. Think seven or eight runs. Go Sox!

The Sox are up 4–0 as the game rolls into the ninth, and I find I can't sit down. As Foulke comes in, I'm muttering the lyrics to his Fenway entrance music, Danzig's "Mother" ("And if you want to find Hell with me, I can show you what it's like"). He gets Edgar Renteria, then has Larry Walker 0-2 when he just lays a fastball in there, and Walker golfs it out. I watch Johnny turn and watch it, then I'm out of the room, swearing and pacing through the house. It's okay, we've got a three-run lead and there's no one on. Foulkie just has to go after hitters and not walk anybody. Pujols gets behind and jaws at the ump after a borderline call, then skies one deep to left (oh crap) that Manny settles under (whew)—that's two. Scott Rolen, 0 for the series, is taking, gets behind, then inexplicably takes the 1-2 pitch, which, while slightly in, is clearly a strike, and the ump punches him out to end the game. We're up 3–0 and I'm jumping around the room.

Petey came through so big, and Manny, and Billy Mueller hitting with two down. We're a game away. I've been a strike away before, so I'm already trying to play it down, but, damn, I didn't expect us to ever be up 3–0 on the Cards. The idea of winning it all sends me romping through the house, bellowing the Dropkick Murphys' "Tessie," even though I don't know all the words: "Up from third base to Hun-ting-ton, they'd sing another vic-t'ry soooooooong—two, three, four!"

Boston has now won seven in a row (tying a postseason record), pushing the Cards to the brink where the Red Sox themselves stood only a week ago. The most amazing thing about the World Series part of the Red Sox run is that the Cardinals have yet to lead in a single game. Their manager, Tony La Russa, certainly knows this, and while his part of the postgame news conference seemed long to me, it must have seemed interminable to him. He looked more like a middle-level racketeer being questioned in front of a grand jury than a successful baseball manager. Part of the reason for La Russa's long face may have had to do with the game's key play, which came in the third inning, when Cardinals base runner (and starting pitcher) Jeff Suppan was thrown out at third.

Suppan led off the inning with a slow roller to third. Mueller handled it cleanly, but not in time to get Suppan at first. Edgar Renteria followed with a double to right that had Trot Nixon falling on his ass because of the wet conditions in the outfield.* Suppan probably could have scored right there, tying the game, but perhaps he was held up by the third-base coach. (We'll give him the benefit of the doubt, anyway.) So with runners at second and third and nobody out, up came Larry Walker, a gent who is absolutely no slouch with the stick. He hit a ground ball to Mark Bellhorn.

At that point the Boston infield was playing back, conceding Suppan's run, which would have tied the score, 1–1. But Suppan didn't score when Walker made contact, nor did he when Bellhorn threw Walker out.

---

*It rained heavily in St. Louis right up until game time, and the warning track was a swimming pool. I hate it when teams are forced to play ball under these conditions, but it's the same old sordid story: when Fox talks, Major League Baseball walks. If this is going to continue, the Players Association ought to consider insisting on pads and helmets (at least for the outfielders) after October 15th.

Instead he broke toward home, broke back toward third base, then broke toward home a *second* time. Meanwhile, Boston's new kid on the block at first base, David Ortiz, in the lineup because the designated hitter doesn't exist in National League parks, was observing all this. From Ortiz's side of the diamond, Suppan must have looked as frantic and disoriented as a bird trapped in a garage. He fired across the diamond to Bill Mueller just as Suppan darted back toward third base a second time. Suppan dove for the bag, but Mueller was able to put the tag on him easily.

The result of this beer-league baserunning was that instead of tying the score against one of the American League's craftiest power pitchers with only one out, the Cardinals found themselves with two outs and no runs scored. Albert Pujols followed Walker, grounding out harmlessly to end the inning. The Cards would not score until the bottom of the ninth, and by then it was too late. The irony (La Russa's long postgame face suggested he did not need this pointed out to him) was that the National League team had been screwed by the very rules that were supposed to tip the scales in their favor. It was *their* pitcher who made the baserunning blunder, and *our* erstwhile designated hitter who saw it happening and gunned him down.

Although Boston got a pair of insurance runs in the fifth, more two-out thunder from Manny Ramirez in the first* and Bill Mueller (batted home by Trot Nixon) in the fourth were all the run support Pedro Martinez needed; he, Mike Timlin and Keith Foulke spun a gem. Following Edgar Renteria's double in the third inning, Red Sox pitching retired eighteen Cards in a row. Larry Walker broke up the string with one out in the ninth, turning around a Keith Foulke fastball to deep left center for a home run.

So now the St. Louis deficit is 0-3. One would like to say that lightning cannot strike twice on the same patch of ground, and certainly not so soon, but in truth, one *cannot* say that. Especially not if one happens to have been a Red Sox fan for the last fifty years and has had the cup snatched

---

*Followed, in the bottom of the inning, by Manny's perfect one-hop peg on a short fly to nail Larry Walker at the plate and keep us up 1–0. This moment of redemption after Manny had made errors on consecutive and very ogly plays in Game 1. Cardinals third base coach Jose Oquendo, like so many other baseball people, mistook Manny's spaciness for lack of ability. Anyone who's watched Manny throw knows he's amazingly accurate and that Walker had no chance. SO

away from his lips so many times just before that first deep and satisfying drink.

I don't think I've ever been so aware of the limitations of this narrative's necessary diary form until today. You sitting there with the finished book in your hand are like an astronaut who can see the entire shape of the earth: where every sea ends and every coastline begins again. I just go sailing along from day to day, hoping to avoid the storms and writing in this log when seas are calm. And now I think I can smell land up ahead. I hope I'm not jinxing things by saying that, but I really think I can. Not just any land, either, but the sweet Promised Land I've been dreaming of ever since my Uncle Oren bought me my first Red Sox cap and stuck it on my head in the summer of 1954. "There, Stevie," he said, blowing the scent of Narragansett beer into the face of the big-eyed seven-year-old looking up at him. "They ain't much, but they're the best we got."

Now, fifty long years later, they're on the verge of being the best of all. One more game and we can put all this curse stuff, all this Babe stuff, all this 1918 stuff, behind us.

Please, baseball gods, just one more game.

SK: Ah, but I begin to smell exotic spices and strange nerds . . . er, nards . . . could these be the scents of the Promised Land? I can only hope they are not scents sent by false sirens on hidden stones beyond a mirage of yon beckoning shore . . .

But I digress.

We rocked tonight, dude.

SO: It's good to be up 3-0 instead of down 0-3, but the job's the same: win the game we're playing. The guys have to stay on top of it.

SK: You must have been eating the postgame spread with Tito. :-)

October 27th/World Series Game 4

It's Trudy's and my twentieth anniversary today. We were supposed to be in Chicago last weekend, eating at Charlie Trotter's and the Billy Goat Tavern (the honest-to-God home of the Cubs' curse as well as the chee-burger, chee-burger skit from *SNL*), but those plans dissolved in the face of Games 1 and 2. Tonight, at Trudy's insistence, I call and cancel our long-standing dinner reservations at the best restaurant in town. I don't tell the maitre d' why. "Enjoy the game," he says.

Signs and portents everywhere. Tonight's the eighteenth anniversary of our last World Series loss—Game 7 to the '86 Mets. Not only is there a full moon, but right around game time there's a total lunar eclipse. By the time I go outside to see the lip of the earth's shadow cross the Sea of Tranquility, Johnny has us up 1–0 with a leadoff home run. Later, when Trot doubles on a bases-juiced 3-0 green light to give us a 3–0 lead, the eclipse is well under way, casting a decidedly red stain—blood on the moon, or is it a cosmic nod to the Sox?

For the third game in a row, Lowe pitches brilliantly, giving up just three hits in seven innings. Arroyo looks shaky in the eighth, but Embree relieves him and is perfect for the second straight outing. As Foulke closes, I'm standing behind the couch, shifting with every pitch as if I'm guarding the line. At this point, for no other reason it seems than to torture us, Fox decides to show a montage combining all the horrible moments in Red Sox postseason history, beginning with Enos Slaughter, moving through Bucky Dent and Buckner, and finishing with Aaron Boone. I hold a hand up to block it out (to eclipse it!). At this moment in Red Sox history, I do *not* want to see that shit. It's not bad luck, it's bad *taste*, and whoever thought it was appropriate is a jerk.

With one down, Pujols singles through Foulke's legs, right through the five-hole, a ball Foulke, a diehard hockey fan, should have at least gotten a pad on. We're nervous—another runner and they'll bring the tying run to the plate—but Foulke's cool. He's got that bitter disdain—that nastiness, really—of a great closer. He easily strikes out Edmonds (now 1 for 15), then snags Edgar Renteria's comebacker and flips to Mientkiewicz, and that's it, it's that simple: the Red Sox have won the World Series!

While we're still hugging and pounding each other (Trudy's crying, she can't help it; Steph's laughing; I'm just going: "Wow. Wow. Wow.") Caitlin calls from Boston. In the background, girls are shrieking. She's at Nickerson Field, formerly Braves Field, where B.U. is showing the game on a big screen. I can barely hear her for the noise. "They did it!" she yells. "They did!" I yell back. There's no analysis, just a visceral appreciation of the win.

I tell her to stay out of the riots, meaning keep away from Fenway, and she assures me she will. It's not until I get off the phone with her that I realize the weird parallel: when I was a freshman there, my team won the World Series too.

It's more than just a win; it's a statement. By winning tonight, we broke the record for consecutive playoff wins, with eight straight. Another stat that every commentator unpacks is that we're one of only four championship teams to have never trailed in the Series.* Thanks to Johnny, O.C., Manny and Papi, we scored in the first inning of every game, and our starters, with the exception of Wake, shut down St. Louis's big sticks. Schill, Petey and D-Lowe combined for 20 shutout innings. Much respect to pitching coach Dave Wallace and his scouts for coming up with a game plan to stop the Cards. As a team, they batted .190, well below the Mendoza Line. Scott Rolen and Jim Edmonds went 1 for 30, that one hit being a gimme bunt single by Edmonds against a shifted infield. Albert Pujols had zero RBIs. Reggie Sanders went 0 for 9. It's not that we crushed the ball. We scored only four runs in Game 3 and three in Game 4. Essentially, after the Game 1 slugfest, we played NL ball, beating them with pitching, and in the last two games our defense was flawless. In finally putting the supposed Curse to rest, we dotted every *i* and crossed every *t*. And to make it all even sweeter, the last out was made by Edgar Renteria, who wears—as a couple of folks noted—the Babe's famous #3.

October 28th

It came down to this: with two outs in the St. Louis half of the ninth and Keith Foulke on the mound—Foulke, the nearly sublime Red Sox closer this postseason—only Edgar Renteria stood between Boston and the end of its World Series drought. Renteria hit a comebacker to the mound. "Stabbed by Foulke!" crowed longtime Red Sox radio announcer Joe Castiglione. "He underhands to first! The Red Sox are World Champions! *Can you believe it?*"

I hardly could, and I wasn't the only one. A hundred miles away, my son woke up *his* five-year-old son to see the end. When it was over and the Red

*Along with Tony La Russa's 1989 A's, the '66 O's and the '63 Dodgers. All three, like the Sox, had a pair of aces—Dave Stewart and Bob Welch with the A's, Jim Palmer and Dave McNally with the O's, and Sandy Koufax and Don Drysdale with the Dodgers.

Sox were mobbing each other on the infield, Ethan asked his father, "Is this a dream or are we living real life?"

The answer, it seems to me this morning, is both. The only newspaper available at the general store was the local one (the others were held up because of the lateness of the game), and the *Sun-Journal*'s huge front-page headline, of a size usually reserved only for the outbreak of war or the sudden death of a president, was only two words and an exclamation mark:

AT LAST!

When the other New England papers finally do arrive in my sleepy little pocket of New England, I'm confident they will bear similar happy headlines of a similar size on their front pages.

A game summary would be thin stuff indeed compared to this outpouring of joy on a beautiful blue and gold New England morning in late October.* Usually when I go to get the papers and my 8 A.M. doughnut, the little store up the road is almost empty. This morning it was jammed, mostly with people waiting for those newspapers to come in. The majority were wearing Red Sox hats, and the latest political news was the last thing on their minds. They wanted to talk about last night's game. They wanted to talk about the Series as a whole. They wanted to talk about the guts of Curt Schilling, pitching on his hurt ankle, and the grit of Mr. Lowe, who was supposed to spend the postseason in the bullpen and ended up securing a magickal and historickal place for himself in the record books instead, as the winner in all three postseason clinchers: Game 3 of the Division Series, Game 7 of the League Championship Series, and now Game 4 of the World Series. And while none of those waiting for the big-time morning papers—the Boston *Globe*, *USA Today*, and the *New York Times*—came right out and asked my grandson's question, I could see it in their eyes, and I know they could see it in mine: *Is this a dream, or are we living real life?*

It's real life. If there was a curse (other than a sportswriter's brilliant

---

*And the summary is simple enough: once again last night we hit and pitched. The Cardinals did neither. Only one Cardinal starter—Jason Marquis—managed to stay in a Series game for six innings, and the heart of the St. Louis batting order (Pujols, Rolen, Edmonds) got only a single run batted in during the entire four-game contest. It came on a sac fly.

MacGuffin for selling books, amplified in the media echo chamber until even otherwise rational people started to half-believe it), it was the undeniable fact that the Red Sox hadn't won a World Series since 1918, and all the baggage that fact brought with it for the team's long-suffering fans.

The Yankees and *their* fans have always been the heaviest of that baggage, of course. Yankee rooters were never shy about reminding Red Sox partisans that they were supporting lifetime losers. There was also the undeniable fact that in recent years the Yankee ownership—comfy and complacent in their much bigger ballpark and camped just downstream from a waterfall of fan cash—had been able to outspend the Red Sox ownership, sometimes at a rate of two dollars to one. There was the constant patronization of the New York press (the *Times,* for instance, chuckling in its indulgently intelligent way over the A-Rod deal, and concluding that the Yankees were still showing the Red Sox how to win, even in the off-season), the jokes and the gibes.

The ball through Bill Buckner's legs in 1986 was horrible, of course, but now Buckner can be forgiven.

What's better is that now the Bucky Dent home run, the Aaron Boone home run and the monotonous chants of *Who's your Daddy?* can be forgotten. Laughed off, even. On the whole, I would have to say that while to forgive is human, to forget is freakin' *divine.*

And winning is better than losing. That's easy to lose sight of, if you've never done it. I can remember my younger son saying—and there was some truth in this—that when the Philadelphia Phillies finally won their World Championship after years of trying, they became "just another baseball team." When I asked Owen if he could live with that as a Red Sox fan, he didn't even hesitate. "Sure," he said.

I feel the same way. No one likes to root for a loser, year after year; being faithful does not save one from feeling, after a while, like a fool, the butt of everyone's joke. At last I don't feel that way. This morning's sense of splendid unreality will surely rub away, but the feeling of lightness that comes with finally shedding a burden that has been carried far too long will linger for months or maybe even years. Cubs fans now must bear the loser legacy all by themselves. They have their Curse of the Billy Goat, and although I am sure it is equally bogus,* they are welcome to it.

*Not so! That one's real, and solidly documented. SO

400

Bottom of the ninth, two out, Albert Pujols on second, Red Sox Nation holding its breath. Foulke pitches. Renteria hits an easy comebacker to the mound. Foulke fields it and tosses it to Mientkiewicz, playing first. Mientkiewicz jumps in the air, holding up the index finger of his right hand, signaling *We're number one*. Red Sox players mob the field while stunned and disappointed Cardinal fans look on. Some of the little kids are crying, and I feel bad about that, but back in New England little kids of all ages are jumping for joy.

"Can you believe it?" Joe Castiglione exults, and eighty-six years of disappointment fall away in the length of time it takes the first-base ump to hoist his thumb in the *out* sign.

This is not a dream.

We are living real life.

While the Babe may be resting easier, I barely sleep, and wake exhausted, only to watch the same highlights again and again, seeing things I missed while we were celebrating. As the Sox mob each other, in the background Jimmy Fallon and Drew Barrymore are kissing, shooting their fairy-tale ending to *Fever Pitch* (nice timing, Farrellys!).* In short center, right behind second base, Curtis Leskanic lies down and makes the natural grass equivalent of a Patriots snow angel. The crawl says RED SOX WIN WORLD SERIES, and I think, yes, yes they did.

It did happen. It was no dream. We're the World Champions, finally, and there's that freeing sense of redemption and fulfillment I expected—the same cleansing feeling I had after the Pats' first Super Bowl win. The day is bright and blue, the leaves are brilliant and blowing. It's a beautiful day in the Nation, maybe the best ever.

And yet, the season's over, too. There will be no more baseball this year, and while I've said I wouldn't mind eating my tickets to Games 6 and 7, it feels wrong that I won't be back in Fenway again until April.

---

*So many story lines wrapped last night: Manny, who went unclaimed on waivers, is the World Series MVP (and very possibly the regular-season MVP as well); Lowe totally vindicates himself, making him an incredibly attractive free agent; the same with Pedro; Terry Francona goes from The Coma to a legendary Red Sox manager; Orlando Cabrera, who stepped up big in the number two slot and fielded brilliantly in the postseason, makes us forget Nomar. The year is signed, sealed and delivered. All that's left now is the Boston Duck Tours parade and the team deciding who gets a World Series share. As always, I hope Dauber's not forgotten.

Just for fun, I go to the website (choked with new World Champions merchandise) and poke around, looking for spring training information. There's a number for City of Palms Park, but when I call it, it's busy. It's going to be crazy there next year. If I want to get in, I'd better start working on it now. I flip the pages of our 2005 calendar to February and March and wonder when Trudy's school has its break. I wonder if there's a nicer hotel closer to City of Palms Park, and whether they'd have any rooms left at this point.

I have to stop myself. Okay, calm down. There's no need to hustle now, the very morning after. I can take a day off and appreciate what we've done—what they've done, the players, because as much as we support them, they're the ones out there who have to field shots we'd never get to, and hit pitches that would make us look silly, and beat throws that would have us by miles. And the coaches and the manager, the owners and the general manager, who have to make decisions we'll never take any heat for. They did it, all of them together, our Red Sox.

Congratulations, guys. And thank you. You believed in yourselves even more than we did. That's why you're World Champions, and why we'll never forget you or this season. Wherever you go, any of you, you'll always have a home here, in the heart of the Nation.

Go Sox!

SO: You know how the papers are always saying you bring the team bad luck? Well, the one year you write a book about the club, we win it all. Another fake curse reversed.

Not in your lifetime, huh? Well, brutha, welcome to Heaven!

SK: How do you suppose Angry Bill is doing?

SO: He's in that box of a room in Vegas, grumbling about something—probably the Bruins.

SK: Are you going to the V-R Day Parade?

SO: No, but tonight I ate that Break the Curse cookie I got on Opening Day. A vow's a vow. Washed that stiff six-month-old biscuit down with champagne and enjoyed every morsel. Life is sweet.

Off to drink more champagne. You (and Johnny D) are still The Man.

SK: No, Stewart, you (and Papi) are The Man. I'm giving you the two Pointy-Finger Salute.

SO: Right back atcha, baby. Keep the Faith.

Acknowledgments

For our baseball widows,

Trudy and Tabby

And for Ted, Johnny, Yaz, Lonnie, Rico, Tony C, Boomer, Luis, Spaceman, Pudge, Rooster, Bernie, Jim Ed, Freddy, Eck, Ned Martin, Ken Coleman, Dewey, Hendu, Bruce Hurst, Sherm Feller, John Kiley, Marty Barrett, The Can, Mo, El Guapo, and yes, for you, Billy Buck, and even you, Rocket, and finally—finally—for you, Babe. All is forgiven.

BOSTON RED SOX 2004 STATS

Regular Season

Player	POS	G	AB	R	H	2B	3B	HR	RBI	BB	K	SB	CS	OBP	SLG	AVG
Johnny Damon	OF	150	621	123	189	35	6	20	94	76	71	19	8	.380	.477	.304
David Ortiz	DH	150	582	94	175	47	3	41	139	75	133	0	0	.380	.603	.301
Manny Ramirez	OF	152	568	108	175	44	0	43	130	82	124	2	4	.397	.613	.308
Mark Bellhorn	2B	138	523	93	138	37	3	17	82	88	177	6	1	.373	.444	.264
Kevin Millar	OF	150	508	74	151	36	0	18	74	57	91	1	1	.383	.474	.297
Jason Varitek	C	137	463	67	137	30	1	18	73	62	126	10	3	.390	.482	.296
Bill Mueller	3B	110	399	75	113	27	1	12	57	51	56	2	2	.365	.446	.283
Doug Mientkiewicz	1B	127	391	47	93	24	1	6	35	48	56	2	3	.326	.350	.238
Gabe Kapler	OF	136	290	51	79	14	1	6	33	15	49	5	4	.311	.390	.272
Pokey Reese	SS	96	244	32	54	7	2	3	29	17	60	6	2	.271	.303	.221
Orlando Cabrera	SS	58	228	33	67	19	1	6	31	11	23	4	1	.320	.465	.294
Kevin Youkilis	3B	72	208	38	54	11	0	7	35	33	45	0	1	.367	.413	.260
Doug Mirabelli	C	59	160	27	45	12	0	9	32	19	46	0	0	.368	.525	.281
Nomar Garciaparra	SS	38	156	24	50	7	3	5	21	8	16	2	0	.367	.500	.321
David McCarty	1B	91	151	24	39	8	1	4	17	14	40	1	0	.327	.404	.258
Trot Nixon	OF	48	149	24	47	9	1	6	23	15	24	0	0	.377	.510	.315
Dave Roberts	OF	45	86	19	22	10	0	2	14	10	17	5	2	.330	.442	.256
Cesar Crespo	SS	52	79	6	13	2	1	0	2	0	20	2	0	.165	.215	.165
Brian Daubach	1B	30	75	9	17	8	0	2	8	10	21	0	0	.326	.413	.227
Ricky Gutierrez	2B	21	40	6	11	1	0	0	3	2	6	1	0	.310	.300	.275
Ellis Burks	DH	11	33	6	6	0	0	0	1	3	8	2	0	.270	.273	.182
Andy Dominique	1B	7	11	0	2	0	0	1	1	0	3	0	0	.182	.182	.182
Adam Hyzdu	OF	17	10	3	3	2	0	1	2	1	2	0	0	.364	.800	.300
Curt Schilling	P	2	7	0	1	0	0	0	0	0	2	0	0	.143	.143	.143
Bronson Arroyo	P	3	6	0	0	0	0	0	0	0	5	0	0	.000	.000	.000

Player	W	L	ERA	G	GS	CG	SV	SVO	IP	H	R	ER	HR	HBP	BB	K
Curt Schilling	21	6	3.26	32	32	3	0	0	226.2	206	84	82	23	5	35	203
Pedro Martinez	16	9	3.90	33	33	1	0	0	217.0	193	99	94	26	16	61	227
Tim Wakefield	12	10	4.87	32	30	0	0	0	188.1	197	121	102	29	16	63	116
Derek Lowe	14	12	5.42	33	33	0	0	0	182.2	224	138	110	15	8	71	105
Bronson Arroyo	10	9	4.03	32	29	0	0	0	178.2	171	99	80	17	20	47	142
Keith Foulke	5	3	2.17	72	0	0	32	39	83.0	63	22	20	8	6	15	79
Mike Timlin	5	4	4.13	76	0	0	1	4	76.1	75	35	35	8	5	19	56
Terry Adams	6	4	4.76	61	0	0	3	6	70.0	84	39	37	10	2	28	56
Alan Embree	2	2	4.13	71	0	0	0	1	52.1	49	28	24	7	1	11	37
Curtis Leskanic	3	5	5.19	51	0	0	4	8	43.1	47	27	25	8	1	30	37
Mike Myers	5	1	4.64	75	0	0	0	0	42.2	45	22	22	5	2	23	32
Ramiro Mendoza	2	1	3.52	27	0	0	0	0	30.2	25	12	12	3	1	7	13
Scott Williamson	0	1	1.26	28	0	0	1	2	28.2	11	6	4	0	3	18	28
Lenny DiNardo	0	0	4.23	22	0	0	0	0	27.2	34	17	13	1	2	12	21
Mark Malaska	1	1	4.50	19	0	0	0	0	20.0	21	11	10	2	1	12	12
Byung-Hyun Kim	2	1	6.23	7	3	0	0	0	17.1	17	15	12	1	2	7	6
Anastacio Martinez	2	1	8.44	11	0	0	0	0	10.2	13	10	10	2	1	6	5
Pedro Astacio	0	0	10.38	5	1	0	0	0	8.2	13	10	10	2	0	5	6
Jamie Brown	0	0	5.87	4	0	0	0	0	7.2	15	7	5	1	0	4	6
Jimmy Anderson	0	0	6.00	5	0	0	0	0	6.0	10	4	4	0	0	3	3
Abe Alvarez	0	1	9.00	1	1	0	0	0	5.0	8	5	5	2	0	5	2
David McCarty	0	0	2.45	3	0	0	0	0	3.2	2	1	1	0	0	1	4
Phil Seibel	0	0	0.00	2	0	0	0	0	3.2	0	0	0	0	1	5	1
Bobby Jones	0	1	5.40	3	0	0	0	0	3.1	3	2	2	1	0	8	3
Joe Nelson	0	0	16.87	3	0	0	0	0	2.2	4	5	5	0	2	3	5

The ALDS

Player	POS	G	AB	R	H	2B	3B	HR	RBI	BB	K	SB	CS	OBP	SLG	AVG
Johnny Damon	OF	3	15	4	7	1	0	0	0	1	2	3	0	.500	.533	.467
Orlando Cabrera	SS	3	13	1	2	1	0	0	3	2	2	0	0	.267	.231	.154
Manny Ramirez	OF	3	13	3	5	2	0	1	7	1	4	0	0	.375	.769	.385
Bill Mueller	3B	3	12	3	4	0	0	0	0	1	1	0	0	.385	.333	.333
Jason Varitek	C	3	12	3	2	0	0	1	2	2	5	0	0	.333	.417	.167
Mark Bellhorn	2B	3	11	2	1	0	0	0	0	5	4	0	0	.375	.091	.091
David Ortiz	DH	3	11	4	6	2	0	1	4	5	2	0	0	.688	1.000	.545
Kevin Millar	1B	3	10	2	3	0	0	1	4	1	1	0	0	.364	.600	.300
Trot Nixon	OF	2	8	0	2	0	0	0	2	2	1	0	0	.400	.250	.250
Gabe Kapler	OF	2	5	2	1	0	0	0	0	0	0	0	0	.200	.200	.200
Doug Mientkiewicz	1B	3	4	0	2	0	0	0	1	0	0	0	0	.500	.500	.500
Kevin Youkilis	3B	1	2	0	0	0	0	0	0	0	1	0	0	.000	.000	.000
Pokey Reese	2B	3	0	1	0	0	0	0	0	0	0	0	0	.000	.000	.000
Dave Roberts	–	1	0	0	0	0	0	0	0	0	0	0	0	.000	.000	.000

Player	W	L	ERA	G	GS	CG	SV	SVO	IP	H	R	ER	HR	HBP	BB	K
Pedro Martinez	1	0	3.86	1	1	0	0	0	7.0	6	3	3	0	1	2	6
Curt Schilling	1	0	2.70	1	1	0	0	0	6.2	9	3	2	2	0	2	4
Bronson Arroyo	0	0	3.00	1	1	0	0	0	6.0	3	2	2	1	1	2	7
Keith Foulke	0	0	0.00	2	0	0	1	1	3.0	2	0	0	0	0	1	5
Mike Timlin	0	0	9.00	3	0	0	0	0	3.0	3	3	3	1	0	1	5
Alan Embree	0	0	0.00	2	0	0	0	0	1.0	0	0	0	0	0	1	0
Derek Lowe	1	0	0.00	1	0	0	0	0	1.0	1	1	1	0	0	0	0
Mike Myers	0	0	27.00	2	0	0	0	0	0.1	0	1	1	0	0	1	1

The ALCS

Player	POS	G	AB	R	H	2B	3B	HR	RBI	BB	K	SB	CS	OBP	SLG	AVG
Johnny Damon	OF	7	35	5	6	0	0	2	7	2	8	2	1	.216	.343	.171
David Ortiz	DH	7	31	6	12	0	1	3	11	4	7	0	1	.457	.742	.387
Bill Mueller	3B	7	30	4	8	1	0	0	1	2	4	1	0	.333	.300	.267
Manny Ramirez	OF	7	30	3	9	1	0	0	0	5	4	0	0	.400	.333	.300
Orlando Cabrera	SS	7	29	5	11	2	0	0	5	3	5	1	0	.424	.448	.379
Trot Nixon	OF	7	29	4	6	1	0	1	3	0	5	0	0	.207	.345	.207
Jason Varitek	C	7	28	5	9	1	0	2	7	2	6	0	0	.355	.571	.321
Mark Bellhorn	2B	7	26	3	5	2	0	2	4	5	11	0	0	.323	.500	.192
Kevin Millar	1B	7	24	4	6	3	0	0	2	5	4	0	0	.379	.375	.250
Doug Mientkiewicz	1B	4	4	0	2	1	0	0	0	0	1	0	0	.500	.750	.500
Gabe Kapler	OF	2	3	0	1	0	0	0	0	0	0	0	0	.333	.333	.333
Dave Mirabelli	C	1	1	0	0	0	0	0	0	0	0	0	0	.000	.000	.000
Pokey Reese	2B	3	1	0	0	0	0	0	0	0	1	1	0	.000	.000	.000
Dave Roberts	–	2	0	2	0	0	0	0	0	0	0	0	0	.000	.000	.000

Player	W	L	ERA	G	GS	CG	SV	SVO	IP	H	R	ER	HR	HBP	BB	K
Pedro Martinez	0	1	6.23	3	2	0	0	0	13.0	14	9	9	2	3	9	14
Derek Lowe	1	0	3.18	2	2	0	0	0	11.1	7	4	4	1	1	1	6
Curt Schilling	1	1	6.30	2	2	0	0	0	10.0	10	7	7	1	0	2	5
Tim Wakefield	1	0	8.59	3	0	0	0	0	7.1	9	7	7	1	0	3	6
Keith Foulke	0	0	0.00	5	0	0	1	1	6.0	1	0	0	0	1	6	6
Mike Timlin	0	0	4.76	5	0	0	0	1	5.2	10	3	3	0	0	5	2
Alan Embree	0	0	3.86	6	0	0	0	0	4.2	9	2	2	0	0	1	2
Bronson Arroyo	0	0	4.00	3	1	0	0	0	4.0	8	7	7	2	0	2	3
Curtis Leskanic	1	0	10.12	3	0	0	0	0	2.2	3	3	3	1	0	3	2
Mike Myers	0	0	7.71	3	0	0	0	0	2.1	5	2	2	1	0	1	4
Ramiro Mendoza	0	1	4.50	2	0	0	0	0	2.0	2	1	1	0	2	0	1

The World Series

Player	POS	G	AB	R	H	2B	3B	HR	RBI	BB	K	SB	CS	OBP	SLG	AVG
Johnny Damon	OF	4	21	4	6	2	1	1	2	0	1	0	0	.286	.619	.286
Orlando Cabrera	SS	4	17	3	4	1	0	0	3	3	1	0	0	.381	.294	.235
Manny Ramirez	OF	4	17	2	7	0	0	1	4	3	3	0	0	.500	.588	.412
Bill Mueller	3B	4	14	3	6	2	0	0	2	4	0	0	0	.556	.571	.429
Trot Nixon	OF	4	14	1	5	3	0	0	3	1	1	0	0	.400	.571	.357
David Ortiz	DH	4	13	3	4	1	0	1	4	4	1	0	0	.471	.615	.308
Jason Varitek	C	4	13	2	2	0	1	0	2	1	4	0	0	.267	.308	.154
Mark Bellhorn	2B	4	10	3	3	1	0	1	4	5	2	0	0	.563	.700	.300
Kevin Millar	1B	4	8	2	1	1	0	0	0	2	2	0	0	.364	.250	.125
Doug Mirabelli	C	1	3	1	1	0	0	0	0	0	1	0	0	.333	.333	.333
Gabe Kapler	OF	4	2	0	0	0	0	0	0	0	0	0	0	.000	.000	.000
Derek Lowe	P	1	2	0	0	0	0	0	0	0	1	0	0	.000	.000	.000
Pedro Martinez	P	1	2	0	0	0	0	0	0	1	2	0	0	.333	.000	.000
Doug Mientkiewicz	1B	4	1	0	0	0	0	0	0	0	0	0	0	.000	.000	.000
Pokey Reese	2B	4	1	0	0	0	0	0	0	0	0	0	0	.000	.000	.000
Bronson Arroyo	P	1	0	0	0	0	0	0	0	0	0	0	0	.000	.000	.000
Alan Embree	P	1	0	0	0	0	0	0	0	0	0	0	0	.000	.000	.000
Keith Foulke	P	2	0	0	0	0	0	0	0	0	0	0	0	.000	.000	.000
Mike Timlin	P	1	0	0	0	0	0	0	0	0	0	0	0	.000	.000	.000

Player	W	L	ERA	G	GS	CG	SV	SVO	IP	H	R	ER	HR	BB	K
Derek Lowe	1	0	0.00	1	1	0	0	0	7.0	3	0	0	0	1	4
Pedro Martinez	1	0	0.00	1	1	0	0	0	7.0	3	0	0	0	2	6
Curt Schilling	1	0	0.00	1	1	0	0	0	6.0	4	1	0	0	1	4
Keith Foulke	1	0	1.80	4	0	0	1	2	5.0	4	1	1	1	1	8
Tim Wakefield	0	0	12.27	1	1	0	0	0	3.2	3	5	5	1	5	2
Mike Timlin	0	0	6.00	3	0	0	0	0	3.0	2	2	2	0	1	0
Bronson Arroyo	0	0	6.75	2	0	0	0	0	2.2	4	2	2	0	1	4
Alan Embree	0	0	0.00	3	0	0	0	0	1.2	1	1	0	0	0	4